HOWDUNIT

FORENSICS

A GUIDE FOR WRITERS

D.P. LYLE, M.D.

WRITER'S DIGEST BOOKS

www.writersdigest.com
Cincinnati, Ohio

W9-ALU-873

Visit our Web sites at www.writersdigest.com and www.wdeditors.com for information on more resources for writers.

To receive a free weekly e-mail newsletter delivering tips and updates about writing and about Writer's Digest products, register directly at our Web site at http://newsletters.fwpublications.com.

12   11   10   09 08   5 4 3 2 1

Distributed in Canada by Fraser Direct, 100 Armstrong Avenue, Georgetown, ON, Canada L7G 5S4, Tel: (905) 877-4411; Distributed in the U.K. and Europe by David & Charles, Brunel House, Newton Abbot, Devon, TQ12 4PU, England, Tel: (+44) 1626 323200, Fax: (+44) 1626 323319, E-mail: postmaster@davidandcharles.co.uk; Distributed in Australia by Capricorn Link, P.O. Box 704, Windsor, NSW 2756 Australia, Tel: (02) 4577-3555

Library of Congress Cataloging-in-Publication Data

Lyle, D. P.

  Forensics : a guide for writers / by D.P. Lyle.

     p. cm. -- (Howdunit)

  Includes index.

  ISBN 978-1-58297-474-3 (pbk. : alk. paper)

  1. Forensic sciences--Popular works. 2. Criminal investigation. 3. Fiction--Authorship--Handbooks, manuals, etc. 4. Criminal investigation in literature. I. Title.

  HV8073.L93 2008

  363.25--dc22

2007029114

Edited by Michelle Ehrhard
Designed by Claudean Wheeler
Production coordinated by Mark Griffin

fw

F+W PUBLICATIONS, INC.

DEDICATION

This book is dedicated to all the clever writers who work to "get it right." I hope this book will help them do just that.

ABOUT THE AUTHOR

D.P. Lyle, M.D. is the Macavity Award-winning and Edgar® Award-nominated author of the nonfiction books, *Murder and Mayhem, Forensics for Dummies*, and *Forensics and Fiction,* as well as the thrillers, *Devil's Playground* and *Double Blind.*

He has worked as a story and technical consultant with many published authors and with the writers and producers of several popular television shows, including *Law & Order, CSI: Miami, Diagnosis Murder, Monk, Judging Amy, Cold Case, Peacemakers, House, Medium,* and *1-800-Missing.*

Through his Web site, The Writers' Medical and Forensics Lab (www.dplylemd. com), he works with writers and readers to enrich their understanding of complex medical and forensic issues in the stories they write and read.

He was born and raised in Huntsville, Alabama, where his childhood interests revolved around football, baseball, and building rockets in his backyard. The latter pursuit was common in Huntsville during the 1950s and '60s due to the nearby NASA/Marshall Space Flight Center.

After leaving Huntsville, he attended college and medical school, and served an internship at the University of Alabama; followed by a residency in Internal Medicine at the University of Texas at Houston; then a Fellowship in Cardiology at The Texas Heart Institute, also in Houston. For the past thirty years, he has practiced cardiology in Orange County, California.

TABLE OF

CONTENTS

FOREWORD

BY MATT WITTEN

Writing crime novels and TV shows is a lot of fun, but there are definitely occupational hazards. For one thing, you tend to have rather odd dreams. Also, your family can get a tad perturbed when you discuss serial killers or methods of strangulation at the dinner table. And last but not least, you can find yourself in the middle of writing a great murder mystery and suddenly realize you have no idea what the hell you're talking about.

Reading *Howdunit: Forensics* may not cure your dreams or make you a more socially appropriate dinner partner, but it will definitely make you feel more knowledgeable. Even better, you'll actually *be* more knowledgeable. This book covers all of the forensics basics, from DNA to gunshot residue to associated legal issues, in a comprehensive way.

Not only that, this book is extremely readable with highly entertaining anecdotes. In fact, my biggest problem with the book is that when I was reading it, my wife kept sneaking it away from me so she could read it. And she's not even into this stuff.

In my work on *Law & Order, Women's Murder Club*, and other crime shows, I have consulted a lot of experts and read a lot of reference books. I have found that most scientists don't *think* like crime writers. Doug Lyle actually does, no doubt because he's been helping crime writers for over a decade and has answered hundreds upon hundreds of our questions. *Howdunit: Forensics* is absolutely the best reference for crime writers I have ever seen.

Best of all, you will probably find that reading this book inspires you to think up new ideas for murder mysteries and plot twists. In fact, I'm thinking of a way to work Lyle's story about "The Shark Arm Murder" into my next TV episode. Maybe I'll try it out on my family at dinner.

> MATT WITTEN has written for several television crime shows including *Law & Order, CSI: Miami, Women's Murder Club,* and *Homicide.* He also wrote the Jacob Burns mystery novels for Signet.

FOREWORD

BY LEE GOLDBERG

When I started out writing TV cop shows, I was taught to avoid the science stuff, the boring exposition that kills the momentum of a good story. Whatever the science was, and there shouldn't be too much of it, you could quickly throw away in a line. You could have one of your cops say "the lab found trace evidence at the crime scene that leads directly to Doug Lyle," and off we'd go to the next car chase, gunfight, or cat-and-mouse game of wits.

The only show I can remember that even showed a passing interest in science was *Hawaii Five-O*. In each episode you could count on blue-suited, lantern-jawed Steve McGarrett going down to see Che Fong who, in his white lab coat, would dryly spout useless exposition based on, at best, questionable science. It was so silly that every *Naked Gun* movie couldn't resist spoofing it.

Nobody wanted science in their cop shows. They wanted good-looking heroes, fast-moving stories, quirky characters, and great action.

Did Columbo ever talk to a crime scene investigator? Hell no.

Did Jessica Fletcher ever consult a lab report? Get real.

How often did the cops of *Hill Street Blues*, *Homicide*, or *NYPD Blue* go down to the lab for a briefing? Almost never. They were too busy dealing with their complicated sex lives, their substance abuse problems, the bureaucracy of the legal system, and the political machinations within their police departments.

Why weren't the TV writers behind those shows paying attention to forensics? Because it was exposition which, by definition, isn't exciting. We believed that viewers didn't care about physical evidence; they cared about people, they cared about passion, they cared about action. They were interested in whodunit, and whydunit, not particularly howdunit.

There simply wasn't anything sexy, thrilling, or suspenseful about test tubes, fingerprints, bodily fluids, DNA, pubic hairs, and autopsies.

Or so it seemed.

Two TV crime shows changed all of that, turning conventional dramatic wisdom upside down: the real-life trial of O.J. Simpson and the fictional series *CSI: Crime Scene Investigation*.

The Simpson trial was a spellbinding education for millions of people into DNA and forensics. It wasn't just a trial, or a media event, it was a classroom, introducing viewers to aspects of science they knew virtually nothing about. And it was utterly captivating.

Then along came *CSI*, a little cop show about crime lab technicians that nobody expected to succeed. But it was the right show at the right time, capitalizing on the audience's discovery of forensics and putting the exposition front and center. The drama was all about the evidence; the people who committed the crimes, and their motives, became secondary in the story telling to whatever microscopic material they left behind at the crime scene. It broke every rule of television.

CSI was a true over-night sensation, a smash hit from the day it premiered. The series and its two spin-offs radically changed the way we tell mysteries on TV (and, I would argue, in movies and books, too). The show has even changed what real-life juries expect to see and hear from prosecutors in a courtroom.

But the fact is that *CSI* and its spin-offs and rip-offs are ridiculously unrealistic. The way the characters behave, the scope of their investigatory responsibilities, their legal authority in a case, their relationship to the police detectives, and the lightning-fast scientific results they achieve have absolutely no basis in reality.

There are no police crime labs on earth that look like the ones on the three *CSI* shows. Most crime labs are financially pinched, sterile, and drab ... they certainly aren't multimillion-dollar architectural wonders stocked with the latest, cutting-edge technology, banks of flat-screen monitors, and illuminated with multicolored, pinpoint halogen mood lighting.

You will never find a real-life crime scene investigator wearing Armani, carrying guns, questioning witnesses, and driving a chrome-plated Hummer.

As a veteran homicide detective I know says: "*Star Trek* is more realistic than *CSI*, and if one of those lab rats ever opened his mouth to question a witness, I'd shoot him."

But success is its own reality to television network executives. So while you and I may know that *CSI* is fiction, it's real to the people who develop TV shows. If you're writing about crime on television, you're required now to incorporate the world according to *CSI* into your fictional universe. More importantly, the audience expects it.

To me, the most obvious example of the inescapable *CSI*-ification of cop shows is the venerable *Law & Order*. If you look at the early episodes of the show, there isn't a single crime scene tech in sight. At most, one of the detectives might refer to information that "just came in from the lab." Now, in every episode, there's a talkative CSI tech at each crime scene and the detectives have to make at least one obligatory stop at CSI HQ to get a multimedia briefing from some colorful tech in a lab coat ... because if they didn't, the audiences wouldn't find the story "realistic."

In the cop show universe, it doesn't matter if CSI is totally fictional, it's the new fictional reality by which all other fictional realities will be measured against for fictional "authenticity"... at least until another cop show becomes a breakout hit and redefines the way we tell crime stories.

Until that time comes, Doug Lyle's book will be a necessary resource for writers crafting crime stories and for mystery fans who want to know more about the fictionalized science they see on cop shows. This is a book about how forensics work in the *real* world, not the magic performed by characters like Gil Grissom and Horatio Caine. And what you will discover is that the real world of forensics is, perhaps, even more compelling than what we are seeing on television every week.

LEE GOLDBERG is a TV writer-producer whose many credits include *Diagnosis Murder*, *Spenser for Hire*, *Psych*, and *Monk*. The two-time Edgar-award nominee is also the author of the *Diagnosis Murder* and *Monk* series of original novels.

INTRODUCTION

The popularity of television crime shows such as *CSI*, *Bones*, and *Law & Order* underscores the public's interest in forensics. Why is forensic science suddenly so interesting? Is it some macabre fascination with death or with the criminal world? Or is it that people are curious by nature and have always had a strong appetite for scientific knowledge? In truth, our fascination with all things forensic is probably a combination of all these. Science and drama can be a powerful mix.

The world of forensic science has proven to be quite fascinating, even to the layman. We are intrigued when we hear of a new forensic technique or a legal triumph due to forensic evidence. Whether it's extracting DNA from a single eyelash, a tear, or a centuries-old mummy, or solving a decades-old murder with a single partial fingerprint, we are glued to the TV to see how it was done.

Forensics is a huge field, encompassing the sciences of anatomy, histology, physiology, pharmacology, chemistry, physics, biology, bacteriology, entomology, anthropology, and psychology, to name a few. It is, of course, impossible to cover every aspect of forensics in this book. In fact, the subject matter covered in each chapter would require several textbooks to thoroughly explore. And the average reader would find such an in-depth exploration confusing and boring.

In this book, I've attempted to open the doors to the world of forensics and provide the reader with a broad understanding of forensic science as well as an in-depth understanding of the most commonly employed forensic techniques. The ones you see on TV, read in the paper, and, for the writer of fiction, the details you want for your stories. For many, this book will supply all the information you need to understand forensic science, both in the present and historically, while others will want to dig deeper. If you are in the latter group, I suggest you simply search in an Internet search engine such as Google (www.google.com) for any subject or name or word you want to explore and see where it takes you.

Above all, I hope this book informs and fascinates, and of course makes you think and ask questions. For the writers among you, I hope it not only gives you the knowledge you need to create a believable story but that it also stirs your creative juices and makes you explore areas of your story you never before considered.

PART I

THE FORENSICS SYSTEM

FORENSIC SCIENCE:
THE HISTORY AND ORGANIZATION

What is forensic science? Where did it originate? What does the term *forensic* mean in the first place?

The short definition of forensic is "of the law." The longer one is "relating to the use of science in the investigation of criminal activity and the analysis and presentation of evidence before the court." Thus, forensic science is the interface of science and the law. *Medico-legal*, a term often substituted for *forensic*, clearly indicates this marriage between law and medical science.

The word *forensic* derives from the Latin word *forum*. In ancient Rome, the forum was the community meeting place within the city or town. It served as an area where merchants, politicians, scholars, and the public could mingle and discuss issues of common interest, and also as the place where justice was meted out in public trials. Over the centuries, the term *forum* evolved into *forensics*.

Today, forensic is applied to anything that relates to law, and forensic science is the application of scientific disciplines to the law. It is important to note that it differs from the term *clinical*, which means "related to a medical clinic."

For example, clinical toxicology is the analysis of medications and drugs in the care of medical patients. Is the level of a drug such as digitalis within a heart patient's bloodstream at the proper level to achieve the desired effect? Are the person's symptoms due to an excess of a particular drug? The clinical toxicologist is concerned with patient care and treatment.

On the other hand, forensic toxicology is the use of the principles and testing procedures of medical toxicology (the study or drugs and poisons) to help resolve legal issues. Did the victim die from a poison or a drug overdose? Was the erratic driver intoxicated? Was a suspect's aberrant behavior due to drug usage? Forensic toxicology helps answer these questions.

A forensics (crime) lab is quite different from a medical (clinical) lab. The latter deals with the living. Testing within the clinical or hospital lab is directed toward aiding the diagnosis and treatment of ill patients. A forensics lab is geared toward evidence testing in the hope of establishing a link between a suspect and a crime.

Another example is the difference between a clinical (hospital) pathologist and a forensic pathologist, who sits at the apex of the forensics investigative system. Just as with labs, the duties of a forensic pathologist and a clinical pathologist vary greatly. A clinical pathologist is concerned with helping other physicians treat the ill. In this regard, he oversees the clinical lab, interprets lab tests, reviews biopsy and surgically removed tissues, and performs medical autopsies. A medical autopsy is designed to determine why someone died and to discover what complicating disease processes may have been present.

The forensic pathologist is concerned with criminal harm and death. He may oversee the crime lab (not always, since more often than not, the crime lab falls under the wing of the police or sheriff's department), interpret forensic tests, and perform forensic autopsies. A forensic autopsy is also designed to explain why someone died or was injured; however, the focus is to determine if either resulted from a criminal act.

THE DEVELOPMENT OF FORENSIC SCIENCE

No one knows for sure when science was first used to help solve criminal cases, but many feel that the origins of forensic science can be dated to Chinese investigator Sung Tz'u (1186–1249), who published the first text on forensic science in 1235. It carried the rather poetic title *Hsi Yuan Lu*, or *The Washing Away of Wrongs*.

The field of forensic science evolved in fits and spurts over the centuries that followed. Some techniques developed early and progressed rapidly, others lagged behind, and still others are truly modern. No forensic technique simply jumped into existence; it followed its own unique evolutionary process.

Modern forensic science rests on a foundation of centuries of scientific discovery. Our knowledge of physical and biological principles had to evolve and expand before it could be applied to the world of forensics. DNA testing could not become an accepted procedure until we knew it existed and understood how it worked. Fingerprints could not be used for identification until we discovered their existence and uniqueness.

Before a technique finds its way into the forensics lab, it must be thoroughly tested and refined by the scientific community. New techniques are sure to face legal challenges, so the scientific community must find them acceptable. Virtually every forensic science technique, including procedures in firearms examination, toxicology, and serology (the study of blood and body fluids), has followed a similar path.

In 1901, Karl Landsteiner (1868–1943) discovered that human blood could be grouped, and he devised the ABO blood group system that we still use today. In 1915, Leone Lattes (1887–1954) used Landsteiner's discovery to develop a simple method for determining the ABO blood group of a dried bloodstain and immediately began to apply his test in criminal investigations. As we will see in Chapter Nine, ABO typing is currently used to identify suspects and exonerate the innocent as well as in paternity testing and crime scene reconstruction.

The history of forensic science is replete with similar examples. Early in the twentieth century, Calvin Goddard (1891–1955) perfected a system for comparing bullets under a comparison microscope in order to determine if they came from the same weapon. This technique remains the mainstay of current firearms examination. Albert Osborn (1858–1946) laid down the principles of document examination in his book *Questioned Documents* (1910). Many of these are still used by modern document examiners.

THE FIRST FORENSIC SCIENTISTS

Interestingly, the first forensic scientists came not from the world of science but from the world of fiction. Not only does art imitate life, but also life imitates art.

Sir Arthur Conan Doyle's Sherlock Holmes frequently uses the sciences of fingerprinting, document examination, and blood analysis to solve the crimes presented to him. In fact, in the very first Sherlock Holmes novel, *A Study in Scarlet* (1887), Holmes develops a chemical to determine whether a stain was blood. Since this technique had not been previously used in a real-life criminal investigation, Holmes was definitely ahead of his time.

In Mark Twain's *Life on the Mississippi* (1883), a thumbprint is used to identify a murderer, and in Twain's *The Tragedy of Pudd'nhead Wilson* (1893–1894), a fingerprint pops up in a court trial. These examples pre-dated the groundbreaking work on fingerprints by Sir Francis Galton (1822–1911) in the 1890s, for which he received knighthood.

Many believe that the first real-life forensic scientist was Hans Gross (1847–1915). His reasoned and methodic approach to criminal investigation and the mind of not only criminals, but also their pursuers, laid the foundation for modern criminology.

In 1893, he published the first treatise on the use of scientific knowledge and procedures in criminal investigations. His classic 1898 work *Criminal Psychology* laid out the principles of criminal behavior and how evidence should be evaluated and used in criminal proceedings. Interestingly, he also used the more modern term *criminalist* to refer to those involved in criminal investigation.

Others soon followed in Gross's footsteps, most notably Edmund Locard (1877–1966), a police officer and professor in Lyon, France. In the early 1900s, he voiced an extremely important observation that became known as Locard's Exchange Principle, which remains the cornerstone of modern forensic investigation.

THE LOCARD EXCHANGE PRINCIPLE

Wherever he steps, whatever he touches, whatever he leaves, even unconsciously, will serve as a silent witness against him. Not only his fingerprints or his footprints, but his hair, the fibers from his clothes, the glass he breaks, the tool mark he leaves, the paint he scratches, the blood or semen he deposits or collects.

All of these and more, bear mute witness against him. This is evidence that does not forget. It is not confused by the excitement of the moment. It is not absent because human witnesses are. It is factual evidence. Physical evidence cannot be wrong, it cannot perjure itself, it cannot be wholly absent. Only human failure to find it, study and understand it, can diminish its value.

—Edmund Locard

An understanding of the Locard Exchange Principle is critical to grasping the true workings of forensic science. As so elegantly stated by Professor Locard, the basic premise is that whenever a person comes into contact with another person, object, or place, an exchange of materials takes place. Blood, fibers, hair, or any other substance is either left behind or picked up and carried away by the individual. If you own a pet, this exchange of materials is well known to you. Look at your clothes and you'll likely see cat or dog hair clinging to the fabric. You may also find that you have transferred these hairs to your car, your office, and any other place you frequent.

The placing of a suspect at the scene of a crime is one of the basic functions of forensic science. The analysis of evidence is to create an association or link between the perpetrator and the crime. In some cases, the mere fact that the suspect was at the scene is an indication of guilt. A fingerprint on the faceplate of a cracked bank vault, semen obtained from a rape victim, or paint from the fender of a car involved in a hit-and-run would place the suspect at a scene where he perhaps had no "innocent" reason to be.

This linkage of evidence is the heart and soul of forensic science. It proves that a person has come into contact with another person, place, or object. Or perhaps it proves that two objects or substances share a common source. For example, if a chip of car paint found in the clothing of a child victim of a hit-and-run is matched to a particular car, this match shows that the car was the source of the paint. Or if blood found at a crime scene matches the DNA profile of blood obtained from a suspect, it proves the blood shared a common source, namely the suspect. Does this make either suspect guilty? Not necessarily. That determination is made in a court of law. The linkage of the evidence simply puts the suspect at the scene. It is up to the police and prosecutors to prove that this linkage is proof of guilt. Or conversely, for the suspect and his attorney to offer an innocent reason for the evidence to be found where it was.

Let's look at another example. A woman is found raped and murdered in her home. DNA from semen found at the scene is matched to the man who lives next door. Doesn't look good for him. But, what if the two were having a clandestine affair? What if he had visited her an hour or so before her murder? Things aren't as clear, are they? The one thing he can't deny is that it was his DNA that was found at the scene. But, he may have another reason for it to be there. So, forensic science can link him to the scene but it cannot always reveal why he was there and what transpired while he was there.

GENERAL ORGANIZATION OF FORENSIC SCIENCE

This book will not deal with the techniques of law enforcement and investigation but rather will look into the functions of the criminalists, the crime lab, and the medical examiner. This is still a huge undertaking, and as we go along you will see that the domain of forensic science involves many scientific disciplines. It is organized in many different ways.

As I said earlier, the development of modern forensic science paralleled advances in science, particularly the physical and biological sciences. The invention of the microscope, the development of photography, the understanding of the physics of ballistic trajectories, and the discovery of blood typing and DNA analysis are examples of such advances. Before these scientific principles and procedures were applied to criminal investigations, they underwent many years of refinement. Some moved quickly, others at a snail's pace, so the various areas of science entered the forensics arena in a more or less haphazard fashion.

It should come as no surprise that the organization of these various techniques into a coherent field of study was neither smooth nor linear, and the use of them in criminal investigation varied greatly from country to country and even from area to area within the United States. This is still true today. Some jurisdictions have complete and sophisticated crime labs, while others are rudimentary by comparison.

For the fiction writer, this is a gold mine of opportunity. The popular horror writer John Saul once said that he set his stories in small towns "because the cops are stupid." What he meant is that if your story is in a rural area, the local police are neither equipped for nor experienced in the handling of major crimes. In a city like Los Angeles, the police, the crime lab, and the coroner's office employs hundreds, even thousands, of people and have a budget, though still woefully inadequate, in the millions. A small town in the rural South may have the police chief, a single deputy, and the local undertaker as the sum total of their forensic team. Sort of like Mayberry with Andy and Barney and Floyd the barber as the coroner. Rich soil for a fiction writer.

Regardless of the level of sophistication in a given jurisdiction, modern forensics integrates the varied scientific disciplines in an effort to solve crimes. This requires extensive coordination among law enforcement, the crime scene technicians, the crime lab, and the medical examiner.

Crime labs have been around for many decades. August Vollmer (1876–1955) used forensics as a police chief in Berkeley, California, and in 1923 he established the first forensic laboratory in the United States when he was chief in Los Angeles. The famous 1929 St. Valentine's Day Massacre (see Chapter Sixteen: Firearms Examination) prompted two Chicago businessmen to help establish the Scientific Crime Detection Laboratory (SCDL), the first independent crime lab, at Northwestern University. In 1932, the Federal Bureau of Investigation (FBI) established a national forensics laboratory, that offered services to law enforcement across the country. It served as the model for all future state and local labs. Now many states have networks of regional and local labs that support law enforcement at all levels.

The scientific services offered by the modern crime lab and medical examiner's office are varied and complex. In reality, the number of services supplied by a particular laboratory depends on its size and budget. State and regional labs may provide a wide array of services while local labs may only provide basic testing. The smaller labs typically outsource more sophisticated testing to the larger regional labs. In addition, the FBI's National Crime Lab offers services to law enforcement throughout the country. Not only does the FBI lab perform virtually every type of test, it possesses or has access to databases on everything from fingerprints to tire track impressions to postage stamps.

At the more local level, larger labs may have separate departments for each discipline, while smaller labs tend to combine services. For example, a large state lab may have separate firearms, tool marks, serology (blood examination), and DNA units, while a local lab may combine firearms with tool marks and DNA with serology. In very small labs, a single technician may do all the work. Obviously, in this circumstance, a great deal of the work must be sent to larger reference labs.

You've no doubt heard of CSI. It stands for Crime Scene Investigation. Larger crime labs may have a special Crime Scene Investigation Unit (CSIU), which consists of individuals trained in evidence recognition, collection, and preservation. They are also skilled in performing many of the "field tests" and screening tests that must be done at a crime scene. Many of these technicians also perform laboratory testing once the crime scene samples are returned to the lab. Smaller jurisdictions do not have a specialized CSIU so the collection of evidence falls to the local police or sheriff.

Two other terms warrant attention because they can create confusion. A *criminalist* is a forensic scientist. *Criminalistics* is synonymous with forensic science. Using either of these terms is correct. Because of the wide range and sophistication of the many scientific disciplines represented in the modern crime lab, many criminalists specialize in a single area of forensic science. They may work in toxicology (drugs and poisons), serology (blood), fingerprint analysis, chemistry, firearms and ballistics, or one of the many other service areas of the crime lab.

CRIME LAB SERVICES

In general, the forensic science services offered by the coroner or medical examiner's office and the crime lab can be divided into biological science and physical science arenas. Each of these areas will be covered in considerable detail in later chapters.

BIOLOGICAL FORENSIC SCIENCE SERVICES

BOTANY: The examination of plant residue by a forensic botanist may be crucial to solving a crime. Plant fragments, seeds, pollen, and soil may place a suspect at the crime. For example, if pollen found on the clothing of a suspect is matched to that of a rural crime scene, it would suggest that the suspect had been in the same area. As with insects, plant and pollen evidence may reveal that a corpse has been moved.

FORENSIC ANTHROPOLOGY: The forensic anthropologist is primarily concerned with the identification of human skeletal remains and is often asked to determine the age, sex, and race of the person, identify any illnesses or injuries the person may have suffered, and establish the time, cause, and manner of death as best he can. Other duties might be to identify victims of mass disasters or those interred in mass graves.

FORENSIC ENTOMOLOGY: Entomology is the study of insects. The forensic entomologist uses his knowledge of the life cycles of flies and various other insects that feed on corpses to determine the approximate time of death. He may also use his knowledge of insect habitats to determine if a body has been moved from one location to another.

FORENSIC ODONTOLOGY: This is forensic dentistry. The forensic dentist helps identify unknown corpses by matching dental patterns with previous X-rays, dental casts, or photographs. Since tooth enamel is the hardest substance in the human body and often survives when nothing else of the deceased remains, the forensic dentist may help with identifying homicide victims, victims of mass disasters, and skeletal remains. He may also be called upon to match a suspect's teeth with bite marks on the victim or on food products, such as cheese or apples, that the perpetrator may have left at the scene.

FORENSIC PATHOLOGY: This is the domain of the forensic pathologist, who is a medical doctor with subspecialty training in pathology and further training in forensic pathology. The medical examiner is usually a forensic pathologist and is called upon to answer many crucial questions. Who is the victim? How did he die? What injuries did he suffer and when and how were they inflicted? The forensic pathologist uses the autopsy, police reports, medical records, suspect and witness interviews, and the results of crime lab evidence evaluations in pursuit of the answers.

The coroner or medical examiner is ultimately responsible for signing death certificates and is charged with determining the time, cause, and manner of death. Many natural and virtually all accidental, suicidal, and homicidal deaths come to his attention. In cases of suspected medical malpractice, his findings as to the cause of injury or death may be crucial to the case's eventual outcome. He may also examine living victims to determine the cause and age of injuries, particularly in cases or assault, rape, or abuse.

FORENSIC PSYCHIATRY: The forensic psychiatrist is often involved in both criminal and civil proceedings, where the state of mind of the perpetrator is important in not only guilt and innocence but also in sentencing. He might be asked to address someone's sanity or competence to stand trial, sign documents, or give informed medical consent. In suicide cases, he may be asked to do a "psychological autopsy" in order to determine possible motivations.

SEROLOGY: The serology department deals with blood and other body fluids such as saliva and semen. Blood typing, paternity testing, and DNA profiling are conducted by the serologist.

TOXICOLOGY: Toxicology is the study of drugs and poisons. The forensic toxicologist is called upon to determine if drugs or poisons are present in both the living and the deceased and perhaps to assess their contribution to the person's aberrant behavior or death. He might be asked to identify confiscated drugs, or to determine if a driver was intoxicated or if a worker has violated company drug use policies.

PHYSICAL FORENSIC SCIENCE SERVICES

DOCUMENT EXAMINATION: Questioned documents are those whose age or authenticity is in doubt. This includes any document that may have been altered. The document examiner uses handwriting analysis to match known exemplars to questioned documents or signatures. He might be asked to analyze the physical and chemical properties of paper and ink as well as expose indented (second-page) writing. Typewritten or photocopied documents that have been altered also fall under the document examiner's area of expertise.

FINGERPRINT EXAMINATION: Fingerprint examiners are charged with matching finger, palm, and foot sole prints. The comparison of a crime scene print may be carried out against a database or a suspect's prints.

FIREARMS EXAMINATION: Firearms examination, commonly but erroneously referred to as ballistics, deals with the examination of weapons, ammunition, fired bullets, shell casings, and shotgun shells. Firearms experts employ the microscope and various chemical analyses in an attempt to identify the weapon type and to match any fired bullets or shell casings to a suspect weapon.

OTHER PATTERNED EVIDENCE: Patterned evidence is evidence that forms a recognizable pattern that can be compared to other patterns. Fingerprints are an example of this type of evidence as are tire and shoe tracks and tool marks.

TRACE EVIDENCE: Examples of trace evidence (any small item of evidence) include hair, fiber, paint, glass, and soil. This evidence may place the suspect at the crime scene or in contact with the victim.

OTHER FORENSIC SCIENCE SERVICES

EVIDENCE COLLECTION UNIT: This unit is also called the Crime Scene Investigation Unit (CSIU) in many jurisdictions. Members of this team are charged with collecting and preserving evidence from the crime scene and transporting it to the lab. Their duties include exposing and lifting latent fingerprints, collecting hair and fibers, and gathering any other articles of evidence at the scene.

EVIDENCE STORAGE: A secure place for storing and preserving evidence is essential. Often materials must be kept for years, even decades, and the chain of custody must remain unbroken throughout or the evidence could be compromised and lose its evidentiary value. Only authorized individuals can examine the evidence and they must sign it in and out and account for it at all times. If the firearms lab needs to check a bullet that is being held in evidence against a suspect bullet, the examiner must take possession of the bullet, signing for its release, and maintain possession until he signs it back into the secure evidence lockup. This is true whether the crime is one day or one decade old.

PHOTOGRAPHY UNIT: This unit photographically records the scene, all evidence, and the body (if one is present). These photos or videos are crucial to crime scene reconstruction and the presentation of evidence in the courtroom.

THE CORONER AND THE MEDICAL EXAMINER

You probably noticed that I've used the terms *coroner* and *medical examiner* (ME) almost interchangeably even though they are often quite different, as you will see. The reason is that whether the person in charge of "all things death" is a coroner or a medical examiner depends upon which system is in place in the particular jurisdiction under discussion. Since this book is designed to give general information that you can use to craft your story in any area, either term could be used. So, I use them interchangeably for the purpose of discussion. If you set your story in a real location, check to see which system is used in that area and then use the proper designation. If your locale is fictional, you can use either term so long as you are consistent.

The term *coroner* comes from the English office of the "crowner of the king" or the "keeper of the pleas of the Crown." It is unclear exactly when the office of coroner came into existence, but it was used prior to the Norman Invasion (1066) and may have been as early as 871 A.D., during the reign of Alfred the Great. King Richard Plantagenet (1157–1199), also known as Richard the Lionheart, officially created the position in 1194. Then, in 1276, the legal document known as *De officio coronatoris* set out the coroner's duties and obligations. This was later replaced and refined by the Coroners Act 1887.

As early as the eleventh century, the crowner performed many judicial functions, including the determination of the cause of death, and even served as a judge in criminal proceedings. In this latter duty, he was an inquisitional judge in that he actually investigated crimes rather than merely tried a case based on evidence brought to his court. That is, he actively pursued evidence and criminals. Such inquisitional judges evolved from ancient Roman law, which is the basis for systems found in Russia, Spain, and France.

But under English law, courtroom judges are non-inquisitional. They are not actively involved in the criminal investigation and do not participate in the evidence gathering. Rather, they hear the evidence provided by others and oversee the proceedings within the courtroom.

The English coroner is an exception to this rule and carries out his duties in a more inquisitional manner. That is, he is an inquisitional judge in a non-inquisitional system. Early English settlers to the New World brought with them the office of the coroner in the 1600s so that the United States has a similar inquisitional coroner system.

The medical examiner (ME), a more modern invention, traces its origins to France and Scotland and was brought to the United States in the late 1800s. By definition, the ME is a medical professional with at least an M.D. degree. Most modern MEs are trained in pathology, particularly forensic pathology. This means that, ideally, an ME is medical doctor with specialty training in pathology, and experience and training in the field of forensic pathology.

Two types of forensic investigative systems exist in the United States. The coroner system is older and in many ways inferior to the more modern medical examiner system. Fortunately, the trend in the United States is toward the latter system.

In England, for centuries, the king appointed the coroner. In the United States, since there was no king, the coroner became an appointed or elected position. What qualifications were needed to run for coroner? Basically, none. At least no special medical or forensic skills were required. The sole criterion was the ability to win an election or to secure an appointment from the county commission or whatever legal body was charged with this appointment. It was, and still is, often more a popularity contest.

The coroner might be the sheriff, newspaper publisher, neighborhood café owner, or local funeral director. As often as not, he possessed little or no medical training or experience. Over the past several decades, this has evolved so that today many jurisdictions require that the coroner be a licensed physician. He may be an internist, an obstetrician, or a dermatologist, but he does not necessarily have to be a pathologist and certainly not a forensic pathologist. Thus, the coroner may not actually be qualified to perform many of his duties. This deficiency led to the creation of the medical examiner system.

In 1877, Massachusetts passed a law that replaced coroners with MEs and required that these MEs be licensed physicians. New York City adopted a similar system in 1915. In the 1940s, Congress established the Commission on Uniform State Laws. One of the laws that came from this commission was the Medical Examiner's Act, which was adopted by most states. This led to the replacement of most coroners with MEs. However, with the exception of the District of Columbia, no program existed for investigating deaths in cases under federal jurisdiction until 1990 when Congress established the Armed Forces Medical Examiner's Office in the Armed Forces Institute of Pathology.

Most medical examiner systems require the ME be a pathologist, while some require that he be trained in forensic pathology. There is a difference. As we saw earlier, most clinical pathologists work in hospitals, where they oversee the hospital laboratory and perform medical autopsies. A medical autopsy is designed to search for diseases and natural causes of death. On the other hand, a forensic pathologist is a clinical pathologist who has taken extra training in the field of forensics. He oversees all aspects of death and criminal injury, perhaps including the crime lab, and performs forensic autopsies. These are designed to help determine the cause and manner of death.

In an ideal world, every jurisdiction would have an ME who is a forensic pathologist. He would be qualified to fulfill all the duties of the office. Yet, even today, in many areas, the coroner system thrives and the non-medically trained coroner continues to be the officer charged with investigating death. This is a practical solution because these areas simply may not have the population base to justify having a forensic pathologist as ME.

In these circumstances, the coroner has several alternatives for acquiring the needed specialized pathological services. He might contract with a larger regional or state ME's office for pathological and laboratory testing. Or, he might hire a forensic pathologist to serve as ME. This pathologist may be given a title such as Deputy Assistant Coroner. Under the legal umbrella of the coroner's office, he would perform autopsies, testify in court, and perhaps oversee the crime lab.

The relationship of the medical examiner to the crime lab varies from jurisdiction to jurisdiction. In some areas the ME oversees the forensic laboratory. In other areas the lab may be under the auspices of law enforcement agencies such as the police or sheriff's department. And as with pathological services, many rural jurisdictions obtain lab services through contracts with major city or state crime labs.

DUTIES OF THE CORONER OR MEDICAL EXAMINER

The coroner or ME wears many hats. Judge, juror, investigator, and scientist are some of the roles he may fill within the medico-legal investigations system. In short, his responsibilities cover every aspect of death investigation and include:

- determination of the cause and manner of death
- determination of the time of death
- supervision of evidence collection from the body
- identification of unknown corpses and skeletal remains
- determination of any contributory factors in the death
- certification of the death certificate
- presentation of expert testimony in court
- oversight of the crime lab (in some areas)
- examination of injuries to the living and determination of their cause and timing

In fulfilling these duties, he uses all available information. Reviewing witness statements, visiting crime scenes, examining collected evidence and the results of crime lab testing, and performing autopsies are part of this endeavor. In addition, he typically has subpoena power to gather whatever evidence he deems necessary and to interrogate witnesses. He often works with the police and homicide detectives to help guide their ongoing investigations by supplying them with the results of any forensic tests he or the crime lab has performed.

THE MEDICAL EXAMINER IN THE COURTROOM

Many of the ME's most important duties take place in the courtroom, for it is in this arena that the world of science is brought to the law. His testimony may make or break a case. In fact, his determination of the cause and manner of death (see Chapter Six) will determine if a case comes to court in the first place. If he states that the manner of death is natural or suicidal, it would not likely become a court case. But, if the death is homicidal or accidental (such as in an industrial setting), the case may very well enter the courtroom. The ME might be called to testify by either the prosecution or the defense and may also face experts with different opinions. His sworn duty is to present the facts and offer an unbiased opinion based on these facts.

He might be asked to discuss and explain the forensic evidence and to offer his expert opinion regarding the evidence to the judge and jury. In this regard he acts as an educator as well as a scientist. Often he is the only person the jury hears from who makes complex scientific information understandable. At other times he must pit his knowledge and communication skills against experts with different opinions.

Our court system is adversarial in nature. This means that each side attempts to outfox or out-argue the other. Each attempts to present evidence that favors their side and "spin" any contrary evidence in a manner that supports their theory of the case. This locking of horns can put the forensic expert in a difficult position. Each side is likely to bring in experts to support or refute the testimony of the ME. These experts may be other forensic pathologists, toxicologists, firearms experts, or someone from any of the other forensic areas.

Each expert should expect to be qualified before the jury. The attorneys will ask questions about his credentials, training, experience, areas of expertise, teaching positions, publications in the field in question, and anything else they deem will support or undermine his true expertise. The side that called him will ask easy, supportive questions, while the other side will ask tougher questions to impeach any testimony he may give. The expert must be prepared for potentially unsettling questions.

The testimony of the expert should be honest and measured. He should avoid over-selling his beliefs, while at the same time making his honest opinions clear and believable. That is, he should be neither too sure nor too unsure of his opinion. The former might alienate the jury while the latter might undermine his credibility.

Depending on his own abilities and knowledge, and depending on the number and types of experts arrayed against or in support of him, the ME may present all the evidence himself or he may ask that members of his staff or the crime lab to present portions of the evidence. For example, the ME may give testimony regarding the autopsy, while a fingerprint expert presents and discusses the prints found and how they were matched. A toxicologist may present the results of the toxicological examinations. A firearms expert might show photos of the two bullets he matched.

It is important for the expert witness to understand that, unlike in his scientific endeavors, the real goal of court proceedings is not to uncover the absolute truth. Rather it is to provide enough evidence so that the jury can come to some understandable version of the truth based on the applicable rules of law. Certain evidentiary items may not be admissible. They might have been improperly obtained or contaminated by mishandling, or they might be deemed overly inflammatory or prejudicial.

So, if some evidence is excluded, how can the absolute truth be found? Isn't that like attempting to solve a math problem with only half the numbers? Mostly, but the expert can't change the law and must work within its confines. He can only present the information he is allowed to present, explain it as fully as he can, and offer his true and unbiased opinion. This will help the jury get as close to the truth as possible.

With expert testimony, the judge typically allows a great deal of leeway in regards to how the information is presented to the jury. Most witnesses are allowed only to answer questions. If they attempt to move too far afield of the question, the opposing attorney will object or the judge himself may rein them in. An expert is allowed to speak more broadly and to teach the jury. The reason for this departure from the normal Q&A method of evidence presentation is that the expert is there for the stated purpose of presenting and explaining any evidence in his area of expertise. Indeed, he is there to teach the judge and jury. For example, it would be very difficult for the average juror to understand the impact of DNA evidence simply from a series of yes and no questions. Allowing the expert to explain what DNA is, how it is tested for, and what the results of the testing means gives the jury the knowledge they need to understand and evaluate the evidence.

In presenting the results of forensic testing, it is rare that an expert is permitted to say that something absolutely, without doubt, matches. Rather he will use phrases such as "similar to," "consistent with," "not dissimilar from," "compatible with," or "shares many characteristics with." Each if these terms speaks to the fact that forensic evidence is rarely, if ever, absolute; rather it states probabilities. For example, no two people have the same DNA, but the testifying expert will not say that the DNA "absolutely matches" that of the defendant. Instead he will say that the probability that it matches is a billion to one. That is almost, but not quite, absolute.

Why is this? Because science is not absolute. It is not static, with the possible exception of mathematics, and even this is subject to debate. Science is built on theories. As scientists attempt to explain why things are as they are, they will develop a theory that explains the given phenomenon and test it. If the theory stands up to the testing process, it becomes an accepted theory. If not, it is altered and retested. As soon as the theory survives rigorous testing, it becomes an accepted theory, or what we might view as the truth. But later, other evidence might come to light that alters the theory yet again. Does this mean that the original "truth" was not true and that the new "truth" is? No, it means that the new theory, as was the old one, is true most of the time. How often does it hold true? It depends on the theory and the results of the testing. The probability that the theory holds true could be 50 percent (coin toss), 90 percent (probable), 99.999 percent (highly probable), or 50 million to 1 (virtually 100 percent probable). As with other branches of science, forensic science deals with probabilities, not absolutes.

EVIDENCE STANDARDS OF ACCEPTANCE

Regardless of who presents the information, how do the judge and jury know that the science behind the presented evidence is real and not junk science? How do they know that the theory or testing procedure has been properly confirmed and that the probabilities cited are real? What's to keep someone from getting on the stand and spouting personal beliefs, which may have no scientific backing? The current standards for accepting evidence in the courtroom resulted from these two landmark cases.

Frye v. United States

In 1923, the District of Columbia Circuit Court addressed the admissibility of polygraph (lie detector) evidence in the case of *Frye v. United States*. This landmark decision set the rules, now known as the Frye Standard, for the presentation of scientific evidence before the court. This standard states that the court will accept expert testimony on "well-recognized scientific principle and discovery" if it has been "sufficiently established" and has achieved "general acceptance" in the scientific community. This allows for new scientific tests to be presented, but only after they have been thoroughly hashed out and accepted by the scientific community.

Frye became the standard for many years and is still followed in many jurisdictions, but more recently it has been replaced by Daubert, or Rule 702.

Daubert v. Merrell Dow Pharmaceuticals

Rule 702 of the Federal Rules of Evidence stated that the "trier of fact," which means the judge, may use expert testimony to "understand the evidence" and to "determine a fact in issue" at his discretion. This was upheld and amplified in 1993 by the United States Supreme Court, which said that the "general acceptance" clause in Frye was not absolute and handed the judge wider discretion as to what expert testimony he would allow in his court in any given case. To help judges in this regard, the court offered several guidelines.

For a new scientific technique or theory to be acceptable to the court it must:

- be subject to testing and to peer review
- be standardized with recognized maintenance of such standards
- have a known and accepted error rate
- attain widespread acceptance

This basically means that the technique or theory must be spelled out, tested, reviewed, accepted, and continually monitored for accuracy.

The admissibility of scientific evidence and testimony is often hammered out in pretrial hearings and motions, which occur away from the jury. If in the eyes of the judge the evidence to be presented by the expert passes the Frye or Daubert standards, he will allow it before the jury. If not, he might exclude it from the trial.

EVIDENCE:
THE HEART AND SOUL OF FORENSICS

If Locard's Exchange Principle is the cornerstone of forensic science, evidence is the heart and soul of the crime lab. Indeed, evidence is the sole reason it exists. Without evidence, what would the lab do? Evidence is used to determine if a crime has been committed, to link a suspect to a scene, to corroborate or refute an alibi or statement, to identify a perpetrator or victim, to exonerate the innocent, to induce a confession, and to direct further investigation.

The modern crime lab attempts to identify and compare any evidence it receives and then links this evidence to a particular individual to the exclusion of all others.

This brings up a critical concept: Evidence is used to eliminate suspects rather than to point the finger at any one person. Individualizing evidence eliminates everyone else and leaves the perpetrator standing alone.

This isn't a modern concept. Again, we look to Sherlock Holmes, who discusses in several of his stories his belief that good evidence and clear reasoning would eliminate all choices but one. My favorite comes from "The Adventure of the Beryl Coronet" in which he states, "It is an old maxim of mine that when you have excluded the impossible, whatever remains, however improbable, must be the truth."

We will look at the discriminatory power of evidence later in this chapter, but first let's see how evidence is classified.

EVIDENCE CLASSIFICATION

DIRECT AND CIRCUMSTANTIAL EVIDENCE

Evidence may be either direct or circumstantial. **Direct evidence** directly establishes a fact. Examples are eyewitness statements and confessions, which are subjective by nature and, as such, are burdened with the problems that plague all subjective information. Eyewitnesses are notoriously incorrect in their identification of a suspect and their recall of events because memory and recall are affected by the witnesses' mental and physical health and abilities, prejudices, experiences, and the emotion of the situation. What if the witness had poor vision or poor hearing, or held racial prejudices, or was highly emotional? Could his perception of who did what to whom, when, and how be distorted? Absolutely. Though most often these distortions are not intentional, they exist nonetheless. Studies of this phenomenon have shown that eyewitnesses may be wrong as much as 50 percent of the time.

On the other hand, **circumstantial evidence** is more objective and is subject to the laws of probability. This leads to the curious fact that circumstantial evidence is often more reliable than direct evidence. Unlike an eyewitness account, accurate science is not altered by subjectivity. Its interpretation might be, but the result is the result.

Circumstantial evidence is any evidence that is not direct. Blood, hair, fibers, bullets, DNA—indeed, all forensic science evidence—are circumstantial in nature. This type of evidence requires that the judge and jury infer something from the presented evidentiary fact. For example, if a fingerprint or hair found at the crime scene is matched to a suspect, the jury may infer that the print is that of the defendant and the fact that it was found at the crime scene links the defendant to the scene. Under most circumstances, this is not absolute proof, but is highly suggestive that he was involved in the crime.

PHYSICAL AND BIOLOGICAL EVIDENCE

Forensic evidence can also be physical or biological. **Physical evidence** might take the form of fingerprints, shoe and tire impressions, tool marks, fibers, paint, glass, drugs, firearms, bullets and shell casings, documents, explosives, and petroleum byproduct fire accelerants. **Biological evidence** would be a corpse, blood, saliva, semen, hair, and botanical materials, such as wood, plants, and pollen.

USING EVIDENCE

Crime scene evidence, as well as other types of evidence, may serve many purposes in criminal investigations:

CORPUS DELICTI: This Latin term means "the body of the crime," or the essential facts of the crime. Evidence will reveal exactly what type of crime was committed.

MODUS OPERANDI (MO): The steps and methods the perpetrator employed to commit the crime. A criminal's methods tend to be repetitive so that identification of his MO can help with uncovering or trapping the perpetrator.

LINKAGE: The association, or linking, of a suspect to a victim, place, or other evidence is critical to solving the crime.

VERIFICATION: Evidence can substantiate or refute suspect or witness statements and show who is lying and who is speaking the truth.

SUSPECT IDENTIFICATION: Evidence such as fingerprints or DNA can often identify the perpetrator.

CRIME SCENE RECONSTRUCTION: The evidence often allows investigators to reconstruct the sequence of events of the crime.

INVESTIGATIVE LEADS: Evidence will frequently direct the lines of investigation that the police and coroner follow and often lead them to the perpetrator.

From a forensic sense, evidence serves many functions. It can identify and compare evidence items, display its inherent class and individual characteristics, reconstruct the crime's sequence of events, and associate or dissociate a suspect from the crime.

IDENTIFICATION AND COMPARISON

The forensic analysis of evidence items is done for two main purposes: **identification** and **comparison**. Identification is done to determine what exactly a particular item or substance is. Is this white powder heroin or crystal methamphetamine or sugar? Who manufactured the shoe that left the print at the crime scene? Are there petrochemical residues present in the debris of a suspicious fire? Is this brown carpet stain dried blood or chocolate sauce?

Identification in such circumstances is critical since, if the powder is sugar and not heroin or the stain is indeed chocolate sauce and not blood, there might be no crime at all. Conversely, if heroin or blood is identified, either may become the crucial evidence in a criminal proceeding. Such identifications make up an important part of the work done by the crime lab. After testing, the examiner may state that the questioned substance is present, not present, or that the testing is inconclusive and the presence of the substance can be neither ruled in nor out.

Comparisons are done to see if a suspect item or substance shares a common origin with a known one. That is, did they come from the same person, place, or object? Did this fingerprint, hair, or blood come from the suspect? Does this paint smudge found on a hit-and-run victim's clothing match that of the suspect's car? Does the bullet removed from a murder victim match the one test-fired from the suspect's gun?

For example, after comparing a crime scene fingerprint to one obtained from a suspect, the examiner may state that the two match (bad news for the suspect), do not match (may exonerate the suspect), or that the comparison was inconclusive, perhaps because the crime scene print was of poor quality. In the last case, the suspect is neither cleared nor condemned.

CLASS VS. INDIVIDUAL CHARACTERISTICS

Some types of evidence carry more weight than others. Hair and fibers can suggest, while DNA and fingerprints can absolutely make a connection. The difference is that some evidence shares **class characteristics** and others **individual characteristics**.

Class characteristics are those that are not unique to a particular object, but rather serve to place the particular bit of evidence into a specific class. For example, if a victim has been shot, the determination that the bullet was from a .38 caliber handgun would make all .38 caliber handguns the possible murder weapon. Other calibers would not belong to this class and would be excluded from consideration. Alternatively, blood recovered from a crime scene could be found to be type B. It could have come from any of the tens of millions of people who share this blood type. If the suspect has type B blood, he remains a suspect and DNA testing will be required to conclusively match the sample to the suspect. But if he has type A blood, he is excluded.

A single piece of class evidence can rarely convict, but it can often exonerate. The above type B blood would exclude all persons with a different blood type.

FORENSIC CASE FILES: THE ATLANTA CHILD MURDERS

In Atlanta, Georgia, during the late 1970s and early 1980s, young black children began disappearing, their bodies turning up along and in nearby rivers. The situation created near hysteria in the area and became racially charged with accusations and speculations about who might be killing the children. The FBI was called in and the story filled newspapers from coast to coast. It was felt that the killer was tossing the bodies into the rivers from bridges, so stakeouts were set up. Early in the morning of May 22, 1981, Atlanta police officers, while staking out a bridge over the Chattahoochee River, heard a splash and found a young black man on the bridge. His name was Wayne Williams. He was questioned and released. Five days later the body of twenty-seven-year-old Nathaniel Cater washed to shore downstream from the bridge and Wayne Williams became a prime suspect. He was arrested on June 21.

In December 1981, Williams was tried for the Atlanta child murders based largely on class fiber evidence. Multiple fibers, twenty-eight different types in all, were found on several of the victims. These fibers chemically and optically matched fibers taken from Williams's home and cars. Blue, yellow, white, and yellow-green fibers of various synthetic types were similar to fibers taken from Williams's kitchen and backroom carpets, bedspread, throw rug, and car liner. Hairs matching those of his dog were also found. Williams was convicted.

They belong to a different class and only those in the class of individuals with type B blood would remain in the suspect pool. However, if multiple types of class evidence are associated with one suspect, the weight of the evidence may make a strong case. A classic example is the Atlanta child murders case.

In cases such as this, the sheer number of the pieces of class evidence makes coincidence extremely unlikely. What are the odds that someone else left behind this combination of fibers and hair? Though class evidence is not absolute proof that a suspect is connected to a particular location, and each bit of class evidence taken alone may not be strong, when a large number of matching evidence is found, the odds that the suspect was present at the crime scene becomes overwhelming.

Individual characteristics are as close to absolute proof of the origin of the evidence item as is possible. The most individualizing types of evidence are fingerprints and DNA, since no two people possess either the same prints or the same

DNA (the exception being identical twins who have the same DNA but different fingerprints). Impression evidence, such as bullet ballistic markings, shoe and tire tracks, and tool marks, may be unique enough to be considered individual evidence. Also, fracture or tear patterns, such as in broken glass, torn paper, or matches ripped from a matchbook, may possess edges that fit perfectly together like a jigsaw puzzle, thus indicating the pieces shared a common source.

The overriding principle in the analysis of individual characteristics is that no two things are exactly alike. No two guns mark a bullet the same way. No two pieces of glass fracture in the same manner. No two pairs of shoes or sets of car tires wear in exactly the same way.

The goal of the criminalist is to identify individualizing characteristics, for these truly "make the case" by positively identifying the source of the questioned evidence. If ballistics matched the markings on a .38 caliber bullet to those from a bullet test-fired by a suspect weapon, these markings are individual evidence. They separate this particular gun from all other .38 caliber weapons and indicate that this particular .38 was the murder weapon. Similarly, in the earlier type B blood example we just discussed, DNA could be used to eliminate all of the people with type B blood except for the one person who actually left the blood at the crime scene.

The bottom line is that class evidence can considerably narrow the field of suspects and individual evidence can narrow it further, perhaps to a single person.

RECONSTRUCTIVE AND ASSOCIATIVE EVIDENCE

Whether the evidence is class or individual in quality, it may be used to reconstruct the events of the crime or to associate a suspect with the crime scene.

Reconstructive evidence is any evidence that helps in reconstructing the crime scene. Broken glass or pried doors and windows may reveal the perpetrator's points of entry and exit. Was the window broken from the inside or the outside? Did the perpetrator use a key or a screwdriver to gain entry? Shoe prints, blood spatters, and the trajectory of bullets may show where in the room everyone was and exactly how and in what sequence the crime occurred. Was the victim attacked from the front or from behind? Was the murder quick or did a struggle occur? Was the prime suspect at the scene at the time of the murder or did he, as he says, stumble into the scene later? Reconstructive evidence helps the ME determine who did what, where, when, and how, as well as helps determine who is being truthful and who might be lying. Crime scene reconstruction is discussed in greater detail later in the chapter.

Associative evidence is evidence that ties the suspect to the crime scene. Fingerprints, shoeprints, hair, fibers, blood and other body fluids, knives, bullets, guns, and paint, among others, may be used to link the suspect to the scene, or prove that the fingerprints, hair, or blood is not his and that someone else must have committed the crime.

This linkage was discussed in Chapter One, but is worth a brief mention here. Evidence is supposed to link a suspect to a person, place, or object. The finding of a victim's hair or fibers from the victim's clothing on the clothing of the suspect suggests that they had some degree of contact, and thus links the two together. A suspect's fingerprint, blood, or semen at the scene of a robbery, murder, or rape strongly links him to the crime scene. A murder weapon that holds a suspect's fingerprints requires a great deal of explaining. Each of these circumstances links elements of the crime to the suspect. The link can be established through the criminalists collecting evidence and the analytical procedures of the crime lab work. When successful, the evidence may find its way into court and result in a conviction.

COLLECTING EVIDENCE

Police, criminalists, and coroner's technicians are charged with locating, protecting, collecting, and transporting evidence to the crime lab or the coroner's office. The coroner and the crime lab technicians then analyze each piece of evidence. Each step in this chain must be done properly, with great attention to detail, or the evidence could be deemed inadmissible in court.

EVIDENCE LOCATION

Before evidence can be collected and processed, it must be located. Often this is straightforward. A caller reports a burglary, and when the police arrive the caller invites them in and shows them the location of the pried window, the family safe, and the open door escape route. But, what if the probable location of the evidence is not associated with a crime scene and the police are not invited into the area where the evidence might be located? To enter and search the location, they need a search warrant.

Search Warrants

The Fourth Amendment to the United States Constitution protects citizens "against unreasonable searches and seizures." This means that police personnel and crime scene investigators need a warrant from a judge before they can search private property for evidence. This warrant must be specific as to time, place, and items to be searched for and must be obtained based on "probable cause." The police petition a judge to sign a search warrant. Only a law enforcement officer may obtain a search warrant; attorneys, private investigators, and private citizens cannot.

The steps required to obtain a valid search warrant are:

PREPARE AN AFFIDAVIT: This must describe the location to be searched, the items to be searched for, and the reasons why the officer expects the items are at the location (probable cause).

PREPARE THE WARRANT: This is the official document that the judge must sign to give permission for the search.

GET THE WARRANT SIGNED: The officer must present the warrant and affidavit to the judge. If the judge feels that probable cause exists, he signs the warrant, making it official.

Often this is simple, but sometimes it can be very difficult. The three issues that can make obtaining and executing a warrant problematic are probable cause, specificity of the search, and the area to be searched.

Probable Cause

Probable cause means that the officer has a strong concrete reason to believe that the items in question are at the location to be searched. A hunch or a mere suspicion won't work.

Let's say an arms supplier has a safe house where he sells his wares. The police have observed known arms dealers come and go with crates that could contain guns. The investigators may even know who has received the illegal weapons. This is more than a hunch. It's fairly solid evidence that the packages coming and going from the house contain weapons. In this case a warrant would most likely be issued.

Another common scenario is for the police to have the word of an informant that some illegal activity has taken place at a certain location. Before the judge issues a warrant on the word of an informant, though, he may require that the police show that the informant has been reliable in the past.

On the other hand, the judge might not issue the warrant if he feels the necessary probable cause does not exist: Maybe the informant is unreliable or has no track record with the police or the evidence submitted in support of the warrant request isn't strong enough. A witness simply seeing a blue SUV near the crime scene would not likely be sufficient to obtain a warrant to search a suspect's blue SUV or his home.

Specificity of the Search

The search warrant must state exactly what the police are looking for. They can't simply say that they are going in to search a house and see what they find. The warrant application should list that they are looking for specific items. In the case of the arms dealer, they would be searching for rifles, handguns, and other ballistic weapons, ammunition, crates containing weapons, and any paper or computer records of arms transactions. Once the warrant is granted, the police could then search any area where these might be found. The house, the attic, the garage, closets, crawl spaces, and anywhere else guns could be hidden would be fair game, as well as any filing cabinets or computers.

What if in the course of their search for the items listed they find other evidence or illegal items? Can these be seized? This is an interesting legal problem and the answer is sometimes yes, sometimes no.

What if the warrant only listed gun crates and not handguns, papers, or computers? The police could then only search areas that could actually conceal a crate. Rooms, attics, closets, and basements would be searchable areas. A kitchen drawer would not. If they opened a drawer and found drugs or a weapon, they could not seize it and use it in court. For this reason, the police attempt to include a number of small items in the warrant since this will allow for a much more inclusive search. In the arms dealer scenario, they would include handguns, papers, and computers, maybe even drugs. These small items can be hidden almost anywhere, which would allow investigators to look through more places.

Area of Search

Another difficulty is the definition of the area to be searched must be explicitly stated. For example, if the warrant identifies a house but does not specifically state that the garage or storage shed can be searched, these areas will be off limits. If the warrant lists a garage but not the car inside, the garage can be searched but not the car.

As you can see, obtaining a proper warrant is not as simple as it appears on television. It requires attention to detail. A case can fall apart when these finer points are overlooked.

Searching Without a Warrant

As previously discussed, the Fourth Amendment requires that a probable cause warrant be obtained in order for a location to be searched, but there are times that a search can be undertaken without a warrant. If a suspect is destroying evidence, or a structure fire is threatening to do the same, can the police save the evidence? Sometimes, yes. The Supreme Court has allowed "warrant-less" searches in some of the following types of situations.

EMERGENCY SITUATIONS: If an emergency exists where someone's life or health is in danger, the police may enter without a warrant. Any evidence found during this emergency entry may be used. But the police cannot make an emergency entrance, leave, and then return at a later date to search for evidence. This second entry would require a warrant.

IMMEDIATE LOSS OF EVIDENCE: This exception would apply in the case of the suspect or some other agent, such as a structure fire, threatening to destroy evidence.

LAWFUL ARREST: If a suspect has been lawfully arrested, he and any property in his immediate control, such as a home or vehicle, may be searched for evidence.

CONSENTED SEARCH: No warrant is needed if the party in question consents to a search of his person or property.

Once the search is done and the evidence is found, what then? The evidence must be protected, collected, and properly preserved.

PROTECTING THE EVIDENCE

Protecting the crime scene and evidence is of paramount importance. Law enforcement's ability to successfully investigate and prosecute a crime can be lost at this critical point. Even the most expensively equipped and sophisticated crime lab can do little with damaged, altered, or contaminated evidence, and courts rarely allow such evidence to be presented to the jury.

This crucial duty of the initial protection of the evidence falls to the first responding officer. He must approach the crime scene in a logical and organized manner. Failure to do this may lead to harm to himself, fellow officers, victims, witnesses, or suspects. For example, a violent perpetrator could still be at the scene or a burned building could be structurally unsound or broken glass could cause bodily injury. Evidence can also be damaged, destroyed, or rendered useless.

The first responding officer detains any witnesses while not allowing them access to the crime scene. Since he has no way of knowing if the person who reported the crime is a witness or a suspect—it is not rare for the perpetrator to report the crime himself, perhaps believing this will make him less of a suspect—allowing entry to the actual scene could lead to loss or contamination of evidence. It is also not uncommon for perpetrators to attempt to destroy or remove evidence.

Once at the scene, personal safety is the officer's primary concern. He makes sure that the perpetrators are no longer present or a threat. If present, they are arrested and secured. Then, he assists any victims, offers first aid as needed, and mobilizes emergency medical services. After that is completed, he begins the process of crime scene preservation.

Concurrent with this he may need to detain and separate all suspects and witnesses in order avoid collusion between them. At this stage he may not know who is a suspect and who is a witness. A witness may turn into a suspect and a suspect may actually be a useful witness. He may have no reason or legal right to detain some witnesses. If this is the case, he must obtain accurate identification and contact information from each person who leaves the area.

At the heart of crime scene protection is our old friend Locard's Exchange Principle in the previous chapter. It states that when any two people come in contact with each other, they will exchange or transfer trace materials. Hair, fibers, and prints are classic examples. The same is true for a crime scene. Every person who enters the scene can leave behind evidence of their presence, take away crucial trace evidence on their shoes, clothes, or hands, or damage or alter any evidence that remains. For this reason, access to the scene must be restricted immediately and all witnesses and suspects are denied entry to the crime scene area.

THE CRIME SCENE

What constitutes a crime scene? Obviously it varies from scene to scene, but the officer must quickly decide its size and boundaries. The scene typically includes the offense site as well as areas of approach, entry, exit, and escape. The offense site might be the body location (in a murder), a safe or cabinet (in a burglary), or an entire structure (in a suspicious fire). The entire scene might include the street in front of a house or the entire block, or an adjacent building or a nearby field or wooded area.

The crime scene is first cordoned off, using crime scene tape, barricades, automobiles, or other officers. Only the personnel absolutely needed to process the scene should be allowed in. This is often more difficult that it seems. Victim's family members and neighbors may be emotionally unstable and difficult to remove from the area. Members of the press are often clever in their methods to gain entry. A lowly patrol officer may have trouble preventing a police captain or other high-ranking official, who has no real reason to be there, from entering the scene. And never underestimate the meanderings of the curious bystander.

Once he has established the perimeter, the officer creates a security log, which must be signed by all visitors to the scene. This helps the investigation in many ways, not the least of which is narrowing the number of people who must be examined when stray fingerprints and shoeprints are found. If the investigators can be ruled out, the print may belong to the perpetrator.

After this, the crime scene investigator does a walk-through examination to get a feel for the scene so he can organize the approach to evidence collection. During this overview, he typically doesn't examine any particular piece of evidence, but tries to see the entire picture.

While processing the scene, everything that transpires is documented in notes, sketches and photographs, and perhaps on videotape. This includes not only the scene and the evidence, but also the surrounding area, particularly any of the perpetrator's possible entry and exit points.

A designated note taker is assigned the job of keeping an accurate account of all activities within the crime scene. Sometimes a tape recorder is used and the tape is later transcribed. Regardless, detailed notes must be kept. A description of the scene and an accurate list of each piece of evidence, noting its description, where, by whom, and at what time it was found, as well as its final disposition, must be made. He also identifies and comments on each photo that is taken.

The crime scene is photographed as early as possible so that it can be preserved in its unaltered condition. Photos should definitely be taken before any evidence, including the body, is moved. Several overview images of the scene and, if outdoors, the surrounding area are taken from multiple angles. Close-ups of each item of evidence and all injuries to the corpse are critical. Videotape has the advantage of including sound so that comments can be added. But if video is used, photographs are also taken since they offer much greater detail resolution.

Full-body photos are taken of any injured parties, including the suspect, as well as close-ups of any injuries. Whether these are done at the scene or at the hospital (even in the operating room) depends on the nature of the injuries.

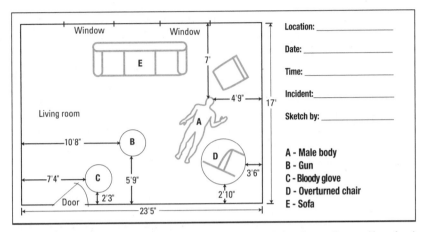

Figure 2-1: Crime scene sketch. The sketch must be clear, complete, and show the coordinate positions of each evidence item.

Bumps, bruises, and scratches can be done at the scene, while major traumas and gunshot and knife wounds will require that the victim be transported to the hospital, so photos can be shot there.

Sketches are extremely important. They show the relationship of each item of evidence to the other items or the body (see Figure 2-1). Each piece of evidence must be indicated and located by its distance from two fixed points, such as a wall, doorway, fire hydrant, or sidewalk. This triangulation gives the exact graphic coordinates of each item. Sketches made at the scene may be rough, but must be accurate. They can later be redrawn for clarity and aesthetics. There are several computer programs available that can help with making clear drawings.

LOCATING AND PRESERVING THE EVIDENCE

Once the crime scene has been defined and protected and the initial walk-through completed, the tedious task of evidence collection begins. This is neither as sexy nor as cool as it appears on television and is, in fact, quite laborious when done properly.

Who has the duty of evidence collection depends upon the size, budget, and organization of the crime lab or law enforcement agency charged with investigating the crime. In smaller, less well-funded jurisdictions, police officers perform this duty, while larger, more sophisticated labs have special evidence-collection units. These are the CSI people. Regardless of who actually gathers the evidence, they should be well schooled in proper techniques.

The first step is to locate the evidence within the crime scene. Corpses and weapons may be readily visible, but other items, particularly smaller materials and bits of trace evidence, must be searched for. Points of entry and exit, as well as the area near the body (in homicides) or open safes, cabinets, or drawers (in robberies), are targeted since these are the areas where most evidence is typically found. The reason for this goes back once again to Locard's Exchange Principle. The perpetrator, of necessity, will have come into close contact with the body or the safe and will have passed through areas of approach, entry, exit, and escape. He might leave behind fingerprints, shoeprints, tire tracks, blood, hair, fiber, bits of broken glass, or paint chips. He might toss the murder weapon or the tool used to gain entrance along his escape route. He might accidentally drop a bloody glove. These items must be searched for.

GATHERING THE EVIDENCE

There is an order to evidence gathering. The first evidence searched for and collected is the most fragile or the most likely to be lost, damaged, or contaminated. This is particularly true in outdoor scenes, where wind and rain may complicate things. Fragile evidence might include blood, fibers, hair, even fingerprints or shoe and tire tracks. It all depends on the situation.

In later chapters, we will look at the techniques for locating and collecting the specific types of evidence typically encountered in criminal investigations. For now we will take a general overview of the collection process.

Obvious and exposed latent fingerprints are photographed and then "lifted" (see Chapter Twelve). The same is true for tool marks and shoe or tire impressions, which are photographed before being lifted or cast. Fibers and hair are searched for with alternative light sources and picked up with tweezers. Carpets and furniture are vacuumed, using a fresh vacuum cleaner bag for each area. This often yields hair, fibers, and other trace material that escape the technician's eye at the scene.

To avoid damage and cross contamination, each piece of evidence must be packaged separately. Most dry trace evidence can be placed in druggist's folds, which are small, folded papers. Envelopes, canisters, plastic pill bottles, and paper or plastic bags may also be used. Documents are sealed in plastic covers for transport to the lab.

Liquid evidence is put into unbreakable, airtight containers. This is also true for solids that may contain volatile evidence, such as fire remnants that are believed to contain residues of hydrocarbon accelerants. Left unsealed, these residues may evaporate before testing can be done. Clean paint cans and tightly sealed jars work well in this situation.

Moist or wet biological evidence must be placed in non-airtight containers so that it may air dry. If not, the moisture can cause mold, mildew, and bacterial growth, which can lead to decay and destruction of the sample. Bloody clothing is often hung up and allowed to thoroughly air dry. After the biological material dries, the evidence is repackaged into sealed containers.

Sometimes it is difficult or impossible to remove the evidence from the scene without damaging it. A tool mark on a pried window seal can be processed at the scene or the entire window frame can be removed and taken to the lab. Bullet holes in a concrete wall may likewise be processed on site or a portion of the wall can be carefully removed for later laboratory evaluation.

Another important aspect of evidence collection is obtaining proper control samples, which are samples used as a standard of comparison for checking or verifying the results of an experiment. These may come from the victim, suspect, or items at the scene. An automobile interior carpet fiber found at the scene is most valuable if control fibers are available from the car of the suspect's vehicle. This way, the identified or control sample can be matched to the unidentified crime scene sample. Control samples of blood taken from the victim and the suspect can be matched to an unknown bloodstain found at the scene to see which one of them, if either, shed the blood.

Sometimes control samples take the form of **substrates** that are identical to the substrate of the evidence item in question. A substrate is any object, material, or environment on which something else acts, is placed, or is combined with. For example, a charred carpet that is suspected of containing residue of an accelerant such as gasoline is best compared against the exact same carpet that is free of the suspect material. A carpet sample taken in an area undamaged by the fire may provide the known sample. If the examiner finds a suspicious hydrocarbon chemical in the charred carpet that is not present in the known sample, he can be more certain that it is indeed a foreign chemical and not a component of the carpet or its adhesive.

Chain of Custody

The **chain of custody** is absolutely paramount in evidence collection. Without this continuity of possession, the evidence may be rendered inadmissible in court. The defense would rightly call into question the authenticity and integrity of the evidence since outside contamination cannot be ruled out. For this reason, every person who handles the evidence must be accounted for and recorded, and this chain of custody must remain unbroken from crime scene to courtroom.

The person who finds the evidence item must mark it for identification. This consists of writing or scratching his initials onto the item itself. Of course, it must be possible for him to do this without damaging the evidence or altering any of its specific identifying characteristics. For example, he may scratch his initials on the side of a shell casing. Later in court, he can then positively identify this shell casing as the exact one he found at the scene. He would not likely do this with a bullet, since the striations on the side of the bullet would be altered, making a ballistic match more difficult. The item is then placed into an evidence bag, which is also marked and initialed by the finder. The identifying information on the evidence bag includes the case number, the name and description of the item, the person who found it, witnesses to the discovery and recovery, and the date, time, and location of the find.

If the item itself cannot be safely marked, it is placed into the appropriate container or packaging. This in turn is placed into an evidence bag. Both the item container and the evidence bag must be marked and initialed. For example, a blood sample may be taken using a moist cotton-tipped swab. After drying, the swab is placed into a sealed glass tube and the tube is marked with the collector's initials and the date. The tube is placed into an evidence bag, which is similarly marked. The collector may then reasonably testify that this is the sample he obtained by identifying his initials on the sample tube and the evidence bag.

Each person who accepts the evidence must initial or sign and date the evidence bag. He is then responsible for the integrity of the item until he passes it to someone else. Let's go back to the example of the shell casing found at a homicide scene. After the finding officer collects it, marks it, and places it into a marked evidence bag, he signs the bag of evidence over to the crime scene coordinator, who then transports it to the lab and signs it over to the crime lab technician. After the testing and evaluation of the item is completed, the technician signs it over to the custodian of evidence, who places it in a secured area until next needed. It is then signed over to the prosecution for

---

presentation in court. If this chain remains intact, each witness—the finding officer, the crime scene coordinator, the lab technician, and the custodian of evidence—can testify that the item presented in the courtroom is indeed the item collected at the scene and tested by the lab.

PRIMARY AND SECONDARY CRIME SCENES

We've looked at how a crime scene is defined and controlled and how evidence is located, preserved, and collected. But what if there is more than one crime scene? What if the criminal moved from place to place during his criminal activity?

Crime scenes can be considered **primary** or **secondary**. The primary scene is where the crime actually occurred, while any subsequent scenes are deemed secondary. In a bank robbery, the bank would be the primary scene while the getaway car and the thief's hideout would be secondary scenes. Or, if a killer commits a murder at someone's home, but transports the victim's body to another location, such as a river for disposal, the home would be the primary scene and the perpetrator's car and the river would be secondary scenes. Primary scenes typically yield more usable evidence than secondary scenes, but not always.

Sometimes only a secondary scene is available. If a body is found at a "dump site," this would be a secondary scene. The primary scene, where the murder actually occurred, is not known. Investigators use the evidence found at the secondary scene in an attempt to identify the killer or to locate the primary scene. For example, fibers from an expensive or unusual carpet may be found on the victim. Investigators might be able to use this evidence to identify the manufacturer and the seller and ultimately to create a list of buyers or locations where that particular product has been installed. This may greatly narrow the focus of the investigation and may lead to the primary crime scene and the perpetrator.

CRIME SCENE RECONSTRUCTION

I mentioned earlier that one of the functions of evidence is to reconstruct a crime scene. **Crime scene reconstruction** is both science and art. The main goals of the reconstruction process are to determine the likely sequence of events and the locations and positions of everyone present during the crime. This information may be critical in determining suspect truthfulness and witness reliability.

The first question the investigators must answer about the crime scene is whether it is **dynamic** (also called active) or **static** (also called passive). This means whether committing the crime involved a great deal of activity. For example, let's say that a murder victim was stabbed multiple times. If the scene is relatively undisturbed with the victim lying on the floor in a pool of blood, this would likely be a static scene. On the other hand, if furniture is toppled over or objects have been knocked off tables or desks, or if a blood trail leads from place to place or room to room, this would indicate a more dynamic scene. It would also indicate that a struggle took place. These are two entirely different scenes and would result from different sequences of events. If suspect or witness statements as to what happened are counter to what is seen, suspicions are raised.

After the investigator does his initial walk-through of the scene, he begins to mentally formulate a hypothesis for the events of the crime. He then looks at each piece of physical evidence to see if it supports this theory. He considers information obtained at the scene and also from the crime lab, the medical reports of any injured persons, and the ME's autopsy examination. Anything that does not fit must be reconciled or the theory must change. This means that the reconstruction of the scene constantly evolves as more evidence is uncovered.

The investigator continually tests his theory not only against the evidence but also against logic and common sense. But he must not make assumptions. It may seem logical that a perpetrator did a certain thing or that a piece of evidence ended up where it did because of some action by the perpetrator, but if the hard evidence doesn't support this belief, the theory must be re-evaluated. If a gun is found just outside the rear door of the house where a homicide occurred, logic suggests that the assailant dropped the gun during his escape. Possible, but what if the gun had been tossed there in an attempt to stage a domestic homicide to make it look as though a breaking-and-entering homicide had occurred? The husband's fingerprints on the gun or the victim's blood on the husband's shoes might change the theory. In reconstruction, all evidence must be considered and explained.

Shoeprints may reveal the perpetrator's every step. Fingerprints may indicate the things he touched. Tool marks are often found at points of entry or where safes or cabinets were pried open. Blood spatters, bullet trajectories, the angle of blows and stabs, and the nature of the victim's injuries as determined by live examination or at autopsy may reveal the actual and relative positions of the assailant and the victim. Reading the pattern of post-mortem lividity of the corpse (see Chapter Five) may confirm that the body was moved several hours after death. The discovery of attempts to clean up the scene may contradict a suspect's story.

The reconstruction of the crime scene must take all of this and more into consideration. As I said, it is both science and art and takes a skilled and experienced investigator to put all the evidence together and create a "picture" of the crime.

THE STAGED CRIME SCENE

Crime scene reconstruction is invaluable in determining that a crime scene has been staged. **Staging** is when the perpetrator alters the scene in an attempt to make the scene look like something it's not. The most common staging scenario is when the perpetrator tries to make a murder look like a suicide or an accident. For example, let's say a husband strikes his wife in the head with a blunt object, killing her. He cleans up the bedroom, moves her into the bathroom, and places her in the tub. He then calls the paramedics and says she fell while bathing. Or he might leave her body in the bedroom and try to make it look like a robbery-murder by breaking windows or prying locks.

Another scenario would be to make a homicide look like a suicide. What if the husband surreptitiously fed his wife enough alcohol and sedatives to kill her and then forged a suicide note?

A self-robbery may be staged to look like breaking and entering. Maybe jewelry is missing and a window is pried—and, of course, the jewelry is insured.

Tearing or removing part or all of a murder victim's clothing may be done to suggest that the crime was sexually motivated when it was not.

Arson may also be considered staging. In this situation, the perpetrator sets the fire to cover another crime, maybe murder, maybe embezzlement. His hope is that the fire will obscure the signs of murder on the body or destroy the papers that show he took the missing money.

In each of these situations, the work of investigators, the medical examiner, and the crime lab may tell a different story than the perpetrator intended. The pattern of the wife's head injury might not match the edge of the tub but the baseball bat in the closet instead—the bat with the faint bloodstain unnoticed by the husband. The forensic document examiner might quickly discover that the suicide note was not written by the victim but rather by her husband. He may also be able to recover information from the burned documents in the fire. The lack of carbon monoxide in the victim's blood and soot in his airways may indicate that he was dead before the fire started. These findings reveal that the sequence of events were not what they initially seemed to be or were claimed to be by the perpetrator.

PART II

THE CORONER AND THE BODY

THE AUTOPSY:
A LOOK INSIDE THE BODY

The terms *autopsy, post-mortem examination*, and *necropsy* are used inter-changeably but mean the same thing—the examination of the dead. The word *autopsy* means "to view one's self." A better term would be *necropsy. Necro* means "death," so *necropsy* means "to look at death." However, *autopsy* is the term that has been traditionally used since the Middle Ages.

HISTORY OF THE AUTOPSY

As early as 3500 B.c. the Mesopotamians conducted autopsies on animals in the hopes of communicating with certain divine forces. They believed that many of the animal's organs, most notably the liver, carried messages from the gods. Ancient Egyptians performed a form of autopsy as they prepared corpses for the journey to the other side. As part of the mummification pro-cess, the abdomen would be opened and the internal organs (except for the heart) would be removed and placed in ceremonial jars within the burial chamber. The brain was extracted in pieces through the nose. These ancient cultures performed these procedures for religious and spiritual reasons and not as a search for medical knowledge.

The first true autopsies done to gain medical knowledge were likely those performed by Erasistratus (c. 304–250 B.c.), founder of Alexandria's school of anatomy, and Herophilus (c. 335–280 B.C.), who discovered that arteries and veins were anatomically different, during the third century B.C. The renowned physician and surgeon to the gladiators Galen (131–200 A.D.) dissected both animals and humans in an attempt to prove that Hippocrates' Four Humours theory of disease causation was correct. For centuries after Galen, the Greeks, Roman, Egyptians, and Medieval Europeans performed autopsies in order to learn anatomy. This was done in a fairly haphazard fashion since medicine was poorly organized and the church cast a wary eye toward such procedures.

Pope Clement VI (1291–1352) ordered that autopsies be done on victims of the Black Death in the hopes of finding a cause for the plague that killed 25 to 35 million people, or between a third and half of Europe's population. It is curious that, even though it was widely believed that this bubonic plague was due to supernatural causes, witchcraft, or as punishment for mankind's evil, the Pope sought an anatomical reason for it. Of course, none was found because the tools and knowledge to uncover the true cause were still centuries away.

In the late 1400s, the first medical schools appeared at Bologna and Padua in Italy, and Pope Sixtus IV (1414–1484) allowed human dissections as a part of medical and surgical training. It would be another 250 years before the autopsy became the useful tool it is today. Giovanni Morgagni (1682–1771), in his long and stellar career as professor of anatomy in Padua, was the first to correlate the findings at autopsy with various diseases. He showed that disease was caused by and in turn caused anatomical changes in the human body. The fields of gross anatomy (the study of anatomy with the naked eye) and pathology were born. Around the same time, Antony van Leeuwenhoek (1632–1723) invented the microscope, an instrument that opened up the microscopic world to scientists. But it would be another two centuries before German pathologist Rudolph Virchow (1821–1902), using Leeuwenhoek's invention, established the roots of cellular biology and anatomy. He found that not only did disease cause visible changes in organs, as Morgagni had pointed out, but also led to changes in the cells of the body.

During a harsh winter on St. Croix Island in 1604, French colonists performed the first documented autopsies in North America when nearly half of the seventy-nine settlers died. Archeological and historical evidence suggests that several autopsies were performed in the hopes of uncovering what was killing so many members of the community.

FORENSIC AUTOPSY MILESTONES

- Erasistratus and Herophilus performed the first post-mortem examinations in order to study disease states in Alexandria in the third century B.C.
- Galen, surgeon to the gladiators in Pergamum, dissected corpses and wrote extensively on human anatomy.
- A Roman physician examined the body of the slain Julius Caesar and determined that of his twenty-three stab wounds only the one to his heart was fatal.
- The first true forensic autopsies were completed in the 1200s at the University of Bologna.
- In 1235, Sung Tz'u's *Hsi Yuan Lu* (*The Washing Away of Wrongs*), a forensic manual, was published in China. In part, it described how to examine murder victims as an aid to solving the crime.
- Ambroise Paré (1510–1590), a famous French military surgeon to four French kings, used cauterization and ligature of arteries rather than amputation for war wounds and pioneered the use of turpentine as a wound antiseptic. He wrote extensively on the anatomical features of war and homicidal wounds.
- In 1642, the University of Leipzig first began offering courses in the field of forensic medicine.
- Giovanni Morgagni performed and carefully recorded many autopsies on victims of murder.
- French physician François-Emmanuel Fodéré (1764–1835) published his *Traité de médecine légale et d'hygiène publique* in 1798, a landmark book in forensic medicine.
- Andrew Duncan (1744–1828) began lecturing on legal medicine at Edinburgh University in 1801, and in 1807, his son Andrew (1773–1832) became the first Professor of Medical Jurisprudence, or forensic medicine.
- In 1813, surgeon James S. Stringham (1775–1817), who studied at Edinburgh, became the first Professor of Medical Jurisprudence in the United States.
- Berlin medical professor Johann Ludwig Casper (1796–1864) published his *Gerichtliche Leichenöffnung* (*Forensic Dissection*) in 1850, and *Practical Manual of Forensic Medicine* in 1856, both becoming international textbooks. He was the first to use color lithographs to illustrate forensic pathology.

THE PATHOLOGIST: CLINICAL VS. FORENSIC

Pathology comes from the Greek words *pathos*, which means "disease," and *logos*, which means "the study of." Thus, pathology is the study of disease.

The medical specialty of pathology began in the 1800s. By the beginning of the twentieth century, gross (naked eye) and microscopic pathology began to drive a rapid progression in our understanding of disease and death. By the mid-1900s, pathologists began to separate along subspecialty lines. The anatomical pathologist dealt primarily with disease states and used the autopsy and tissues removed at surgery to conduct his studies. The clinical pathologist involved himself primarily with laboratory testing and the diagnosis of disease. Today, general medical or clinical pathologists are concerned with both areas.

The clinical pathologist oversees the hospital lab to assure quality and to interpret lab tests. He consults with treating physicians in all specialties and helps them with the diagnosis and treatment of the living. The post-mortem exams He performs are medical autopsies, which are designed to determine the cause of death and to search for the presence of any other diseases.

On the other hand, a forensic pathologist is concerned with the interface of pathology and the law. He is more likely to deal with injuries and death than he is with disease. He performs forensic autopsies and is often required to testify in court regarding his findings and opinions.

THE FORENSIC AUTOPSY

A forensic pathologist typically performs forensic autopsies, though in some areas, a medical pathologist may be the designated ME and be charged with this duty.

The forensic autopsy is performed to answer four questions (covered more extensively in other chapters).

1. What is the cause of death? What illness or injury led to the death? (Chapter Six)
2. What is the mechanism of death? What physiological derangement actually resulted in death? (Chapter Six)
3. What is the manner of death? Was the death natural, accidental, suicidal, or homicidal? (Chapter Six)
4. What was the time of death? (Chapter Five)

WHO GETS AUTOPSIED?

The coroner typically investigates any death that is traumatic, unusual, sudden, or unexpected. In most areas, approximately 1 percent of the population dies each year. About one quarter of these will come to the attention of the coroner or ME. In most deaths, the physician who has cared for the person will sign the death certificate and the coroner will accept his determination that the death was natural. If the attending physician is uncomfortable with a particular situation or if he feels that the death is in any way suspicious, he may request the ME's involvement.

The ME may or may not perform an autopsy in any particular situation. Whenever he reviews a case, he has several options for handling it. In the case of a terminally ill individual or one that is very old and chronically ill, he may perform no testing and deem the death a natural occurrence. In other cases, such as victims of automobile or industrial accidents, he may perform a cursory exam and order toxicology testing to see if the person was chemically impaired in any way. If neither of these suggests something more sinister than an accidental death, he may sign it out as exactly that. Sometimes he will perform a partial autopsy. If the victim died from a head injury in a fall or in an industrial accident, the ME may only examine the head and brain before filing his report. Or he may perform a complete forensic autopsy. It's his call.

The laws that govern situations in which the coroner will perform an autopsy vary among jurisdictions, though most operate under similar guidelines. The terms **reportable death** or **coroner's case** mean any death that must, by law, be reported to the coroner for his investigation. The following are common situations that would lead to involvement of the coroner and the performance of a post-mortem examination:

- violent deaths (accidents, homicides, suicides)
- deaths at the workplace (either traumatic or from poison or toxin exposure)
- deaths that are suspicious, sudden, or unexpected
- deaths that occur while incarcerated or in police custody
- deaths that are unattended by a physician, that occur within twenty-four hours of admission to a hospital, or that occur in any situation where the victim is admitted while unconscious and never regains consciousness prior to death
- deaths that occur during medical or surgical procedures

- deaths that occur during an abortion, whether medical, self, or illegal
- a found body, whether known or unidentified
- before a body can be cremated or buried at sea
- at the request of the court

But not all cases that fall into one of these categories will be autopsied. The coroner or ME has the final say. If the cause of death is obvious and the circumstances are not suspicious, the coroner may accept a cause of death and a death certificate signed by any physician.

For example, a physician may believe that the death of his patient was a natural occurrence even though the patient died unattended at home or within the first twenty-four hours of hospital admission. If the patient had severe heart disease or cancer or any disease where death is likely, the physician may sign the death certificate and the coroner may accept it. No autopsy or further investigation is done.

THE AUTOPSY PROCEDURE

An autopsy is a scientific procedure. Its purpose is to examine the corpse for evidence of the cause and manner of death. This is done through a gross (naked eye) and microscopic examination of the body as well as toxicological (drugs and poisons), serology (blood), and any other ancillary testing the ME deems necessary. It may seem obvious, but it is worth mentioning, that the autopsy must be performed before the body is embalmed. Embalming fluid alters the appearance of wounds and prevents accurate toxicological testing.

The timing of the autopsy depends upon many factors. It may be done immediately or several days after the body is collected. Weekends and holidays, excessive workload, and the need to ship the body to a larger lab may cause a delay. During this time period, the body is stored in a refrigerated vault. Storage of up to four or five days results in little noticeable deterioration of the corpse.

Each pathologist has his own method of doing things, but for the most part, the forensic autopsy follows a common protocol. Many of the steps overlap and some may be performed in a different order, depending upon the nature of the situation. The steps typically include:

- identification of the deceased
- photography of the body, clothed and unclothed

- removal of any trace evidence
- measuring and weighing the body
- x-raying all or parts of the body
- external examination of the body
- dissection of the body
- microscopic examination of any tissues removed during the examination
- toxicological and other laboratory examinations

After the ME has completed the autopsy exam and reviewed all the ancillary materials, he will file a final report and give his opinion.

Let's look at each of these steps in greater detail.

IDENTIFICATION: Identification of the deceased is critical. If the death becomes the subject of a criminal proceeding, there must be no doubt as to who the deceased was. If the identification is not confirmed, the evidence gleaned from the body will be of little use in court.

Usually, the identity of the person is not in question. Family members or friends come forward and offer this information. If not, photos, fingerprints, and dental records may be used.

PHOTOGRAPHY: The body is photographed, both clothed and unclothed. Frontal and profile photos of the face and body are important, particularly if the victim's identity hasn't been thoroughly established. Every injury, scar, birthmark, tattoo, and unusual physical feature must be adequately recorded.

TRACE EVIDENCE: Before the body is moved for measuring and weighing and before any other examination is done, a diligent search for trace evidence is undertaken. This is to avoid the loss or contamination of these delicate evidence items during the other examinations. The ME carefully scrutinizes the corpse and any clothing for hairs, fibers, fluid stains, and other bits of trace evidence. He employs a magnifying glass and often an alternative light source such as laser or ultraviolet or infrared light. The clothing is carefully removed, packaged, and taken to a clean environment for further examination and a more diligent search for trace evidence.

MEASURING AND WEIGHING: This is the first step in the actual post-mortem examination of the body. The ME records these measurements along with age, sex, race, and hair and eye color.

X-RAYS: X-rays of traumatized areas often reveal bony and some types of internal soft-tissue injuries, as well as foreign bodies whose general shape and size may help identify the murder weapon. In stab wounds, they may reveal that the tip of the knife broke off and remained behind. They are extremely useful in gunshot wounds. Bullets are unpredictable and move in unusual paths through the body, particularly if they strike bones. X-rays may help locate the bullet's final resting place so that the bullet can be retrieved for ballistic examination. For example, a bullet may enter the chest, strike a rib or the spinal column, deflect downward through the diaphragm, and settle in the pelvic area. An extensive search of the chest will not find the bullet, but an X-ray of the abdomen or the entire body can reveal its location.

Also, bullets tend to deform and break up, leaving behind chips and fragments, which show the bullet's path through the body. This may be useful in crime scene reconstruction, since knowing the bullet's path may indicate where the victim and the assailant were standing in relation to each other at the time the gun discharged.

EXTERNAL EXAMINATION: The external examination of the body should commence at the crime scene if at all possible. The ME should visit the scene before the body has been moved but this is not always practical. The advantage is that this will give him an overall view of the body and the crime scene. He can see the body's position and its relationship to other crime scene evidence such as the perpetrator's points of entry and escape, weapons, or blood spatters. Photographs help, but being there gives a clearer picture.

It is important to note that this crime scene examination does not include the ME touching or moving the body any more than is absolutely necessary. This helps to avoid the loss or contamination of any evidence related to the body.

For the same reasons, when the body is removed from the scene, it must be done carefully. In traumatic deaths, the hands of the victim should be covered with paper bags to protect any trace evidence on the victim's hands or beneath the fingernails before the body is moved. Usually the body is wrapped in clean plastic sheets and then placed in a clean body bag. These wrappings collect any trace evidence that falls from the body while at the same time prevent the accumulation of any foreign materials that could confuse or contaminate any evidence later retrieved. Once in the lab, the body is removed from the transport wrappings and placed on the autopsy table. The sheets are then taken to the crime lab where a search for trace evidence is done.

The pathologist focuses on the body. During his initial exam, the body is clothed. He searches for trace evidence such as hair, fibers, gunshot residues, semen, saliva, or bloodstains. Any findings are photographed and collected. He also looks for damage to the clothes that might correspond to injuries on the body. For example, do the defects in the victim's shirt match the gunshot or stab wounds found on the body? If not, it brings up the possibility that the corpse was re-dressed after death in an attempt to stage the scene. After his exam, the clothing is carefully removed, in order to avoid the loss of any trace evidence, and sent to the crime lab for processing.

Next, the ME determines the state of rigor mortis and the presence and location of any livor mortis (see Chapter Five: Time of Death, "Livor Mortis"). Knowing the position the body was in at the time it was discovered and knowing the location of the livor mortis may indicate whether the body was moved after death.

He searches for scars (traumatic or surgical), tattoos, birthmarks, and any skin lesions or abnormalities, which are photographed and diagramed. These may be particularly useful if the body has yet to be identified.

Trace evidence found on the corpse is examined, photographed, and collected, just as with the examination of the clothed body. In cases of traumatic death, the victim's fingernails are clipped and scraped. Hair, blood, and tissue from the assailant may be found if the victim struggled with the attacker. In a sexual assault case, the pubic hair is combed to search for hair from the rapist. Also, vaginal and anal swabs for semen are obtained. The ME takes samples of the victim's head, eyebrow, eyelash, and pubic hair for comparison with any foreign hair found on or around the body. All collected trace evidence is then sent to the crime lab for further evaluation.

Fingerprints are taken after all trace evidence, particularly fingernail clippings or scrapings, has been obtained. This is delayed until this time because the mere action of opening or prying open the hand for printing may result in loss of small bits of evidentiary material.

Injuries, whether old or recent, are examined and photographed. A diagram showing the location of the wounds on the body and their positions is marked relative to anatomical landmarks. For example, a stab wound to the chest is located by its distance from the top of the head, the heel of one foot, the midline of the body, and the nipple on the same side as the wound. This detail may be important in crime scene reconstruction. The exact location of the wound may suggest that the assailant was a certain height or was right- or left-handed. This may also help exonerate a suspect. What if the suspect is simply too short to have stabbed the 6-foot-4 victim in the neck with a downward motion?

Contusions (bruises) from blunt trauma are measured and photographed. If widely scattered over the arms, legs, and torso of the victim, they may suggest that a struggle took place or that the victim was tortured before death. Bruises and cuts on the arms and hands may indicate that the victim attempted to defend himself from his attacker. Such injuries are called defensive wounds. Contusions may be seen around the throat in cases of manual or ligature strangulation (see Chapter Eight: Asphyxia, "Ligature Strangulation").

If the murder weapon is available, the ME might compare it to the injuries in order to determine if it is the device that caused the injuries. He may use X-rays to help. In a death from blunt force trauma (see Chapter Seven: Bodily Harm, "Blunt Force Trauma"), a depressed skull fracture or a series of fractured ribs whose dimensions mirror that of the suspected murder weapon can be important evidence.

In stabbings, the ME carefully determines how many wounds are present, if possible. In some passionate or "overkill" homicides, there may be so many wounds that an accurate count isn't possible. If so, the ME determines the minimum number of wounds. He then measures the width, thickness, and depth of each. This examination includes an attempt to determine if the blade or blades were single- or double-edged and which wound was the killing thrust (see Chapter 7: Bodily Harm, "Sharp Force Injuries"). This information may be critical if there was more than one assailant, since it may directly impact any charges levied against the perpetrators. The perpetrator whose wound actually caused the death of the victim might face the more serious charges. Hesitation wounds often accompany suicide attempts involving a knife. These are small nicks and cuts inflicted by the person as he gathers the courage to make a real cut.

Gunshot entry wounds are measured and photographed. The ME makes an assessment of the angle of entry and the gun's distance from the body at the time of discharge (see Chapter Seven: Bodily Harm, "Guns and Bullets"), since these can be critical in distinguishing suicide from homicide. As I pointed out before, X-rays are helpful in following the bullet's path through the body and in locating its final resting place. This information is used during the dissection to find the bullet and to assess the extent of any organ and tissue damage it may have inflicted.

DISSECTION: Dissection is the opening of the body for internal examination. This is accomplished by making a Y incision (see Figure 3-1). This incision has three arms: Two extend from each shoulder down to the lower end of the sternum (breast bone), the third continues down the midline of the abdomen to the pubis. The ribs and clavicles (collarbones) are then cut with a saw or shears and the breastplate is removed, exposing the heart, lungs, and blood vessels of the chest.

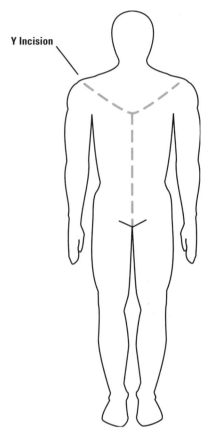

Y Incision

Figure 3-1: The Y incision. This incision allows access to the abdominal contents as well as the removal of the breastplate for examining and removing the heart and lungs.

The heart and lungs are sequentially removed, though most often they are removed en bloc (in one unit). Blood for typing, DNA analysis, and toxicological testing is often taken from the heart, the aorta, or a peripheral vessel. One blood sample is placed in a tube containing sodium fluoride, which retards bacterial growth. This is important because some yeasts and bacteria actually produce alcohol as a byproduct of their metabolic processes. If testing is de-

FORENSICS

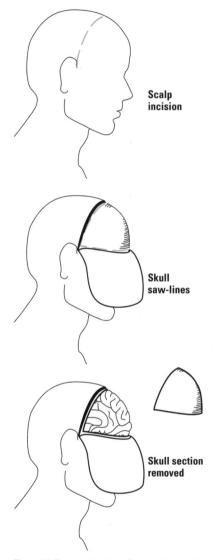

Scalp incision

Skull saw-lines

Skull section removed

Figure 3-2: Removing the brain. The steps include the incision and forward reflection of the scalp, and the sawing and removal of a portion of the skull.

layed several days, the blood alcohol level may be falsely elevated. Sodium fluoride lessens this likelihood.

After this, the ME turns his attention to the abdomen. Each organ is weighed and examined, and samples are taken for microscopic examination.

Stomach contents may help in the determination of the time of death if the content and timing of the victim's last meal is known (see Chapter 5: Time of Death, "The Last Mean"). Stomach contents, ocular (eye) fluid, bile from the gall bladder, urine, and liver tissue samples may be taken for toxicological testing.

Lastly, the ME looks for evidence of head trauma or skull fractures, and then he examines the brain. To do this he must open the skull. First, the scalp is incised from just behind one ear, over the top of the head, to just behind the other ear (see Figure 3-2). The scalp is then peeled forward, exposing the skull. A saw is used to remove a portion of the skull and expose the brain. He first examines the brain *in situ* (in place), then he removes it for a thorough inspection and to take tissue samples.

After each organ has been examined and samples have been taken for later microscopic examination, the organs are returned to the body and the incisions are sutured closed. The body might then be released to the family for burial, unless further examination is necessary for the investigation.

MICROSCOPIC EXAMINATION OF TISSUES: The removed tissue samples are "fixed" in a formalin solution and then imbedded in a block of paraffin. These paraffin blocks make slicing the specimen into very thin sections easier. The slices are placed on a glass slide and stained with biological stains such as hematoxylin and eosin (H&E) for viewing under a microscope.

TOXICOLOGICAL EXAMINATIONS: Any collected body fluids and tissues are sent to the toxicology lab for drug and poison testing. Stomach contents and ocular fluid may reveal any drugs the victim ingested in the hours before death. Urine and bile may indicate what drugs the victim used during the past several days. Hair may show signs of chronic heavy metal (arsenic, mercury, and lead) ingestion. Blood is particularly useful for alcohol levels and for many other drugs. Urine can reveal barbiturates and other sedatives as well as marijuana and nicotine.

THE OFFICIAL AUTOPSY REPORT

The final report consists of the anatomical and microscopic findings, along with attachments that contain the results of any ancillary tests, such as toxicological, serological, or DNA analyses. Using this information, the ME then offers his opinion as to the cause and manner of death (see Chapter Six).

The report may be filed immediately or may be delayed until all ancillary testing has returned. This may take days or weeks. At times, the ME may file a preliminary statement and await the return of these reports before filing his final report. Since his findings and opinions can affect the police, prosecutors, suspects, and families of all involved, the ME is typically cautious in both preliminary and final reporting.

Even his final report is not "written in stone" and can be altered at any time. If he uncovers evidence that changes his opinion, he can revise his opinion and the report. For example, if a chronically ill, elderly woman died in a nursing home and the cause of death appeared to be natural, the coroner could decide that an autopsy was not necessary and file his report stating that the manner of death was natural. But what if a large inheritance or insurance policy was at stake and someone came forward with evidence that suggested that the woman had been murdered? The coroner could exhume the body (if the burial had already occurred) and search more diligently for signs of injury or poisons. If he found trauma or toxins that could have caused the death, he could amend his report to state that the manner of death was not natural but homicide. A police investigation would then ensue.

Each pathologist has his own method and style of preparing the final report, but certain information must be included. A typical format would be:

- external examination
- evidence of injury
- central nervous system (brain and spinal cord)
- internal examination of chest, abdomen, and pelvis
- toxicological examinations
- other laboratory tests
- opinion

The opinion includes his assessment of the cause, mechanism, and manner of death.

IDENTIFYING THE BODY:
WHO IS THE VICTIM?

All too often the police and the medical examiner are confronted with identifying an unknown corpse. In movies this process usually takes only a few minutes of screen time, but in the real world it may take weeks, months, or years. Not infrequently, the body is never identified.

The corpse in question may have been dead for hours, days, months, or many years. Depending upon the time since death, the identification may be as easy as on television or it may be very complex and involve many different forensic disciplines and techniques.

If the body is more or less intact, size, sex, race, scars and tattoos, facial photographs, fingerprints, and DNA examination as well as the victim's clothing might help with identification. But, if the body is significantly decayed, much of this identifying information may not be available.

If the body is skeletal, the problem of identification is further magnified. The help of a forensic anthropologist, a forensic odontologist (dentist), and a forensic artist may be needed. They will work together to establish the person's identity, estimate the time since death, and, it is hoped, determine the cause and manner of death.

Whether the investigation centers on a single murder victim or found body, victims of a mass disaster such as a plane crash or hurricane, or a collection of corpses found in a mass grave, the skills of these experts are crucial. These same professionals might also be asked to reconstruct the face of the victim from the facial bones.

THE IMPORTANCE OF IDENTIFICATION

Besides the desire to reunite the deceased with his family and to allow a proper burial, there are many police and forensic issues that make corpse identification critical. In the case of a homicide victim, his identity will be the single most important factor in solving the crime. Ninety percent of the time, people are killed by people they know—a family member, lover, friend, business associate, or by some other person they have a relationship with. One factor that makes serial killers so difficult to track is that these are usually stranger killings, that is, the killer and the victim had no long-term relationship. But most killers and victims do, so identification of the corpse will allow investigators to dig into the relationships the victim had.

BASIC CONSIDERATIONS

Mother Nature and time are not kind to the dead. From the moment of death, extreme weather, bacteria, insects, and predators work to destroy the body. The condition of the body when it is found depends upon how long ago the death occurred and whether it is left exposed to the elements or buried.

If exposed to the elements, the damage to the corpse is more rapid and more severe. Not only is an unburied corpse affected directly by water and extremes of temperature, it is also a target for predatory animals and insects. In warm, moist climates bacteria and insects can reduce a corpse to bones in short order, while in colder, drier areas, this may take many months, even years (see Chapter Five: Time of Death). And when animal predators enter the picture, as is often the case with exposed corpses, the body can be literally eaten and the bones scattered far and wide. Sometimes only a bone or two, or perhaps a skull, is found and the remainder of the corpse is never located. As we will see later in this chapter, this presents a difficult problem to the forensic anthropologist.

Though burial provides some protection, this protection is incomplete. The most important factors in the destruction of a buried body are the time since burial, the burial container, and the depth of the grave. Other than time, which is an uncontrollable factor, the container is of paramount importance. A body simply buried with no coffin will deteriorate much faster than one in a metal coffin. Obviously, a cardboard box or plastic bag provides little protection. A shallow grave will attract more insects and predators than will one that is "six feet deep."

A body tossed into water presents similar problems. Whether weighted down or not, a corpse almost always sinks initially. It will remain submerged until enough decomposition gas collects within the tissues and body cavities to make it buoyant, at which time it will rise to the surface and become a "floater." The time required for this depends mostly on the water temperature. We will look at this process more closely in Chapter Five.

WAs you can see, what happens to a corpse and the time it takes for a corpse to decay completely varies with its location. The general rule is that one week in the open equals two weeks in water equals eight weeks in the ground.

PRESERVED CORPSES

Not all bodies decay and become skeletal. Sometimes conditions within the environment will lead to incredible degrees of preservation, even after many years. Soils high in acid or alkali content may delay or prevent bacterial growth, and thus putrefaction (decay). This is the situation with bodies found in boggy areas. These "bog people" may remain in remarkably good condition for decades. Frozen bodies are often very well preserved, as are those that undergo mummification. Mummification occurs when a body is exposed to hot and dry conditions that desiccate (dry out) the body, removing the water that bacteria need to grow and putrefy the corpse. What remains is a dark-colored corpse that looks as though leathery skin has been shrunk over a skeleton. These processes will be dealt with in Chapter Five.

In addition, conditions within the body may delay putrefaction and promote preservation. The presence of high levels of poisons such as arsenic may kill off the bacteria and delay putrefaction so that even bodies that have been dead for many years appear as if they have been dead only weeks.

GETTING RID OF THE BODY

Some criminals attempt to destroy corpses, the primary pieces of evidence in homicides. They think that if the police never find the body, they can't be convicted. This isn't true, since convictions have in many cases been obtained when no body is found. And destroying a body is no easy task.

Fire seems to be the favorite tool for this effort. Fortunately, this is essentially never successful. Short of a crematorium, it is nearly impossible to create a fire that burns hot enough or long enough to destroy a human corpse. Cremation uses temperatures of around 1,500°F for two hours or more and still bone fragments and teeth survive. A torched building would rarely reach these temperatures and would not burn for this long. The body inside may be severely charred on the surface, but the inner tissues and internal organs are often very well preserved.

Another favorite is quicklime. Murderers use this because they have seen it in the movies and because they don't typically have degrees in chemistry. If they did, they might think twice about this one. Not that quicklime won't destroy a corpse; it just takes a long time and a lot of the chemical. Most killers who use this method simply dump some on the corpse and bury it, thinking the lime will do its work and nothing will remain. Quicklime is calcium oxide. When it contacts water, as it often does in burial sites, it reacts with the water to make calcium hydroxide, also known as slaked lime. This corrosive material may damage the corpse, but the heat produced from this activity will kill many of the putrefying bacteria and dehydrate the body. This conspires to prevent decay and promote mummification. Thus, the use of quicklime may actually help preserve the body.

Acids are also used in this regard, and once again the criminal hopes the acid will completely dissolve the body. Serial killer Jeffrey Dahmer tried this with little success. Indeed, powerful acids such as hydrochloric acid (HCl), sulfuric acid (H_2SO_4), and chlorosulfuric acid ($HClSO_3$) can destroy a corpse, bones and all. If enough acid is used over a sufficient period of time, that is. But this is not only difficult but also extremely hazardous. The acids will indeed destroy the corpse, but they will also "eat" the tub the body is in and chew up the plumbing. Acid fumes will peel the wallpaper and burn the perpetrator's skin, eyes, and lungs.

FORENSIC CASE FILES: THE ACID BATH MURDERER

John George Haigh came to the English public's attention in the 1940s when he confessed to not only multiple murders, but also to drinking his victims' blood and destroying their corpses with acid. He seemed to favor sulfuric acid, which he kept in a vat in his workshop. He took the victims' money and, through forgery, their property and businesses, and then basically laughed at the police as he admitted to the killings, believing they could not prosecute him without a corpse. He was wrong. He was convicted through forensic evidence and was hanged at Wandsworth Prison on August 10, 1949.

So, whether it's Mother Nature or the work of the perpetrator, something almost always remains for the ME and the other forensic scientist to work with. It may be an intact body, a partially destroyed corpse, or a single bone, but it will give them something to use in identification. Let's take a look at how they do this—first with a body and then with only skeletal remains.

CORPSE IDENTIFICATION

An intact or only partially decayed body gives the coroner a great deal to work with—in this case, the age, race, sex, and stature of the person are usually obvious. Also, a facial photograph of the corpse can be compared with photos or descriptions of any reported missing persons. Once a presumptive match has been made, family or friends may be able to make the final identification. If no missing person matches the general characteristics of the corpse, descriptions and photos can be circulated to law enforcement and the media.

If it were always that easy, the identification of a corpse would be a simple task. But all too often this is not the case, and the ME and his staff must resort to other means.

BURIAL ARTIFACTS

Corpses are often buried along with their clothing, jewelry, and other items. Needless to say, a wallet, ID card, or military dog tags would be helpful. Medic Alert medallions or bracelets can usually be traced to the owner. Not always, though, since some are inscribed only with the needed medical information, while others bear the person's name or an ID number. A locket might contain a picture of a loved one, and rings and bracelets are often inscribed with names, initials, or dates.

Clothing may be distinctive in either style or manufacturer. For example, designer clothes and shoes may lead the police into one area of search while the ragged clothes of a homeless individual may lead in another. Laundry marks can often be traced to a particular cleaner, and then to the owner of the item.

The person may have been buried in a coffin or in a blanket or some other material. An expensive metal coffin would bear the manufacturer's name and maybe a serial number, but rarely are unidentified victims of accidents and murders placed in such coffins. A makeshift, wooden coffin might provide information from its construction materials and methods, or from any distinctive markings it might bear. The same is true for blankets or sheets, which often have manufacturer or seller tags. A plastic bag might offer up the prints of the perpetrator, which could then lead to the identity of the corpse.

BODY MARKS, DISEASES, AND SCARS

Body marks, such as birthmarks and tattoos, are often so distinctive that they supply strong identifying evidence.

Birthmarks come in many varieties. One distinctive type is called a port-wine stain (naevus flammeus), a reddish or purplish discoloration that may be small or cover a large area such as an entire shoulder or half of someone's face. Former Soviet President Mikhail Gorbachev has such a mark on his forehead. Port wine stains are typically very irregular, like an amoeba, and thus have a pattern that is distinctive, no two being exactly alike. If the unknown corpse has such a mark, an old photo revealing the mark could be used to make a positive identification.

Tattoos may be just as distinctive, and at times, a family member or friend will recognize the design. Some tattoos can be traced to the artist, particularly today since tattoos are considered body art and some tattoo artists have very individual styles. Followers of such art can often identify a particular artist's work.

Though far from a universal practice, the tattoos and other body marks seen on those who have been arrested are often sketched or photographed as part of the booking process. If such sketches or photos exist from a previous arrest, they can be compared to those on the corpse.

Gang tattoos, which identify a person as a member of a particular gang, may narrow the search. If the deceased has had a previous brush with the law, a former cellmate, corrections officer, or arresting officer might recognize the tattoo and be able to supply at least a presumptive identification. In addition, many police jurisdictions maintain files of the tattoos associated with the gangs that operate in the area. For example, California's CAL/GANG, established in 1987, is a database of information on known gang members throughout the state, including descriptions and photos of members' tattoos. Outside California, many states use the similar GangNet. A search of these databases may yield a hit and supply the needed identification.

A forensic chemist can also help. Many tattooists use black pigments that contain carbon, reds that contain mercuric chloride, and greens with potassium dichromate. Others use aniline-based dyes. It is possible to extract and analyze some of the pigment from the corpse's skin and help confirm that a particular artist did the work.

The usefulness of tattoos is underlined in a famous Australian case that became known as the Shark Arm Case.

FORENSIC CASE FILES: JAMES SMITH—THE SHARK ARM CASE

In April 1935, two fishermen caught a large tiger shark off the coast of Sydney, Australia, and donated the creature to a local aquarium. A few days later the shark regurgitated a well-preserved, muscular, Caucasian human arm. The shark was sacrificed and an autopsy was performed, but no more human remains were found.

The arm appeared to have been removed by a knife rather than by the shark's teeth. Further, the knife wounds appeared to have occurred postmortem. The arm bore a tattoo of two boxers squaring off. Through meticulous work, fingerprints were obtained, and they indicated that the victim was James Smith, an ex-boxer with a criminal past. His wife identified the tattoo.

Further investigation led the police to Patrick Brady, a known forger and drug-trafficker, who had gone on a fishing trip with the victim just before his disappearance. Police theorized that Brady killed Smith, hacked him to pieces, and stuffed his remains into a trunk that was missing from the fishing shack the two men had shared. Smith's arm must have slipped free in the water and been swallowed by the shark. Under questioning, Brady implicated another man named Reginald Holmes, who was himself shot to death the day before the inquest into Smith's death was to begin. Brady's attorneys obtained an injunction from the court, halting the inquest on the grounds that an arm was not sufficient evidence to bring murder charges. The police charged Brady with murder anyway, but a jury, likely influenced by the court ruling, acquitted him.

Occasionally, broadcasting the description of the victim and his clothing, jewelry, and tattoos or birthmarks over the media is all that is needed to identify the unknown corpse. You've seen TV reports in which the police request help Occasionally, broadcasting the description of the victim and his clothing, jewelry, and tattoos or birthmarks over the media is all that is needed to identify the unknown corpse. A reporter may give a description such as a 6-foot-2, 180-pound, white male, thirty to forty years of age, with brown hair, brown eyes, and a tattoo that says "Martha" on his upper arm. He may add that the victim was wearing blue jeans and a red plaid shirt and that he was wrapped in a blue wool blanket. A photo of the corpse may be shown. The hope is that someone will recognize the photo, the tattoo, the clothing, or the blanket and come forward to identify the corpse.

If all this fails, at autopsy, the ME might discover that the victim had some disease or previous surgical procedure that may narrow the search. Medical conditions such as acromegaly, neurofibromatosis, scleroderma, and others are uncommon yet easily identifiable. A search of missing persons with these unusual conditions may lead to a quick identification. Some diseases have national registries and support groups, and the deceased could have a membership. Checking with these organizations could prove helpful.

If the victim has had an appendectomy or a gallbladder removal, a search of missing persons' reports of the same age and sex who also had these procedures might help. This is particularly true if the surgery was fairly recent, since the ME can often determine the age of surgical wounds.

Any repaired wound, whether surgical or from a knife fight, will follow the same healing pattern. During the first week, the wound has sutures (stitches) in place. And for several months after suture removal, the telltale pattern of the suturing can be seen.

For several weeks, any scar will be slightly pink to brownish red due to the microscopic blood vessels that invade the area to aid with the healing process. Over the next few months, as the body repairs the damage by laying down collagen (thick strands of connective tissue), the color gradually fades and the scar shrinks considerably. As the scar matures, it finally becomes a faint white line by four to six months. The collagen continues to shrink for about one year. Thereafter, the scar remains unchanged for life. This means that the age of a scar can be approximated in the first four to six months or so.

A surgical appliance is any artificial, manufactured device used in surgical treatment. They typically bear unique markings. For example, if the corpse in question has had a hip replacement, the ME can remove the artificial hip at autopsy and examine it. Such prosthetic joints possess engraved serial numbers, which can be traced to the manufacturer, the hospital where the replacement was done, and to the person who received it. Pacemakers, implantable defibrillators, heart valves, and other cardiac devices also have traceable serial numbers.

FINGERPRINTS OF THE DEAD
Unless the corpse is severely deteriorated, fingerprints can usually be obtained and matched against known missing persons and national fingerprint databases; this would lead to a quick and absolute identity (see Chapter Twelve: Fingerprints). Fingerprints can even be obtained from mummified bodies in some circumstances. The finger pads of such corpses are shriveled and have the texture of old leather, but soaking them in water or glycerin may swell them enough for fingerprints to be obtained. Or saline can be injected into the tips of the fingers, which swells the pads and reveals the friction ridges. Alternatively, the skin over the pads of the fingers can be carefully sliced away and placed between two microscopic slides for viewing and photographing.

DENTAL COMPARISONS
Forensic odontologists are frequently involved in the identification of corpses. The value of dental comparisons lies in their being almost as individual as fingerprints. Everyone's teeth are different. You and I may have the same number and types of teeth, but the length, width, and shape of each shows great variability. Missing, misaligned, and reconstructed teeth (fillings, crowns, and bridges) as well as chips, furrows, and wear patterns, add even more individuality.

When faced with an unidentified corpse, the ME often makes a set of dental X-rays, which can then be compared with the most recent dental X-rays of a missing person who fits the corpse's general description as to age, sex, and size. With a match, the identity of the corpse is confirmed.

This points out the main problem with dental comparisons: having something to compare the corpse's dental pattern against. If the police have no clues as to who the person might be, such as a missing person's report of someone who fits the general description of the unknown corpse, they can't obtain that person's dental records for comparison.

Newer techniques allow for the chemical analysis of filling materials, which could lead investigators to the manufacturer of the material or the dentist who uses it. This might be an important step in ultimately identifying the corpse. Let's say only one local dentist used the type of filling material found in a corpse and he had only used it on two dozen patients. A comparison of those patients' dental records with the dental pattern of the corpse might lead to a positive identification.

The dentist might see changes that relate to the person's occupation. This information can help narrow the list of possibilities or move the investigation down a new path. The mouthpiece of certain wind instruments can alter the teeth of those who frequently play them. Nails can chip the teeth of the carpenter who holds them in his mouth as he works.

Using teeth as a method of identity is not a modern endeavor. In the first century A.D., the Roman Emperor Claudius demanded to see the teeth of his beheaded mistress to assure her identity. She apparently had a distinctively discolored front tooth. William the Conqueror used his crooked teeth to bite, and thus identify, the wax seal on his letters. In 1776, Paul Revere identified the body of a friend after the Battle of Bunker Hill. It seems that Revere had made a pair of dentures for the man and recognized his own handiwork.

FORENSIC CASE FILES: DR. JOSEPH WARREN'S TEETH

Paul Revere was a gifted metal smith and engraver and had been schooled in the art of dentistry. In 1775, he made a set of dentures for his friend Dr. Joseph Warren.

Dr. Warren fell in the Battle of Bunker Hill in June of that year and was buried in a mass grave for those killed in action. Warren's family wanted his body disinterred for a private burial. To do this, Dr. Warren's corpse had to be distinguished from all the others. A positive identification came when Revere recognized the dentures he had made for his friend.

Today, in the case of mass disasters or where mass graves are uncovered, X-rays taken from each of the corpses are matched with X-rays from suspected victims, if these X-rays are available. This greatly speeds up the identifying process. Though dental records are still used in such situations, DNA is replacing this technique in many areas.

BLOOD TYPE AND THE CORPSE

The forensic use of blood typing is dealt with in Chapter Nine, but blood type can also help with identifying a corpse. At least it can exclude certain possible identities. This is based on the fact that a person's blood type is determined by the blood type of his parents and certain pairings cannot produce children of certain types. For example, if a corpse that is thought to be John Smith is found to have type B blood and John's parents are type O and type A, the corpse is not John. The two parents could not bear a type B child. So, blood typing excludes John. But if the corpse had type A or type O blood, John remains a possibility. This does not confirm that the corpse is John, but it doesn't exclude that possibility either. This will become clearer after you read Chapter Nine.

DNA AND THE CORPSE

DNA will be discussed in detail in Chapter Ten. Its usefulness in identifying an unknown corpse is limited but, when possible, it can make an absolute identification. Why is it limited? The simple reason is that, like fingerprints and dental comparisons, DNA from the corpse must be compared against the DNA of the person suspected of being the corpse. But, as with fingerprints, there is a national databank that might help in some circumstances. The DNA databank known as the Combined DNA Index System (CODIS), though still woefully inadequate, is growing, and if the victim's DNA profile is in CODIS, a match can be made. If not, DNA from a corpse may still be useful to the ME.

Let's say the ME suspects that the corpse on his table is John Smith, who has been missing for a few months. The corpse is severely decayed, so visual identification is impossible and fingerprints cannot be obtained. Further, John has no dental records. John's family may bring in his hairbrush or toothbrush or

FORENSIC CASE FILE: XIANA FAIRCHILD'S DNA

On December 19, 1999, Antoinette Robinson reported that her seven-year-old daughter, Xiana Fairchild, was missing. After an extensive search of the area, neither the girl nor her body could be found, so the police had little to go on. Then in January 2001, a construction worker found a partial skull and jawbone near a mountainous road some sixty miles south of Xiana's Vallejo, California, home.

The bones were recognized as being from a child around Xiana's age. DNA from one of the molars in the jawbone was compared with DNA obtained from Xiana's toothbrush, and the skull and jaw fragments were identified as those of Xiana. It was also determined that even though she had been abducted in December 1999, her murder did not take place until around August 2000.

Ultimately, Curtis Dean Anderson, a cabdriver who had been fired a few days before Xiana's abduction, was charged with the crime. When charged, he was already in prison serving a 251-year sentence for the abduction and molestation of an eight-year-old girl who escaped from him just days before Xiana's disappearance. Ominously, Anderson had been to Xiana's house a few weeks before her disappearance, visiting Robert Turnbough, a fellow cabdriver and boyfriend of Xiana's mother.

perhaps envelopes or stamps he had licked, and the ME might be able to extract DNA from these to compare with that taken from the corpse. With the newer DNA techniques of PCR and STR (see Chapter 10: DNA, "The DNA Fingerprinting Process"), this type of identification is becoming increasingly common.

If none of the above information leads to identification of the corpse, the coroner must resort to other, more creative, methods. The case of Abraham Becker and Reuben Norkin illustrates just how clever an astute ME can be.

FORENSIC CASE FILES: ABRAHAM BECKER, REUBEN NORKIN, AND THE CANAPÉS

Abraham Becker and his wife, Jennie, had a rocky marriage at best. On April 6, 1922, in New York City, they attended a party at a friend's home. Jennie ate canapés, almonds, grapes, and figs. After they left the party, Jennie was never seen alive again. Becker said that she had run off with another man. The police investigation led to Reuben Norkin, a business associate of Becker's. Under pressure, Norkin admitted that he had helped Becker bury the missing woman's body. He said that Becker had killed her with a wrench and buried her body in a shallow grave, sprinkling it with lime in the hopes of hastening its destruction. He led police to the shallow grave.

When confronted, Becker said that the corpse was not that of his wife. He said that his wife was larger than the corpse and that the clothes were not the ones she had been wearing when she was last seen. Medical examiner Dr. Karl Kennard performed an autopsy and found that the victim's stomach was very well preserved. Within it he found almonds, grapes, figs, and meat-spread canapés. Becker countered that any woman could have eaten these foods, but when the meat-spread was tested its ingredients were identical to the spread served at the party. It was an old family recipe. Both men were convicted of first-degree murder.

CAUSE OF DEATH

After examining the body, the ME might be able to determine the cause, which might help identify the victim. A drug overdose would lead to a canvassing of local dealers and users. A distinctive knife wound might instigate a search into where such a weapon could be purchased and ultimately to who bought it. The victim of a gunshot wound would be x-rayed in an attempt to locate the bullet, which could then be removed and examined by ballistics experts. This could lead to the murder weapon and the shooter.

The point of these investigations is that identifying the perpetrator may allow identification of the victim since most murders occur between people who know each other. Even if the perpetrator refuses to talk, an investigation into his background, acquaintances, and business dealings may help identify the victim.

SKELETAL REMAINS

Sometimes the forensic team doesn't have a body to work with, only a skeleton. In this situation, the expertise of a forensic anthropologist and a forensic odontologist are usually brought into play. As with a corpse, the investigators follow a logical sequence in attempting to identify the remains. They are asked to answer several questions:

- Are the bones human?
- What are the victim's biological characteristics (size, age, sex, and race)?
- How long has the person been dead?
- What is the cause and manner of death?

Though the science of anthropology has been around for a long time, the field of forensic anthropology can be dated to 1939 and the publication of Dr. W.M. Krogman's classic article on the examination of human skeletal remains in the *FBI Law Enforcement Bulletin*. In 1972, the American Academy of Forensic Sciences established the Physical Anthropology Section, and in 1977, the American Board of Forensic Anthropology (ABFA) began to professionally certify workers in this field. The field has expanded rapidly since then.

The skeletal remains the forensic anthropologist deals with might be in the form of an intact skeleton, a partial skeleton, a handful of bones, or just a single bone. They may be scattered on the ground, buried, or found within a structure.

HUMAN VS. ANIMAL

The first question that must be answered is whether the bones are human. Sounds easy, and most of the time it is—if a complete adult skeleton is present. But with time and the effects of nature and various animal predators, which can scatter and destroy portions of the skeleton, a complete set of bones is not always available. This can lead to great difficulties for the examiner. For example, the front paw bones of a bear are similar to those of a human hand, shell fragments from some turtles often resemble skull fragments, and the ribs of sheep and deer appear similar to human ribs.

If the victim is an infant or young child, determining that the bones are human may be even more difficult. Infant bones and teeth are much smaller and are easier to confuse with small animal bones and teeth. An infant's skull is not completely fused (joined together into a single structure) so that an intact skull will not be found.

Yet, with careful examination, a skilled forensic anthropologist can usually distinguish human bones from those of other animals. This is a highly technical endeavor that requires great experience, so it is beyond the scope of this text.

BIOLOGICAL CHARACTERISTICS

Once it has been established that the bones are of human origin, the anthropologist turns his attention to identifying the person by first looking into the corpse's biological characteristics before moving on to assessing the time, cause, and manner of death.

PHYSICAL CHARACTERISTICS

Any hope of identifying an unknown corpse rests with determining the deceased individual's biological characteristics. Age, stature, sex, and race

---

are crucial; these determinations alone narrow the field greatly. Simply determining the sex of the deceased will cut the possibilities in half. If the bones are those of a fifty-something, six-foot, Caucasian male, the search can exclude any persons not fitting this profile. Once these characteristics are determined, the search turns toward individualizing characteristics. The presence of bony evidence of disease, congenital defects, or trauma is very important.

With an intact adult skeleton, the determination of sex can be made nearly 100 percent of the time, age to within five to ten years, height to within 1½ inches, and race much of the time. With only a partial skeleton or just a few bones, the accuracy of each of these determinations diminishes.

AGE

To determine the age of the person when only bones are available, the forensic anthropologist looks at the teeth, the skull, and the maturity of the bone growth centers, as well as the normal age-related changes in the bones and joints. Since the analysis of each of these gives only an estimate of age, the examiner must in the end make his best guess. Age can be more accurately estimated in the young than in the mature individual. The teeth and bones in children and adolescents follow a predictable growth and maturation pattern. By assessing the stage of this development, a fairly narrow age range can be determined. Later in life, after the maturation process is completed, changes in the teeth and skeleton occur at a much slower rate. This leads to much broader ranges of age assessment.

Teeth are often examined first. Humans have two sets of teeth: twenty deciduous (baby) and thirty-two permanent (adult). Tooth development begins before birth. The formation, appearance, and loss of baby teeth and the appearance of permanent teeth occur in a known sequence. Charts are available that reveal this order; they can be used to estimate the age of a victim who was less than twelve years old at the time of death. With the exception of the third molars (wisdom teeth), the loss of deciduous teeth and the appearance of the permanent teeth are completed by about age twelve. The last teeth to appear are the wisdom teeth, which typically erupt by age eighteen.

This general timeline helps with assessing the age of any individual who was eighteen or younger at the time of death. For example, a skeleton that has all its permanent teeth, except the wisdom teeth, was likely between twelve and eighteen at the time of death. If the third molars have appeared, the teeth aren't as useful to the examiner in determining age.

In adults, the skull is of little use for age estimation, but in infants it may be of some help, though not as much as once believed. An infant's skull is actually in several pieces that with time fuse or meld together along jagged lines of separation known as **suture lines**. Logically, the pattern of the closure of these sutures would be useful, but unfortunately this fusion occurs in a widely variable pattern, so that age estimation is not that accurate.

If available, the anthropologist turns his attention to the body's long bones in the arms and legs. These bones consist of three parts: the diaphysis (shaft) and the epiphyses at each end (see Figure 4-1). The growth plates (epiphyseal plates or ossification centers) are located near each end where the diaphysis and the epiphyses come together. Bones can continue to grow as long as these epiphyseal plates are "open." When they "close" or ossify (become hard bone like the shaft), growth is no longer possible. The timing of this varies among individuals, but is typically completed by the time the person is in his mid–twenties, and it tends to occur a little earlier in females than in males. If the skeleton in question is small, with no fusion of the epiphyses, the person was likely a child. If the bones are that of a nearly grown individual, and if these growth plates are partially fused, then the person would have been a teenager or in his early twenties at death. If the growth plates are fully fused, the person was probably over twenty-five years of age.

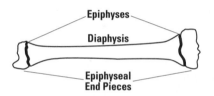

Figure 4-1: Long bones. Human long bones consist of the diaphysis (shaft) and two epiphyseal end pieces. The two epiphyses (growth plates) bind these segments and are the location of bone growth. At maturity, the plates fuse and growth ceases.

Pubic symphysis

Figure 4-2: Pubic symphysis. The pubic symphysis is the frontal union of the right and left halves of the pelvis. Straightening and narrowing of the junction occurs with aging.

The complete closure of the epiphyses in the various bones of the body occurs at different and predictable times. For example, the plates near the elbow close between ages twelve and fourteen, those of the hip and ankle around fifteen, and those of the shoulder between eighteen and twenty. This allows for fairly accurate age determination between the ages of about twelve and twenty.

Another marker of age is the changes that occur in the pubic symphysis (see Figure 4-2). The right and left pelvic bones join to the spinal column in back at the sacroiliac joints, and in the front to each other at the pubic symphysis. This union is by way of a thin band of cartilage that is slightly scalloped. With age, this cartilage band becomes more of a straight line. The straightening of this line is a rough indicator of age, but this is only useful to about age fifty.

Another important area to examine is the sternal end of the ribs. This is where the ribs join the breastbone (sternum). Early in life, the ends of the ribs are smooth and rounded, but with age they become pitted and develop sharper edges. The standard is to look at the ends of the third, fourth, and fifth ribs. Examination of these junctions can narrow age predication to one and a half years up to age thirty and within five years up to age seventy. After that, these changes are of little use. Also, the cartilage that connects the ribs to the sternum tends to ossify (become bony) with age, so this can be used as a crude indicator of age.

With age, bones tend to lose calcium and become less dense. That is, they weaken, soften, and become more prone to fractures. X-ray, photon absorptiometry, CT scanning, or MRI examination of the bones will reveal the density of the calcium and may help with determining the age. Diseases such as osteoporosis and malnutrition will lessen the bone density at any given age, and this fact must be considered in determining age from skeletal remains. Since this demineralization of the bones is affected by so many factors, this is only marginally useful for age determination.

Age also leads to the development of arthritis and other joint abnormalities. Arthritis is not commonly seen before age forty. After age sixty or so, ossification progresses in the cartilage of the ribs and larynx (voice box). This means that if significant arthritis changes are seen, the person was probably beyond age sixty at the time of death.

STATURE

You might think that in order to determine the unknown person's height you could simply measure the skeleton from top to bottom and that would be that. If a complete skeleton is present, that would work. But with only partial remains, this isn't possible. Also, the height is just one part of the person's stature. Was the person of slight or muscular build? That could make a crucial difference in identification. A 6-foot male who is thin would suggest one group of possible matches, while a 6-foot male who is muscular or obese would suggest another.

If one or more of the long bones are available, measurement of these can lead to an estimate of height. This technique is called allometry. For example, one rule of thumb is that the height is equal to five times the length of the humerus (upper arm bone). But there are also tables and formulas for each of the long bones available to help in estimating height. Though any long bone can be used, the best and most accurate are the femur (upper leg bone) and tibia (larger of the two lower leg bones). One set of formulas was developed by Genoves in 1967.

Using Femur and Tibia Length to Estimate Height in Centimeters
(2.54 centimeters = 1 inch)

Male:

femur length × 2.26 + 66.38 = height in centimeters

tibia length × 1.96 + 93.75 = height in centimeters

Female:

femur length × 2.59 + 49.74 = height in centimeters

tibia length × 2.72 + 63.78 = height in centimeters

But, what if the examiner only has fragments of these bones? Fortunately, other formulas have been worked out that allow the estimation of the bone length from fragments, and once this is determined, the estimated length can be used to calculate the overall height of the individual.

Once the height is estimated, the examiner tries to determine the person's body type. There are no formulas here, just an experienced guess. If the bones are thick, particularly in the areas where muscles attach to the skeleton, the person was most likely to have had a muscular physique. If not, a slighter build is likely. Unfortunately, this is inexact at best.

Similarly, handedness can often be determined since the dominant side tends to have thicker, stronger bones. That is, the right arm and leg bones of a right-handed individual are usually thicker than the left.

SEX

As opposed to the situation with age estimation, determining sex from skeletal remains of infants and children is more difficult than it is in adults. The reason for this is that gender-specific changes in the skeleton do not appear until puberty. After this, male and female bones grow differently and begin to take on sex-identifying characteristics. If the needed bones are available, the forensic anthropologist can use these variations to accurately determine the sex of skeletal remains.

The overall size and bone thickness of the male skeleton is greater than that of the female. This is not universal, though, since bone size and thickness is related to many things other than sex. Better nutrition and heavy physical activity lead to stronger bones regardless of sex. So a female who ate well and preformed manual labor might have a more male appearing skeleton than a male who had poor nutrition and rarely worked physically.

Still, the thickness of certain areas of some bones may be used to distinguish between males and females. In general, the diameters of the heads of the humerus, the radius (lower arm bone on the thumb side), and the femur are larger in males.

The most reliable bones in sex determination are those of the pelvis. The male pelvis is designed only for support and movement, while the female pelvis is adapted for childbirth (see Figures 4-3A and B). The female pelvis is wider and possesses an increased diameter of the pelvic outlet, which allows passage of the infant during childbirth. Also, the sciatic notch (where the sciatic and

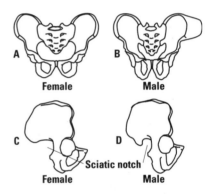

Figure 4-3: Pelvic bones. The female pelvis (A) is wider than the male (B). In addition, the sciatic notch is broader in females (C) than in males (D).

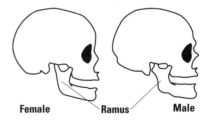

Figure 4-4: The mandible. The posterior ramus of the mandible is curved in males, but straight in females.

other nerves pass through on their way to the leg) is wider in females than in males (see Figures 4-3C and D). In addition, the backside of the pubic bone in women who have delivered a child may be scarred and irregular. This is due to the tearing and regrowth of ligaments that occurs during childbirth.

The skull is also helpful. Male skulls tend to have more distinct ridges and crests and to be larger and thicker, particularly in areas where facial and jaw muscles attach. In addition, the posterior ramus of the mandible (jawbone) in males is slightly curved, while in females it tends to be straight (see Figure 4-4).

As you can see, the ability to determine the sex of skeletal remains depends upon how many and which bones are present. If the skeleton is intact, the accuracy is extremely high. If only a hipbone or a mandible is found, the job of the forensic anthropologist is more difficult, but he can still provide a fairly accurate guess.

RACIAL CHARACTERISTICS

The racial background of the person is very difficult, if not impossible, to determine since no single skeletal trait is racially distinct. Any classification is rough at best and is greatly altered by racial mixture. There are only three groups to which a given skeleton can be assigned: Caucasoid, Negroid, or Mongoloid.

Caucasoid individuals tend to have high, rounded or square skulls, straight faces, and narrow, protruding noses. On the other hand, those of Negroid or Mongoloid descent tend toward lower and narrower skulls and wider, flatter noses. Negroids tend to have proportionally longer arms and legs than do Caucasoids, while in Mongoloids the limbs are shorter. Also, Caucasoid individuals have a forward curve to their femurs, while in Negroid persons this bone is straighter.

The skeleton of an individual of mixed racial origin shares characteristics of the individual races in his ancestry. Often this racial admixture makes racial assignment impossible.

INDIVIDUAL CHARACTERISTICS

The estimation of the age, stature, sex, and race of the remains greatly narrows the search for the identity of the unknown person, but to establish the true identity requires more information. Just knowing that the remains are those of a twelve- to eighteen-year-old, five-foot, left-handed, Caucasian female does not absolutely identify the individual, but it might narrow the focus to a handful of individuals. As with a corpse, this information is compared to the characteristics of anyone reported missing (except, with a skeleton rather than a body, this review would need to go back several years) and if someone with similar characteristics is found, a closer look is taken.

As with a more intact corpse, clothing remnants, jewelry, and burial artifacts, if present, may add information. Evidence of previous injuries, such as healed fractures or knife or gunshot wounds, which can fracture and nick bones, might be the key to identifying the remains. Comparing these types of findings with old medical records or X-rays of potential individuals may lead to a positive identification. As with intact corpses, many surgical appliances, such as artificial hips and pacemakers, can be found among the bones, and since these often possess traceable serial numbers, the identification can be secured from these.

Several diseases leave behind skeletal evidence. Primary bone cancers and those that metastasize (spread) to bone and such infectious processes as tuberculosis, syphilis, and osteomyelitis (bone infection) may leave behind characteristic findings. Bone disorders such as Paget's disease and rickets are usually easily identified.

The finding of any of these injuries or diseases further narrows the possibilities. Of course, each of these indicators are much weaker identifying characteristics than are fingerprints, dental patterns, and DNA.

Although fingerprints are not available in skeletal remains, DNA and teeth often are. Dental patterns can be compared to old dental records, X-rays, and sometimes photographs. An entire set of teeth is not usually necessary for this comparison, but is preferred. In many cases DNA can be extracted from bones and teeth. Of course, both of these techniques require that old records or known samples of DNA exist.

One newer technique for identification is through the use of mitochondrial DNA (mtDNA), which will be discussed in Chapter Ten. Mitochondrial DNA is inherited unchanged along maternal lines for many centuries. It is very hardy and survives for great periods of time in decayed and skeletal remains. It is found in all the cells of the body, the pulp of the teeth, and even in the shaft of hair, a place that does not contain normal, or nuclear, DNA. If the identity of the corpse is suspected to be a particular individual, the mtDNA obtained from maternally related relatives, such as siblings, can be matched against that of the unknown corpse. If they share a common maternal ancestry, the mtDNA from each will match.

FACIAL RECONSTRUCTION

When all of the above fails to identify the remains, facial reconstruction must be considered. If a likeness of the individual can be created and circulated, someone might recognize the person. Alternatively, if the search has been narrowed to a few individuals, photographs of these persons can be compared to the skull in question. This is called skull-to-photo superimposition.

Facial reconstruction is a fascinating art that often involves a forensic anthropologist, dentist, and artist or sculptor. Facial reconstruction from a complete or partial skull involves recreating a two-dimensional image on paper or a computer screen or sculpting one that is three-dimensional. In either case, the goal is to produce an image that is an approximate likeness of the deceased.

For the sculptor, the skull or a cast of the skull serves as the framework. A clay model is then created one layer at a time. Studies have determined the average skin thickness over certain bony landmarks of the skull. Small spacers of this thickness are placed in these areas and are then connected by strips of clay. This latticework is then filled in and contoured. Needless to say, this requires the hand and eye of an artist.

FORENSIC CASE FILES: JOSEF MENGELE'S SKULL

Josef Mengele, the Nazi Angel of Death, conducted an array of unspeakable human experiments on prisoners of Hitler's Third Reich and alone oversaw the deaths of perhaps 400,000 people. Yet, when the Russians took the concentration camps at Auschwitz, few people knew the name Mengele. In fact, it was not until many years later, with the capture of Adolf Eichmann, that Mengele became the prime target of Nazi hunters.

From the 1960s through the 1980s, sightings and rumors placed Mengele at various times in Argentina, Brazil, and Paraguay, and he became the world's single most sought-after war criminal. In 1985 rumors of his impending capture took on a fever pitch. Would the Angel of Death finally be brought to trial and be forced to answer for his crimes? Unfortunately, no. Wolfram and Liselotte Bossert, a German couple living in Brazil, showed authorities a grave near the village of Embu, stating that the body beneath the soil was Josef Mengele.

Scientists from the United States and Germany, as well as a team of experts from the Simon Wiesenthal Center in Vienna, Austria, took part in the examination of the skeletal remains. They determined that the bones were that of a Caucasian male, whose size and age matched that of Mengele. Unfortunately, Mengele's SS file was sketchy at best and in particular his hand-drawn 1938 dental chart was inexact. It revealed that Mengele had twelve filings, but did not pinpoint their locations. Also, it made no mention of his gap-toothed smile.

German forensic anthropologist Richard Helmer had been working with photographic superimposition. He took a photograph of the skull from the grave and marked over thirty identifying points. He then superimposed a known photo of Mengele over the skull photo and determined that the match was perfect. He was convinced that the bones were those of Mengele. Final confirmation came in 1992 with DNA matching of materials obtained from the bones with samples taken from Mengele's relatives.

However, many problems plague this process. Hair and eye color, hairstyle, and the presence or absence of facial hair is not known. Some features, such as the nose and ears, are made of cartilage and may be absent. To draw or sculpt these features requires a "best guess." Similarly, the thickness of the skin and the amount of body fat must also be estimated, and errors in this estimation may greatly affect the final model.

If a missing individual who fits the general characteristics of the remains is identified, and if a photograph of this person is available, a skull-to-photo superimposition may be used to confirm the identification. Basically, the photo is superimposed over a similar-sized photo of the skull and the bony landmarks are compared. This can rarely provide a conclusive match but it can eliminate certain candidates. If the photo reveals that the eyes are too widely spaced, the nose too long, or the chin is of a different contour, the skull is not that of the suspect individual. On the other hand, if all these features match, the suspect individual cannot be excluded.

This technique was used to help solve one of the greatest mysteries of the twentieth century: Was Josef Mengele really dead?

PHOTOGRAPHIC COMPARIS ONS AND AGE PROGRESSIONS

Most often, the forensic anthropologist is involved with identifying skeletal remains, but he may also be asked to determine if two photos are of the same person. Often these photos were taken years or decades apart and vary widely in quality and technique. Sometimes one photo is from a surveillance camera, while another a family snapshot. Though everyone's face undergoes age-related changes, there are certain features that do not change.

FORENSIC CASE FILES: JOHN LIST'S FACE

In 1971, John List lived in a large home in Westfield, New Jersey, with his wife, his three teenage children, and his mother. Neighbors noticed that they had not seen the List family for some time and that the home seemed deserted except for the fact that lights throughout the house blazed brightly every night. The police investigated and found the bodies of Helen List and the three children neatly placed on sleeping bags in a room near the back of the house. In an upstairs bedroom, they found the body of John's mother, Alma. Each had been shot. John List was nowhere to be found.

The police did find five addressed envelopes that contained letters explaining List's rationale for committing the multiple murders. Apparently, he was on the brink of bankruptcy and did not want his family subjected to the humiliation of a life on welfare, so he spared them this by killing them. Two days later, his car turned up in the long-term parking at New York's John F. Kennedy International Airport.

Thirteen years later, Bernard Tracy, who was still investigating the case, was no closer to finding the fugitive, so in an attempt to rekindle interest in the case he approached *Weekly World News*, a supermarket tabloid. They ran a story on the John List case on February 17, 1986. Again, no new information came forth.

However, Wanda Flannery of Aurora, Colorado, thought the printed photograph that accompanied the story resembled her neighbor, Bob Clark. She mentioned this to Bob's wife Delores, who scoffed at the idea that her churchgoing husband could be a murderer. Shortly thereafter the Clarks ran into financial difficulty due to Bob's poor handling of their money and relocated to Richmond, Virginia.

In 1987, FBI specialist Gene O'Donnell was asked to join the effort. Using the latest computer technology and the photograph of John List, O'Donnell was able to "age" the photo by adding gray, receding hair and fleshly jowls. He also included thick-rimmed glasses similar to those List wore in the photo. Bernard Tracy then approached the TV show *America's Most Wanted*; they hired forensic sculptor Frank A. Bender to fashion a bust of what John List might look like some eighteen years after his last known photograph. Criminal psychologist Dr. Richard Walter was brought in to offer a profile of John List as an aid to reconstructing his likely current image. He felt that List's religious background would make it unlikely that he had undergone any plastic surgery and that his lifestyle would not be one of diet and exercise. This was valuable information since either could alter List's pattern of aging.

On May 21, 1989, *America's Most Wanted* aired the John List case along with O'Donnell's "aged" photo and Bender's bust. Over 250 calls came in. One came from an anonymous caller in Colorado who said that John List was living in Richmond, Virginia, under the name of Bob Clark. The caller later turned out to be a relative of Wanda Flannery. Fingerprints proved that Bob Clark and John List were the same individual. On May 1, 1990, nearly two decades after murdering his family, John List received five life sentences.

The examiner superimposes one photo over the other and compares fixed structures such as orbital ridges (eyebrow area), nasal openings, and chin contour. A match suggests that the photos could be of the same individual. This is not conclusive, but suggestive evidence.

The forensic anthropologist or artist may also be asked to "age" a photograph. Let's say a suspect or a missing person has not been seen for years, even decades. Using an old photograph of the individual, the examiner attempts to determine what the individual might look like years later. This has been successful in finding missing persons and tracking down suspects on many occasions. Mostly this "aging" process is guesswork, but, in recent years, experience has increased so that a number of individuals have become quite skilled in this technique. There are even computer programs to aid the process.

Often, a psychiatric profile will be done on the missing person. This is a look into the type of person he was, what type of work he did, what his dietary and exercise habits were, whether he is likely to undergo cosmetic surgery or not, and many other things. The artist uses the information from the psychiatric profile to help speculate what facial changes have likely occurred in the individual over the years.

A major triumph of this technique was realized in the case of John List.

TIME SINCE DEATH

Taphonomy comes from the Greek words *taphos*, which means "grave or burial," and *nomos*, which means "rules or laws." So, taphonomy means the "rules of burial" and is the study of what happens to the human body after death. How the body decays, if it does, and how it becomes skeletonized (deteriorated to the point that only bones remain) are the domain of taphonomy. As we will see in Chapter Five, this field of study might involve the forensic anthropologist and odontologist, as well as the ME, archeologist, climatologist, botanist, entomologist, and others. Here we will look at older skeletal remains, and then, in Chapter Five, we will address more recent deaths where the examiner studies more or less intact bodies.

When confronted with skeletal remains, one of the first questions the anthropologist must answer is: How old are these bones? This is critical to any forensic involvement. Bones that are hundreds of years old have no forensic use. But those that are two years or twenty or even fifty years old may very well have forensic use.

Let me make one thing very clear so you won't make this mistake in your story: When reduced to bones, the corpse does not look like an intact skeleton. You won't find a skeleton sitting in chair, or behind the wheel of a submerged car. The reason is that, as the body's tissues decay, so do the tendons and ligaments that hold the skeleton together. This means it will disarticulate and be a pile of individual bones.

So, how long does it take for a corpse to become completely skeletonized? As previously mentioned, it depends on the environment, with temperature and humidity being the most important factors. In a swamp in Florida, it can take as little as two weeks, while in the deep forests of the north, it could take years.

For the forensic anthropologist, estimating the time since death is never easy and it becomes increasingly more difficult with each passing day. There are a few things that can help, however.

Artifacts of the burial site might offer telling clues. Clothing, jewelry, casket materials, and burial artifacts may indicate the period of the burial. For example, arrowheads, or musket balls would suggest a different time frame than would synthetic materials and plastic objects. Pages from a newspaper or a magazine would set the outside range for the time of death.

Chemical analyses of the bones, such as determining their **nitrogen** levels, can also help. Nitrogen is found in proteins and in their amino acid building blocks. Bones consist of a protein matrix to which calcium is attached. As bones slowly deteriorate, the protein, and thus the nitrogen, level decreases. Measuring the level of the remaining nitrogen can give an estimate of how many years or decades the bones have been interred. This is inexact since the rate of protein and nitrogen loss is affected by temperature and moisture, the same two elements that most affect body decay rate.

Bones tend to absorb **fluorine** and **uranium** from the soil and from ground water. Measurement of these levels may also be a crude indicator of time.

Another measurement is based on the fact that different **amino acids** disappear from bones at different rates. Analysis of fresh bones may yield as many as fifteen different amino acids, while those that are a hundred or more years old may have only seven. Two of the longest surviving amino acids are **proline** and **hydroxyproline**. Their absence would suggest that the bones had been buried many hundreds of years.

Ultraviolet (UV) light is another useful tool. Fresh bones **fluoresce** (glow) a pale blue color under UV light. If the bone is cut crosswise, this glow can be seen across the full thickness of the bone. This fluorescence is lost over time, starting with the surface and then inside the bone. Since the long bones are hollow, this loss of fluorescence occurs from the outside surface and the inside surface toward the middle area of the bone. A bone that is less than one hundred years old may glow across its full thickness, but with time, this fluorescent band becomes progressively thinner until, after several hundred years, it disappears (see Figure 4-5). This offers only a crude estimate of bone age and is of more concern to anthropologists than to forensic scientists.

Radioactive isotopes help age bones. Carbon-14 (C-14) dating is of little use in forensics since its ranges are too broad. The half-life (time it takes to decay by 50 percent) for C-14 is 5,700 years. It is useful for dating something that is many hundreds or thousands of years old, but not for shorter time periods. However, other radioactive materials may be helpful. With the testing and use of nuclear devices in World War II and the continued testing throughout the 1950s and 1960s, the global environment saw an increase in C-14, strontium-90, cesium-137, and tritium (a radioisotope of hydrogen). The finding of

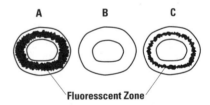

Figure 4-5: Bone fluorescence. Bones lose their fluorescence under UV light from the exterior and interior surfaces inward. (A) A bone less than one hundred years old will fluoresce through its full thickness. (B) After several hundred years all fluorescence is lost. (C) In between these time limits, the central band grows progressively thinner.

increased amounts of one or more of these in bones means that the victim died after about 1950. Those who died before this were not exposed to the environmental increase in these isotopes and would show no such elevation.

BURNED BONES

Bones that have been burned, either before or after complete skeletonization of the corpse has occurred, present special problems for the anthropologist. Under normal circumstances, he will use the texture and color of the bones to help with his estimate of age, but with burning, this texture and color is altered. However, these changes might provide clues regarding the intensity and the duration of the fire, and this might provide some useful investigative clues as to the cause and manner of death. Indirect or brief exposure to the fire causes only yellow-brown discoloration of the bones with or without streaks of soot. With direct exposure to the fire, the bones char and blacken and might crack or splinter. With prolonged direct contact, the bones can be reduced to white ashes. Under these circumstances, the anthropologist may have only a few remnants to work with. To complicate things further, the dessication (drying out) of the bones by the heat of the fire causes them to shrink, making an accurate estimate of stature very difficult.

CAUSE AND MANNER OF DEATH

Occasionally, the skeleton offers clues to the cause and manner of death. As with the intact corpse, this determination can open pathways of investigation. And whether the victim died from blunt trauma or a gunshot might prove critical to the investigation and ultimate solution of the crime.

With blunt-force injuries, such as falls or blows from a blunt object, the injured bone may show fractures, fragmentation, and impact marks (dents and depressions). Sometimes these bony injuries suggest what type of object was used. A baseball bat, a tire iron, and a hammer each leave behind different depressions in a skull.

With sharp-force injuries, such as with an axe or a knife, cut surfaces, nicks, and chips where the blade struck the bone might be visible. Occasionally, metallic remnants from the weapon can be seen along the cut surface.

Gunshots may leave entry and exit holes in the skull, and gouges and other defects in the ribs, spine, and other bones. Finding a bullet or two would help. Sometimes, measuring the entrance hole will estimate the caliber of the bullet that caused the injury. Tracking any injuries to the bones or finding an imbedded bullet may allow for an estimation of the bullet's path and, thus, a determination of which organs were likely damaged.

Of course, blunt objects, knives, and bullets can lead to death without impacting the skeleton, and many deaths by strangulation and most natural deaths leave behind no skeletal evidence. This means that the skeleton might not offer any clues as to the cause and manner of death.

One of the problems facing the examiner is whether the bony injuries he sees occurred around the time of death or many years earlier. For example, a skull fracture that occurred years before death and one that occurred at the time of death may mean two entirely different things. Often, the forensics team can make such a distinction.

Fractured bones heal in time. This healing is by way of **callus** (scar) formation at the area of injury. Callus formation takes months to complete. And, of course, no healing occurs after death. So, a fracture with a robust callus must have occurred months before death. On the other hand, perimortem (around the time of death) fractures show no signs of healing, so there is no callus formation. Thus, a skull fracture that showed no signs of healing could have occurred around the time of death and may indeed be related to the cause of death. This means that a blow to the head or a fall could have led to the individual's death. Conversely, well-healed fractures could not be directly related to the cause of death.

But, what of fractures that occur years after death, after the skeleton has been exposed to nature for a considerable time period? Bones left in nature tend to undergo trauma from natural forces as well as from predators. Often, the examiner can determine when the fractures occurred.

Living bones possess moisture, living protein, and fat, which make them less brittle. Fractures tend to be spiral or "greenstick" in nature. Bones that have desiccated are very brittle and tend to crumble more readily and fracture cleanly, usually parallel or at a cross section to the long axis of the bone. By examining the nature of any fractures, the forensic anthropologist may be able to distinguish premortem from distant post-mortem fractures.

Based on the timing and nature of skeletal injuries, the forensic anthropologist and the ME might be able to determine the cause of death and whether it was self-inflicted, accidental, or homicidal in nature, but determining the manner of death is not always easy or accurate. What if the findings suggest that the individual died as a result of a skull fracture? Was this from a blow to the head (homicidal), a fall (accidental), or a fall after a heart attack or stroke (natural)?

BODY LOCATION

With the exception of some photographic comparisons, all these forensic identification techniques require a corpse or skeletal remains. No body, nothing to work with. Often a discovered body is what instigates this identification process. But sometimes, investigators know a homicide has occurred, or has likely occurred, but they can't find the corpse. The Laci Peterson case is an example. When Laci, who was eight months pregnant at the time, went missing on Christmas Eve 2002, in Modesto, California, it was not long before it became obvious that she had been murdered. Authorities launched a search of her neighborhood and the bay where her husband, Scott, had been fishing. In April 2003, the bodies of Laci and her unborn son Conner washed up on shore in San Francisco Bay. Scott Peterson was later convicted of the double murder.

In homicides, finding and examining the corpse is critical. Searchers use a number of low- and high-tech location methods. All evidence is used to narrow the search area, including the victim's work and leisure habits and witness statements. The victim may work several miles from home, so searching along this route would be undertaken. Maybe he frequently ran or walked in a nearby wooded area. Or maybe the suspect's vehicle was spotted or some of the victim's clothing was found in a remote area. These bits of information can greatly focus the search.

One basic rule is to "look downhill" for a burial site. Let's say it is believed that the body in question was buried near a remote roadway. In the area, the terrain rises above the road on one side and falls away on the other. Search downhill. Why? It is much easier to carry a body downhill than up. It's just that simple.

Once the area of search has been defined, a systematic approach to covering the area should be followed. Freshly turned dirt, trenches, elevations or depressions in the terrain may be helpful. Fresh graves tend to be elevated above the surrounding area, while older ones may be depressed. This is due to settling of the soil, decay of the body, and collapse of the skeleton. Interestingly, the depth of the depression is greater if the body is deeply buried. This is likely due to the larger amount of turned dirt, which is subject to a greater degree of settling. Another factor could be that in deeper graves, the increased weight of the dirt over the corpse causes earlier and more complete skeletal collapse.

Tracking dogs, if provided with an article of the victim's clothing, may be able to follow a scent trail to the burial site. Specially trained cadaver dogs search for the scent of decaying flesh. They can often locate bodies in shallow graves or in water. Deeper graves may present problems.

Another important clue may come from changes in the vegetation over the gravesite. The turning of the soil in the digging process and the presence of the body change the soil conditions in the area over the grave. Changes in compaction, moisture, aeration, and temperature may attract plant species that differ from those around the grave. Or, the plants typical for the area may be present but the changed soil conditions may increase the thickness and richness of their growth. This may be visible, particularly from the air.

Aerial reconnaissance and photography can be coupled with thermal imaging. Freshly turned dirt loses heat faster than normally compacted soil; it appears "colder" by such a device. Alternatively, a decaying body releases heat, which may reveal a measurable difference when compared to the surrounding area. So, the thermal images are inspected for either cold or warm spots, and these areas are then subjected to a more aggressive search.

If a suspect area such as a mound or depression is found, special devices that locate sources of heat and nitrogen, both byproducts of the decay process, or that measure changes in the physical properties of the soil, may be employed. Ground-penetrating radar can "see" into the ground and often locate a buried body. Measurement of the electrical conductivity may prove helpful—a buried body often adds moisture to the soil, and the moisture increases the soil's electrical conductivity. Two metal probes are placed in the soil, and an electrical current is passed between them and measured. Changes in this current may indicate where the body is buried.

Magnetic devices may also be employed. A simple metal detector may locate the victim's jewelry or belt buckle.

A special device called a magnetometer, which measures the magnetic properties of soil, can also be helpful. Soil contains small amounts of iron, so it possesses a low level of magnetic reaction. Since the area where the body is buried has proportionally less soil (the corpse takes up space), it will exhibit a lower level of magnetic reactivity. The magnetometer is passed above the soil and locates any areas that have low magnetic reactivity.

MULTIPLE CORPSES

If identifying a single skeletal corpse is difficult, mass graves and scenes of major catastrophic events obviously present special problems for the forensic anthropologist. Not only will he have difficulty identifying whose bones are present, but he may have trouble determining exactly how many bodies are present. This is particularly difficult in mass graves where a jumble of skeletal remains is found. The forensic anthropologist may never be able to ascertain the exact number of victims, but he can at least determine the minimum number. For example, if he finds ninety skulls, jawbones, or hip girdles, he can conclude that a minimum of ninety people were interred in the site. There could be more, but not less.

In these situations, each bone must be analyzed using whichever of the techniques discussed in this chapter is deemed appropriate. This is why identifying skeletal remains found in mass graves is a long and arduous process.

TIME OF
DEATH:
A CRITICAL PART OF THE TIMELINE

Just about every murder mystery you read or watch on television has a question about the time of death. The same is true for news stories about real-life murders. Why do the police spend so much time on making this determination? Why is the time of death argued about in court, each side trying to tweak the timeline to its advantage? Because the time of death can exonerate a suspect or focus suspicion on him. It can substantiate or refute witness and suspect statements. It can literally make or break the case. It is one of the most important functions of the ME.

Before we look at why this estimation is so important, let's first understand what we mean by the term *time of death*.

DEFINING TIME OF DEATH

There are several times of death. Let me repeat that: There are several times of death. Time of death seems to be a simple and straightforward term that obviously means the exact time that the victim drew his last breath. Unfortunately, it's not quite that simple. There are actually three different times of death: the **physiologic** time of death, when the victim's vital functions actually ceased; he **legal** time of death, the time recorded on the death certificate; the **estimated** time of death, the time the ME estimates that death occurred.

It is important to note that the estimated time of death can vary greatly from the legal time of death and the physiological time of death.

The only absolutely accurate determination of the time of death is the uncommon circumstance in which a person died with a physician or other skilled medical professional present. The doctor could make the determination and mark the time, and even this is assuming his watch or the clock on the wall was accurate. But that little inaccuracy aside, a death witnessed in this fashion is the only time that the three above times of death would correlate with one another.

Otherwise, it is impossible to determine the exact time of death. But what if someone witnessed the fatal blow or gunshot or what if the event was recorded on a timed surveillance camera; wouldn't that accurately mark the time of death? The answer is a qualified yes. If the witnessed event led to immediate death, the witness would have seen the actual death. If not, the witnessed event is simply the trauma that led to death but not the actual moment of death. People can survive massive and apparently lethal injuries for hours and even days or years.

But most deaths are not witnessed. Natural death may come during sleep, and accidental and suicidal deaths often occur when the victim is alone. In homicides, the perpetrator is typically the only witness and he rarely checks his watch, and even if he did, he's not likely to talk about it. This means that when the ME must determine the time of death he can only estimate the approximate time.

These times of death may differ by days, weeks, or even months if the body is not found until well after physiological death has occurred. For example, if a serial killer killed a victim in July, but the body was not discovered until October, the physiologic death took place in July, but the legal death is marked as October, since that is when the corpse was discovered and the death was legally noted. The ME estimated that the time of death could be July, or it could be June or August. It is only an estimate and many factors can conspire to confuse this determination. But, it is critically important for the ME to be as accurate as possible.

THE IMPORTANCE OF THE TIME OF DEATH

An accurate estimation of the time of death can lead to discovering the identity of the assailant. In criminal cases, it can eliminate some suspects while focusing attention on others. For example, a husband says that he left for a business meeting at 2 P.M. and returned at 8 P.M. to find his wife dead. He says that he was home all morning and that she was alive and well when he left. If the ME determines the time of death was between 10 A.M. and noon, the husband has a great deal of explaining to do. On the other hand, if the estimation reveals that the death occurred between 4 and 6 P.M., and the husband has a reliable alibi for that time period, the investigation will move in a different direction.

Notice that in the above example the ME gave a range rather than an exact time for his estimated time of death. He didn't say 4:30 P.M. but rather said between 4 and 6 P.M. Simply put, that's the best he can do and that's why it's called the estimated time of death. It's a best guess.

The time of death is not confined to criminal investigations; it can also come into play in civil situations. Insurance payments may depend upon whether the insured individual was alive at the time the policy went into effect or if he died before the policy expired. Even a single day can be important. Likewise, property inheritance can hinge on when the deceased actually died. Suppose two business partners die near the same time. Their contract may read that the company assets go to the survivor if one of them dies. In this case, the heirs of the one who died last would own the company assets. Similarly, the dispersal of property under a will might be affected by which partner died first.

DETERMINATION OF THE TIME OF DEATH

Determining the time of death is both an art and a science and requires that the ME use several techniques and observations to make his estimate. As a general rule, the sooner after death the body is examined, the more accurate this estimate will be.

Unfortunately, the changes that a body undergoes after death occur in widely variable ways and with unpredictable time frames. There is no single factor that will accurately indicate the time of physiological death. It is always a best guess. But when the principles are properly applied, the ME can often estimate the physiological time of death with some degree of accuracy.

To help with his estimation, the ME utilizes various observations and tests, including:

- body temperature
- rigor mortis
- livor mortis (lividity)

- degree of putrefaction
- stomach contents
- corneal cloudiness
- vitreous potassium level
- insect activity
- scene markers

The most important and most commonly used of these are body temperature, rigor mortis, and lividity. French physician Dr. Alexandre Lacassagne (1843–1924), director of Legal Medicine in Lyon, France, wrote extensively on **algor mortis** (the temperature of death), **rigor mortis** (the stiffness of death), and **livor mortis** (the color of death).

BODY TEMPERATURE

Normal body temperature is 98.6°F After death, the body loses or gains heat progressively until it equilibrates with that of the surrounding medium. Since corpse temperature can be easily and quickly obtained (we'll look at how shortly), the search for a formula that uses this parameter to define the time of death has been sought for years. As early as 1839, English physician John Davey undertook the study of corpse heat loss in London, and as late as 1962, T.K. Marshall and F.E. Hoare attempted to standardize this analysis when they established a computerized mathematical formula known as the Standard Cooling Curve. In the intervening years, and even since Marshall and Hoare, many others have attempted to devise similar schemes. Unfortunately, none of these have proven to be any more accurate than the current formula for heat loss of 1.5 degrees per hour.
The formula is:

Hours since death = 98.6 - corpse core temperature / 1.5

This approximate rate of heat loss continues until the environmental temperature is attained, after which it remains stable. That sounds simple enough.

Unfortunately, it's not quite that straightforward. The 1.5-degrees-per-hour factor varies, depending upon the environment surrounding the body, the size of the corpse, clothing, and other factors. For example, a body in a temperate room will lose heat much more slowly than will one in an icy, flowing stream. And a body in a hot environment, such as an enclosed garage in Phoenix, Arizona, in August, where the ambient temperature could be 125°F or more, will gain heat. The key is that the corpse will lose or gain heat until it reaches equilibrium with its environment.

The coroner's technician who processes the corpse at the scene takes a body temperature, and also measures the temperature of the surrounding medium—air, water, snow, or soil (if the body is buried). Ideally, the body temperature is taken either rectally or by measuring the liver temperature, which may be a more accurate reflection of the true core body temperature. This requires making a small incision in the upper right abdomen and passing the thermometer into the tissue of the liver. This should only be done by a trained individual and under the direction of the ME. Care should be taken not to alter or destroy any existing wounds on the body. Some people have suggested measuring the core temperature by inserting the thermometer into a knife wound or gunshot injury to negate the need to make a new incision. This should never be done because the introduction of any foreign object may contaminate or alter the wound, which can be key evidence in the case. For practical reasons, the rectal temperature is usually taken.

The sooner after death the body is found, the more accurately the time of death can be assessed by this method. Once the body reaches ambient temperature, all bets are off. But even if done correctly and soon after death, body temperature determination is subject to several sources of inaccuracy.

One assumption made in the calculations is the initial body temperature. The normal 98.6°F is an average and varies from person to person. Some people have higher normal temperatures than others. Women tend to run higher temperatures than do men. Illnesses associated with fevers can markedly elevate the temperature of the person at the time of death, while chronic illness, dehydration, or the presence of prolonged shock may lower initial body temperature. There is also some diurnal (basically, morning versus evening) variation in body temperature in most people. All this means that the calculation begins with some degree of error.

A dead body loses heat passively by three distinct mechanisms: **radiation** (heat lost as infrared heat rays), **conduction** (heat passed on to any object that contacts the body), and **convection** (heat lost into the moving air). The state of the corpse and the environmental conditions greatly affect the rate of heat loss.

Obesity, heavy clothing, warm still air, exposure to direct sunlight, and an enclosed environment slow heat loss. Fat and clothing make good insulators, so an obese person in a sweater will lose heat much more slowly than would a thin, unclothed corpse exposed to cold or moving air, water, or shade. Children and the elderly tend to lose heat faster, as do those who are chronically ill or emaciated. If the body is in contact with cold surfaces such as marble or cool concrete, heat loss will be greater.

There's still one more curveball: Several days after death, as fly maggots begin to feed on the corpse, their activity and internal metabolic processes can at times raise the temperature of the corpse. This should not be a problem for the forensic investigator, though, because once this insect activity is that far advanced body temperature is no longer of use.

As you can see, heat loss is fraught with inaccuracies. Still, with early and careful measurement of the core body temperature and consideration for the conditions surrounding the corpse, a reasonably accurate estimate can be made.

Let's say two people are murdered in a home in Houston, Texas, during late summer. The bodies are discovered four hours after death. One body is left in the garage where the ambient temperature is 110°F, while the other is in the living room where air conditioning holds the temperature at 72. The corpse inside would lose heat at about 1.5 degrees per hour, so that if the ME had evidence that the death had occurred four hours earlier, he would expect to find a core body temperature of approximately 92°F to 93°F.

1.5 degrees / hour x 4 hours = 6 degrees

98.6 − 6 = 92.6

If he found a different core temperature, he would revise his estimate. But what if the victim were very old or young, thin, unclothed, or lying on a cold tile floor near an air conditioning vent? Under these circumstances, the heat loss would be more rapid. The core temperature could be 88°F to 90°F, perhaps even less. If the ME failed to consider these mitigating factors, an erroneous estimate of the time of death could result. For example, if the core temperature was 88°F and he failed to adjust for the environmental conditions around the body, he could estimate that approximately seven hours had elapsed since death.

98.6 − 88 = 10.6 / 1.5 = 7.1 hours

An estimate of six to eight hours is quite different from an estimate of three to five hours. The killer may have an ironclad alibi for the former time period, and easily could since he hadn't arrived at the crime scene at that time. He could have been having lunch with twenty people. But only four hours later, he might not have such an alibi.

What of the body in the garage? The ME would expect the corpse to gain heat at the same rate of 1.5 degrees per hour. Thus, the core temperature should be approximately 104°F, or perhaps even higher.

RIGOR MORTIS

Rigor mortis is the stiffening and contraction of the muscles due to chemical reactions that take place within the muscle cells after death. The chemical reaction that causes this is the loss of adenosine triphosphate (ATP) from the muscles. ATP serves as energy for muscular activity. Without it, our muscles could not contract. The presence and stability of ATP depends on a steady supply of oxygen and nutrients, which are lost with the cessation of cardiac activity that occurs at death. When the ATP levels fall, the muscles contract and stiffen, producing the rigidity of rigor. The later loss of this rigidity and the appearance of flaccidity (relaxation) of the muscles occur when the muscle tissue itself begins to decompose as part of the putrefaction process.

It is important to note that rigor begins throughout the body at the same time but the appearance of the actual rigidity doesn't. It typically follows a predictable pattern, being detectable first in the small muscles of the face, neck, and hands before progressing to the larger muscles. The reason for this progression from smaller to larger muscles is simply that smaller muscles possess less ATP so the loss is relatively more rapid, and smaller muscles will exhibit stiffening more readily than will larger ones.

The rigor begins in about two hours and the entire contracting process takes about twelve hours. At that time, the body is completely stiff and is fixed in the position of death; it tends to remain so for another twelve hours. This is called the **rigid stage** of rigor mortis. The process then reverses itself with rigidity being lost in the same fashion, beginning with the small muscles and progressing to the larger ones. This process requires another twelve or so hours. The muscles are now flaccid (relaxed); this is termed the **flaccid stage** of rigor mortis.

A good general rule for rigor mortis is 12-12-12: it maximizes at twelve hours, remains unchanged for twelve hours, and resolves over the next twelve hours. So, rigor is only useful in the first thirty-six hours or so after death. Under normal conditions, that is. There are wide variations from corpse to corpse and from situation to situation. These variations make rigor one of the least reliable methods of determining the time of death. To understand these variations, let's look at the physiology behind this process.

Sometimes rigor mortis comes on very quickly after death. This occurs in any situation that leads to a premortem (before death) depletion of ATP. If the muscles are already very low on ATP at the time of death, the contraction and stiffening of the muscles will occur more rapidly.

Muscular activity and excessive body heat are the two most important conditions that lead to ATP depletion. Any severe muscular activity around the time of death quickens the onset of rigor. For example, the victim could have been running, fighting with an assailant, struggling to prevent drowning, or suffering from violent seizures. Each of these would consume most, if not all, of the muscular ATP and rigor could come on within minutes of death. Interestingly, a victim who was chased prior to death may show the first signs of rigor in the legs, where the ATP would be most depleted in this circumstance. Strychnine is a drug that causes convulsions and muscular spasms, conditions that mimic severe physical activity. Victims of strychnine poisoning may develop rigor almost immediately.

Since an elevated body temperature also causes increased ATP consumption, any drugs or infectious processes that increased the body temperature could cause a rapid onset of rigor. Victims of sepsis (infection throughout the bloodstream), pneumonia, or any other febrile (fever) process, as well as those that succumb to heat stroke, may develop rigor very rapidly.

The opposite is also true. Cold conditions slow the process of ATP loss considerably and will delay the onset and development of rigor. A victim who dies from exposure in a cold clime or one that is frozen immediately after death may not develop rigor for days, perhaps not until the body is warmed or thawed.

In addition, for reasons that are not well understood, obese people tend to develop rigor at a slower pace than do thin individuals. In fact, obese persons sometimes don't develop rigor at all.

Rigor can be broken by bending and stretching the corpse, which breaks up the muscle fibers. Once broken, rigor will not return.

Cadaveric spasm is the instantaneous onset of stiffness throughout the body, which locks the corpse in the exact posture it was in at the moment of death. The corpse could be frozen sitting, kneeling, reaching, or in virtually any position. Cadaveric spasm occurs under extremely violent physical and emotional situations. A victim may be holding a knife at the moment of death and cadaveric spasm will cause the hand to get a death grip on the weapon.

Though somewhat controversial, cadaveric spasm is best viewed as simply instantaneous rigor. This makes sense since the conditions that cause cadaveric spasm are similar to those that cause early onset of rigor.

LIVOR MORTIS

Corpses typically contain a dark discoloration of portions of the body. This discoloration is **livor mortis** (also called **lividity** or **post-mortem hypostasis**). It is important for two reasons: It can help determine the time of death and, as important if not more so, can indicate whether a body was moved after death.

Lividity is a purplish hue of the tissues and may be mistaken for bruising by the inexperienced. It is caused by stagnation of blood in the vessels. At death, the heart stops beating and the blood ceases to move. Gravity then causes the stagnant blood to settle into the dependent (lower) areas of the body. This means that a supine corpse (lying with the face upward) will develop lividity along the back and buttocks. A corpse lying on its left side will show lividity along the downside of the left shoulder, arm, hip, and leg.

However, any dependent area that presses against a firm surface will appear pale and will be surrounded by the lividity. For example, a corpse lying on its back will show lividity along its entire lower surface except where the body actually contacts the hard floor. The back of the head, shoulder blades, buttocks, and calves will show pale points of contact, because the weight of the body compresses the blood vessels in these support areas and prevents the accumulation of stagnant blood. Tight clothing may do the same thing. A belt, waistband, or brassiere may leave a pale track through an area of lividity.

Why is the lividity this dusky color? Blood that is rich in oxygen (O_2) is bright red, whereas blood that is depleted of oxygen is purple. At death, when the heart and circulation cease, no fresh blood reaches the cells of the body. In a futile attempt to survive, the cells of the body extract all the oxygen they can, leaving the blood depleted of it. This oxygen-poor blood is dark purple, and when it settles it produces purple lividity.

But, not all lividity is bluish or purplish in color. In carbon monoxide (CO) and cyanide (CN) poisoning (see Chapter Eleven), the lividity may take on a cherry-red or pinkish coloration. Carbon monoxide combines with hemoglobin creating carboxyhemoglobin, which is bright red in color. Similarly, cyanide combines with hemoglobin to produce cyanohemoglobin, also bright red in color. In addition, cyanide is a "metabolic" poison that prevents the body's cells from using oxygen. Since the cells no longer take in oxygen, the blood remains rich in oxygen, which also gives it a bright red color. So blood that is rich in carboxyhemoglobin, cyanohemoglobin, or oxygen is bright red and the resulting lividity reflects this.

Another common situation that may produce red lividity is when the victim is exposed to very cold conditions near and after the time of death. In this case, the cold slows down all cellular activities, including the post-mortem removal of oxygen from the blood, which leaves the blood rich in oxygen and red in color so any lividity will be red or pink.

In individuals who exsanguinate (bleed to death), there may be little or no lividity, since there is little blood remaining that can settle. Typically, the entire body will be pale. Alternatively, people dying from severe heart failure, shock, or asphyxia may develop deeply purple lividity. The blood in these situations is usually poorly oxygenated during life and is thus deeply purple in color, which means any lividity will be also.

Lividity typically appears between thirty minutes and two hours after death and reaches its maximum by eight to twelve hours. Initially, this discoloration can be shifted by rolling the body to a different position. If a body is supine for a couple of hours and then rolled to its left side, the lividity that had begun accumulating along the back will shift and begin accumulating along the left side. But, by six to eight hours, the lividity becomes fixed. This means that rolling the body to another position will not result in a shifting of the discoloration. The reason is that after about six to eight hours, the blood vessels in the area begin to break down, and the blood seeps from the vessels and stains the surrounding tissues. As opposed to the blood that remains within the vascular system, this blood in the tissue is fixed in position. The ME can use shifting and fixed lividity to estimate time of death and to determine if the body has been moved or repositioned, something the dead do not do without assistance.

If a body is found face-down with fixed lividity along the chest, abdomen, and front of the legs, the ME can conclude that the death was at least six to eight hours earlier. It may be longer but it is not likely sooner. If the lividity can still be shifted, death likely occurred less than four hours or so earlier. On the other hand, if a body is found face-down, but with fixed lividity along the back, then the body was moved at least six hours after death, but not earlier or the lividity would have shifted to the newly dependent area. This means the body lay on its back for at least six hours after death, long enough for the lividity to become fixed, and was then rolled to its stomach or moved to an entirely different location and deposited on its stomach.

This fixing process is not an all-or-nothing phenomenon. It occurs gradually. This means that by four to six hours some of the lividity might be fixed and some still able to shift. If the ME finds that the corpse has some faint areas of fixed lividity along the back and true fixed lividity along the front, he might conclude that the body laid on its back for around four hours and was then moved and placed face-down, where it laid for six or so hours more.

This same process occurs in the internal organs. At the autopsy of a person found supine, the ME would expect to find a settling of the blood along the posterior (back) areas of the lungs, liver, spleen, brain, and other internal organs. This may present a problem because a victim left in the supine position accumulates blood along the back of his scalp and the back of his brain. Blood may even seep into the subdural space (between the brain and the skull). At first examination, this may appear similar to someone who was struck in the back of the head with a blunt object, contusing (bruising) the scalp and brain. The ME must make the distinction by using his knowledge and experience.

From this you can see that the careful examination of the lividity pattern of a corpse can provide critical evidence in homicide cases. It can help reconstruct the sequence of events surrounding the death. If the patterns and the body position don't match, it suggests that someone had reason to move the body. That someone is most likely, but not always, the killer. Sometimes a family member who finds a loved one dead will want to clean up or reposition the body to a more acceptable position or place before calling the police.

All these mental gymnastics presume normal circumstances. Since body decay depends primarily on the ambient temperature, and since the fixing of the lividity is due to breakdown of the blood vessels and the seepage of the released blood into the tissues, anything that hastens or slows the decay process will do the same for the fixation of lividity. In hot and humid environments this fixation may occur in as little as three or four hours, while in colder climes, it may take as long as thirty-six hours.

THE RATE OF BODY DECAY

Putrefaction is the term used for decay or decomposition of a body. Under normal circumstances it follows a predictable pattern, which the ME can use in his estimation of the time of death.

At death, all vital processes within the body stop. The heart doesn't beat, the blood doesn't flow, and all body processes cease. For many years it was believed that the hair and nails continued to grow for a while after death. This was actually stated as fact by Charles Meymott Tidy in his book *Legal Medicine* (1882). The reason for this erroneous belief is that as fluids are lost from the corpse, the tissues retract or shrink so that it appears as if the nails and hair are longer several days after death than they were at the time of death.

The decomposition of the human body begins immediately after death and involves two distinct processes: autolysis and putrefaction. **Autolysis** is basically a process of self-digestion. After death, the enzymes within the body's cells begin the chemical breakdown of the cells and tissues. As with most chemical reactions, the process is hastened by heat and slowed by cold. **Putrefaction** is the bacteria-mediated destruction of the body's tissues. The responsible bacteria mostly come from the intestinal tract of the deceased, though environmental bacteria and yeasts contribute in many situations. Bacteria thrive in warm, moist environments and become sluggish in colder climes. Freezing will stop their activities completely. A frozen body will not undergo putrefaction until it thaws.

Putrefaction is an ugly and unpleasant process, which under normal temperate conditions follows a known sequence. During the first twenty-four hours, the abdomen takes on a greenish discoloration, which spreads to the neck, shoulders, and head. Bloating, caused by the accumulation of gas within the body's cavities and skin as a byproduct of the action of bacteria, soon follows. This begins in the face where the features swell and the eyes and tongue protrude. The skin will then begin to marble, and a web-like pattern of blood vessels forms over the face, chest, abdomen, and extremities. This marbling is green-black in color and is due to the reaction of the blood's hemoglobin with hydrogen sulfide. As gases continue to accumulate, the abdomen swells and the skin begins to blister. Soon, skin and hair slippage occur and the fingernails begin to slough off. By this stage, the body has taken on a greenish-black color. The fluids of decomposition, or **purge fluid**, begin to drain from the nose and mouth. This may look like bleeding from trauma, but is due to extensive breakdown of the body's tissues.

However, the rate at which this process occurs is almost never normal because conditions surrounding the body are almost never normal. Both environmental and internal body conditions alter this process greatly. Obesity, excess clothing, and a hot and humid environment speed this process, while a thin, unclothed corpse lying on a cold surface with a cool breeze follows a much slower decomposition process. Very cold climes may slow the process so much that, even after several months, the body appears as if it has been dead only a day or two. Freezing will protect the body from putrefaction if the body is frozen before the process begins. Once putrefaction sets in, even freezing the body may not prevent its eventual decay. If frozen quickly enough, the body may be preserved for years.

Sepsis (blood infection) is particularly destructive to the body and might accelerate the decay process so much that, after only twenty-four hours, the corpse could appear as if five or six days had passed. The reason is that not only would the body temperature be higher at death in this circumstance, but also the septic process would have spread bacteria throughout the body. This allows the decay process to begin quickly and in a widespread fashion.

The internal organs tend to decay in a predictable order. The ME can use this in his estimation of time of death. The stomach and intestines, which hold many bacterial species, decay first, followed by the liver, lungs, and brain, and then the kidneys. Lastly, the uterus and prostate succumb to the bacteria.

Left unchecked, the decomposition process will ultimately leave behind only a skeleton. The time required for a body to completely skeletonize is determined by the environmental conditions we've been discussing. And the process is not always uniform. Occasionally, the decomposition is spotty so that portions of a body decay while others are left more or less intact.

Another important factor in the rate of decay is the location of the body. A body exposed to the environment will decay faster than will one that is buried or in water. The general rule is that one week exposed above ground equals two weeks in water and eight weeks in the ground. Also, bodies left exposed or in shallow graves are subject to predators.

Dead bodies attract dogs, cats, bears, hogs, rats, and other predators. They might feed on the flesh and carry away portions of the corpse. The remaining flesh and bones may reveal claw and tooth marks that might reveal the predatory species. For example, dogs and cats tend to remove V-shaped wedges of tissue, while rodents tend to leave shallower, smooth-edged wounds. Rodent incisors (front teeth) leave parallel grooves on the surface of gnawed bones. The ME looks for evidence of predator activity since their activities may bear on his estimated time of death.

But decomposition is not the only way a body can change after death. Under certain circumstances mummification or adipocere formation may occur.

Mummification occurs when the body desiccates (dries out) in a hot, dry environment. The low humidity inhibits bacterial growth and putrefaction, while at the same time sucking the moisture from the tissues. In ancient Egypt, spices and salts were rubbed on the corpse to hasten the drying process so that the corpse would mummify rather than decay. A leathery, dark-colored corpse results. Its appearance is as if the flesh had been "shrink-wrapped" over the bones. This is a similar process to the making of beef jerky. The internal organs may dry and shrivel or become a dark brownish-black putty-like material. Mummified corpses tend to remain intact for long periods of time.

Adipocere is the result of a chemical process called **saponification**, which is basically soap making. Adipocere is caused by a reaction between certain bacteria and the body's adipose (fatty) tissues. Bacteria such as *Clostridium perfringens*, the bacterium that causes gas gangrene, convert body fat into oleic, stearic, and palmitic acids, the primary constitutes of adipocere. The result is a brownish gray, greasy or waxy substance, which can cast the body into a statue-like form. On first glance, the corpse may appear as a mannequin, or as if it had been carved from a large bar of soap. Adipocere most often occurs in bodies found in water or warm, damp areas and usually takes several months to form so it is a broad indicator of time of death. A corpse that has significant adipocere formation could not have been dead only a couple of weeks.

Bodies may not decompose uniformly. A corpse may be partially skeletonized, partially mummified, and partially converted to adipocere. Incomplete embalming may lead to partial preservation and partial skeletonization.

One other decomposition state worth covering is the bloated condition of **floaters**, bodies of people who either die in water or are dumped into water shortly after death. Initially the body sinks, but as putrefaction occurs and gases accumulate in the body's tissues and cavities, the body rises to the surface and floats. Since the production of these gases is a byproduct of the action of bacteria, it is greatly affected by the temperature of the water. In the warm waters of the Gulf of Mexico, where the warmth accelerates bacterial growth and gas formation, a body may float after only a week or two, while in cold waters, where bacteria multiply more sluggishly, it may take weeks or months.

In general, bodies found in temperate water display:

- swollen hands and face after two to three days
- separation of skin from the body after five to six days
- loss of fingernails after eight to ten days

- floating after fourteen or so days in warm water and after three or four weeks in cooler water

The appearance of each of these physical signs is extremely variable and depends on many conditions within the corpse and in the water.

TIME SINCE DEATH

One of the most difficult tasks for the ME is determining the approximate time of death in a corpse that is weeks or months old. In this situation, body temperature, rigor mortis, and lividity are no longer useful, so the ME will use the expected stages of post-mortem decay and then modify that timeline according to the local conditions where the body is found.

The average temperature and humidity are key to his assessment. A corpse dumped in a cool mountain cave decays much more slowly than one left lying in a sunny field. A buried corpse decomposes at a slower rate than one that is exposed to the open air. Bacterial growth tends to be less vigorous in a buried corpse, and predators and climate changes are less likely to damage the body. Shallow graves, less than two or three feet deep, suffer some temperature variations that parallel the environmental temperature changes, while those buried more deeply are exposed to relatively stable temperatures.

The ME might consult with a **forensic climatologist** to see what the recent daily high and nightly low temperatures have been and use this information to refine his time estimate. For example, a corpse left in a wooded area in the Colorado mountains decomposes much faster if the average daily high and low was 85°F and 65°F, respectively, as compared to 65°F and 45°F. A corpse exposed to a heat wave for four or five days might look like one exposed to more normal temperatures for ten to fourteen days.

In buried corpses, the moisture in the soil affects the rapidity of decay, with more moisture translating to more rapid decay. The amount of moisture in the soil at a burial site depends on the relative humidity, the amount of rainfall, and the degree to which the soil drains. Graves in moist, rainy, and low-lying areas would contain more water than those on a hillside in a drier area. The ME must consider these variables in his estimation.

To further complicate things, the body's location and degree of exposure might change at any point after death. Murder victims may be stored for a few days prior to burial or dumping and are sometimes moved from one site to another. The killer simply might not have had enough time to get rid of the body at the time of the murder and might return later after he has developed a plan for disposal. Or the corpse might be moved because the police are getting too close to locating it, or as part of a serial killer's sick fantasy. The body might even be moved by nonhuman agents, such as water or landslides.

The passage of several days between the death and the burial of the victim presents the ME with changing exposure conditions that can introduce errors into his time of death estimation. He looks for evidence that the body has been moved and attempts to analyze each place where the body lay, estimating how long it lay there in order to make an educated guess of time of death. This is quite difficult, and often impossible.

Consider a body dumped in a lake that is then retrieved two days later and buried. Or one that is weighted down and dumped in a cold river, then breaks free from its bonds and washes downstream, and finally comes to rest on an isolated sunny shore where it is found four days later. Or a body that is buried for a week, and then dug up and moved to another burial site with entirely different soil and water conditions. Or a body in a cave that is dragged into the sunlight by predators. In each of these situations, the corpse is exposed to varying environmental conditions for varying amounts of time.

THE LAST MEAL

The ME can often use the contents of the victim's stomach to help determine time of death. After a meal, the stomach empties in approximately two hours, depending on the type and amount of food ingested. If a victim's stomach contains largely undigested food material, then the death likely occurred within an hour or two of the meal. If the stomach is empty, the death likely occurred more than four hours after eating. Additionally, if the small intestine is also empty, death probably occurred some twelve hours or more after the last meal.

If the medical examiner can find out through witness statements when the last meal was consumed, he can use this to determine the time of death. Let's say a man is found dead in a hotel room and the ME determines that his stomach is full of undigested food materials. If he had dinner with a business associate from 8 to 10 P.M., then returned to his room, the finding of a full stomach would indicate that the death occurred shortly after he returned to his room. The ME might place the time of death between 10 P.M. and midnight.

These calculations depend on a number of factors. Heavy meals and those rich in protein and fat digest more slowly than do small meals and those high in carbohydrates, sugars, and liquids. The consumption of alcohol or many sedative and narcotic drugs, as well as some medical conditions, tend to slow digestion and gastric emptying, while other drugs and medical conditions hasten these processes. Also, there is great individual variation in rate of digestion. Therefore, gastric contents are of marginal help in time of death determinations.

THE EYES

The clear covering over eye pupils are called **corneas**. At death they become cloudy and opaque. This may occur in a very few hours if the eyes are open at death, or it may take up to twenty-four hours if they are closed.

The **vitreous humor** is the clear, thick, liquid substance that fills the eyeballs. After death, the concentration of potassium within the vitreous increases at a constant rate over the first few days. This increase is due to release of potassium from red blood cells into the vitreous. Though the determination of the vitreous potassium level is only useful in the first three or four days, as opposed to many other post-mortem changes, it is independent of ambient temperature.

INSECTS

Besides animal predators, a dead body attracts numerous insects. These are typically flies and beetles that feed off the corpse's flesh. They tend to appear at predictable times and in a predictable sequence, which the ME will use to aid in his determination of the time of death. Unfortunately, these patterns vary greatly by geographic region, specific locale, time of day, and season. Because of the complex nature of the bug world, the ME will often request the assistance of a **forensic entomologist**. **Entomology** is the study of insects and forensic entomology is the study of the insects that populate a dead body.

The first use of insects to solve a crime dates back to thirteenth-century China. In the first forensic text in 1235, Sung Tz'u described the case of a murder using a sickle. The villagers were forced to line up and lay their sickles on the ground before them. Flies congregated around one attracted by the remnants of the victim's blood on the blade. Thinking this must be some divine finger pointing at him, the killer confessed. Modern forensic entomology began in France in the mid-1800s, culminating with the publications of two forensic entomological texts by Jean Pierre Mégnin (1828–1905): *Faune des Tombeaux* (*Fauna of the Tombs*) in 1887 and *La faune des cadavres application de l'entomologie à la médecine légale (The Fauna of Cadavers in Forensic Entomology)* in 1894. The American Board of Forensic Entomology was founded in 1996.

During the first seventy-two hours after death, the ME employs all of the non-entomological methods for determining the time of death and makes his best guess. After that time, entomology is the most accurate method of making this determination.

Insects help to determine the time of death in two basic ways: The first method uses the predictable developmental stages of insects, most notably the blowfly; the second addresses the predictable succession of insect species that populate the corpse.

Numerous species either feed on the dead body, on the insects that are attracted to the body, or both. Each has a preferred time and order of appearance and a different life cycle. It is well beyond the scope of this text to consider this subject in any great detail, so let's confine ourselves to the most common species, the blowfly. An understanding of this insect will give you a feel for the problems the forensic entomologist faces.

When a body is left exposed, blowflies appear early, often within the first hour after death. They seek out the moist areas of the corpse, such as the nose, mouth, armpit, groin, and open wounds, to lay their eggs. The eggs hatch to larvae (maggots) within hours. Over the next ten days, the larvae feed, grow, and repeatedly molt. There are tables that show the growth rate of these larvae so that the entomologist can compare those found at the scene with the tables of length, and therefore estimate the age of the larvae. Using this method he can usually say whether the larvae are three days old or nine days old. After the larval stage, the maturing flies become pupae, which is when their outer covering hardens. Approximately twelve days later adult flies emerge. So, this entire cycle takes from about eighteen to twenty-two days. The mature flies will then lay eggs and the cycle repeats.

Under normal circumstances, if the ME or the entomologist finds only eggs, the death likely occurred less than forty-eight hours earlier. If he finds maggots but no pupae, the death occurred between two and ten days earlier. The finding of pupae indicates that ten or more days have passed, while the presence of mature hatchlings indicate that death occurred two to three weeks earlier.

As you might suspect, it's not really that easy. Blowflies do not deposit eggs at night, and they are less plentiful and even absent in winter. So, if the victim was murdered at midnight, the blowflies may not appear until dawn, and if it

---

is cold out, they may not appear at all. In unfavorable conditions, the maggots may go dormant for extended periods of time. If the body is in an area that is warm during the day and very cold at night, they may be dormant half of each twenty-four-hour period. Also, if it turns cold for several days, the developmental process may be put on hold for that time period. The entomologist might consult a forensic climatologist, who can provide information regarding the temperature and weather conditions over the past days and weeks.

Fly activity is typically delayed in a corpse enclosed in a structure. It may not occur at all if the corpse is in a container, such as a car trunk or barrel or plastic sheeting. While a buried corpse may not attract flies, other insects do attack the corpse. Each of these situations must be considered when insect activity is used to determine the time of death.

Most of the time, insect studies can only give a minimum time since death occurred. If pupae are found, the corpse must be *at least* six to ten days old. It can't be less since the pupae would not have had time to appear, but if the weather is inhospitable to the larvae, it could be much longer. Another compounding factor is that the insects appear in waves and new generations appear all the time. The adults produced after two weeks will themselves lay eggs and these eggs will follow a similar cycle. So a three-week-old corpse may show fly eggs, maggots, pupae, and adults. Sorting all this out is no easy task.

Insects might also show that the corpse has been moved. A corpse found to be populated with insects that are not found in the area of its discovery suggests that the corpse had at one time been where these species of insects live, and therefore, must have been moved.

Another use of insects is in the field of toxicology (see Chapter Eleven). Insects feeding on the tissues of the corpse ingest whatever chemicals are contained within the tissues. If a corpse is too decayed for adequate toxicological testing, the insect larvae might reveal the presence of a toxin. Some chemicals retard the maturation rate of the larvae, while others accelerate it; this might alter the estimation of time of death.

Live maggots, pupae, and empty pupal cases, are collected as samples for the entomologist to evaluate the types of insects present and where each is within its developmental cycle, and estimate how many cycles have occurred. Some maggots should be placed in a KAAD solution (a mixture of alcohol, kerosene, and other chemicals) or alcohol. This will preserve them in a state that reflects the scene.

SCENE MARKERS

The ME uses everything at his disposal to estimate the time of death, including many non-scientific findings. Scene markers include any information at the scene or from witnesses or family and friends. The last time the person was seen alive serves as a starting point. The individual must have died at some time after the sighting—if that sighting is accurate. Family and friends can speak to the person's habits and any changes they have observed.

Missed appointments or work, missed daily walks or visits to the coffee shop, uncollected mail or newspapers, and dated sales receipts can be useful. In assaults, a broken watch or clock may give the exact time of the event. The absence of home lights or the lack of smoke from a chimney might strike the neighbors as odd.

The victim's clothing might be helpful. For example, if the victim has missed work for two days and is found near the front door of his home, dressed in work attire and carrying his car keys, it is logical to assume that he was headed to work at the time of his death. Or perhaps he had a racquetball game scheduled but never showed. He is then found in his garage, wearing his exercise gear. In this case, he likely died as he was leaving for his game.

Let's say a neighbor knows that the person goes for a walk every morning at 7 A.M., but has not done so for two days. Lights are on in the house but no one answers the door, so the police are called. They enter to find a corpse sitting in a chair, facing the television that is on and tuned to a certain channel. Next to his chair is a *TV Guide*, opened to the listings for three days earlier and a show on the very channel the television is tuned to is circled. This evidence suggests that the victim died three days earlier around the time of the show in question. Or not. It's a best guess situation and the ME would add this information to the more scientific determinations discussed earlier before making a final estimate. But these scene markers can help him narrow the time.

PUTTING IT ALL TOGETHER

As you can see, determining the time of death is not an easy matter. No single test or observation will give an exact time, so the ME uses all available testing and puts it together in an attempt to arrive at some reasonable range for the time of physiological death.

Let's say a body is found at 6 A.M. The on-scene analysis reveals that the body temperature is 90°F, lividity is fixed, rigor is full, and no appreciable insect activity is noted. How would the ME use this to determine the time of death? The body temperature suggests that death occurred six or so hours earlier, and the lividity would give a range of six to eight hours. Typically, full rigor would take eight to twelve hours to occur. The lack of insect activity is expected since the death took place after sunset. Since none of these are absolute times, the ME combines them for a best guess. He might conclude the most likely range would be six to nine hours and place the time of death between 9 P.M. and midnight the previous day. That's the best he could do, but it might be enough if the prime suspect has no alibi for that time period.

THE BODY FARM

No discussion of the time of death would be complete without mention of the **Body Farm** (officially the University of Tennessee Forensic Anthropology Facility) and its contribution to the field of taphonomy (see Chapter Four: Identifying the Body, "Time Since Death").

In 1971, Dr. William M. Bass, a forensic anthropologist, established the Body Farm at the University of Tennessee in Knoxville as a place where he could study the rate and pattern of decomposition of bodies under various environmental conditions. He basically created an outdoor taphonomy laboratory.

Bass began with a single body, but now has studied hundreds. At any one time, the three-acre farm may have as many as 150 bodies decomposing in the open in either sun or shade, buried at various depths and in varying soil conditions, in water, in the trunks of cars, stuffed in trash bags, rolled in carpeting, interred beneath concrete slabs, or hanging from scaffolding. With each body, our understanding of the decay process increases. In fact, virtually everything we know about corpse decomposition came from Bass's farm.

The FBI regularly uses Bass's expertise and the information obtained from the research at the Body Farm. They even send agents there for training. In the future, the Body Farm wants to produce an atlas of body decomposition for law enforcement and help perfect ground-penetrating radar and other body-locating techniques, including an "electronic nose" for sniffing out corpses. The main goal is to understand the chemistry of decomposition better so that more accurate estimations of the time of death become possible.

CAUSE, MECHANISM, AND MANNER OF DEATH:
HOW DID THE VICTIM DIE?

From a forensic sense, the **cause** and **manner** of death are of paramount importance. Somewhere death occurs every minute of every day, but only a small portion of these attracts the attention of the medico-legal investigative system. Before we look at the forensic aspects of death, let's first look at death itself.

THE DEFINITION OF DEATH

Death is when someone "ceases to be alive," right? That's as good a definition as any, but then again ... what does "cease to be alive" mean? And when exactly does that happen? How does one determine when life leaves the body? When and how is someone pronounced dead?

The determination of death has never been straightforward, and before the last one hundred years it was nearly impossible. In fact, as we learned in the previous chapter, the exact moment of death is still controversial.

In the seventeenth century, physicians knew that the living breathed and had a pulse, but that was about it. If you had these you were alive, and if not, you were dead. Sounds easy enough. But some people might appear dead when they are actually ill or intoxicated. Alcohol, drugs, heart attacks, serious infections, bleeding, shock, dehydration, and other situations might render the victim comatose, cold to the touch, and with shallow respirations and weak pulses. Signs of life may be difficult to ascertain. Not uncommonly, people who were thought to be dead woke up.

To overcome this problem, several methods for determining the presence of death were devised. Tongue and nipple pulling, tobacco smoke enemas, and the insertion of hot pokers into various body orifices were each used. I'd suspect that, if alive, the hot poker deal would get the person's attention. Tongue pulling was so popular that a device for performing this was developed. It consisted of a clamp for the tongue and a crank that, when turned, would yank the tongue back and forth. After an hour or so of this, if the person didn't respond, death was proclaimed.

Still, the occasional seriously ill, but living, person who was pronounced dead proved not to be.

Finally, a system of **vitae dubiae asylums**, or "waiting mortuaries," was established. Here the suspected dead would be placed on cots and watched until decay set in. Once the corpse began to smell, death was certain. Though this was unpleasant for the family of the deceased, this system at least allowed for a confident proclamation of death and avoided premature burials, which weren't unheard of in the seventeenth century.

Two hundred years ago, physicians would listen to a patient's heart by placing an ear directly against the patient's chest. This was called direct auscultation. But this was rarely allowed when the patient was female. In 1816, French physician René-Théophile-Hyacinthe Laënnec (1781–1826) found himself in such a situation, so he solved the problem by rolling several sheets of paper into a tube, placing one end to his ear, and the other to the woman's chest. He found that with this indirect method he could hear the beating heart even more clearly than with the old direct method. The stethoscope was born. It later evolved into its current form.

This invention gave physicians a tool to better hear the *lub-dub* of the beating heart and allowed for a more accurate determination of death. No heartbeat and no air moving to and fro in the lungs, no life. But still, in people with very shallow breathing and very weak pulses, these sounds might not be heard even when faintly present.

Willem Einthoven (1860–1927) won the 1924 Nobel Prize in Medicine for constructing the first crude electrocardiographic machine (ECG or EKG). This device actually recorded the electrical activity of the heart and gave physicians some objective measure of death. No electrical activity in the heart, no heartbeat, no life. Finally, a true definition of death was available. Or was it?

The twentieth century saw the development of ventilators and pacemakers that could keep the heart and lungs working well after death. This would be artificial life, but if the definition of life was the presence of breathing and a heartbeat, this was life nonetheless. The water suddenly became muddier.

This brought about the concept of **brain death**, that is, the heart and lungs may be working but the brain is dead. Currently, a death pronouncement in someone with a heartbeat or a pacemaker and on a ventilator requires the absence of brain electrical activity as determined by an **electroencephalogram** (EEG), a device that measures brain activity.

The concept that the brains of living creatures possessed electrical activity was first proven by Richard Caton (1842–1926) in 1875 when he recorded the electrical waves emitted by the exposed brains of monkeys and rabbits. In 1924, German psychiatrist Hans Berger (1873–1941) recorded the first human EEG by attaching electrodes to the scalp. This gave physicians and scientists the first objective test of brain activity. But even this is controversial since definitions for brain death vary among states today.

As you can see, from the earliest of times to today, the definition of death is not straightforward. But, why is this important to the coroner? Isn't this a medical and not a forensics question? Not exactly. What if the person in the ICU on a ventilator had been shot in the head or hit by a drunk driver? The charges that could be filed against the shooter or the driver become measurably more serious if the victim dies. The fact that the victim was shot or was hit by the car of a drunk driver makes his death of interest to the coroner and the prosecutors. While alive, the shooter or the driver might face assault or vehicular injury charges, but if the victim dies, the charges could rise to manslaughter or murder. Before the physicians caring for the victim "pull the plug" on the ventilator, they must be absolutely sure the individual has no hope for survival. Otherwise, they could be implicated in the death. And you can bet that prosecutors and defense attorneys would be on opposite sides of any dispute surrounding when to take the victim off life support. The Terri Schiavo case would be an example of such legal jousting.

Another controversy would arise if this same brain-dead individual were to be an organ donor. Before the donation, the donor must be brain dead. But, at the moment that occurs, the corpse falls under the jurisdiction of the ME, and if any organs are then removed without his permission, it could be considered tampering with the death investigation. Fortunately, since time is critical in these situations, the coroner's office offers an automatic consent in most jurisdictions so that the organs can be removed and donated.

Still, the defense could argue that the death was not due to the gunshot but rather to the removal of the organs or the ventilator. It isn't the shooter who is guilty but the physicians. And so on and so on. Death is never easy.

Despite these problems with the exact definition of death, once it occurs, it falls in the lap of the ME or coroner. Whenever possible, he must determine the **cause**, **mechanism**, and **manner** of death in any unexpected or suspicious death. To do this, he uses evidence from the crime scene, the autopsy, and the crime lab.

CAUSES AND MECHANISMS OF DEATH

Simply put, the **cause** of death is why the individual died. A heart attack, a gunshot wound, a traumatic brain injury—they are the diseases or injuries that caused the physiological derangement that lead to death.

The **mechanism** of death is the actual physiological derangement that caused the cessation of life. In the heart attack victim, the mechanism could be a lethal change in heart rhythm (cardiac arrhythmia), or the heart could be so severely damaged that it can no longer pump adequate amounts of blood to sustain life (cardiogenic shock). Rarely the mechanism of death in a heart attack victim is a rupture of the heart muscle (ventricular rupture). Each of these mechanisms can lead to death from the same cause—a heart attack.

The gunshot victim could also die by several mechanisms. The bullet could directly damage the heart or the brain. Here, the mechanism would be penetrating trauma to the heart or brain. Or the bullet could cause extensive bleeding, which would lead to death. The mechanism of death would be exsanguination (bleeding to death). Also, the wound could become infected, leading to sepsis (infection throughout the bloodstream and the body) and death. Here, the mechanism would be sepsis, the cause a gunshot wound.

Similarly, the victim of a blow to the head could die from direct trauma to the brain (cerebral contusion), bleeding into the brain itself (intracerebral hemorrhage), or bleeding around the brain (subdural or epidural hematoma), which could lead to compression of the brain and result in the stoppage of breathing (asphyxia). Again, one cause can lead to death by several mechanisms.

Conversely, one mechanism can result from several different causes. Exsanguination (the mechanism of death) can result from such divergent causes as a gunshot, stabbing, bleeding ulcer, bleeding lung tumor, or excessive ingestion of blood-thinning medications such as warfarin. In each case, blood loss and shock are the physiological derangements.

From these examples you can see that a single cause may result in death by varying mechanisms, and a single mechanism can result from several different causes. The coroner must make these determinations and his conclusions can greatly impact any criminal proceedings.

For example, let's say a man is struck by an intoxicated driver's car and is severely injured. The paramedics arrive and transport him to the hospital where he dies as a result of his injuries. If the ME determines that the blunt trauma from the car caused severe and lethal brain injuries, the driver may be charged in the man's death. But, what if the ME determines that the injuries were not that severe and that the victim died from internal bleeding, which the paramedical and hospital personnel failed to recognize and treat appropriately? Who's responsible for the man's death? In each of these scenarios, the cause of death is blunt trauma from the automobile impact. But, the mechanism is either a brain contusion or exsanguination. The ME's assessment of the mechanism will determine what legal actions might follow. One could lead to a charge of vehicular manslaughter and the other to a malpractice suit.

Let's take this a step further. What if, during his investigation, the ME discovers that the man had been distraught and that he actually threw himself in front of the car? Would the death then be a suicide?

The answer to this question leads to the **manner** of death, which is how, why, and by whose hand the cause of death came about. The ME must also make this determination.

THE FIVE MANNERS OF DEATH (ACTUALLY FOUR PLUS ONE)

The manner of death is the root cause of the sequence of events that leads to death. In other words, how and why did these events take place? Who initiated the events and with what intention? Was the death caused by the victim, another person, an unfortunate occurrence, or Mother Nature? There are four main manners of death:

NATURAL: Natural deaths are due to the workings of Mother Nature in that the death results from a natural disease process. Heart attacks, cancers, pneumonias, and strokes are common natural causes of death. This is by far the largest category of death that the ME sees.

ACCIDENTAL: Accidental deaths result from an unplanned and unforeseeable sequence of events. Falls, automobile accidents, and in-home electrocutions are examples of accidental deaths.

SUICIDAL: Suicides are deaths that come by the person's own hand. Intentional self-inflicted gunshots, drug overdoses, or self-hangings are suicidal deaths.

HOMICIDAL: Homicides are deaths that occur by the hand of another. Note that a homicide is not necessarily a murder. Homicide is a determination of the ME; murder is a legal charge that is determined by the courts. Though each would be ruled a homicide by the ME, the legal jeopardy is much different for a court verdict of negligent homicide as opposed to first- or second-degree murder.

UNDETERMINED OR UNCLASSIFIED: This extra category is used in situations where the coroner can't accurately determine the appropriate category.

Just as a cause of death can lead to many different mechanisms of death, any cause of death can have several different manners of death. A gunshot wound to the head can't be a natural death, but it could be deemed homicidal, suicidal, or accidental.

Only natural deaths are due to disease. The other categories involve trauma and could lead to civil or criminal proceedings. Of course, even a natural cause of death may be deemed accidental, homicidal, or, rarely, suicidal. How is this possible? What if a critically ill person is prevented from visiting a doctor or hospital? Maybe an inheritance is at stake. The individual who prevented the victim's receiving health care could be charged with homicide.

Another scenario could be death from a heart attack because of some error during surgery. Though the cause of death would be a heart attack (a natural event), the manner might be deemed accidental and could lead to malpractice litigation. Or this same person could have severe heart disease and be assaulted on the street. During his struggles with his assailant, he could suffer a heart attack and die. The cause of death would again be a heart attack, but the manner would be homicide, since, but for the attack, he likely would not have suffered a fatal heart attack. At least not at that time and place.

THE CORONER'S DETERMINATION

It is imperative that the ME attempts to accurately classify the manner of death, as this determination will decide what happens next. When faced with a sudden and unexplained death, the ME will take a series of systematic and logical steps to evaluate the case. This approach is similar to that taken by physicians who treat the ill. The sequence a good physician follows is to take a complete history, perform a physical exam, order the appropriate laboratory tests, and make a diagnosis. Only after this can treatment begin.

When confronted with a homicide, the ME follows a similar approach. He obviously cannot obtain a direct history from the deceased, but he can get information from police reports, medical records, witness statements, and interviews with family, law enforcement, and medical personnel. To help him gather the needed information he may have subpoena power (in some jurisdictions) and usually the blessing of the court. He then performs a "physical exam." This is the autopsy. He examines the body externally, internally, and microscopically. Based on the findings in his "history and physical exam," he orders laboratory tests. These may include microscopic examinations of the tissues of various organs, toxicological testing, ballistics evaluations, or any other tests indicated and available in the crime lab. After all this, he makes the "diagnosis"—his statement of the cause and manner of death.

If no overt trauma is seen, the ME first looks for natural causes of death. He reviews medical records, perhaps discusses the situation with the deceased person's physician, and performs an autopsy if he feels it is necessary. These investigations may lead him to believe that the person died as a result of a heart attack, an infection, the failure of organs such as the liver or kidneys, diabetes, or any number of other diseases. In this case he deems the death to have been natural.

If no natural cause is present, the other manners of death are considered. He then looks for less obvious trauma, poisons or drugs, and other signs of accidental, suicidal, or homicidal death.

What about undetermined or unclassified deaths? How do these come about? Let's consider the example of a drug abuser who dies from a drug overdose. Heroin and several other illicit drugs when taken in excess amounts can lead to coma, cessation of breathing, and death from asphyxia (see Chapter Eight). Here, the cause of death is a drug overdose and the mechanism is asphyxia. But what is the manner?

What if the victim has a history of overdoses, both accidental and as previous unsuccessful suicide attempts? If he dies from a drug overdose (cause), was it an accident or suicide (manner)? To the ME, the autopsy and laboratory findings would be the same, regardless of the victim's intent. The ME might order a **psychological autopsy** in which a forensic psychiatrist delves into the person's personal history in an attempt to find any hidden motives for suicide. Even after this, the intent or lack of intent of the deceased may not be apparent and the manner of death might be listed as undetermined or unclassified. Simply put, there is no way to know for certain whether the person overdosed accidentally or purposefully.

But it gets even cloudier. What if the victim was a police informant or was due to testify against a local dealer? What if the dealer knew this and sold him a bag of 100 percent heroin, while the usual stuff he gets is only 15 percent? How would he know? Not being a chemist, he would simply melt and shoot up the same amount of the powder and would not know that he was actually taking six times his usual dose. Here the manner of death would be homicide. As we saw above, to the ME and the forensic toxicologist, this death would appear identical to one due to an accident or suicide.

The key point: It's the intent and by whose hand the event occurred that determines the manner of death.

THE CORONER'S REPORT

Once the coroner or ME completes his analysis, he files a report in which he lays out the essentials of the case and comes to some conclusion regarding the cause, mechanism, and manner of death. The manner of death is an opinion expressed by the ME after he has looked into all the circumstances leading to and surrounding the death. His opinion may or may not be accepted by the courts, law enforcement, attorneys, or the victim's family. Even if he concludes that a death was a homicide, prosecutors may not agree and may not file criminal charges. There are many reasons a family might sue to change the manner of death, particularly in situations where the manner of death has been ruled a suicide. Changing the manner of death to accidental may help them accept the loss or perhaps affect any insurance payments.

The ME's determination of the manner of death has no time limit. For example, a victim who was shot by a perpetrator during a robbery and admitted to a hospital could have a very long hospitalization. During the course of his treatment, he could develop pneumonia and die as a result. The cause of death may be the pneumonia, but the manner of death would be homicide. How can this be? Isn't pneumonia a natural cause of death? After all, the perpetrator may have shot him, but he didn't cause the pneumonia that killed him. Well, actually he did, just not directly. The event that began the "cascade of events" that led to death was the gunshot. If not for that, the victim would not be in the hospital and would not have developed the pneumonia that led to his death. The time lag between the inciting event and the actual death, which could be days, months, years, or decades, does not affect the final determination of the manner of death.

The ME's opinion is not written in stone and may change if more evidence comes to light. Perhaps evidence is presented to suggest that a natural death may not have been so natural. The body is exhumed and high levels of arsenic are found in the remains. With a natural death ruled out, the question then becomes, was this death a suicide, a homicide, or the result of an accidental ingestion? The coroner then shares this information with law enforcement and an investigation begins. Once further information is uncovered, the ME might be able to classify the death into a specific category. If the family uncovered a suicide note, suicide might be favored. If the husband suddenly has a pocketful of insurance money, a new girlfriend, and a bottle of arsenic-containing pesticide hidden in his closet, homicide may be the ruling. But, what if family members come forward with information that the victim possessed the odd belief that a little arsenic taken each day was good for arthritis? Would an accidental death be more likely?

Tackling these types of complex problems is common for the ME. How effective he is depends upon his training, skill, and experience.

BODILY HARM:
IDENTIFYING WOUNDS

Trauma to the human body comes in many forms: gunshots, stabbings, blunt-force injuries, thermal and electrical burns, and bite marks. Rape and abuse, traumatic events themselves, also frequently involve one or more of these types of injuries. In this chapter we will look at each of these.

GUNS AND BULLETS

If you've ever fired a high-powered handgun, rifle, or a shotgun, you're likely to have vivid memories of the first time you pulled the trigger. The shock of the sudden explosive discharge and the kick of the recoil were probably more jolting than you anticipated. Even more shocking is the damage a bullet can do to a human.

Gunshot wounds (GSWs) are a common cause of death in accidental, suicidal, and homicidal shootings (see Chapter Six). The mechanism of death depends upon the location and the severity of the injury the bullet produces. For a gunshot to be immediately fatal, extensive trauma to the brain, the heart, or the upper spinal cord must occur. Otherwise death is slower and is typically due to exsanguination (bleeding to death) or a secondary wound infection. The manner of death depends upon the intent of the person discharging the weapon. Obviously, death from a gunshot wound can't be a natural death, but if the shooter did not intend to harm himself or others, it would likely be deemed accidental in nature. If someone else shot him it could be accidental or homicidal.

As we saw in Chapter Three when discussing the autopsy, bullets that strike a human can be tricky and behave in all sorts of odd ways. A gunshot wound to the head does not necessarily result in damage to the brain. The bullet can flatten against the skull and never penetrate the bone or enter the brain, or it can ricochet off the skull and leave the body entirely, or it can burrow beneath the scalp and be found some distance from the entrance wound. The bullet is more likely to burrow beneath the scalp if it approaches from an angle of less than 90 degrees. For example, a bullet may strike the victim's forehead, penetrate the skin, career off the skull, burrow beneath the scalp, and come to rest at the back of the person's head.

The same thing can occur if the victim is shot in the chest. The bullet might strike the sternum or a rib and flatten against the bone, or ricochet in any direction. It might leave the body or burrow beneath the skin, never entering the chest, or be deflected upward into the neck or downward into the abdomen. It's very unpredictable.

For this reason, whether the victim is among the living in a hospital emergency department or on the coroner's autopsy table, if the bullet or bullets cannot be readily located, X-rays are taken of the chest, abdomen, and sometimes the entire body. Since lead bullets are readily visible under X-rays, the surgeon or the ME can locate them in this manner.

When the coroner examines a gunshot victim, he must determine how many wounds are present. He must locate all entrance and exit wounds (if any) and trace the path of each bullet through the victim's body, if possible. Only with this information can he determine which bullet, if any, led to the victim's death. This information may be critical to the prosecution of the crime.

DETERMINING RESPONSIBILITY

Let's say a man is shot several times in the arm, the leg, twice in the chest, and once in the head. The shooter claims the victim threatened him and he was merely protecting himself. But, the crime scene analysis reveals that the limb and chest wounds occurred while the victim was standing and the shot to the head came after he was on the floor. The initial shots could indeed be self-defense, the headshot less so, since the "attacker" was down and the shooter could have fled or called for help.

But, which was the fatal shot? If one of the bullets to the chest severely damaged the heart and led to death, the subsequent shot to the head would be of less consequence since the victim would have died anyway. In this case, a first-degree murder conviction might be difficult. But, if neither of the chest wounds was immediately fatal, the shooter could be facing a murder charge. The prosecution would likely contend that the shooter did not have to fire the fatal bullet and that he did so in a calculated and premeditated fashion. What charges are brought depends upon how the ME assesses the injuries.

This becomes even more important if two shooters are involved. If one assailant fired the shots to the victim's limbs and chest and the other the single shot to his head, the ME's opinion as to which was the fatal shot would be crucial to the prosecution. The person who fired the lethal shot would likely face the more serious charges.

ENTRY WOUNDS

A bullet that harms someone always leaves an entry wound, simply because to do harm the bullet must strike, and usually enter, the person at some point. However, if the bullet remains within the victim, there will be no exit wound.

Though not always easy, the ME must attempt to distinguish entry wounds from exit wounds and determine which bullets followed which path through the victim.

The characteristics of wounds produced by a gunshot depend on several factors, including the distance between the victim and the gun's muzzle, the caliber and velocity of the bullet, the angle at which the bullet enters, and whether the bullet remains within the victim or passes completely through and exits the body. This later situation is often termed a "through-and-through" gunshot wound.

When a gun is fired, the gunpowder or smokeless powder explodes, forcing the bullet from the cartridge and down the gun's barrel. But, the bullet is not the only thing that leaves the barrel. Hot gases and particles of burned and unburned gunpowder are also ejected from the muzzle.

The gases are predominantly carbon monoxide, carbon dioxide, and nitrogen oxide. Mixed with these gases are certain components of the primer. The most important of these are the heavy metals lead, bismuth, and antimony,

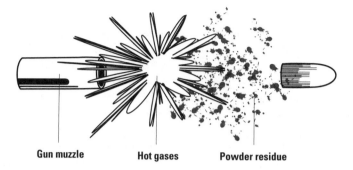

Gun muzzle   **Hot gases**   **Powder residue**

Figure 7-1: Gun muzzle output. A fired gun expels the bullet, burned and unburned powder, and hot gases. Which of these mark the entry wound depends on the distance between the muzzle and the victim.

which are useful when testing for gunshot residue (GSR). The particulate matter is predominantly burned and unburned powder and soot.

Each of these ejected materials travels a different distance from the muzzle (see Figure 7-1). The hot gases may travel only a few inches, the particulate matter a foot or two, and, of course, the bullet a considerable distance. The character of the entry wound is affected by which of these components actually contact the skin. The ME can use this information to determine the distance between the gun's muzzle and the point of entry at the moment the gun discharged.

The anatomy of the entrance wound is different depending on how close the muzzle is to the skin (see Figure 7-2). The resulting wound is different from weapon to weapon, but in general if the muzzle is two or more feet away from the victim, the entrance wound is a small hole, smaller than the bullet due to the elastic quality of skin. A blue-black bruising effect forms a halo around the entry point (called an **abrasion collar**) along with some black smudging where the skin literally wipes the bullet clean of the burned powder, grime, and oil residue it picks up as it passes through the barrel. This smudging is often easily wiped away with a wet cloth.

If the muzzle is between six inches and two feet from the point of entry, there might also be **tattooing** or **stippling** of the skin. This is due to burned and unburned powder that is discharged from the muzzle. These tiny particles embed in the skin and cause tiny hemorrhages (red dots of blood within the skin) in a speckled pattern around the wound. These cannot be wiped off because the particles are actually embedded (tattooed) into the skin. The breadth of scatter, or spread, of this stippling increases as the distance between the muzzle and the entry point increases (see Figure 7-2B). The tattooing resulting from a gunshot inflicted from a distance of ten or twelve inches will be compact and dense, while that from a shot delivered from eighteen to twenty-four inches will be broader and less dense.

If the muzzle is only a few inches away (see Figure 7-2C), the stippling will be very compact and partially obliterated by the charring from the hot gases. Here, the skin around the entry wound is burned and blackened by the heat from the expelled gases. In addition, the carbon monoxide in the gases combines with hemoglobin and myoglobin (iron-containing compounds that reside in the blood and muscle tissues, respectively). This combination produces carboxyhemoglobin and carboxymyoglobin. These compounds are bright red in color and impart this to the surrounding tissues. Thus, a gunshot from a very close distance will produce a hole, a compact area of stippling, a surrounding area of charring, and a bright red hue to the wounded tissues.

A contact gunshot wound (see Figure 7-2D) occurs when the gun's muzzle is pressed against the skin as it is fired. In this circumstance, the hot gases and particulate matter are driven directly into the skin, producing greater charring. Also, the rapidly expanding gases rip the skin in a star-shaped or **stellate** pattern. Since the gases cannot expand the gun's metal barrel, nor can they force their way very deeply into the tissues, they take the path of least resistance by expanding laterally in every direction and tearing the skin in a jagged star

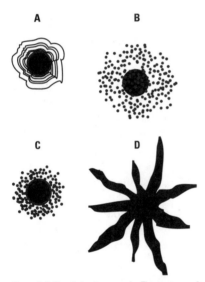

Figure 7-2: Gunshot entry wounds. The anatomy of an entry wound depends on the distance between the muzzle and the entry point. If far away (A), the wound may be a simple hole with a faint abrasion collar. If closer (B), there might be stippling or tattooing, which becomes more dense the shorter the distance is (C). With contact wounds, the skin is torn by the hot gases into a stellate pattern (D).

pattern. This is particularly true if the contact wound is over a bone such as the skull. Thus, a contact wound rips the skin in a classic stellate pattern, chars the skin severely, and produces the bright red tissue color as described above.

The entry wound made by the bullet is not always round. If the bullet enters at an angle other than 90 degrees, the wound may be somewhat elliptical. Or if the bullet strikes another object, such as a window or wall or another person, and then ricochets into the victim, it may lose its spin and begin to tumble or gyrate. This is called **yawing**. The wound in this circumstance may be difficult to distinguish from the typically larger and more irregular exit wounds.

So, why is all this important? If the person is dead and the gun that fired the bullet is found, who cares how far away it was? Let's look at a simple scenario to see why this determination is critical.

Say that a victim is found shot in the head, the gun is lying on the bed beside him, and a suicide note is spread open on the dresser. But what if the ME's examination of the entry wound indicates that the muzzle was not held against the victim's head but rather was at least two feet away? Try holding your hand such that the tip of your finger is two feet from the side of your head. If not impossible, it is at least awkward and not the position someone would likely hold a gun.

Further, what if the angle of entry indicates that the gun muzzle was not only two feet away, but was also such that the muzzle must have been pointed at the back of the victim's head? It simply isn't possible for the victim to have held the weapon in that position. This means that someone else did. The suicide might now be a homicide.

EXIT WOUNDS

Exit wounds are typically larger than entry wounds and result from the bullet lacerating (cutting or tearing) the tissues as it forces its way up and out through the skin. The shape and size of the wound depends on the size, speed, and shape of the bullet. Soft lead bullets are easily deformed as they enter and pass through the body, particularly if the bullet strikes any bony structures during its passage. If so, the bullet may become severely misshapen and produce more extensive tissue damage, often resulting in a gaping, irregular exit wound. Similarly, if the bullet strikes a hard surface such as a brick wall or metal railing before entry, it might be significantly deformed before it enters the victim. This may lead not only to a large irregular exit wound, but also a larger entry wound. Hollow-point bullets have a depression or hollowed area in their noses, which causes greater deformation of the bullet, more tissue damage, and larger exit wounds.

The opposite is true with jacketed bullets. Such bullets might be completely or partially covered with a metal, Teflon, or other hard material. These are typically high-velocity bullets with extraordinary penetrating power and they tend to pass directly through the victim with little change in their structure. In this case, the exit wound may be small and resemble a typical entry wound. The ME might not be able to distinguish between the entry and the exit wound. These types of jacketed bullets can also pass through protective bulletproof vests and have earned the name "cop killers."

A **shored** exit wound, where the tissues at the exit point are supported, may also give the ME problems in distinguishing entry wounds from exit wounds. The typically ragged nature of most exit wounds is due to the bullet ripping its way through the skin. But if the skin is supported by tight clothing made of materials like leather or woven fabrics, or if the victim is against a wall or other structure, the skin will be less likely to tear and the exit wound will be smaller and less ragged, and will appear more like an entry wound.

SHOTGUN WOUND PATTERNS

A shotgun expels a cluster of shot (small round beads) rather than a single bullet, which leads to multiple entry wounds. As with other guns, it might be critical to determine the distance between the muzzle and the victim, since this may distinguish between a murder and a suicidal or accidental shooting. It may also support or refute a suspect or witness statement.

Rather than the characteristics of the wounds, the most important factor in making this determination is the spread pattern of the shot. A general rule is that the shot spreads an inch for every three feet it travels. This depends greatly upon the choke applied to the barrel. The choke is an alteration in the diameter of the end of the barrel, which concentrates the shot pattern. There are four degrees of choke (from narrowest to widest): full, modified, improved cylinder, and cylinder-bore. The last is no narrowing or choking of the barrel at all. The barrel may be sawed off, which greatly increases the scatter of the shot.

There is no truly scientific way to determine the distance between the muzzle and the victim for shotgun blasts. The best way is to fire the suspect weapon, using the same ammunition type, from several distances until you find the distance that most closely matches the shot pattern found at the crime scene. This will approximate the distance from which the murder weapon was fired.

The estimated distance between the victim and the muzzle is often critical in the ME's assessment of the manner of death. For example, if the shotgun that caused the death of the victim is tested and the spread pattern indicates that the muzzle must have been approximately six feet from the victim, then suicidal and accidental shootings are ruled out. This would likely lead the ME to state that the shooting was homicidal.

SHARP-FORCE INJURIES

Sharp-force injuries, also called penetrating injuries, come from any weapon that is pointed or possesses a sharp edge. Knives, scissors, axes, swords, ice picks, forks, wooden stakes, and other edged or pointed instruments fit the bill. Other than a stab wound to the brain or to the upper part of the spinal cord, both of which are very rare, only a stab wound to the heart could cause immediate death. Otherwise, death arrives more slowly and is most often due to excessive bleeding. Much later, death can result from secondary wound infections.

Just as we saw with gunshot wounds, when faced with fatal penetrating injuries, the ME must determine the cause and manner of death. To do this, he examines the corpse and locates each and every wound, then determines what types of weapons were likely used and which wounds were potentially lethal. With a single stab wound to the heart, this is easy. But if the victim has received multiple wounds, the ME's work becomes more difficult.

In this situation, the ME's goal is to determine the sequence of the injuries and to estimate which wound or wounds were the likely killing injury. Again, in homicides with more than one assailant, this becomes critical, since the deliverer of the fatal wound could face the more serious charges.

Once he has nailed down the actual cause of death, the ME looks at the manner of death. Stabs, cuts, and chopping wounds can be accidental, suicidal, or homicidal in nature. The ME will use the nature, location, and number of wounds to make this distinction whenever possible.

Sharp-force wounds can be divided into three general types: stab wounds, incised or cut wounds, and chop wounds.

STAB WOUNDS

Stab wounds are caused by pointed instruments—knives are the most common. Other instruments frequently used are ice picks, scissors, swords, and even screwdrivers.

Deaths from stab wounds are most often homicidal, but can also be accidental. They are rarely suicidal. If the victim slipped and fell onto a pointed object, causing a fatal wound, the manner of death would be accidental. The ME would need to determine that such a fall took place and exclude the possibility that the victim had been pushed onto the object, or that he had been stabbed and then fell. These latter two situations would be homicidal.

The reason that suicide by stabbing is uncommon is that it is extremely difficult for someone to stab himself with enough force to be fatal. Not to mention that it hurts. For this reason, if the wounds are suicidal, the deeper, more severe punctures are typically associated with smaller, shallower wounds called **hesitation wounds**. These vary greatly in size and depth, as if the individual were working up the courage to make the final stabs. When the ME encounters these hesitation wounds, suicide must be considered.

The main characteristics of stab wounds are that they are deeper than they are wide. For the ME, measuring the depth of the wound is much easier than assessing its width. Using a probe and very carefully plumbing the depth of the wound, being careful not to alter it, he can fairly accurately estimate its depth. But this doesn't give him the exact length of the blade. Only half of the blade could have been thrust into the victim, so this measurement is only the minimum length of the blade. It can be longer, but not shorter.

If the knife had been thrust to the hilt, it could have left a patterned abrasion of the hand guard around the wound. The hand guard is the piece of metal between the handle and the blade that keeps the user's hand from sliding down onto the blade. If this impacts the skin with enough force, it can leave a bruise or abrasion that matches the guard in shape and size. In this situation, the ME can state that the measured depth of the wound reflects the actual length of the blade. This also gives him the shape and size of the hand guard, which might help determine the type of knife used.

The width of the blade is more problematic. The elastic nature of human skin often causes it to contract around the wound once the weapon is removed, making the wound much smaller in appearance. On the other hand, some people, particularly the elderly, have poor skin elasticity and the wound may actually gape open and appear larger than it is. The blade also may be removed at an angle that is different from its entry angle, thus distorting the wound. Sometimes a knife twists or turns as it is withdrawn. This may produce Y- or L-shaped wounds.

Other factors that affect the character of the wound are the angle of the stab, movement of the knife within the wound, and the characteristics of the blade itself. And of course, the victim might move and distort the wound. The victim may turn, twist, deflect the blows, strike back, or try to run. Each of these actions could change the nature of any wounds received.

This brings up the subject of **defensive wounds**. These are the wounds inflicted by the attacker on a victim who is attempting to defend himself. Stabs, cuts, and slices on the victim's hands and arms indicate that he tried to parry the stabs. These are usually found on the palms of the hands and the ulnar side (little-finger side) of the forearms. They effectively rule out an accidental or suicidal manner of death.

Most of the time, determining the nature of the blade that made the wound is impossible. But with a clean stab wound, the ME might be able to measure the depth and width of the wound and occasionally determine if the blade were straight, curved, or serrated on one edge. If a double-edged blade was used, the wound might be pointed on each end, whereas with a single-edged blade, one end might be pointed and the other squared. Most of the wounds the ME sees are single-edged, since double-edged blades are rarely used.

Some stabbing instruments leave behind distinctive wounds. An ice pick makes small, round wounds; a barbecue fork leaves paired, uniformly spaced wounds; and a kitchen fork marks four evenly spaced punctures. Screwdrivers may leave wounds that distinguish a Phillips-head instrument from a standard slotted one. The wounds left by scissors depend on whether the two blades were separated at the time of use or not.

By looking at these wound characteristics, the ME can usually determine the type of instrument used and can easily distinguish a knife wound from one made with an ice pick or screwdriver. He might be able to assess the exact dimensions, shape, and style of the blade, but identifying the exact weapon is virtually impossible because the marks left are specific to a certain weapon. There are, however, two notable exceptions.

If the tip of the knife blade breaks off and remains in the wound, the crime lab might be able to match the broken edge to that of a suspect weapon. This would be strong individualizing evidence that this weapon made the wound. Or blood may provide the link. If the victim's blood can be matched through DNA (see Chapter Ten) to blood found on the weapon, that would again be powerful evidence. Murderers often overlook small flecks of blood on the blade or handle or blood that has seeped into the groove between the blade and the hand guard. Wiping down or rinsing the knife will not always remove such traces.

The pattern of blood loss may be helpful in determining the sequence of the injuries and which wounds were potentially fatal. Post-mortem wounds do not bleed, so wounds associated with a large amount of blood loss must have occurred while the victim was alive. This is the general rule, anyway. But, if a person suffers multiple stab wounds and bleeds profusely, some wounds may be delivered after he has lost a great deal of blood and has slipped into shock. These wounds may show little or no bleeding. Alternatively, a wound to a large blood vessel in a dependent area may bleed significantly even after death. This is due to the force of gravity. Regardless, the ME uses the pattern of blood loss to help reconstruct the sequence of events surrounding the murder as best he can.

INCISED WOUNDS

Incised wounds or cuts are caused when a sharp instrument is drawn across the skin. Unlike stab wounds, they have no characteristic width or depth, and thus reveal little of the nature of the weapon. These wounds are not usually fatal, but when they are, they are usually suicidal or homicidal. Accidental, suicidal, and homicidal incised wounds are usually in different areas of the body and show different cut patterns. Knowing these locations and patterns helps the ME reconstruct the death scene and determine the manner of death.

Accidental incised wounds typically involve the hands and are rarely fatal. To be lethal, an accidental cut would have to involve the neck or a major artery. Falling or flying glass fragments make up the majority of such serious wounds, though this can happen with falls onto sharp instruments or edges, or injuries suffered in a car accident, or with the use of power tools such as band, circular, or chain saws.

Suicidal wounds are usually found on the victim's wrists. As with stab wounds, suicidal incised wounds are frequently accompanied by hesitation marks. Right-handed individuals typically cut their left wrist and left-handers their right.

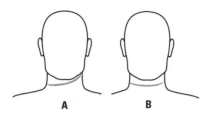

A   **B**

Figure 7-3A: Rear assault incised neck wound. The path of the blade is from high on one side of the neck, down and across the throat, and slightly upward again. Here the assailant was right handed, since the wound begins high on the left side of the neck. With a left-handed attacker, the path would be opposite.

Figure 7-3B: Frontal assault incised neck wound. When an assailant faces his victim, the slashing wound is typically horizontal or slightly angled.

Homicidal incised wounds are typically seen on the neck. If the assailant is behind the victim, the cut usually extends from high up on one side near the ear, sweeps downward across the front of the throat, and then back up on the opposite side (see Figure 7-3A). The cut tends to end up lower than it began. The path of this sweep is left to right in a right-handed assailant and the opposite for a left-handed one.

If the attacker is facing his victim, the cut is usually shorter and horizontal or on a slight angle (see Figure 7-3B). Defensive wounds on the hands and arms are more common in frontal assaults.

CHOP WOUNDS

Heavier, sharp-edged implements such as axes and meat cleavers produce **chop wounds**. The wounds tend to be deep and wedge-shaped and are often accompanied by fractures, grooves, and chips in underlying bones. Lethal chop wounds are usually accidental or homicidal and are very rarely suicidal. But it's not uncommon for someone to accidentally injure himself while using an axe to chop wood. If the blow severs a major artery in the leg, death can follow from extensive blood loss unless medical help is quickly available.

BLUNT-FORCE TRAUMA

Blunt-force trauma occurs whenever someone is struck with a blunt object, including fists, shoes, sticks, skillets, floors, stairs, bathtubs, steering wheels—any instrument that does not have a sharp or cutting edge. Blunt trauma can come from an assault, a fall, an automobile accident, or a number of other situations.

The injuries produced by such traumas vary based on the location, the force, and the number of the blows inflicted. The greater the force of the blow, the greater the resulting injury, while the greater the surface area struck by the blow, the less the injury. Thus, a board or boat oar will produce less injury than would a baseball bat swung with the same force. The greater surface area of the board spreads out and lessens the degree of injury.

The ME is often asked to determine what object caused a blunt-force injury. This is not always easy to do since similar wounds can be produced by very different objects. A hammer and certain brass statuettes could produce very similar wounds, or they may not. But the accurate determination of the type of weapon is critical since this might lead to identifying the assailant. For example, if the ME determines that a ball-peen hammer caused the victim's skull fracture and the prime suspect has one in his possession, this could be useful information. The ME must also determine the age of the injury. If a victim's cuts, bruises, and abrasions are two days old, they could not have occurred at the time of the assault in question but rather must have occurred prior to the current event. This may greatly affect the charges filed against the assailant.

As we saw with someone attacked with a knife, the victim of a blunt-trauma assault also attempts to mount a defense by trying to block the blows with his hands and arms. For example, if pummeled with a baseball bat, the victim raises his arms to prevent the blows from striking his head. The blows impact against the palms and the ulnar side (little finger side) of his forearm. Abrasions, contusions, lacerations, and even broken bones can be defensive wounds.

Blunt-force injuries are of four types:

- abrasions
- contusions
- lacerations
- fractures

ABRASIONS

Abrasions (scrapes) are injuries where the superficial layer of the skin is removed. Abrasions are classified as:

- scrape abrasions
- impact abrasions
- patterned abrasions

Each of these comes from a different mechanism. **Scrape abrasions** occur when an object scrapes or brushes away the skin. Common examples are scratches from thorns or fingernails and slides across pavement, such as occurs when a vehicle strikes a pedestrian. Rope nooses and various types of strangulation ligatures can also cause neck scrape abrasions.

Impact abrasions occur when a blunt object strikes the skin, crushing it, and leaving behind a raw area. These injuries tend to be small and discreet.

Patterned abrasions are a special type of impact abrasion. Sometimes the object will leave behind its pattern or the pattern of any clothing between the object and the skin. A chain may leave abrasions that reveal the link pattern, or the grill pattern of a car in a hit-and-run may be seen on the victim. A neck abrasion left by the braid of a rope used in a murder by strangulation might be readily visible (see Chapter Eight). Or perhaps the assailant wore a ring with a large initial or unusual pattern, and when he struck the victim he left a distinctive patterned abrasion. If the victim is wearing clothing with a coarse weave, the impact may imprint the pattern of the weave on the victim's skin. The ME can often use these autopsy findings to suggest the type of object that caused the injury. And if a suspect weapon or object is found, he might be able to match the object to the patterned abrasion on the victim.

Abrasion Healing
The dating of abrasions is difficult; the estimation is based on the typical healing pattern of such injuries. Unfortunately, the process doesn't always move at the usual pace. The ME visually inspects any wounds in both the living and the deceased, but in the deceased he can also examine the wounded tissues microscopically, which can better help him see how far along the abrasions are in the healing process.

The healing process can be divided into five stages:

- scab formation
- cell regeneration
- cell growth
- remodeling
- return to normal

Scab formation begins almost immediately, though it is not visible for about six hours. The area appears dark red and, under the microscope, large numbers of specialized white blood cells called polymorphonuclear cells (PMNs or polys for short) are seen. This is followed by evidence of cell regeneration, which is marked by the reappearance of lost epithelial (skin) cells. This stage begins around one and half days after the injury, but is not clearly visible until about

---

three days. Cell regeneration begins in surviving hair follicles at the edge of the injured area and spreads inward. Epithelial cell growth continues over the next five to ten days, and by about day twelve, the skin is **remodeled**. This remodeling is a thinning of the skin, which takes on a slightly pale appearance. Over the next week or two, the skin completes its repair and all remnants of the wound disappear. Rarely do abrasions leave permanent scars.

The ME can only guess the general age of an abrasion. His analysis of the injuries is based on these general healing stages, but the stages vary greatly from person to person and from different injuries in the same person. This still may be helpful in supporting or refuting suspect and witness statements.

Let's say a suspect in an assault that occurred the previous night has scrape abrasions that appear to be from fingernails on his face and arms. He says the injuries are thorn scrapes that he got a week ago while hunting. If the examining physician finds that the scratches could not be more than twenty-four hours old, the suspect's explanation doesn't add up.

CONTUSIONS

Contusions (bruises) occur after blunt trauma as a result of damage to the small blood vessels in the tissues. When damaged, these injured vessels leak blood, which imparts a blue-black color to the injured area. If the blood collects in a pocket beneath the skin (goose egg) it is called a **hematoma**. *Heme* means "blood" and *toma* means "tumor." So, a hematoma is a tumor or mass of blood.

It is important to point out that the absence of a contusion does not mean that no trauma occurred. Sometimes, the trauma simply does not leave a bruise, or if it does, the bruise is deep and is not visible on the surface. The opposite is also true. The presence of bruises doesn't necessarily mean that the person was intentionally injured. The reason is that some people, particularly children and the elderly, bruise more easily than others. The same is true for those with bleeding disorders, liver cirrhosis, or who take aspirin or other blood-thinning medications.

Some contusions reflect the object that caused them. As with abrasions, a chain, rope, or ring may leave behind a contusion that reveals its link pattern. A board may leave a broad bruise with straight parallel edges. A car grill pattern might be seen on the body of a car versus pedestrian collision and a handprint might be easily visible from slaps to the face or body on the injured party.

In blunt-force injuries, internal organs as well as skin can be contused. The liver, spleen, muscles, and other organs and tissues can be bruised in falls, automobile accidents, and some assaults. The liver and spleen are particularly prone to such injuries; these are easily identified at autopsy.

Contusion Healing

As with abrasions, the dating of bruises is inexact at best and depends on the sequence of color changes that a contusion goes through as it is reabsorbed by the body. A bruise changes from blue-black to greenish-yellow to brownish-yellow before it finally fades. Why does this happen?

Once blood has left the vascular system and has leaked into the tissues, enzymes in the body break down the hemoglobin in the blood. It is these breakdown products that cause the changes in color. Then, scavenger cells, called macrophages, and the circulatory system remove these remnants. As this occurs, the contusion fades. This process follows a more or less predictable pattern and takes about two weeks to complete.

Contusions are initially blue-black in color and tend to darken and increase in size over the first forty-eight hours. The reason for this is that leakage of blood from the damaged vessels continues for that long, and thus enlarges and deepens the bruise. This is particularly true of contusions of the face and around the eyes, where the tissues are more lax and vascular (filled with blood vessels). Over the next four or five days, the contusion lightens somewhat, and by day seven it begins to change color. The color sequence is typically from dark blue to a lighter blue to a greenish-yellow to a brownish-yellow, after which it fades by about day fourteen.

The estimation of the age of bruises may be critical to the diagnosis of child and elder abuse. Abusers tend to repeat their abusive behavior again and again, so an abuse victim often shows multiple contusions of varying ages. Physicians must always be alert to the possibility of abuse when a child shows such an array of injuries. Similarly, when evaluating the accidental death of a child, the ME must diligently search for signs of repeated injury. Finding any may make him suspicious that the death was not truly accidental, but was the final insult in a series of abusive acts.

Besides assessing the age of contusions, the ME is often asked to determine when the injuries occurred. Was the victim battered before or after death?

Premortem, Perimortem, or Post-Mortem Trauma?

Premortem means before death, **post-mortem** after death, and **perimortem** around the time of death. Trauma administered during these time frames cause differing results, and the ME can use these changes as a general guideline for dating contusions.

Since a bruise takes several minutes to appear, if the victim suffers a contusing blow many minutes or hours before death, the resulting bruise will be fairly diffuse and widespread around the area of impact. However, if the blow is struck during the perimortem period, the bruise will be smaller and more clearly defined. The perimortem period may be defined as seconds or a very few minutes before or after death. Perimortem bruises are smaller because it takes time for the blood to seep into and spread through the tissues. If death interrupts this process, the bruise will be smaller and have more distinct edges.

It's possible to bruise a corpse, but it is difficult. Since a contusion results from a leakage of blood from injured vessels, a bruise requires that blood be flowing into the injured vessel. At death, the heart stops, the blood ceases to circulate, and blood clotting occurs in a few minutes. Any injury to the vessel after death would not produce a bruise. The ME can use this to determine if a particular blow was struck before or after death—most of the time, anyway. But if a blow to a corpse is delivered with sufficient force, vessels may be damaged and any blood stagnated within them might leak into the area of impact. Again, with no blood flow, this bruise would be smaller than one that formed before death. Unfortunately, the ME is not always able to determine if the blow was premortem or post-mortem.

Sometimes a body suspected of having suffered blunt-force trauma shows no evidence of bruising on the surface. This may be the case if the bruising has occurred deeply within the tissues and muscles and if the victim did not live long enough for the bruising to seep up to the surface where it would be visible. In this situation, during the autopsy, the ME makes a series of deep cuts into the muscles and down to the bones along the back, arms, and legs in a search for deep bruising. He also looks for contusions of the internal organs such as the liver, spleen, heart, and lungs. If he finds contusions or hematomas in these areas, he then knows that the victim had indeed suffered blunt-force trauma.

Examining the contusions carefully, the ME must determine if they occurred pre-, peri-, or post-mortem, and if any of the contusing blows were potentially lethal. As with gunshot and stab wounds, these determinations can directly impact the cause and time of death, as well as substantiate or refute a suspect's account of events.

LACERATIONS

Lacerations (tears or rips) from blunt trauma occur when the skin is crushed or sheared by the blow. Basically the skin is torn or ripped by the impact. These are more common in areas where the skin lies close to the bone, such as the scalp. Lacerations may occur not only to the skin but also to internal organs. An **avulsion** is a severe laceration where a section of the skin is actually torn away from the underlying tissues or bone. This most often occurs when the blow strikes the skin at an oblique or tangential angle.

Sometimes the nature of the laceration and any associated contusions gives the ME a clue as to the type of instrument that caused the injury. A board or a baseball bat would leave a broader bruise and a larger area of skin disruption than would a thinner metal rod or a thicker car bumper.

FRACTURES

Fractures are breaks in the bones. A **simple fracture** is a single break, a **comminuted fracture** is where the bone breaks in two or more places, and a **compound fracture** is one in which the bone protrudes through the skin. These may result from either **direct** or **indirect** trauma.

Fractures From Direct Trauma

When an object directly strikes a bone, it can cause a single **transverse** fracture or a **crush** fracture, which tends to be comminuted (see Figure 7-4). A transverse fracture is one that is perpendicular to the long axis of the bone, and a crush fracture is one where the bone is broken into pieces, like cracking or crushing ice. A crush fracture often produces a **compression wedge**, which may indicate the direction of the blow, with the point of the wedge pointing in the direction of the force. Knowing the direction of the compression wedge helps the ME reconstruct the blow and perhaps the sequence of multiple injuries. In automobile versus pedestrian accidents, this type of fracture is often termed a "bumper fracture" since it results from the impact of the vehicle's bumper against the victim's legs.

Fractures From Indirect Trauma

Indirect fractures are not due to a direct blow but occur when some other force is applied to the bone with sufficient force to cause it to break. Traumatic indirect fractures can be divided into four basic types (see Figure 7-5):

- angulation
- rotational
- compression
- combination of these types

Angulation fractures (see Figure 7-6A) occur when a bone is bent to the point of breaking. These tend to be simple transverse breaks.

Rotational fractures (see Figure 7-6B) follow the twisting of a bone as when an arm or leg is violently rotated. These tend to be **spiral** fractures, which literally spiral down the long axis of the bone. The path of the spiral indicates the direction of the twisting force. These types of fractures are frequently seen in sports injuries, as well as in abused children.

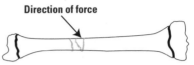

Direction of force

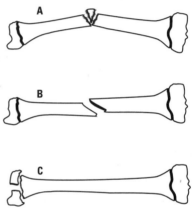

Figure 7-4: Direct fractures. Direct fractures can be either a simple transverse break or a crush fracture. The latter often produces a compression wedge that indicates the direction of the applied force.

Figure 7-5: Indirect fractures. Indirect trauma may result in fractures that are angulation (A), rotational (B), compression (C), or a combination of these types.

Compression fractures (see Figure 7-6C) result when a force is applied along the long axis of the bone. This drives the bone into its end and results in T- or Y-shaped break. This is common in automobile accidents where the knee is driven into the dashboard or when someone falling from a sufficient height lands on his feet.

Sometimes a bone is subjected to many types of forces and the resulting fractures can be any combination of these three. Multiple fracture types are often seen in automobile accidents and falls from high places.

Assessing the age of fractures is easier than aging abrasions and contusions. Initially there is bleeding into the fracture site, followed by the accumulation of various types of blood cells. By the end of the first week osteoblasts—bone-forming cells—appear. By week two or three, a **callus** forms. This is a fibrous capsule-like structure that surrounds the area of fracture. Bone formation and the closing of the fracture within the callus takes four to six weeks, and complete healing may take five months. This sequence of events varies with age and from person to person. Healing is faster in the young and slower in the old.

Aging fractures is extremely important in the evaluation of individuals who have suffered multiple injuries over a period of time, such as in cases of child or elder abuse. In these situations, X-rays might show fractures that are years old, others that are weeks old, and still others that are fresh, indicating the ongoing nature of the abuse. As with bruises, whenever a physician sees a child or elderly person with fractures of varying ages, the likelihood of repeated abuse must be considered.

TRAUMA TO INTERNAL ORGANS

The ME often evaluates internal injuries resulting from blunt force trauma, as well. This is a broad and complex subject, and is far beyond the scope of this book, but a few general statements are in order. In examining internal trauma, the ME attempts to determine the cause and mechanism of the injuries, estimate the sequence of the injuries, and determine the manner of death. When there are multiple injuries, he assesses which injury, if any, was the proximate cause of death. For example, did death come from the blow that ruptured the spleen or from the one that contused the heart and lungs? This determination can implicate or exonerate a suspect, confirm or repudiate suspect or witness statements, and assign blame for the death in any situation where there were multiple attackers.

BLUNT TRAUMA AND HEAD INJURIES

Head trauma is always dangerous. Even though most blows to the head don't result in death, a lot of nasty and deadly injuries can result. In fact, the head is the single most dangerous location for blunt-force trauma. Head and brain injuries and skull fractures are most often accidental, usually from falls or motor vehicle accidents, but they can also be from assaults or from suicide attempts where the individual jumps from an elevation or purposefully crashes his car.

When faced with a death in which head trauma is present, the ME must evaluate how the injury occurred. This includes a determination of what instrument caused the trauma and whether the manner of the injury was accidental, suicidal, or homicidal.

Blunt head trauma may result in anything from a simple bump on the head (contusion) to loss of consciousness (concussion) to death. To cause death, bleeding would most likely have to occur. Bleeding anywhere inside the cranium (skull) is called **intracranial bleeding**. It may occur with the rupture of an artery, a vein, or multiple small capillaries, any one of which can follow trauma.

Intracranial Bleeds

Several different membranes (thin sheets of tissue) cover the brain. The most important is the dura mater, which separates the brain from the skull. The space between the dura mater and the skull is called the **epidural space**, while the space between the dura mater and the brain is the **subdural space**.

Intracranial bleeds are of three basic types (see Figure 7-6):

INTRACEREBRAL BLEEDS: bleeding within the brain tissue itself

EPIDURAL BLEEDS: bleeding between the dura mater and the skull

SUBDURAL BLEEDS: bleeding between the dura mater and the brain

Intracerebral bleeds typically result from strokes, ruptured aneurysms (swelling in the arteries that are prone to rupture and death), and blunt or penetrating head trauma. Both epidural and subdural bleeds occur in the space between the brain and the skull. Epidural bleeds typically follow skull fractures, which result in injury to or laceration of the epidural arteries that course over the surface of the brain. Subdural bleeds can occur with ruptured aneurysms or with trauma, where the bleeding is usually due to

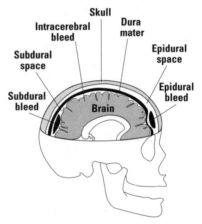

Figure 7-6: Intracranial bleeds. Any bleeding within the skull is called intracranial bleeding. Subcategories include intracerebral bleeds (within the brain), subdural bleeds (between the brain and the dura mater), and epidural bleeds (between the dura mater and the skull). All are potentially deadly.

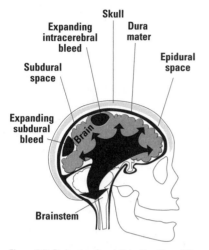

Skull
Expanding intracerebral bleed
Dura mater
Epidural space
Subdural space
Expanding subdural bleed
Brain
Brainstem

Figure 7-7: Brain stem herniation. Bleeding within the rigid skull can elevate the pressure and force the brain downward into the foramen magnum. This deadly sequence of events is called herniation of the brainstem

torn veins in the subdural space. They may occur with or without fracture of the skull. All these bleeds are potentially lethal.

The skull is a rigid capsule. It's designed that way to protect the brain. But in traumatic injuries, this rigidity is the proverbial double-edged sword, since when bleeding occurs within the skull or within the brain itself, the bony skull cannot expand. This causes the pressure inside the skull to rise rapidly, effectively squeezing the brain. The only outlet is the hole (called the foramen magnum) at the base of the skull where the spinal cord exits (see Figure 7-7). It lies near the back juncture of the skull and the neck. The mounting pressure first shuts down all brain function and ultimately pushes brain material into the opening and down along the spinal cord. We call this herniation of the brainstem. Not only is consciousness lost, but the part of the brainstem that controls breathing shuts down, respiration stops, and death follows. This process can occur over minutes, hours, or days.

At autopsy, the ME can easily determine that a blow to the head occurred and can locate bleeding into and around the brain. He might then conclude that the cause of death was blunt-force injury to the brain with bleeding. The manner of death depends on whether the blow was accidental or intentional.

Skull Fractures

Significant brain injury can occur with or without a fracture of the skull. Also, a fractured skull may or may not be associated with injury to the brain. Skull fractures may be **simple linear**, **circular**, **stellate**, or **depressed** (see Figure 7-8).

Simple linear fractures occur with low-impact injuries such as falls or a blow to the head. Circular fractures require more force and may result from

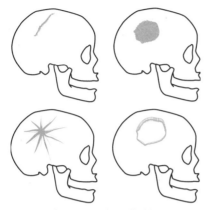

Figure 7-8: Skull fracture types. Skull fractures may be simple linear, circular, stellate, or depressed. The type of fracture seen reflects the weapon or injury that caused it.

a blow with a pipe, hammer, or similar object. Depending on the angle and the force of the blow, a circular fracture might be a complete or incomplete circle. With an even more powerful blow, the fracture may take on a stellate or star-like shape. This results when the force of the blow bends the skull inward, causing it to fracture along multiple lines of stress.

A depressed skull fracture is one in which a section of the skull is pushed inward against the brain. This requires a blow of considerable force, enough so that the skull is fractured through its entire depth. A hammer can produce such a fracture by forcing a circular segment of the skull inward.

The ME determines the nature of the fracture and then attempts to estimate what instrument likely caused it. This may help him establish the manner of death. Let's say a man is found dead, sprawled at the bottom of some stairs, and his wife says he fell. At autopsy the ME finds a depressed skull fracture that suggests that the fatal blow came from a hammer and not from the stairs or the floor. If a hammer is found at the scene he might be able to determine that the shape and size of the hammer's head matches the depressed portion of the skull exactly. He would then likely state that the manner of death was homicidal and not accidental.

Coup and Contrecoup Brain Injuries

Coup and contrecoup injuries constitute special types of brain injuries that occur in situations characterized by rapid acceleration or deceleration. This means that the organ either collides with a stationary or slower-moving structure or a faster-moving structure collides with a stationary or slower-moving organ. Picture a car involved in a rear-end collision. Damage results because the two cars are moving at different speeds. A similar situation occurs with head injuries if the brain and the skull are moving at different speeds. The brain sits within the skull and is surrounded by several layers of membranes and fluid (cerebrospinal fluid). Like an egg yolk within the shell, the brain is suspended to some degree and can move a little.

When someone is struck in the head or when a head is moving and strikes an object, two types of lesions (injuries) may occur. The first is called a **coup** lesion and is at the site of the impact. The second type of injury, a **contrecoup** lesion, often called an **acceleration-deceleration** injury, involves the side of the brain opposite the blow. Contrecoup lesions can occur with or without a fracture of the skull. The mechanism by which this happens is complicated, but essentially the blow to the skull imparts some motion to the brain, which then collides with the opposite side of the skull, causing injury to that area.

When a blow is applied to one side of the head, the brain absorbs some of the blow's energy and may be injured. This is a coup injury. The blow also causes the brain to move, and it might bounce off the other side of the skull. This is a contrecoup injury and can be in the form of a contusion, tear, or bleeding of the brain and is often worse than that of the coup injury.

When the head is moving and strikes an object, such as in an auto accident, the brain is moving as well. A coup injury might occur at the site of impact, such as the forehead striking the dashboard (see Figure 7-9). The brain then bounces backwards and strikes the back of the skull, causing a contrecoup injury. .

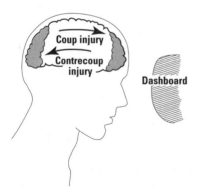

This type of injury is also seen in shaken baby syndrome. The violent back and forth movement of the infant's head repeatedly bangs the brain against the skull and can lead to severe brain damage and death.

At autopsy, the ME might find a contusion at the site of the traumatic blow as well as of the brain beneath that area (coup injury). He might also find contusions, lacerations, and bleeding of the brain on the side opposite the blow. This

Figure 7-9: Coup and contrecoup injuries. When the head strikes the dashboard the brain in the area of impact is injured (coup). The brain might then bounce backwards and strike the back of the skull (contrecoup).

would be a contrecoup injury. Sometimes the coup injury is not evident and the ME only finds evidence for the contrecoup damage. In these situations, the contrecoup injury might be mistaken for a direct injury, which could lead the ME to draw the wrong conclusion as to how the injury occurred. He might say the victim was struck from behind when in fact the blow came from the front. This could confuse the reconstruction of the crime scene (see Chapter Two).

ELECTRICAL INJURIES

Electrical current can be considered either low or high voltage. **Low-voltage** currents, found in residential electrical systems, are less than 600 to 1,000 volts. **High-voltage** currents, most often found in industrial situations, are in the range of 1,000 to 8,000 volts. Virtually all deaths from electrical current are accidental since it is rarely used for suicide or homicide.

Most people know not to touch a live wire or stick anything into an electrical outlet, yet every year thousands of people suffer shocks from just such actions. And some of these are deadly.

When electricity enters the body, it flows from the point of entry to the point of grounding by following the shortest path. Electricity can kill by several different mechanisms. Whether a particular shock is deadly depends on its voltage and the duration of contact. A low-voltage current can take several minutes to do harm while a high-voltage one can kill instantly.

LOW-VOLTAGE SHOCKS

Residential alternating current (AC) is low voltage and causes only minor burns if the exposure is brief. With longer exposures, severe burns may result and internal organs such as the liver and bone marrow may be severely and irreparably damaged, which may cause death. But the greatest danger of a low-voltage shock is its effect on the heart.

The normal heartbeat is due to a rhythmic pulse of electrical current that originates in the heart's internal pacemaker and flows through the heart muscle in a well-organized pattern. A low-voltage AC shock can interfere with this rhythmic pulse and lead to deadly cardiac arrhythmias (changes in heart rhythm) such as ventricular tachycardia and fibrillation. Death is typically instantaneous when this occurs.

HIGH-VOLTAGE SHOCKS

High-voltage electrocutions occur in industrial settings and from the high-tension lines that carry currents across the country and into neighborhoods. Local suburban and urban lines typically carry 7,000 to 8,000 volts, while the transcontinental lines carry 100,000 or more volts. Contact with these high-tension lines usually occurs when they fall to the ground in storms or in vehicle accidents. Direct contact with these high-voltage cables is not necessary since the current can arc or "jump" from the line to a person standing nearby. Also, any tall metallic object, such as a ladder, a crane arm, a cherry picker, or TV cameras, can carry the current to the victim.

High-voltage AC shocks usually result in severe internal and external burning with even very brief exposures. But they are less likely to cause dangerous changes in the heart's rhythm. The reason is that higher voltage currents are defibrillatory rather than fibrillatory. **Defibrillatory** means that they convert an abnormal rhythm back to a normal rhythm rather than the other way around. In a cardiac arrest, the external shock that physicians give to the patient is higher voltage. It is intended to restore a normal rhythm where a deadly, abnormal rhythm exists. However, high-voltage shocks can paralyze the respiratory center in the brain and death can follow from asphyxia.

At autopsy, the ME typically finds several signs of electrical injury. In some low- and all high-voltage deaths, charred skin is seen at the point of contact, the point of grounding, or both. For example, if the victim grabbed an electrical cable with his right hand, the current might flow through his body and exit into the ground through his left foot. Here the ME would likely see burning or charring of the right hand and left foot. Sometimes in low-voltage electrocutions there is no charring but instead redness and blistering at the contact point. In the case of a high-voltage arc, there might be multiple small areas of burning, which represent the contact points of the arcing electricity.

One interesting phenomenon of electrocution deaths is the appearance of localized rigor mortis. The spasm of rigor mortis results when the adenosine triphosphate (ATP) in the muscles falls low after death (see Chapter Five: Time of Death, "Rigor Mortis"). With electrocution, the muscular spasm caused by the electrical current may consume the ATP and cause a more sudden onset of rigor in the affected area. In the above example, the victim's right arm and left leg could show signs of rigor long before the rest of the body.

In the rare cases where electrocution is used as a tool for homicide, it usually involves the tossing of an electrical device into a tub where someone is sitting in water. In this situation, there are no burns to the body, and if the device is removed before the body is found, the ME may not be able to determine the cause of death. This is less common than in the past since all such devices are required to have ground-fault circuit interrupters (GFCIs), which break the electrical circuit as soon as a spike in the current or resistance is detected.

LIGHTNING

Lightning never strikes twice—because once is usually enough to do in the victim. Of course, lightning can strike twice, such as at lightning rods, and many people do survive being hit by lightning. There are some cases of individuals surviving multiple strikes. Needless to say, all deaths from lightning are accidental.

Lightning strikes come in four varieties:

DIRECT STRIKE: The lightning hits the victim directly. This is the most serious type and more likely if the victim is holding a metal object such as a golf club or umbrella.

FLASHOVER: The lightning travels over the outside of the body. This is more likely if the victim is wearing wet clothing or is covered with sweat.

SIDE FLASH: The current splashes from a nearby building, tree, or other person and then spreads to the victim.

STRIDE POTENTIAL: The lightning strikes the ground near the victim with one foot being closer to the strike than the other. This sets up a potential electrical difference between the legs, which is called a **stride potential**. Here the current enters through one leg, spreads through the body, and exits via the other leg.

Lightning, which is a direct current (DC), is extremely high voltage in the range of 3 million to 200 million volts. Fortunately, the current is very brief, averaging from 1 to 100 milliseconds (thousandths of a second). This is why some people do survive lightning strikes.

The injuries that result are primarily due to the body's conversion of the electrical energy to heat. This heat can burn and char the skin, scorch the

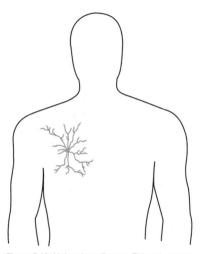

Figure 7-10: Lichtenberg figures. This arboresque pattern of skin discoloration is seen only in lightning strikes.

clothing, fry various internal organs, and even fuse or melt metal objects in the victim's pockets, buttons on his shirt, belt buckles, and the fillings in his teeth. All the organs and tissues of the body are susceptible to injury. Survivors often suffer significant damage to the heart, liver, kidneys, bone marrow, brain, spinal cord, and muscles.

One interesting, though rare, sign of lightning strikes are Lichtenberg Figures (see Figure 7-10) on the body. Lichtenberg Figures are branching electric discharges first described in 1777 by German physicist Georg Christoph Lichtenberg (1742–1799). They appear as a painless, red fern-like or arboresque pattern over the back, shoulders, buttocks, or legs. It appears quickly and tends to fade over twelve to forty-eight hours, leaving behind no scars or discolorations. Their cause is unclear, but when they are seen, they are **pathognomonic** (absolutely indicative) of lightning strikes, which aids the ME in determining the cause of death.

BITE WOUNDS

Bite injuries occur in cases of murder, rape, torture, assault, and child or spousal abuse. They also might be used for self-defense. In fact, bite wounds are characterized as either offensive or defensive.

Offensive bite wounds are inflicted on the victim by the perpetrator. They tend to be well defined and can be single or multiple. Defensive bite wounds are inflicted by the victim on the attacker as an attempt to ward off the assault. These tend to be more diffuse and can result in tearing and ripping of the skin.

Using bite mark patterns to solve crimes is not new, as witnessed by the famous Gordon Hay Case.

On August 7, 1967, the body of missing fifteen-year-old Linda Peacock of Biggar, Scotland, was found in a cemetery. She had been beaten and then strangled with a rope. There was no evidence of rape, but a bruise near her right breast turned out to be a bite mark, which revealed that one of the killer's teeth was unusually jagged.

The town of Biggar had only two thousand residents and the police interviewed virtually all of them, as well as members of nearby communities. The investigation led the police to a local low-security detention center for juvenile offenders. Twenty-nine residents of the center were asked to give dental impressions and these were matched against the wound found on the girl. This narrowed the suspect list to one person—Gordon Hay.

Hay had a rare disorder called hypocalcination, which causes pits and craters in the teeth. The defects in Hay's teeth were matched to the pattern of the bruises on the girl's corpse and he was convicted of the murder.

Bite mark evidence was first allowed into a United States courtroom in Texas in 1954 in *Doyle v. Texas*. Since then many cases have revolved around bite patterns on victims or in food materials.

The biting of victims seems to be particularly favored by some serial killers, such as Ted Bundy. In fact, it was bite marks that ultimately led to his conviction.

FORENSIC CASE FILES: TED BUNDY

Between 1969 and 1975, a series of brutal sexual homicides swept through the Pacific Northwest, Utah, and Colorado. The female victims each possessed dark hair, parted down the middle. The killer used various ruses to entrap his victims, often wearing a fake cast or feigning some injury to elicit the victim's help with some task. Once the unsuspecting woman stepped into his tiny Volkswagen Beetle, the killer would overpower her and take her to some remote area where he would torture, rape, and murder her.

As police in various jurisdictions worked the cases, one name kept cropping up: Theodore Bundy. On November 8, 1974, eighteen-year-old Carol DaRonch found herself inside Bundy's VW, but when he attempted to handcuff her, she fought him off and escaped. Nearly a year later, on August 16, 1975, police stopped a VW driver for suspicious behavior. They found handcuffs and a crowbar in the car and identified the driver as Ted Bundy. Carol DaRonch identified him, and he was convicted of kidnapping and given fifteen years in prison.

In June 1977, Bundy was extradited to Colorado to face a murder charge, but he escaped, only to be recaptured eight days later. On December 30, he escaped again and this time made his way to Florida.

On the night on January 15, 1978, Bundy entered the Chi Omega sorority house on the campus of Florida State University in Tallahassee where he assaulted and raped four co-eds, killing Lisa Levy and Margaret Bowman. Less than two hours later another student was attacked. She survived.

One month later, police arrested Chris Hagen for driving a stolen vehicle and quickly discovered that Chris was actually Ted Bundy, who was wanted for murder in several states. He would first be tried in Florida for the Tallahassee murders.

Unfortunately for prosecutors, Bundy had left little evidence at the Chi Omega house. No fingerprints, blood, or semen, and neither of the two surviving victims could identify him as the attacker. The single piece of evidence the police had was a bite mark on the buttocks of Lisa Levy. Bundy refused to give an impression of his teeth, but a court order soon forced him to comply. Bundy's teeth were misaligned and chipped, and they matched perfectly the bite mark bruises found on Lisa Levy. On July 23, 1980, Bundy was convicted and finally visited Florida's electric chair on January 24, 1989.

It's disturbing that people like Bundy exist or that we must even discuss the art of bite mark analysis. But bite mark comparison is an important forensic tool. It involves not only the marks left on a human victim but also bite patterns left on food.

If a perpetrator bites into an apple or a piece of cheese, or uses his teeth to tear a piece of tape, he might leave a valuable clue at the crime scene. The ME might be able to use these to match the dental pattern of any suspect.

Bite marks on human flesh are similar, except that flesh, unlike an apple, is elastic and recoils somewhat, so that the details are less clear. Still, a match between the punctures and bruises left on the skin and the dental pattern of a suspect can often be made. If, as in Ted Bundy's case, the individual's teeth are damaged, chipped, or in an unusual pattern, an individualizing match can sometimes result.

Not all bite injuries occur to harm, control, or torture the victim. For some serial killers, post-mortem biting is part of their fantasy, their signature (see Chapter Nineteen: Criminal Psychology, "MO vs. Signature"). As with blunt-force contusions, the ME can often distinguish among bite marks made before death (ante- mortem), around the time of death (perimortem), and those that are inflicted after death (post-mortem). The key to this determination is the degree of bruising.

As discussed earlier, contusions (bruises) are due to bleeding within damaged tissues and occur only in the living. A human bite might puncture the skin or simply contuse it and often both types of injuries are present. Puncture wounds can occur whether the victim is alive or not, but bruising requires that the bite be delivered ante-mortem.

Bites that are inflicted many minutes before death tend to leave behind a diffuse bruising pattern. This happens because the blood has sufficient time to spread away from the actual injury site. Perimortem bite marks possess a more distinct or well-defined bruise pattern. Since death occurs shortly after the bite, the bleeding has less time to spread, resulting in this more concentrated pattern. Post-mortem bites have no bruising. They might show punctures or indentations, but since there is no blood flow, bruising simply doesn't occur.

Once a bite mark is located on a victim, it is carefully photographed, using both black-and-white and color film. Swabs are obtained for saliva so that amylase testing (Chapter Nine), ABO blood typing (Chapter Nine), and DNA analysis (Chapter Ten) can be done. Additional swabs are taken and placed into a culture tube designed to grow any anaerobic bacteria, which are common inhabitants of the mouth. Since each individual grows slightly different combinations of bacteria in his oral cavities, comparing the types of bacteria found in the bite wound with those found in the suspect's mouth might provide another link between him and the victim. This is not strong evidence, but it is helpful in some cases.

Once a suspect is identified, a mold of his teeth can be made and from these a model can be created. This casting can then be compared with the bite marks on the victim. The lack of a match can exclude the suspect. If a match is made, it is suggestive, but confirmation that the suspect is the perpetrator requires more definitive testing such as DNA matching, which can often be done using saliva left in the bite wound.

RAPE INVESTIGATION

Rape is rarely about sex, but is rather about violence, control, and humiliation. Rape is a legal term and not a medical diagnosis. The physician can determine if penetration has likely occurred, if trauma is present, and if semen is found in or on the victim, but the courts must decide whether the sexual encounter was indeed a rape. In other words, the court must decide the "intent" of both parties. In order for rape to be charged, three things must have occurred: actual penetration, the use of force, and the lack of consent.

Penetration does not need to be complete, since only slight penetration is needed to meet the definition of rape. Force may be applied through violence, the threat of violence, or coercion. All too often, rape is accompanied by homicide, either as part of the violent act or following it to prevent the victim from identifying the assailant. Rape is often part of the act of homicide by a serial killer, particularly the sexually sadistic types. In this case, the rape is almost always part of the killer's fantasy or his need to humiliate the victim.

ASSAULT SURVIVORS

In a living rape victim, it is critical that a complete rape exam be done as soon after the act as possible. Unfortunately, because the act is so humiliating for the victim, she will often wait days, if not months or years, before reporting it. At other times, the victim will shower or bathe before going to authorities or to a hospital. On the surface this may seem to be odd behavior for an assault victim, but rape is not like a punch in the face. It carries with it an array of emotions and social baggage that no other crime does. Often the victim feels ashamed, even guilty, and wants to avoid the inappropriate, but real, feeling of social stigmatization. Remnants of Puritanical thinking and a court system that all too often puts the victim "on trial" play a role in these feelings.

Ideally, a medical doctor experienced in rape examinations examines the victim. If possible, a law enforcement officer should be present so that the chain of evidence can be maintained. The examination consists of a history, complete physical exam, photographs if indicated, and evidence collection. Of course, the treatment of any serious or life-threatening injuries to the victim takes precedence over evidence collection.

The physician examines the victim's entire body, including the genitalia, for evidence of trauma such as bruises, abrasions, or lacerations. He carefully notes and photographs each. Note that the absence of signs of trauma or violence in no way negates or diminishes the claim that a rape has occurred. Any bite marks are photographed and swabbed for saliva, which may yield DNA evidence. Any stains are likewise swabbed since they could represent saliva or semen. As guided by the history the victim gives as to what transpired during the assault, the examining physician obtains vaginal, anal, and oral swabs for DNA-containing materials. The victim's pubic hair is combed for foreign hairs and fibers. Lastly, the victim's clothing is examined for stains; if any are found, samples are taken and the clothing is packaged and taken to the crime lab for evaluation. All evidence collected is turned over to law enforcement for transport to the crime lab for study.

Once the examination is completed, the victim's injures are treated and she is given medications to prevent pregnancy and to treat any possible venereal diseases. The philosophy is to treat these as soon as possible, not wait and see if they arise. HIV testing is obtained and repeated over the next several months. A rape counselor usually becomes involved immediately to help the victim with the psychological fallout from the assault.

At the crime lab, a search for spermatozoa in the vaginal, oral, or anal samples is undertaken. In living victims, motile (moving) sperm may be seen up to twelve hours after intercourse and rarely up to twenty-four hours. Non-motile sperm may persist for two or three days. As sperm die off, they initially lose their tails, leaving behind only sperm heads. These may be seen up to seven days after intercourse. So if the victim states that she last had consensual intercourse three days earlier, the finding of non-motile sperm or sperm heads is of little help, but any motile sperm could not have come from that episode and must be related to the rape.

Even if no sperm are found, intercourse cannot be ruled out. The assailant may have used a condom, had a previous vasectomy, have failed to ejaculate, or be azoospermic—a condition in which no sperm are produced.

FATAL ASSAULTS

In rape-homicides, many of the same examinations are taken except that a history of the events is typically absent and the ME rather than a physician performs the examination. As with any homicide, it is best if the ME sees the body at the crime scene, but for practical reasons this is not always possible (see Chapter Two). At the scene, the coroner's technicians are charged with transporting the body and protecting the evidence. Paper bags are secured over the victim's hands and the body is placed in a clean body bag or wrapped in clean sheets for transport. This prevents the loss of trace evidence and lessens the likelihood that the corpse will pick up any trace materials during transport.

At the lab, the ME initially examines the victim while clothed. He will look for trace evidence and stains and attempt to match any defects in the clothing with injuries to the victim. Only then are the clothes removed and sent to the crime lab for further processing. The ME then turns his attention to the body.

The body is searched for foreign hair, fibers, or other trace evidence. Stains are examined and swabbed. After the protective bags have been removed, the ME carefully examines the hands and collects nail clippings and scrapings. Often the assailant's hair, blood, or skin tissues are found clutched in the victim's hand, or beneath her fingernails. All injuries, including those to the genitalia, are examined and photographed. A diligent search for evidence of penetration follows, and vaginal, anal, and oral swabs are obtained.

Even if no overt genital trauma is found, the ME looks for signs that sexual intercourse took place. Vaginal fluids are examined for semen; this is done both chemically and microscopically (see Chapter Nine: Serology, "Other Body Fluids."). Tests for **acid phosphatase**, an enzyme found in abundant quantities in semen, and **p30**, a semen-specific glycoprotein, are done. Acid phosphatase may be present up to seventy-two hours after intercourse. A problem arises when the victim has had consensual sex during the two or three days before the assault. There is no method for determining if elevated levels of acid phosphatase are remnants of this consensual act or of the rape itself.

As in the living victim, sperm are searched for in the vaginal, anal, and oral samples taken at autopsy. Sperm survive longer in a corpse than in a living victim because, in a living woman, the vagina produces certain chemicals that destroy sperm, while in a corpse, sperm are destroyed only through decomposition, which requires many days. Sperm can sometimes be found for up to two weeks in a corpse.

ASPHYXIA:
DEPRIVING THE BODY OF OXYGEN

Asphyxia is defined as the deprivation of oxygen to the cells of the body. It can occur in many ways. Under normal circumstances, air contains an adequate amount of oxygen (O_2). Once in the lungs' air sacs, the oxygen crosses into the blood, combines with the hemoglobin of the red blood cells, and is transported throughout the body, where the cells extract the oxygen from the hemoglobin. An interruption of the supply of oxygen at any step in this process can lead to asphyxia.

Asphyxia may result from:

- suffocation
- strangulation
- toxic gases
- drowning

SUFFOCATION

Suffocation occurs whenever sufficient oxygen is unable to reach the bloodstream. The air might be poor in oxygen or some blockage or obstruction might prevent it from entering the lungs or the bloodstream. Suffocation may be divided into five general categories:

- environmental suffocation
- smothering
- choking
- mechanical asphyxia
- suffocating gases

ENVIRONMENTAL SUFFOCATION

This occurs whenever the environmental air possesses very low levels of oxygen. The lungs and circulatory system may be perfectly normal, but if the oxygen content of the air is deficient, it is of little use to the body. Normal air is approximately 21 percent oxygen. When this percentage drops to 10 to 15 percent, judgment and coordination suffer, and below 10 percent loss of consciousness occurs, and at around 8 percent death is all but assured.

Deaths from an oxygen-poor environment are almost always accidental, though homicide is a possibility. The classic example of an accidental death of this type is a child who locks himself in an old refrigerator. Once the oxygen is consumed, the child dies from asphyxia. This was once common, but it is now mandated that modern refrigerators have some mechanism that enables them to be opened from the inside simply with a firm push. Still, a child might not be strong enough or might not know to do this.

Another type of environmental suffocation occurs when a victim enters an enclosure that is poor in oxygen, such as some underground chambers and mines. If someone unknowingly enters, he may succumb before he is able to escape. The same is true in structure fires, where the fire consumes the oxygen and some victims die from suffocation.

There are no specific autopsy findings in most cases of environmental suffocation, so the determination of the cause and manner of death relies more on an analysis of the circumstances surrounding the death. In other words, if the victim is found in an oxygen-poor environment or an air-tight enclosure and there is no evidence of trauma or toxin exposure, and if natural causes are ruled out, the ME would likely deem the death to be an accidental suffocation.

SMOTHERING

Smothering occurs when some external device prevents air from entering the nose or mouth. This is distinguished from choking in which the obstructing material is within the mouth or throat. Smothering deaths are usually homicidal or suicidal, but might be accidental, though that is rare.

Ambrose Tardieu (1788–1841) first described the pathological findings of suffocation. He identified small blood spots in the lung tissues of suffocation victims and named them "Tardieu spots," a moniker that is still used today. Though not present in all cases of smothering, when present, they help the ME assess the cause of death.

Suicidal smothering usually employs a plastic bag such as a trash bag or those used by dry cleaners. The individual places the bag over his head and secures it with tape or a rope. This securing is not necessary since the plastic typically clings to the person's face, obstructing the mouth and nose. Occasionally, the victim will bind his own hands. This is particularly true in cases of "suicide pacts" where two or more people commit the act together.

Plastic bags may also cause accidental smothering, particularly in children. Rarely, an intoxicated individual may lose consciousness face-down on a pillow and die from smothering.

Homicidal smothering usually employs a pillow, bedding, a plastic bag, or the killer's hands. When a pillow or a plastic bag is used, marks on the victim are typically not present unless the victim puts up a struggle. If so, abrasions or bruises are often left on the victim's face or arms by the killer's attempts to control the victim. If there are no external bruises, no microhemorrhages (blood spots) in the lungs, and if the pillow or bag is removed before the body is found, the ME might not be able to determine the cause of death, since smothering itself leaves behind little physical evidence.

One form of homicidal smothering is when the assailant places a gag or tape over the victim's mouth and nose. This can block the entry of air and lead to death from suffocation. On occasion, the gag may be removed before the body is found, but bruises from its application may remain. As with pillow smothering, if no bruising is found, the true cause of death can be difficult to determine.

In smothering deaths where the victim struggles, rigor mortis may appear early. Just as with deaths that occur during exercise, the struggle consumes the muscular adenosine triphosphate (ATP) and leads to earlier onset of rigor (see Chapter Five: Time of Death, "Rigor Mortis").

CHOKING

As opposed to smothering where the blockage is outside the body, **choking** requires a blockage within the mouth or airways. Here the cause of death might be natural, homicidal, or accidental.

A natural choking death could result from **acute fulminating epiglottitis** or **diphtheria**. The former is an acute infection and inflammation of the epiglottis, which is the flap at the upper end of the trachea (main airway) that closes to prevent the aspiration of food and water when we swallow. It may rapidly swell and block the airway. This is a true medical emergency and must be treated immediately, usually with a **tracheotomy**. This is an incision into the trachea below the larynx (at the Adam's apple) that allows air to reach the lungs.

Diptheria is a bacterial infection of the throat, caused by the bacterium *Corynebacterium diphtheriae*. It causes the formation of a thick, tenacious scab-like sheet called a **pseudomembrane**, which can peel away from the throat and obstruct the airway, causing death from asphyxia. Thanks to childhood immunization programs, diphtheria is now rare in the United States, but one hundred years ago it was a deadly childhood disease that claimed thousands of lives every year.

Homicidal choking deaths are rare. However, if the assailant gags the victim by placing a sock, cloth, ball, or other object in the victim's mouth before the gag is applied, the victim may choke and die. As with deaths from smothering, if the choking device is removed before the body is found, the ME might not be able to determine the exact cause of death.

Most choking deaths are accidental. Children get small objects such as pieces of balloons, parts of toys, and food materials into their airways and choke. With adults, the culprit is almost always food. In fact, this is so common that it has been given the moniker "café coronary." Typically, the victim is eating, suddenly stops talking, perhaps grabs his throat, and collapses. On the surface it looks like a heart attack, or coronary. In reality, the airway is obstructed, the victim cannot breathe, the oxygen level in his blood drops dramatically, and he collapses and dies. Cardiopulmonary resuscitation (CPR) is not effective in this situation because attempts to offer mouth-to-mouth respiration are futile while the airway is blocked. The **Heimlich Maneuver** was designed for just this situation.

With natural and accidental choking deaths, the ME usually has little difficulty in determining the cause of death, although finding food material within the victim's airways does not absolutely indicate that the victim choked to death. Many individuals will aspirate food into their airways and lungs as they die. In this situation, obtaining a detailed history from witnesses of what happened might be the ME's most useful information. However, if the airway is completely obstructed with a piece of meat or other firm food product, the ME should be able to state that the death was indeed from choking.

MECHANICAL ASPHYXIA

Mechanical asphyxia results when some external force is applied to the body that prevents the expansion of the chest and thus respiration. A person trapped beneath a heavy object such as a car or a collapsed wall or ceiling can die from this mechanism. A similar circumstance occurs when people are crushed during a riot or trampled by a stampeding crowd. In this situation, the external pressure is so great that the victim literally can't take a breath.

Boa constrictors kill exactly this way. This muscular species of snake wraps itself around its prey. With each exhalation by the prey, the snake coils a little tighter, making each successive breath increasingly shallower until the prey is trapped permanently in the position of exhalation and is unable to take another breath. Death follows quickly.

Tragically, infants may die from mechanical asphyxia when a parent rolls onto them during sleep. Such deaths are often deemed to be the result of Sudden Infant Death Syndrome (SIDS), and some of them may well be from this poorly understood syndrome. True SIDS appears to be due to a defect in the brain's respiratory center while a parent rolling onto an infant is a form of mechanical asphyxia.

A bizarre form of mechanical suffocation is known as **burking**, causing suffocation by covering the victim's nose and mouth so that no marks are made on the body. This first case of this arose in the 1820s from the nefarious activities of William Burke and William Hare.

FORENSIC CASE FILES: BURKE AND HARE

William Burke was a merchant in Edinburgh, Scotland, in the early 1800s. He bought old shoes, fixed them up, and sold them. He also trafficked in old clothes, skins, and human hair. In 1827, he hooked up with William Hare, who ran a beggar's hotel in Tanners Close in West Port. In December of that year, a resident of the hotel named Donald died and Burke arranged to sell his body at Surgeon Square to Professor Robert Knox, who needed corpses for his dissection demonstrations.

To pull off their scam, the two men loaded Donald's coffin with bark and it was buried in front of many witnesses. They then delivered the body to Professor Knox and received seven pounds and ten shillings in return. A business was born. Burke and Hare became grave robbers, supplying pilfered corpses to the doctor for eight pounds in summer and ten in winter.

Greed did them in. The local populace refused to die fast enough, so they resorted to kidnapping and killing people who were not likely to be missed. Burke would sit on them and hold their mouths and noses closed until they suffocated, after which he and Hare would deliver the corpse and collect their fee. Over the next year, at least sixteen people died at their hands.

Finally, a lodger at the hotel notified authorities when she discovered their last victim beneath a bed. Apparently the two men had stashed the body there while awaiting an opportunity to transport it to Surgeon Square. The two men were arrested. Hare then turned "King's evidence" on Burke and testified against him. Burke was convicted and hanged on January 28, 1829.

SUFFOCATING GASES

Deaths from suffocating gases can be accidental, suicidal, or homicidal, but most are accidental.

Suffocating gases are not in and of themselves toxic. That is, they are not poisons. Rather, their presence diminishes the percentage of the oxygen in the air. To understand this, let's look at the physiology of respiration.

When you breathe, you take air and oxygen into your lungs. The oxygen then diffuses from the **alveoli** (air sacs of the lungs) into the bloodstream where it binds to **hemoglobin**. Hemoglobin is the molecule within red blood cells that carries oxygen from the lungs to the tissues and transports **carbon dioxide (CO_2)** from the body's cells back to the lungs. In the lungs, oxygen combines with hemoglobin to produce **oxyhemoglobin**, which imparts a bright red color to the blood. In the tissues of the body, carbon dioxide combines with hemoglobin to produce **carbaminohemoglobin**, which turns the blood dark purple. This exchange process is essential for life. Thus, arterial blood (blood rich in oxygen that is pumped out to the body through the arteries) is red, while venous blood (blood low in oxygen and high in carbon dioxide that returns to the heart through the veins) is dark purple.

If the oxygen content of the breathed air is low, the concentration of oxyhemoglobin in the blood falls rapidly. Low blood oxygen content is called **hypoxia**. Any gas added to air will, of necessity, lower the percentage of the air that is oxygen. Room air is approximately 21 percent oxygen. If an equal amount of a gas such as **methane** is added, the percentage of air present in the environment drops by 50 percent; so, the percentage of oxygen lowers to 10.5 percent. Oxygen levels this low can lead to lethargy, confusion, disorientation, loss of consciousness, and ultimately coma and death.

Carbon dioxide and methane are common examples of suffocating gases. Both are odorless, making them undetectable to the person exposed. Methane is the principle component of natural gas. The odor of household natural gas is an additive so that leaks can be detected.

High levels of methane and carbon dioxide may arise in sewers and mines. The victim enters the area, becomes hypoxic and confused, falls into unconsciousness and dies. At autopsy, there are no specific findings in deaths from suffocating gases. However, in methane-related deaths, the crime lab might find high levels of methane in the victim's blood. Carbon dioxide is another story. Since carbon dioxide is a normal constitute of blood and its levels in the blood often rise around the time of death, it may be impossible to determine the cause of death when this is the culprit. Here the circumstances of the death might be

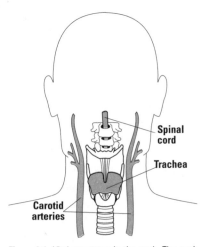

Figure 8-1: Vital structures in the neck. The neck connects the brain to the body, the mouth and nose to the lungs, and the heart to the brain.

the only thing that allows the ME to make the proper determination of the cause of death.

A particularly tragic case of mass carbon dioxide poisoning occurred in 1986 at Lake Nyos in Cameroon, in Africa. An odd geological event known as a limnic eruption caused a large cloud of carbon dioxide-laden water to rise up from the depths of the lake. Since carbon dioxide is slightly heavier than air, it settled like an invisible and odorless fog over a wide area, killing nearly 1,800 people and 3,500 livestock by asphyxia.

STRANGULATION

The neck is a fragile conduit of life and a vital link between brain and body (see Figure 8-1). All neurological communication between the brain and the body passes through the neck by way of the spinal cord. All the brain's blood supply from the heart must pass through the arteries of the neck, most importantly the two **carotid arteries** that lie on either side of the larynx. Air must traverse the neck in order to reach the lungs. But this highway of life is exposed and vulnerable to injury, both accidental and intentional. Asphyxia may occur if there is an obstruction to the arteries of the neck, which prevents oxygen-filled blood from reaching the brain. This is what happens in strangulation deaths.

MECHANISM OF STRANGULATION ASPHYXIA

The cause of death in all strangulations is **cerebral hypoxia**, which is a low level of oxygen in the brain. This results because strangulation blocks the airway, preventing the victim from breathing, and occludes the carotid arteries, preventing the flow of blood to the brain. Of these two, the occlusion of the arteries is the predominant cause of unconsciousness and death. A person can remain awake and alive for several minutes without breathing, but if the blood supply to the brain is interrupted or severely limited, loss of consciousness can follow in a few seconds, and death in a minute or so. As we will see later in this chapter, the unexpected rapidity with which consciousness is lost during carotid compression is an important factor in deaths and brain injury from chokeholds and during autoerotic asphyxiation.

A common, though not universal, finding in all types of strangulation is **petechial hemorrhages**, also called **petechiae**, in the conjunctivae (the pink parts around the eyeball) and the sclera (the white part) of the eyes. These are small red dots or streaks that result from blood leaking into the soft conjunctivae and sclera of the eyes. With strangulation, the pressure within the veins of the neck rises suddenly and dramatically. This pressure is transmitted to the veins of the eyes, causing them to leak blood and produce the petechial hemorrhages.

In strangulations, some outside force compresses the airways and blood vessels of the neck. This compression prevents blood from reaching the brain and air from entering the lungs. There are three basic types of strangulation:

MANUAL STRANGULATION: strangulation using only the hands

LIGATURE STRANGULATION: strangulation using rope, cord, wire, or other flexible material

HANGINGS: strangulation in which the body weight is used to tighten the ligature, most often a rope

Manual and ligature strangulation are essentially always homicide, while hangings are predominately suicidal (except for judicial hangings). Each of these strangulation types results in the same mechanism of death.

MANUAL STRANGULATION

Manual strangulation occurs when pressure from a hand, forearm, or other limb is applied to the victim's neck, compressing the airway and the carotid arteries. Since it is virtually impossible to manually strangle yourself, manual strangulations are homicidal.

The marks found on the victim's neck are a combination of contusions and abrasions. The pressure from the assailant's fingers and thumbs often leave bruises in the shape of fingers or, more often, round bruises that match the tips of the fingers and the pads of the thumb. These are typically found on the sides of the victim's neck, but not always. If the assailant is facing the victim, he might press his thumbs into the recesses where the carotid arteries lie. In this case, the major bruising may be on either side of the trachea (windpipe), with smaller finger bruises on either side or the back of the victim's neck.

Our understanding of these anatomical findings date back Sung Tz'u's forensic book *Hsi Yuan Lu*, published in 1235. Believed to be the first written statement on using medical knowledge in criminal investigation, it described how to distinguish between strangulation and drowning. These strangulation marks, as well as the fracture of the **hyoid bone** that often occurs during manual strangulation, were more fully delineated in 1897 by French physi-

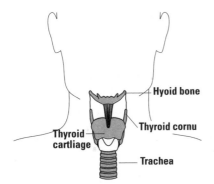

Figure 8-2: The thyroid cornu and the hyoid bone. These delicate structures are often fractured during manual strangulation, but less often in ligature strangulation and hanging

cian Paul Brouardel (1837–1906) in his book *La Pendaison, la strangulation, la suffocation, la submersion*.

In addition to bruising, abrasions can result from the assailant's fingernails. Since the tips of the fingers are used to grip the victim's neck, the assailant's nails can dig into or scratch the victim's flesh. These nail abrasions often appear as linear scratches or as thin, semicircular marks where the nails dug in.

In manual strangulation, the victim's face is typically congested and petechial hemorrhages are commonly seen. Since most assailants use a great deal more force than is necessary, there may also be injury to the neck muscles and the ME will often find bleeding into these muscles at autopsy. Also, the small bones of the neck are often injured. Fractures of the cornu (horn) of the thyroid cartilage (Adam's apple) and the tiny hyoid bone are frequently seen in manual assaults (see Figure 8-2).

When a suspect is located, it is important to examine him carefully for signs of injury since victims often put up a fight and scratch or bruise the attacker. Such injuries are typically seen on the assailant's fingers, hands, forearms, and face. If the attack is a rape-strangulation, scratches may be seen along the attacker's flanks or over his back.

Another form of manual strangulation is the **chokehold**, which is at times employed by law enforcement to subdue a combative subject. There are two basic types: the bar arm hold and the carotid hold. The purpose of both is to collapse the carotid arteries and render the individual unconscious. In the former, the officer places his forearm across the front of the subject's throat and, using his other hand, grasps his wrist and pulls back, applying pressure to the neck with his forearm. Sometimes the officer uses his baton rather than his forearm. In the carotid hold, the officer places the crook of his elbow against the center of the subject's neck and again grasps his wrist and pulls back. This produces a pincher or scissors effect that occludes the two carotid arteries. Unconsciousness and brain damage or death can occur with such holds much more quickly than is often appreciated.

The ME often becomes involved in situations where these holds have been used and a police brutality complaint is filed. If too much force is used, the thyroid cartilage and the hyoid bone may fracture, and bleeding may occur in the strap muscles of the neck. In either a living or deceased subject, the ME must evaluate the injuries and determine their cause.

LIGATURE STRANGULATION

Ligature strangulation occurs when a constricting band is tightened around the neck. The tightening force is some force other than the victim's body weight, as occurs in hangings. Most ligature strangulations are homicides, though some are accidental, even suicidal.

Devices used for homicidal ligature strangulations are ropes, wires, electrical cords, and clothing such as neckties, belts, bras, and stockings. If the ligature is soft, such as a towel, bed sheet, or silk scarf, it might not leave visible marks on the neck, and if the device is removed before the victim is found, the ME will have a more difficult time determining the exact cause of death.

If the ligature is thin, such as an electrical cord, a **groove** or **furrow** will remain in the tissue of the victim's neck. This furrow is a deep impression that matches the width of the particular ligature used. With thicker devices like ropes, the groove is wide and shallow and, not uncommonly, there are associated bruises and abrasions. Occasionally, these will reveal the pattern of the ligature used, such as the braid pattern of a rope or the link pattern of a chain.

In ligature strangulation, as with the manual variety, the victim's face is typically congested and scleral and conjunctival petechial hemorrhages are seen. However, in contrast to manual strangulation, bleeding into the neck muscles and fractures of the thyroid cartilage and the hyoid bone are much less common. This difference is probably due to the thickness of fingers and the diffuse pressure they apply as opposed to the thinner area of compression with a ligature.

Even in severely decomposed corpses, the ligature mark may be preserved.

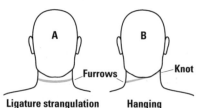

Ligature strangulation   Hanging

Figure 8-3: Ligature strangulation and hanging marks. With ligature strangulation the furrow tends to be horizontal (A), while with hanging, it angles across the neck with the higher end toward the knot (B)

The compression of the tissues within the furrow collapses the underlying blood vessels. After death, the bacteria that cause putrefaction tend to migrate through the blood vessels as they disseminate throughout the body. The crushed vessels in the furrow lessen the number of bacteria that reach the area, which in turn slows the putrefaction process within the furrow.

As opposed to hangings, the furrow in ligature strangulations tends to be directed horizontally around the neck (see Figure 8-3A). The reason for this is that whether the assailant is facing the victim or approaching from behind, he will tighten the ligature by pulling laterally on its ends.

At autopsy, it is also important to examine the victim's hands and nails since strands of the assailant's hair might be found clutched in the victim's hand and his blood and tissue might be present beneath the fingernails. ·

Suicide by ligature strangulation is rare, but not unheard of. Since it takes approximately fifteen seconds or so to lose consciousness, the victim has time to secure the ligature in place by either tying a knot or wrapping the cord around several times. In the latter situation, the overlapping loops secure the ligature in place. Once the victim loses consciousness, he cannot loosen the ligature and death from asphyxia follows.

Accidental ligature strangulation is also rare. It typically occurs when a scarf, tie, or other article of clothing becomes entangled in a piece of machinery or a moving vehicle. Ski lifts, elevators, motorcycles, and cars are often involved. Perhaps the most famous victim of accidental ligature strangulation was Isadora Duncan.

FORENSIC CASE FILES: ISADORA DUNCAN

Isadora Duncan was born May 27, 1878, in Oakland, California, and became a worldwide icon. Isadora began to experiment with new forms of dance at a very early age, but recognition of her genius did not occur until the family moved to Europe when she was a teenager. As her reputation grew, she became known as the "mother of modern dance" for her bold development of a new system of interpretative dance. She lived a flamboyant lifestyle and dressed the part, developing a fondness for very long scarves that flowed along behind her. This fashion statement led to her death when, on September 14, 1927, in Nice, France, her scarf became entangled in the wheels of a moving automobile, strangling her.

HANGINGS

As opposed to strangulation, asphyxia in hangings results from a noose or other ligature that is pulled tight by the body's weight. This means that the victim must be completely or partially suspended. Hangings are almost always suicidal; homicidal hangings, though they do occur, are rare. Accidental hangings are uncommon and most often involve children who become entangled in a rope or clothing and find themselves in a position of complete or partial suspension.

Though the airway can be compressed and breathing can be interrupted, the real cause of death in most hangings is compression of the carotid arteries. Except for judicial (legally directed) hangings, fractures of the cervical vertebrae (spinal bones of the neck) are uncommon.

Judicial Hangings

Though there are seven cervical vertebrae, the one that is typically fractured in a judicial hanging is the second cervical vertebra, called C-2 (also called the axis). The first (C-1—also called the atlas) is melded with the base of the skull, so the C-2 vertebra takes the brunt of the force of the fall (see Figure 8-4). In fact, a fracture of C-2, regardless of its cause, is called the "hangman's fracture." Death is usually immediate, even though it may take fifteen minutes or so for the heart to stop. These fractures require that the body drop a sufficient distance, which is very unusual in suicidal hangings.

How far does the drop need to be to fracture the cervical bones? Several factors come into play here. Obese persons and those with little neck musculature or who have arthritis of the cervical spine may suffer neck fractures quite easily. The opposite is true for muscular, thick-necked persons. In judicial hangings, these factors are considered in gauging the distance of the drop.

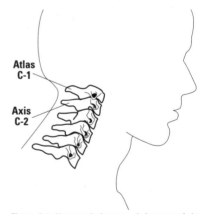

Figure 8-4: Hangman's fracture. A fracture of the second cervical vertebra (C-2), which occurs during judicial hangings, is called the "hangman's fracture."

Too little drop and the condemned person strangles to death, too far and he could be decapitated.

Suicidal and Homicidal Hangings

In suicidal hangings, the victim typically makes a noose with whatever is handy. Ropes, belts, bed sheets, clothing, and electrical cords are common. In jails, bed sheets and clothing are common.

It might seem obvious that if the victim's hands are bound, someone else must have facilitated the hanging. This would point to homicide or at least that someone aided in the suicide. However, this is simply not the case. Suicide victims frequently bind their own hands to prevent a change of heart. Otherwise, they might attempt to loosen or undo the noose, which would leave scratches and gouges of the flesh near the ligature.

If the victim's hands are bound, the ME should closely examine the knots of these restraints. What if the knots are such that the victim could not have tied them himself? This means that someone else did and would lead to a stronger consideration of homicide, or at least an assisted suicide.

The ME might bring in a forensic knot specialist to offer an opinion. This is an individual with specialized knowledge of ligatures and knots who might be able to determine whether the knot was self-tied. He might also be able to characterize the knot in such a way as to narrow the suspect list.

People tie knots based on their knowledge, skill, and habits. Certain knots may indicate certain professions or hobbies. For example, knots used in nautical situations are very different from those used on a farm or cattle ranch and would vary widely from the common "bow" or "granny" knot the average person uses on packages.

In addition, if the binding ligature is of unusual manufacture, this might offer useful leads. Or, if the ends have been cut, the cut ends might provide valuable tool mark evidence (see Chapter Fourteen).

Autopsy Findings in Hanging Deaths

The neck markings seen after hanging depend mainly on the nature of the noose used. Soft nooses such as sheets may leave little or no markings, and if the victim is discovered fairly quickly and cut down, the ME may not be able to find any marks at all. Similar to ligature strangulations, a rope or cord may leave a very deep and distinct furrow in the victim's neck. The longer the body hangs, the deeper the furrow. Abrasions and contusions are also common with these types of nooses. Occasionally, the furrow and any associated bruising may reveal the braid pattern of a rope or the link configuration of a chain. Because the noose compresses the flesh in the furrow so severely and basically "squeezes" out any blood in the area, the furrow may appear pale yellow. With time it will darken to a brownish color.

The furrow found in hanging victims follows an inverted V course and tends to be diagonal across the neck with its high end where the knot is located (see Figure 8-3B). This means that if the knot is to the victim's left side, the furrow will be lower on the neck and much deeper on the right side and will angle upward toward the left ear. Near the knot, the furrow typically shallows and disappears. This pattern is due to the body hanging by the bottom of the noose. This differs from that found in ligature strangulation, where it is typically horizontal.

If found several hours after the hanging, the victim's face may be pale and his tongue may be dark purple and protrude from his mouth. If lividity has appeared, it will be in the dependent areas, which in this situation would be the legs, forearms, and hands.

At autopsy, the ME will not usually find facial congestion or petechial hemorrhages that are common in manual and ligature strangulations. Nor is he likely to find bleeding into the neck muscles or fractures of the thyroid cartilage or the hyoid bone. In a suicidal hanging where the victim did not tie his own hands, the ME might see abrasions and claw marks on the neck. However, he would not expect to see any other trauma to the body, and if he did, he might consider homicide as the manner of death. For example, if he found bruises that suggest that the victim had been beaten or restrained before the hanging, homicide becomes a more likely possibility. This is not universally the case, however. The victim may have harmed himself prior to the suicide or he may have thrashed around as he strangled on the rope and bruised himself against walls or furniture.

Another factor to consider is that the victim could have been subdued with drugs or alcohol and then hanged. This might be an attempt to stage the death to look like a suicide (see Chapter Two: Evidence, "The Staged Crime Scene"). For this reason, a toxicological analysis should be performed on all victims of hanging. Clouding the issue is the fact that the victim may have taken alcohol or drugs in order to "get the courage" to do himself in. Here the ME might be able to determine if the level of drugs and alcohol found in the victim were enough to "knock him out" or merely enough to impair his judgment. The point is that if the victim had enough drugs in his system to render him unconscious, he could not have hanged himself (see Chapter Eleven).

The ME examines the rope or ligature in place around the neck after it is removed from the victim. The nature of the ligature used and the type of knot employed could be valuable information, particularly if homicide is considered. As with the restraining ligatures mentioned previously, a forensic knot expert may be brought to the case.

Autoerotic Asphyxia

Autoerotic or **sexual asphyxia** is a special type of asphyxia. The mechanism involved in such asphyxias are typically either smothering or strangulation. The victims are most often males involved in some masturbation ritual. Occasionally, sexual asphyxiation is part of partner sexual activities.

The concept is that partial asphyxia somehow accentuates sexual enjoyment. One of the first symptoms of cerebral hypoxia (low oxygen in the brain) is giddiness; this sensation is believed to accentuate sexual arousal. It is also a very dangerous game.

The most common method employed is hanging, but non-hanging ligatures and plastic bags are also used. The victim rigs up a situation where the rope or chosen ligature compresses the neck "on demand." It may be an elaborate setup or something as simple as leaning one way or the other. This often involves some form of "self-rescue device." The victim may be able to move a certain way to relieve pressure or may have an instrument for cutting a ligature or slicing open a bag.

Unfortunately, miscalculations can lead to tragedy. Cerebral hypoxia can result in poor judgment, poor assessment of the level of hypoxia, and sudden loss of consciousness. Once unconscious, the victim is unable to save himself. In partner sex, a miscalculation by one can lead to the death of the other.

Sometimes, the ritual involves the inhalation of various gases that lead to hypoxia and other physiological derangements. For example, nitrous oxide and amyl nitrate, both not uncommonly used in sex play, can cause a sudden and profound drop in blood pressure, which can lead to loss of consciousness and death. When coupled with partial asphyxia, these inhaled gases can be particularly treacherous.

The typical scene is a male victim, partially suspended by a hanging noose. He may be wearing female clothing or be surrounded by erotic magazines, photos, or paraphernalia. At times, his hands will be bound, which may bring up the possibility of a homicide staged to look like an accidental death. But, such binding may be part of the ritual. As with other types of hanging deaths, an examination of the bindings may reveal whether the victim could have bound himself or not.

TOXIC GASES

As opposed to what we saw with suffocating gases, which simply replace oxygen in the breathed air, toxic gases interact with the blood or tissues of the body in a manner that prevents oxygen transport or utilization. Certain toxins interfere with the uptake of oxygen by the blood or its utilization by the cells of the body. The most common chemical asphyxiant gases encountered by the ME are **carbon monoxide (CO), hydrogen cyanide (HCN)**, and **hydrogen sulfide (H₂S)**. Deaths due to carbon monoxide may be suicidal, accidental, or homicidal; those due to cyanide are usually suicides; and those involving hydrogen sulfide are typically accidental. We'll look at each of these toxic substances.

CARBON MONOXIDE

Deaths from carbon monoxide poisoning are usually suicidal or accidental. It is an uncommon method for homicide, but it has been reported.

Carbon monoxide is stealthy, treacherous, deadly, and common. A family is found dead and the cause is a faulty heater or fireplace. A suicide victim is found in his garage with the car engine running. Campers are found dead in a tent, a kerosene lantern burning in one corner. Each of these is due to carbon monoxide poisoning.

Carbon monoxide is a tasteless, odorless, colorless gas that is completely undetectable by humans. It results from the incomplete combustion of carbon-containing fuels—paper, wood, gasoline, and many other combustible products. Complete combustion of one of these fuels yields carbon dioxide (CO_2). If there is a deficiency of oxygen or if the fire is smoldering and doesn't produce enough heat to drive the reaction to completion, incomplete combustion occurs and the result is the production of carbon monoxide.

Wood, coal, and gas are common carbon-containing fuels. Faulty stoves, heaters, and fireplaces, as well as the exhaust from a car engine, can fill the air with carbon monoxide. Carbon monoxide poisoning is a more common cause of death in fires than is the fire itself. Charcoal briquettes are particularly dangerous as they are designed to smolder rather than burst into flame and are also good sources for carbon monoxide. Using a charcoal grill in an enclosed space such as a garage or tent can lead to carbon monoxide buildup very quickly. Faulty butane and propane camp stoves and heaters can also be deadly.

Carbon monoxide's treachery lies in its great affinity for hemoglobin, the oxygen-carrying molecule within our red blood cells (RBCs). When inhaled, CO binds to hemoglobin producing carboxyhemoglobi. It does so three hundred times more readily than does oxygen, and thus it displaces oxygen. The result is that the blood that leaves the lungs and heads toward the body is rich in carbon monoxide (carboxyhemoglobin) and poor in oxygen (oxyhemaglobin).

This strong affinity of hemoglobin for carbon monoxide means that very high blood levels can occur by breathing air that contains only small amounts of carbon monoxide. For example, breathing air that contains a carbon monoxide level as low as 0.2 percent may lead to blood carbon monoxide saturations greater than 60 percent after only thirty to forty-five minutes. So, a faulty heater or smoldering fire that produces only a small amount of carbon monoxide becomes increasingly deadly with each passing minute.

This powerful attraction for hemoglobin explains how certain individuals succumb to carbon monoxide poisoning in open areas. Most people believe that carbon monoxide is only toxic if it is in an enclosed area, but this is not true. There have been cases of individuals dying while working on their cars in an open area, such as a driveway. Typically the victim is found lying near the car's exhaust. Similarly, the newly recognized problem of carbon monoxide poisoning in swimmers and water skiers who loiter near a dive platform on the back of a powerboat with an idling engine.

The degree of exposure to carbon monoxide is typically measured by determining the percent of the hemoglobin that is carboxyhemoglobin. The signs and symptoms of carbon monoxide toxicity correlate with these levels. The normal level is 1 to 3 percent, but may be as high as 7 to 10 percent in smokers. At levels of 10 to 20 percent, headache and a poor ability to concentrate on complex tasks occur. Between 30 and 40 percent, headaches become severe and throbbing, and nausea, vomiting, faintness, and lethargy appear. Pulse and breathing rates increase noticeably. Between 40 and 60 percent the victim becomes confused, disoriented, and weak, and displays extremely poor coordination. Above 60 percent, coma and death are likely. These are general ranges since the actual effect of rising carbon monoxide levels varies from person to person.

In the elderly and those with heart or lung disease, levels as low as 20 percent may be lethal. Victims of car exhaust suicide or those who die from fire in an enclosed room may reach 90 percent.

A running car engine in an enclosed garage is a common method for suicide, but it could also be used for homicide. If the killer subdues the victim by force or by way of intoxication, he could place the victim in his car and let the carbon monoxide actually do him in. When determining the manner of death, the ME looks for evidence of trauma to the victim as well as performs a toxicology screen. Finding trauma, such as evidence of a blow to the head, might change the manner of death from suicide to homicide, but finding drugs may not. Some people use multiple suicide methods to assure success and a drug overdose combined with carbon monoxide inhalation is not rare.

When more than one person is found dead in a house or a car and there is no evidence of trauma, carbon monoxide toxicity is considered. The odds of two or more people dying from natural causes at the same time and the same place are extremely remote.

Carboxyhemoglobin is bright red in color and imparts this hue to the blood. When the ME performs an autopsy and sees bright cherry-red blood, he suspects carbon monoxide poisoning as the cause of death. This finding is not absolutely conclusive since cyanide inhalation or ingestion can also result in bright cherry-red blood and tissues. Also, individuals dying from cold exposure or corpses exposed to very low temperatures may show bright red blood. Livor mortis in these situations may also be red or pink rather than the usual blue-gray color (see Chapter Five: Time of Death, "Livor Mortis").

At autopsy, the internal organs in victims of carbon monoxide intoxication are also bright red. Interestingly, this color does not fade with embalming or when samples taken by the ME are fixed in formaldehyde as part of the preparation of microscopic slides. At times the presence of carbon monoxide can be found in the blood as long as six months after death.

Individuals who survive carbon monoxide intoxication may have serious long-term health problems. The brain is particularly vulnerable since it is extremely sensitive to lack of oxygen. Symptoms and signs of brain injury can begin immediately or be delayed for several days or weeks. The most common aftereffects include chronic headaches, memory loss, blindness, confusion, disorientation, poor coordination, and hallucinations. The ME may be asked to evaluate a living victim in this situation if the exposure was due to a criminal act or if a civil lawsuit is involved.

HYDROGEN CYANIDE

In books and movies, cyanide is often used for murder. In real life, this happens rarely. It is more likely to be used for attempted suicide, particularly mass suicides. Accidental poisoning of individuals or groups can occur in industrial settings. Cyanide salts are used in metal electroplating, jewelry making, and X-ray recovery industries. The plastic manufacturing industry uses solvents called nitriles, which contain cyanide. When burned, these nitriles can release hydrogen cyanide gas.

FORENSIC CASE FILES: JIM JONES AND THE PEOPLES TEMPLE

Christian pastor Jim Jones established his Peoples Temple in the 1960s in Indianapolis, Indiana, where his outlandish claims that he could cure cancer, heart disease, and other maladies, drew criticism. So, in the 1970s he moved his congregation to Northern California, San Francisco, and Los Angeles, where he warned his congregation of the coming end of the world. Suspicions arose about many of Jones' financial dealings and when an exposé appeared in a California magazine, he moved his followers from the United States to the makeshift town of Jonestown, Guyana.

Rumors of human rights abuses followed, and this attracted the attention of some members of Congress. In 1978, U.S. Congressman Leo Ryan and members of the press visited Jonestown and after talking with many of the Peoples Temple members, several members requested to leave with the Congressman and return to the United States. As they awaited a plane at Port Kaituma Airport, they were ambushed by several of the Temple's security guards. Congressman Ryan and five others were killed and eleven people were wounded. Fear of retribution led Jones and the Temple leaders to arrange a mass suicide.

Jones fed his congregation a fruit drink laced with cyanide and the sedatives Valium and chloral hydrate. Over 900 people perished, including over 250 children.

Hydrogen cyanide gas is the most deadly form of cyanide. The most common cyanide salts are sodium and potassium cyanide, which are white powders. When ingested, these powders react with the acids in the stomach to produce hydrogen cyanide gas. This is also the agent used in gas chamber executions.

Cyanide is a metabolic poison, which means it poisons the cells of the body. It reacts with the iron in cytochrome oxidase, an enzyme necessary for the cell to be able to use oxygen. This reaction prevents the body's cells from using oxygen and they begin to die rapidly. It is as if all the oxygen was suddenly removed from the body—it's still present, but the cells can't use it.

Since the cells no longer remove oxygen from the blood, the blood remains very well oxygenated (rich in oxyhemoglobin) and thus bright red. Another contributor to this cherry-red color is the reaction of cyanide with the blood's hemoglobin to produce cyanohemoglobin, a bright red compound. Similar to carbon monoxide poisoning, the blood of victims of cyanide exposure is bright red in color.

At autopsy, if the ME sees bright red blood, a reddish hue to the internal organs, and pinkish lividity, he would suspect the presence of cyanide or carbon monoxide and would test for both. In addition, he might detect the typical bitter almond odor of hydrogen cyanide. That is, if he is capable. Curiously, the ability to detect this odor is genetically determined and about 50 percent of people cannot smell it.

SEWER GAS

Hydrogen sulfide is a byproduct of fermentation and is often found in sewers and cesspools. The combination of the two toxic gases hydrogen sulfide and carbon monoxide and the suffocating gas methane is called **sewer gas**. When inhaled or ingested, hydrogen sulfide converts oxyhemoglobin (hemoglobin rich in oxygen) into **methemoglobin**, which does not release oxygen to the tissues, thus effectively suffocating the cells of the body. Methemoglobin imparts a dark purple color to the blood, which can be seen at autopsy, where the ME is also likely to find high levels of sulfide in the blood of sewer gas victims. These deaths are almost always accidental and occur when the victim enters an area rich in sewer gas.

DROWNING

Drowning is a form of asphyxia in that the victim dies from lack of oxygen. As the lungs' bronchial tubes (airways) and alveoli (air sacs) fill with water, the ability to oxygenate the blood is lost. Initially, the victim struggles to breathe, and while doing so forces water into the nasal sinuses. Coughing triggers an inhalation reflex, which pulls even more water into the lungs. With the loss of air supply and the energy consumption in the struggle for survival, the oxygen level in the blood rapidly falls and loss of consciousness occurs in one to two minutes. The heart stops shortly thereafter.

Drowning is almost always accidental, but can be suicidal or homicidal. For the ME, the determination of the manner of death is often difficult. Whether the victim fell, jumped, or was pushed into the water, drowning is drowning. It all looks the same.

Even determining that the victim actually drowned is difficult and is mostly a diagnosis of exclusion. The circumstances of the death are often more important than any autopsy findings. If there is no evidence of trauma or natural disease to explain the death, and if the victim is found in water, the ME may determine that the death was from drowning. The reason for this confusion is that there are few, if any, pathological findings at autopsy that can definitely indicate that the person drowned.

You might think that if the lungs are full of water, the victim must have drowned. Not true. The lungs and airways of any corpse submerged in water for several hours will passively fill with water. For this reason, the ME may not be able to determine if the victim was dead or alive when he entered the water and he can't say whether the victim drowned.

Further confusing the situation, there are several medical conditions, including heart attacks and certain drug overdoses, that cause pulmonary edema (water-filled lungs). So, if a victim suffered a heart attack and developed severe secondary pulmonary edema before falling into the water, or if he died from a certain type of drug overdose and was dumped into water, the autopsy findings might be similar to those of someone who drowned. For this reason, a complete toxicological analysis should be performed on all suspected drowning victims.

Another confusing circumstance is that as many as 15 percent of deaths by drowning are "dry drownings." In this situation, the intake of water into the throat causes laryngeal spasm, where the larynx reacts to the water by spasming (constricting or closing). This shuts down the passage of air into the lungs, and the victim asphyxiates. This closing of the airway also prevents water from entering the lungs so that they are dry at autopsy. This may be more common in salt water than in fresh water drowning.

There are a few tricks the ME can use to identify a drowning victim. If the victim is conscious when he enters the water, the struggles to breathe cause a great deal of pressure trauma to the sinuses and the lungs. The ME would expect to find hemorrhaging (bleeding) into the sinuses and airways, as well as debris from the water, which is sucked into the sinuses and lungs with attempted breathing. Such findings suggest that the victim was alive when he went into the water. The finding of plants or rocks from the bottom of the body of water clutched in the victim's hand would be important. This would be presumptive evidence that he grabbed them during his struggle to survive.

The ME might also find clues to indicate that the victim was conscious before drowning by examination of the bone marrow. This might sound odd at first, but the key is in finding tiny creatures called **diatoms** within the marrow. Diatoms are tiny single-celled organisms that scurry around in both salt and fresh water. They have silica in their cell walls and are very resistant to degradation. If the victim's heart is still beating when he enters the water, any diatoms in the inhaled water will pass through the lungs, enter the bloodstream, and be pumped throughout the body, where they tend to collect in the bone marrow. If a microscopic analysis of the marrow reveals diatoms, the victim must have been alive at the time of water entry. This technique may be useful in severely degraded or skeletal remains where no lungs or sinus tissues are available for examination. Unfortunately, diatom testing is not exactly that straightforward and is controversial. Some experts feel that diatoms are an inexact tool for determining if a drowning occurred. Some bodies of water contain no diatoms. Also, they are found in air and soil and even on the clothing of the examiner. This makes contamination of the tested sample a possibility.

The **Gettler chloride test** is another controversial test available to the ME. Some pathologists believe that testing the chloride content of blood taken from each side of the heart can distinguish fresh water from salt water drowning. If the chloride content in blood from the right side is higher, the drowning was in fresh water. If higher on the left, the drowning took place in salt water. The physiological explanation for this is complex and not universally accepted.

As the victim struggles to survive and sucks water into his sinuses and lungs, he also drags in other things—dirt, gravel, plant materials, sand, and microscopic plants and animals. The medical examiner might employ a forensic chemist, a botanist, or a geologist to help identify and determine the site of origin of these materials. For example, the finding of pine pollen and bits of pine needles within the lungs suggests that the victim drowned in a nearby pine-shaded pond, not the backyard swimming pool. Or the absence of these and the finding of high chlorine levels in the water taken from the victim's lungs suggests the opposite.

An analysis of the sand in a victim's mouth might be traceable to a particular beach. It could be the chemical nature of the sand itself or any associated insects or bits of leaves, animal fur, or bird feathers that pinpoint the location of the drowning. This can be extremely important in cases where the body has been moved.

The bottom line is that the determination as to whether a victim drowned or not is often a best-guess situation. The ME may depend more on the circumstances of the death than any autopsy or laboratory findings.

SEROLOGY:
BLOOD AND OTHER BODY FLUIDS

Serology is the science that deals with the examination, characterization, and analysis of blood and other body fluids, such as semen, saliva, and tears. It overlaps with other scientific disciplines, including biology, biochemistry, medical science, and cellular anatomy and physiology and is a critical component of forensic scientific investigation. Serology is a large and complex field, but I will try to keep it simple and address only those issues that relate to the field of forensics.

Blood is by far the most common biological fluid left at a crime scene because many crimes, from assaults to homicides, include the spilling of blood. It is also the most useful fluid since it offers many avenues of investigation to the forensics team. Some of these avenues depend on blood's physical properties (how it behaves as a liquid), while others depend on its chemical and biological behaviors.

The physical properties of blood will be dealt with when we look at bloodstain patterns in chapter thirteen. The goal of the forensic bloodstain analyst is to reconstruct the crime scene, determine the sequence of events surrounding the crime, and follow the actions of the perpetrator, the victim, and the witnesses. This analysis can in turn link a suspect to a crime scene and support or refute suspect and witness statements.

After this evaluation of the bloodstains is completed, the **serologist** steps in to conduct chemical and biological tests of any blood samples retrieved from the scene. A serologist is a scientist who analyzes blood and body fluids. He attempts to characterize each bloodstain with an eye toward individualizing each stain. That is, he tries to determine whose blood it is and hopes to tightly link the suspect to the scene. Was the suspect far away at the time the crime occurred, as he states, or is the stain on his sock the victim's blood? Is the blood beneath the victim's fingernails that of the suspect or did it come from someone else? The coroner uses the science of serology to determine the truth.

I should point out that since the advent of DNA testing, the serological evaluation of blood and other body fluids has diminished as a forensics tool. The reason, as you will see in this and the following chapter, is that DNA testing offers much greater individualization. Yet, serology remains a useful tool for the forensic scientist.

To begin our understanding of this subject, let's first see what blood is.

THE CHARACTERISTICS OF BLOOD

Blood is a complex substance. The liquid portion of whole blood is called **plasma**. It contains proteins, enzymes, clotting factors, and electrolytes, as well as cells of three basic types: **leukocytes**, or white blood cells (WBCs), **erythrocytes**, or red blood cells (RBCs), and **platelets** (tiny cells involved in blood clotting). If whole blood is allowed to clot and the clot is removed, the yellowish liquid remaining is called **serum**. It contains most of the proteins and enzymes of plasma, but none of the cells or clotting factors, which have been consumed in forming the blood clot.

For years, physicians attempted to perform blood transfusions from one person to another. Each attempt failed. The blood would clot within the recipient's veins and cause almost immediate death. In 1901, Karl Landsteiner revealed one of the most important medical discoveries in history. He had earlier observed that all blood was not the same in that blood from different people reacted in varying ways when combined with blood from another. Sometimes there would be a reaction, and other times there would be none. To explain these observations, he embarked on a course of extensive experimentation and ultimately discovered that human blood could be classified into four types, which he designated A, B, AB, and O. For this reason, Landsteiner called his classification scheme the **ABO blood group system**.

He learned that if a person received blood from a donor with the same type of blood, he was much less likely to have a reaction. But if he received blood from a donor of a different type, the reaction was essentially universal.

In the decades following Landsteiner's pivotal discovery, we have gained a much better understanding of the ABO system, which is still in use today. It not only serves as the basis for all blood transfusions, but also for matching blood samples in the forensic lab.

THE ABO SYSTEM

The two most important components of blood from a forensics point of view are the **red blood cells** and the **serum**. Using these two components, we can determine the ABO type of a blood sample and most bloodstains.

The red blood cells are the cells that contain hemoglobin, which is the molecule that transports oxygen from the lungs to the tissues. The hemoglobin resides within the red blood cell. On the surface of the red blood cells are other extremely important molecules called **antigens**. These antigens determine the blood type.

There are only two types of antigens; they are designated as either A or B. A person with type A blood will have A antigens on his red blood cells; type B blood has B antigens; type AB blood has both A and B antigens; and type O blood possesses neither antigen.

Landsteiner also discovered another antigen in the blood, the D antigen. Whether a person has this antigen is known as the rhesus or **Rh factor** because Landsteiner's studies were performed in rhesus monkeys. The presence of this factor in a person's red blood cells means he has Rh-positive blood, and if not, it is Rh-negative blood. Thus, a person with type A positive blood possesses the A antigen and the Rh (D) antigen on their red blood cells. Persons who are type O negative have neither the A, B, nor Rh antigen on his red blood cells.

Another important factor is that the serum contains specialized proteins called **antibodies**. The key point in understanding blood typing is that for every antigen there is a corresponding antibody. An antibody is highly specific in that it only recognizes and reacts with its specific antigen and not with any other. When an antibody meets its matching antigen, it combines with it to form an **antigen-antibody complex**. This reaction is what causes transfusion reactions and is the basis for the blood-typing procedure.

BLOOD MATCHING AND TYPING

As stated above, the surfaces of red blood cells possess either A or B antigens, both, or neither. The serum contains antibodies that are termed either anti-A or anti-B, depending upon which antigen they recognize. That is, if an anti-A antibody comes into contact with an A antigen, a reaction will occur. Since it is highly specific for the A antigen, it will not react with a B antigen.

These anti-A and anti-B antibodies are found in the serum, but which one, if any, a person has depends upon his blood type. Logically, a person with type A blood cannot possess anti-A antibodies, since this would lead to an antigen-antibody reaction that would be deadly. So, each person has antibodies that are directed against the blood antigens that differ from the ones on her own red blood cells.

That is, if a person has antigen A on his red blood cells (type A blood), he then has anti-B antibodies in his serum (see Figure 9-1). If he has antigen B (type B blood), then he has anti-A antibodies in his serum. Likewise, a person with both A and B antigens (type AB blood) has neither anti-A nor anti-B antibodies. And a person with neither A nor B antigens (type O blood) has both anti-A and anti-B antibodies.

TYPE	ANTIGENS ON RBCS	ANTIBODIES IN SERUM
A	A	Anti-B
B	B	Anti-A
AB	AB	None
O	Neither	Anti-A and anti-B

But type O blood is considered to be the "universal donor." This means that in situations where time does not allow for cross matching, type O is given. But, even though type O possesses both anti-A and anti-B antibodies, it does not react with blood types A, B, and AB because the red blood cell antigens of the donor react with the serum antibodies of the recipient to cause transfusion reactions. Since type O has no red blood cell antigens, no reaction occurs.

The reaction of the recipient's serum antibodies with the red blood cell antigens of the donor's blood is what causes transfusion reactions. For example, a person with type A blood cannot receive a transfusion of type B blood without risking a severe reaction; he has anti-B antibodies in his serum, so if he is given type B blood, these anti-B antibodies will immediately react with the B antigens on the red blood cells of the donor's blood. This is a transfusion reaction and results is **agglutination**, or clumping, of the blood cells, which can lead to rashes, kidney damage, and death.

Agglutination occurs because the serum antibodies are **bivalent**. This means that they have two reactive ends. If each end of the antibody reacts with a red blood cell surface antigen, it forms a complex of two red blood cells and one antibody. Sort of like a dumbbell, with the red blood cells being the two end-weights and the antibody the handle. As the reaction continues, the red blood cells are bound into a latticework and clump together (see Figure 9-2).

Figure 9-1: Blood type antigens and antibodies. In a person with type A blood, A antigens cover the surface of red blood cells. The serum would contain anti-B antibodies, which would not react with the A antigens but would react with B antigens found on types B or AB blood.

Blood typing makes use of this reaction. Serum that contains antibodies is called **antiserum** (plural is antisera). If the serum contains anti-A antibodies, it is called anti-A serum; if it contains anti-B antibodies, it is anti-B serum. In the lab, these two types of antisera are used to determine blood type.

For example, if a given blood sample agglutinates when exposed to anti-A serum but not with anti-B serum, the cells contain only antigen-A and the blood type of the sample is A.

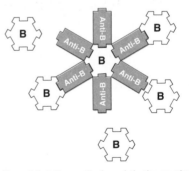

Figure 9-2: Antigen-antibody agglutination reaction. If type B blood is transfused into a type A individual, the anti-B antibodies in the serum of the recipient react with the B antigens on the surface of the red blood cells in the transfused blood, causing the cells to agglutinate, or clump together.

Similarly, if the sample reacts only to anti-B serum and not anti-A serum, it is type B. If it reacts to both, it is type AB, since this would mean that the red blood cells possess both the A and the B antigens. Finally, if it reacts to neither, the red blood cells possess neither antigen and the type is O.

REACTS TO ANTISERA	BLOOD TYPE
A only	A
B only	B
Both A and B	AB
Neither A nor B	O

Remember these two key points:

1. The antisera contain antibodies that "test for" or react with antigens on the red blood cells.
2. The antigen (or antigens) on the red blood cells determine the blood type.

This means that which antisera react with a particular blood sample reveals which antigens are present and thus the blood type of the sample.

The serologist tests each submitted crime scene sample separately and determines the type of each. In situations where more than one person shed blood, this information may help with crime scene reconstruction. Blood typing was critical to crime scene reconstruction in the Jeffrey MacDonald case.

FORENSIC CASE FILES: THE JEFFREY MACDONALD CASE

At 3:40 A.M. on the morning of February 17, 1970, U.S. Army Captain Dr. Jeffrey MacDonald called the military police (MPs) to his home at Fort Bragg, North Carolina. They found MacDonald lying on his bedroom floor next to his wife, Colette. He wore only blue pajama bottoms, its matching pajama top spread across Colette's chest. She had been brutally and repeatedly stabbed to death. Above them on the bed's headboard was the single word "pig" written in blood. Down the hall the bodies of the two MacDonald children, five-year-old Kimberly and two-year-old Kristen, lay in pools of blood. Only Jeffrey MacDonald was alive, having suffered only a single knife wound to his chest.

MacDonald stated that he was asleep on the living room sofa when he heard Colette screaming. He was immediately attacked by three men and a woman, who he described as hippies and who chanted, "Acid is groovy, kill the pigs," while they slashed him with a knife. They tore his pajama top, which he then used to parry the thrusts from the knives. He was ultimately knocked unconscious, then later awoke to find his family slaughtered. He attempted mouth-to-mouth resuscitation on each of his daughters. He then found Colette with a knife protruding from her chest. He removed the knife, covered her with his pajama top, and phoned the MPs.

The MPs were immediately suspicious. Why were MacDonald's injuries minimal while his family had been severely brutalized? Colette had been stabbed over thirty times; Kristen and Kimberly were beaten and repeatedly stabbed. Another question the MPs had was why was the living room, where four people allegedly attacked MacDonald, so neat? Only an upended coffee table and a turned-over flowerpot were out of place. And how could MacDonald, who needed glasses to correct his poor vision, provide such detailed descriptions of four assailants whom he only saw in the dark? Why was the torn fingertip of a latex surgical glove found in Jeffrey and Colette's bloodstained bed? Interestingly, the MPs found a copy of *Esquire* magazine with an article on the recent Manson family murders in the living room. In these murders, messages, including the word "pig," also had been written in blood at the crime scenes.

Unfortunately, the investigation was less than perfect and evidence was lost, so charges against MacDonald were dropped. The story might have ended there, except that MacDonald went on *The Dick Cavett Show* and berated the military, accusing them of gross incompetence. This led to a renewed interest in him.

The FBI entered the investigation and turned up a wealth of information. First, in a coincidence that defies odds, each family member had a different blood type. This allowed investigators to track the movements of each, particularly those of Jeffrey MacDonald. His blood was found in small quantities in only three places: on his glasses in the living room, on a cabinet where a box of surgical gloves were stored, and on the bathroom sink, where investigators believe he inflicted his own minor wound. There was no blood, or even fingerprints, on the two phones he used to call for help. Also, no prints were found on the knife that MacDonald said he had removed from his wife's chest, nor were any prints on the knife and ice pick found outside near the back door. Had they been wiped clean?

Blue fibers from MacDonald's pajamas were found everywhere. Almost. They were in the two girls' rooms and all over, around, and even beneath Colette's body. Yet, none were found in the living room, where MacDonald was allegedly attacked and the shirt was ripped.

But the most damning evidence came from the FBI's crime lab. Analysts showed that the holes in the blue pajama top exactly matched the wounds to Colette when the garment was folded over her chest. More importantly, each of the punctures was round and smooth, indicating that the garment was stationary when the blows were struck. Had the top been in motion as it would have been if MacDonald were using it for defense, it would have shown ragged and irregular holes.

Lastly, Collette's blood had stained both halves of the torn pajama top. When the two pieces were placed side by side, like two adjacent pieces of a jigsaw puzzle, the stain pattern matched, suggesting that the stain occurred before the top was torn. This directly contradicted MacDonald's statement that he had placed the pajama top over his wife's body after it was torn.

In July 1979, nearly a decade after the murders, Jeffrey MacDonald went on trial for the triple murder and received three consecutive life terms.

BLOOD AND THE SEROLOGIST

Fresh blood is usually red, but what does a bloodstain look like? Is it red or purple or brown? Can it be confused with grease, paint, or chocolate? The truth is that its color depends upon its age and what conditions it has been exposed to. Sometimes blood looks like chocolate and chocolate looks like blood. Even to the experienced eye, bloodstains may look like stains left by many other materials. When the serologist analyzes a liquid sample or a stain that could be blood, he must answer three questions:

- Is it blood?
- Is it human blood?
- Whose blood is it?

His first task is to determine if the specimen is blood or some other rusty brown stain such as oil, paint, or ketchup. If the stain isn't blood, no further testing is required, but once the serologist is sure that blood is present, he must determine if it is human or not. After that, he must match it to a suspect if it is to be of forensic value.

For blood to be useful to the serologist, it must be found in sufficient amounts and in good enough condition to allow testing. Many modern techniques require only minute amounts of blood, but if the blood is severely degraded, even large quantities may prove useless. Many chemicals can damage blood to the point that typing and DNA profiling can't be performed. Also putrefaction, which is due to bacterial growth, can degrade the sample beyond repair. Since warmth and moisture promote bacterial growth, putrefaction proceeds much more rapidly in warm and wet conditions. In cooler and drier areas, the blood is less likely to decay and the dried stain may last for decades, even centuries.

If the serologist obtains a usable sample, he possesses many analytical tools that will tell him if the sample is indeed blood.

IS IT BLOOD?

Testing a liquid or stain to determine if it is blood is not new. The microscope has been used for this purpose for centuries, since visually identifying blood cells is proof positive that the substance is blood. Of course, the blood must be in a liquid state, since clotted blood or dry bloodstains contain no identifiable cells. Several other tests appeared in the late 1800s, including Ambrose Tardieu's olfactory test. He set out to prove that blood could be identified by its distinctive smell. He failed, though, because the sense of smell is too variable and unreliable in this regard.

Like microscopic examination, the old hematin test, developed in 1853 by Polish scientist Ludwig Teichmann (1823–1895), also required liquid blood. In this test, the suspected blood sample was mixed with acetic acid and salt crystals, heated and viewed under a microscope for the presence of the characteristic rhomboid crystals. This test is similar to the present-day Teichmann and Takayama tests, which we'll look at shortly

Dutch scientist Izaak van Deen (1804–1869) developed the guaiacum test in 1862. Guaiac comes from the resin of a West Indian shrub and was the best test of its time. It is also the precursor of the present day phenolphthalein test. In the guaiacum test, the suspected blood sample was mixed with hydrogen peroxide and guaiacum and, if it were indeed blood, a blue color would ap-

---

pear. In fact, in the very first Sherlock Holmes novel, *A Study in Scarlet*, published in 1887, Holmes used a similar test to identify a stain as blood.

In 1863, German scientist Christian Friedrich Schönbein (1799–1868) developed another simple screening test for liquid blood when he found that hydrogen peroxide would oxidize blood in a reaction that produced foam.

Each of these tests proved useful for testing liquid blood, but most blood samples obtained at crime scenes are dried. The advantage of dried blood is that it is much more resistant to decay than is liquid blood. But it presented a major problem for investigators. How could they identify the dried stain as blood? The microscope was useless since dried blood had no intact cells to view. All the above tests offered no help since they required liquid blood. Obviously, other techniques were needed and many were developed, some of which have been around for over one hundred years.

To determine if a given sample is blood, the serologist conducts tests of two basic types: **presumptive** and **confirmatory**. Presumptive tests are typically cheaper and faster. When results are negative, the sample is not blood, and no further, more expensive testing is necessary. When positive, they indicate that blood is likely present, but do not absolutely establish that as fact. That requires confirmatory testing.

Presumptive Tests

Presumptive tests for blood fall into two broad categories: those that yield a **color** reaction and those that cause a **fluorescent** (glowing) reaction. Those that cause a color change are benzidine, o-toluidine, phenolphthalein, tetramethylbenzidine, and leucomalachite green. Those that cause fluorescence include fluorescein and luminol.

Tests That Cause a Color Change

Benzidine and **o-toluidine** (3.3'Dimethylbenzidine) are no longer used, though at one time they were very popular. Benzidine was the chemical in the old **Adler test**, which was developed in 1904 by Oskar and Rudolf Adler. When applied to a bloodstain, it would become blue, and then slowly turn brown. O-toluidine was the original chemical on Hemastix, which were manufactured by Miles Laboratories. These dip-sticks were used to test urine samples for the presence of blood. O-toluidine also yields a blue color when exposed to blood. However, by the mid-1970s, both benzidine and o-toluidine were found to be potentially carcinogenic (cancer producing) and faded out of use.

Phenolphthalein is the active compound in the popular **Kastle-Meyer color test.** The reaction in this test rests on the fact that the hemoglobin in blood possesses what is called a peroxidase-like property. Peroxidases are enzymes that accelerate the oxidation of certain compounds by peroxides. One such compound is phenolphthalein. When blood, phenolphthalein, and hydrogen peroxide come together, the hemoglobin in the blood causes the peroxide to react with the phenolphthalein and produces a dark pink color. The major advantage of the Kastle-Meyer test is that the reaction is very quick, with the color change appearing within a minute or two. The major disadvantage is that certain vegetable products, such as potatoes and horseradish, may also cause the reaction to occur. Of course, potatoes and horseradish are not typically found at scenes where blood has been shed.

Tetramethylbenzidine (TMB) was derived from benzidine after the latter was proved to cause cancer and also replaced o-toluidine in Hemastix. At a crime scene, the presumed bloodstain is sampled with a moistened cotton-tipped swab and then applied to the Hemastix strip. If it immediately turns blue-green, blood may be present.

Leucomalachite green (LMG) has been available since the early 1900s. When in contact with blood, it produces a green color.

Tests That Fluoresce

Fluorescein has also been used since the early 1900s. It reacts with the hemoglobin (the iron-containing molecule) in red blood cells and glows when exposed to ultraviolet light. At the crime scene, it is sprayed where blood is believed to be, the lights are lowered, and an ultraviolet light source is directed over the area. Bloodstains will glow in the dark. Not only can the likely presence of blood be established, but also its area of distribution can be clearly defined. Spurts, spatters, drag marks, and foot and handprints jump into view.

Fluorescein has two advantages over luminol, which is discussed below. It does not react with household bleach, as does luminol, which makes it better suited for stains that have been cleaned up. Perpetrators often attempt to scrub walls and floors clean in the erroneous assumption that if the blood can't be seen it can't be found. Fortunately, that's not true. Another advantage of fluorscein is that it is a thicker liquid than luminol and tends to drip less. This means it will stick better to walls, doors, and other vertical surfaces.

Luminol (3-aminophthalhydrazide) also reacts with the blood's hemoglobin and fluoresces under ultraviolet light. It is also applied by spraying and is viewed under ultraviolet light after the area has been darkened. As with fluorescein, it can reveal bloodstain patterns.

Its major advantage is that it is extremely sensitive and can reveal blood that is present in extremely small amounts, as little as one part per ten million or less. Unless chlorine bleach or a chlorine-containing cleaning fluid was used, luminol can detect blood in areas that have been thoroughly cleaned, and even on walls that have been painted over. Though it may interfere with some serological testing procedures, it does not affect later typing or DNA analysis.

When luminol is used, the area is darkened. Indoors, the lights are turned off and the window shades drawn. Outdoors or in rooms that cannot be darkened, waiting for nightfall might be necessary. Once dark, the examiners put on protective goggles, spray the area with luminol, and look for areas that glow. The fluorescence appears immediately and fades quickly so photographs or videos are used to capture the images of the blood patterns.

Using luminol, it is often possible to track the movements of the perpetrator by following his bloody shoeprints. Shoes that appear clean but hold minute traces of blood do not leave visible prints, but their tracks glow brightly under the influence of luminol.

Confirmatory Tests

Once one of the presumptive tests indicates that blood is likely present, a confirmatory test is used to confirm or deny that fact.

The most commonly used confirmatory tests are the **Teichmann test** and the **Takayama test**. Both rely on a reaction between a chemical and the hemoglobin molecule found within the red blood cells. This reaction results in the formation of crystals, which are then viewed under a microscope. A major advantage of both tests is that they work well with very old stains.

The Teichmann test involves the heating of the suspected blood sample with acetic acid and a chloride compound, which causes the chloride compound to react with the blood's hemoglobin to produce a hemoglobin-chloride crystalline compound. Under the microscope, brown, rhomboid-shaped crystals are seen if the substance is indeed blood. Care must be taken not to overheat the preparation or the crystal-forming reaction may not occur.

To perform the test, the sample is placed on a glass slide and the acetic acid-chloride solution is added. The slide is then carefully heated. If blood is present, crystals, which can be seen under the microscope, quickly form.

The Takayama test (also called the pyridine test), developed by Masaeo Takayama in 1912, is performed in a similar manner, except that the suspect sample is heated with pyridine and glucose (sugar). The reaction that occurs causes the formation of pyridine ferriprotoporphyrin or hemochromogen crystals, which are viewed under a microscope.

Once confirmatory testing has proven that the sample is blood, the next step is to determine whether it is human blood or that of another species.

IS IT HUMAN BLOOD?

Humans aren't the only creatures that shed blood at a crime scene. It falls to the serologist to determine if the blood is human or from a dog, cat, or some other animal. Only after this determination is made can further testing be done to discover whose blood it is.

The technique for distinguishing human blood from animal blood dates to 1901 when German professor Paul Uhlenhuth (1870–1957) published a paper on his precipitin method. Similar to the typing of blood, the tests used for species determination are antigen-antibody reactions. The difference is that an antiserum that reacts with antigens specific for humans rather than with the A and B red blood cell antigens must be created. That is, a specific antibody to a specific human antigen is created and the resulting reaction, or lack of reaction, determines whether the blood is human. In that same year, Uhlenhuth was called on to use his new test in a double murder case.

FORENSIC CASE FILES: LUDWIG TESSNOW AND THE WEREWOLF MURDERS

In 1901, the battered and dismembered bodies of two young boys were found on the German coastal island of Rugen. The victims had been ripped apart and their limbs scattered far and wide. One boy's heart was missing and the skulls of both had been crushed. The murder weapon appeared to be a bloodstained stone. Ludwig Tessnow, who had been seen earlier with the boys, was arrested and a search of his home turned up clothing with suspicious dark stains. Tessnow said they were wood dye stains. Interestingly, this was the same thing he had said about some clothing stains three years earlier when he was suspected in the murder and dismemberment of two young girls in Osnabruck, Germany. Even more bizarre, a local farmer said he had seen a man who looked like Tessnow fleeing from his fields after ripping the limbs from several of his sheep. Though it is unclear whether the term was ever applied to Tessnow, these types of savage killings of humans and animals were often believed to be the work of werewolves and were sometimes called Werewolf Killings.

The police investigating the deaths of the two young boys knew of Professor Uhlenhuth's new test and asked for his help. He did, indeed, find wood dye on Tessnow's clothing, but he also found both human and sheep blood. Tessnow was convicted and executed.

Developing and Using an Antiserum

In order to determine if the blood in question is human, an anti-human serum that only reacts with uniquely human antigens must be created. To do this, the human antigen (human blood) is injected into a rabbit or other animal and then enough time is allowed for the animal to produce sufficient antibodies against the antigen. The animal's blood, which is now rich in anti-human antibodies, is removed and the antiserum is isolated. This antiserum can now be used to test blood samples and determine if they are from humans.

In the laboratory, if a solution containing an antiserum is brought into contact with one containing the antigen it was designed to react against, a reaction will occur. This reaction produces an antigen-antibody complex that precipitates or falls out of solution. This results in a visible line of precipitation along the line of contact between the two solutions. For example, if the antiserum to human blood made with the rabbit contacts a solution that contains human blood, the reaction occurs and a visible line of precipitation results. On the other hand, if the blood is not human, no reaction occurs and no line of precipitation is seen.

The contact between the two solutions can be accomplished by simple diffusion or by electrophoresis. With simple diffusion, the two liquids are placed in contact or near contact with each other, and they simply flow toward each other by the laws of diffusion. The precipitation reaction will occur along the line of contact. Electrophoresis is the application of an electric current to the test material. This quickens the rate of movement of the components of each solution and thus hastens the precipitation reaction. Either way, the reaction is highly specific for human blood.

The most commonly used tests for human blood are the ring precipitin test, the Ouchterlony double diffusion test, crossover electrophoresis, and anti-human hemoglobin. The first three use antisera to human blood proteins, while the latter uses an antiserum to human hemoglobin.

RING PRECIPITIN TEST: In this test, the anti-human antiserum is placed in a test tube. The blood sample is dissolved in a liquid and carefully poured into the tube. It will float over the denser antiserum much as vinegar floats above the oil in many salad dressings. If the sample is human blood, a reaction occurs and a thin white band of solid precipitate forms at the interface of the liquids. If not, no precipitate ring is seen.

OUCHTERLONY DOUBLE DIFFUSION TEST: This test uses a gel agar plate. This is a plastic plate that contains a jelly-like gel. Wells (holes) are arranged in the gel so that there is a central well surrounded by an array of other wells. The antiserum is placed in the center well and the samples to be tested are placed in the surrounding ones. Each solution slowly diffuses outward in every direction. This leads to several lines of contact with the central solution and each of the surrounding solutions. Each sample solution that contains human blood yields a faint line of precipitation along the line of contact. Those that do not contain human blood show no such reaction.

CROSSOVER ELECTROPHORESIS: A gel plate is also used in this test, except that in this case two rows of wells are cut into the gel. The antiserum is placed in all the wells of one row and the samples are placed in the rows opposite them. An electrical current is applied, which causes the two liquids to move toward each other. As with the other tests, a positive result is indicated by a line of precipitation along the line of contact.

ANTI-HUMAN HEMOGLOBIN: This test utilizes an antiserum that specifically reacts with human hemoglobin. Unfortunately, these are often only primate specific and not human specific. It can discriminate between human and dog or cat blood but not human and gorilla blood. Its major advantage is that it can be used with very old and degraded samples. But, unless the location where the blood is found is known to house a gorilla or other primate, a positive test means the blood is human.

The modern crime lab contains antisera to a variety of common animals' blood, such as dog, cat, deer, cow, and sheep. Using these, the serologist can determine the species that shed the blood. This may be important evidence in and of itself.

WHOSE BLOOD IS IT?

Once the serologist has determined that the blood is human, he will set about trying to discover whose it is. The first step is to determine its type. This is similar to the typing protocol described earlier in this chapter with one major exception. Standard blood typing utilizes liquid blood and a positive reaction is indicated by agglutination or clumping of the red blood cells. This means that agglutination can only occur if the blood is liquid and if the red blood cells are intact.

But, as I said earlier, crime scene blood is more likely to be either clotted or a dried stain. When blood clots, the red blood cells break up, and if they are not intact they can't agglutinate, which means that any antigen-antiserum reaction can't be verified. Even though the blood in the stain has clotted, dried, and the RBCs have disintegrated, the antigens on the surface of the red blood cells remain. They simply need to be extracted for testing.

The serologist makes use of these facts by employing the clever **absorption-elution technique**. This technique offers a roundabout or indirect way for determining exactly what antigens are present in the bloodstain, which will in turn reveal the blood type.

Absorption-elution is a four-step process.

STEP 1: The bloodstained material is treated with blood antisera. The antibodies in the antisera combine with and are bound to the antigens.

STEP 2: The material is then washed to remove any excess antiserum. This leaves behind the blood antigens and the specific antibodies to those particular antigens.

STEP 3: The sample then undergoes elution. This is a process whereby the sample is heated to 56°C. This breaks the antigen-antibody bond and frees the antigen and the antibodies from one another.

STEP 4: The eluted antibodies are then tested against known blood antigens and their reaction is observed. Because of the extreme specificity of antibodies for a particular antigen, whichever antigens the antibodies react with must be identical to the antigens present in the original unknown sample.

Let's say the serologist is confronted with a bloodstained shirt. He has determined that the blood is human and goes through the above steps. Let's assume the stain is from a type A individual. In the first step, both anti-A and anti-B serums are added. The stain has only A antigens and so only reacts with the anti-A antibodies in the anti-A serum. It does not react with the anti-B antibodies of the anti-B serum. After washing, only the complex of the stain's A antigens and the anti-A antibodies remain. Elution separates these two, freeing the anti-A antibodies from the stain. Testing these antibodies against blood samples of known type result in a reaction only to type A blood. This means that the original sample must also have been type A.

Using the Results

Simply determining the ABO type of the blood at a crime scene can narrow the suspect list and completely exonerate some suspects. For example, the population distribution of the four ABO types is:

O	43%	B	12%
A	42%	AB	3%

If the blood is AB, it will narrow the focus to 3 percent of the population and will exonerate any suspects with types A, B, or O. Of course, everyone with type AB blood could still be considered suspect.

By adding the Rh factor to the mix, the serologist can narrow the list further. The approximate percentages of people with the various ABO-Rh combinations are:

O-Pos	33%	B-Pos	10%
O-Neg	8%	B-Neg	3%
A-Pos	33%	AB-Pos	5%
A-Neg	7%	AB-Neg	1%

This means that if the blood found at the scene is AB-Neg, 99 percent of the population has been eliminated as the source of the blood. But that's not the end of it since the serologist has a few other tools to further individualize the sample. It has been discovered that red blood cells contain more proteins, enzymes, and antigens than just the A and B antigens. These include antigens

---

with such catchy names as Duffy, Kell, and Kidd, and intracellular enzymes such as adenylate kinase, erythrocyte acid phosphatase, and the very useful **phosphoglucomutase (PGM)**. Each of these also has a known distribution in the population. Let's take a closer look at PGM.

Many enzymes are **polymorphic**, which means that they come in varying forms. These polymorphic types are called **isoenzymes**. PGM comes in many different isoenzymes with at least ten of them being fairly common. As with ABO antigens, these enzymes are inherited independently. This means that regardless of ABO type, a particular individual could have any combination of the isoenzymes of PGM. The serologist can use this fact to further narrow the list of suspects who could have left a particular bloodstain.

For example, let's say a stain has been found to be ABO type AB-Neg and to possess PGM 2. The AB-Negative blood type is found in only 1 percent of the population and PGM 2 is found in only 6 percent of people. Since these two factors are inherited independently, the probability of a particular individual being type AB-Neg, PGM 2 is only 0.06 percent or about 6 per 10,000.

The math: 6% = 0.06 and 1% = 0.01

0.06 × 0.01 = .0006 or 0.06%

If the police find a suspect that possesses type AB, PGM 2 blood, the probability that he is the perpetrator is 6 in 10,000, or 1 per 1,667 people. Not perfect, but better than ABO typing alone. Though too involved to cover in this book, there are several other blood enzymes and proteins that can be used in a similar manner to further whittle at the suspect list. DNA testing, which will be discussed in the next chapter, can then be used to further individualize the sample.

PATERNITY TESTING

Each of us inherits our blood type from our parents, which allows the serologist to use ABO blood typing to assess paternity in many cases. To understand how this works, let's look at a thumbnail sketch of some genetics basics.

BASIC GENETICS

Essentially all of our cells contain genetic material, which we call DNA. Our DNA is packed into units we call **genes**, which are the basic units of inheritance. The genes are arranged on thread-like structures we call **chromosomes**. Humans have forty-six chromosomes that are arranged into twenty-three pairs. On each chromosome every gene has its own specific location, which we call a **locus** (pleural is **loci**). When the chromosomes pair up, so do these loci. This means that our genes pair up in what is called an **allelic pair**.

Each of the genes in an allelic pair can be, and usually are, different. And they usually possess different "strengths." That is, one will have a greater say in the particular trait governed by the pair than will the other. We call the stronger of the two **dominant** and the weaker **recessive**. So in any gene pair, one gene may be dominant and the other recessive. Some genes are of equal strength and are termed **co-dominant**, meaning that they are equally powerful in their expression and neither "takes a back seat."

Blood Type Inheritance

There are two other important terms to consider. **Phenotype** is what we look like physically or how a gene is expressed. **Genotype** is what our genes are like. In blood grouping, the phenotype is simply the blood type. This can be A, B, AB, or O. But this blood type does not tell us the genotype, or what gene alleles the person actually possesses.

Our ABO blood groups, or phenotypes, come in only four types: A, B, AB, O. But, for some of these four types there are two possible gene pairings, or genotypes. It is important to know that in this system, A and B are co-dominant while O is recessive. This means that a person who receives an A gene from one parent and an O gene from the other will have type A blood, but not type O, since the A gene is dominant.

At conception, we receive one ABO gene from each parent and this allelic pairing of genes (genotype) determines what blood type (phenotype) we will express.

PHENOTYPE	POSSIBLE GENOTYPES
A	AA or AO
B	BB or BO
AB	AB
O	OO

As you can see, individuals with type O blood must have an OO genotype. They can't possess either an A or a B gene since this would dominate the O gene and produce either type A or type B blood, respectively. This means that they received an O gene from each parent.

A type A person could have received an A gene from each parent (and thus would be an AA genotype) or an A gene from one and an O gene from the other (an AO genotype). Remember, A is the dominant allele, so when it is paired with the recessive O gene, the A gene is the one that is expressed. Outwardly, the AA and the AO individual would be the same in that each would have type A blood when tested. But genetically, they would be different. One would have an AA allelic pairing and the other an AO.

From this you can see that a type A parent who is AA can only give an A gene to their offspring since all their eggs or sperm have an A gene. But, a type A parent who is AO could give either an A or an O gene since half their eggs or sperm would be A and the other half O. If both parents are type A, there are several possibilities for the genotype, and thus the phenotype, of their offspring. These are:

Both parents AA:	Child must be AA
One parent AA and other AO	Child can be either AA or AO
Both parents AO	Child can be AA, AO, or OO

The same situation exists if both parents are type B. Simply substitute B for A in the above pairings.

If both parents are type O (genotype by definition OO), they can only have type O (genotype OO) children, since neither has an A nor a B gene to donate.

DETERMINING PATERNITY

Blood typing can exclude paternity, but cannot absolutely verify it. For example, a man with type AB blood could not father a child with type O blood. If the child in question possessed type O blood (genotype OO), the type AB man (genotype AB) could not be the father of the child and he would be excluded from consideration. A type A (genotype AA or AO) man could be the father, but only if he were an AO genotype. If he were AA, he would also be excluded. But, even if he is AO, he still may not be the father. He simply cannot be excluded.

Another genetic marker, the human leukocyte antigen (HLA), can also be useful in paternity testing. HLA is the same antigen that plays a major role in matching transplant donors with recipients. If the father and child share the same HLA markers, there is a 90 percent chance of paternity. If testing combines HLA and ABO typing with another genetic marker called haptoglobin, the accuracy approaches 95 percent.

However, DNA matching, which offers 99 percent certainty when properly done, is the gold standard for assessing paternity.

OTHER BODY FLUIDS

Though blood is the most common biological fluid found at the crime scene, semen, saliva, and, rarely, vaginal fluid are also seen. During sexual assaults, the attacker's semen and saliva are commonly transferred to the victim, the victim's clothing, or nearby surfaces. Saliva can be obtained from the stamp and envelope of a threatening letter or an extortion or ransom note. Cigarette butts and food items found at crime scenes can yield saliva from which DNA can be obtained. Even tearstains have yielded usable DNA.

But before these materials can reach the lab and undergo analysis, they must be located. Sometimes stains are apparent; other times they are invisible to the naked eye. The first and simplest step in locating these fluids is an examination of the crime scene with an **alternative light source (ALS)**. This simply means any light source that isn't standard ambient sun or room light. Under alternative sources, such as laser or ultraviolet light, these fluids will often fluoresce (glow).

Once located, these materials must be carefully collected and preserved. If the sample is moist, it must be air dried before packaging, since moist, biological materials are susceptible to putrefaction from bacterial growth. If already dried, the sample can simply be packaged. For example, if panties are found at the scene of an alleged rape, they will be collected for analysis. If a stain is seen and it is dry, the garment can be packaged for transport. If still damp, it is hung up, allowed to dry, and then placed in a paper evidence bag. Plastic is not used since it tends to hold any residual moisture and can cause decay of the sample, where a paper bag will "breathe" somewhat.

Let's look at how several common biological fluids are located, identified, and analyzed.

SEMEN

Semen is an exclusively male fluid that comes from ejaculation. It consists of fluids from the seminal vesicles and the prostate gland as well as spermatozoa. There is an exception, however. The semen of men who suffer from **oligospermia** (low sperm count) or **azoospermia** (no sperm) may possess little or no sperm. The same is true if the man has undergone a successful vasectomy.

At the scene of a sexual assault (see Chapter Seven: Bodily Harm, "Rape Investigation"), a search for semen includes the corpse (in cases of murder), underwear, condoms, bed sheets, mattresses, carpeting, and flooring. In the case of a corpse, all body orifices are tested for semen residue. The victim's clothing is collected, dried if necessary, and placed in clean paper bags for transport. The same is done with the suspect's clothing (if one is identified) as well as bed sheets or the surface where the assault occurred (if possible). Sofas, countertops, carpets, car seats, and other places where rape could have occurred may not be easily transported. Sometimes an entire sofa or car seat will be taken to the lab; other times sections of carpet or a countertop may be removed.

As discussed in Chapter Seven, it is important that a living victim undergo a rape exam by a physician. The sooner after the event this is done, the better, as biological evidence tends to degrade and diminish over time. The physician performing the exam looks for and documents any signs of trauma or orifice penetration. All samples taken are documented and controlled by a police officer so that the chain of evidence remains unbroken.

As with other testing, the tests for semen are either presumptive or confirmatory. Presumptive testing is based on the fact that semen contains a very high level of the enzyme acid phosphatase. Confirmatory testing relies on demonstrating the presence of spermatozoa or prostate-specific antigen (PSA).

Presumptive Testing: The Brentamine Fast Blue Test

Acid phosphatase (AP) enzymes are a class of proteins that are very common in nature and are found in many animals and plants. Semen contains a high level of acid phosphatase, which is produced by the seminal vesicles. This type of acid phosphatase, called **seminal AP (SAP)**, was discovered in 1935 by W. Kutscher and H. Wolbergs. When SAP is found in a crime-scene fluid sample or stain, it provides presumptive evidence that semen is indeed present. Unfortunately, certain fruit and vegetable juices such as watermelon and cauliflower,

---

some fungi, contraceptive creams, and even vaginal fluid itself can give a false-positive acid phosphatase test.

Many methods for semen identification have been devised over the years, but the Brentamine Fast Blue test is currently the primary presumptive test used. Typically, a moist cotton swab or piece of filter paper is used to collect the sample, which is then treated with a combination of alpha-naphthyl phosphate and Brentamine Fast Blue. If a bright purple color appears within two minutes, the test is positive. The above-mentioned substances that can lead to a false positive tend to react very slowly, while SAP reacts quickly. If the color change is strong and occurs within thirty seconds, the identification of semen is virtually certain.

Other, less-used, presumptive tests search for the presence of two other components of semen: **spermine** and **choline**. Each of these tests is positive if crystals form after the sample is exposed to certain chemicals. The **Florence test** uses potassium triiodide and tests for choline while the **Barberio test** uses picric acid and tests for spermine. If either of these tests is positive, semen is likely present.

Confirmatory Testing

If one of the presumptive tests suggests the presence of semen, one or more of the confirmatory tests are then done. The two most commonly used are microscopic examination and prostate-specific antigen.

Microscopic Examination

Since spermatozoa are present only in semen, finding them is absolute proof that semen is present. Antony Van Leeuwenhoek first described the presence of spermatozoa in semen in 1679 and by the mid-1980s finding motile sperm was the method of choice for semen identification. It remains so today.

The sample is placed on a microscope slide and treated with one of several stains. A commonly used one is a combination of **nuclear fast red** solution and **picroindigocarmine (PIC)**, which stains the spermatozoa red and makes them readily visible. The viewer typically will see a combination of intact and fragmented spermatozoa. The finding of a single sperm or sperm head confirms that the sample is semen.

The sperm do not have to be motile (moving), merely present. In the living victim, motility of sperm is usually lost within four to six hours after the semen is deposited.

Prostate-Specific Antigen (PSA)

If no spermatozoa are seen, the examiner must resort to testing for **prostate-specific antigen (PSA or p30)**, which is highly concentrated in semen. It was first identified as a useful test for semen in 1978 by George Sensabaugh.

Testing involves an antigen-antibody reaction and is quick and simple. When PSA is found, it confirms the presence of semen. Though vasectomy and one of the low-sperm-count syndromes mentioned above may markedly reduce or completely eliminate spermatozoa from the semen, it has no effect on the PSA level. This is because PSA is produced in the prostate gland, which lies "downstream" from where the vasectomy procedure is done.

This test is highly specific for semen and is very sensitive in that very old semen stains can often be analyzed for PSA. In many cases, even if the clothing or bed sheets have been washed, PSA can still be detected.

Once the presence of semen is confirmed, the serologist attempts to match the semen to a particular individual by using ABO blood typing and DNA analysis. Usable DNA depends on whether the sample is damaged or degraded, and ABO blood typing requires that the perpetrator be a secretor.

Secretor Status

A **secretor** is someone who secretes his ABO proteins in other body fluids. A **non-secretor** does not. Approximately 80 to 85 percent of individuals are secretors. Their body fluids, including seminal fluid, saliva, and tears, contain proteins that reflect their ABO blood type. Non-secretors have no such proteins in these fluids. In rape cases, the material swabbed from the vagina of the victim is a mixture of fluids from the victim and the attacker. The ABO types found in this fluid can be used much as blood typing to eliminate a suspect in a rape, but cannot accurately identify him.

Secretors with blood type A secrete type A antigens in their saliva, semen, vaginal secretions, and other body fluids; blood type B persons secrete type B antigens; blood type AB individuals secrete both A and B antigens; and persons with type O blood secrete neither. Non-secretors, likewise, secrete no antigens, so in this regard they are similar to type O individuals. Non-secretors may have any of the four blood types, but since they do not secrete their ABO antigens in their body fluids, their blood type cannot be determined without a blood sample.

It is important to note that secretor status has no bearing on whether DNA testing can be done. DNA can be obtained from the semen of both secretors and non-secretors.

Let's suppose that a rape victim is a secretor of type B, while the prime suspect is a secretor of type A. Let's further suppose that semen is found in the victim's vaginal swab and when tested shows only type B antigens. These B antigens could have come from the victim, the perpetrator, or both. But, the prime suspect is not the attacker since he is a type A secretor and would have left behind type A antigens. He is exonerated and the police must now search for a suspect who is type B, type O, or a non-secretor. That is, the perpetrator either left behind B antigens (type B) or no antigens at all (type O or non-secretor status). In the later case, the B antigens found would be from the victim.

Similarly, if the victim is a type A secretor and the vaginal swab reveals types A and B, the perpetrator must be either type B or type AB. He cannot be type O or a non-secretor, since the type B antigen could not have come from the victim and must have come from the attacker.

If the victim is type O and no antigens are found in the vaginal smears, then the perpetrator must be either type O or a non-secretor. If he were a secretor of type A, type B, or type AB, he would have left antigens behind.

If the vaginal material matches the ABO group of the suspect, he cannot be eliminated, but neither can he be convicted. For example, if the victim is type A and the vaginal sample shows only type A and the suspect is a type A secretor, he cannot be eliminated from the suspect list. He could be the perpetrator, but so could anyone who is a type A or type O or a non-secretor. In the case of a type A suspect, the type A antigens found in the vaginal swabs could come from both him and the victim, while in the case of a type O secretor or a non-secretor, all of the type A antigens would have come from the victim.

Thus, secretor antigen matching is similar to blood typing. It can eliminate someone but cannot conclusively identify him as the assailant. It is too crude a test. DNA testing must be employed to make a conclusive match (see Chapter Ten).

Time Since Intercourse

The timing of sexual intercourse or rape is often critical in forensics and courtroom proceedings. An accurate determination can implicate or exonerate a suspect. But, can the time lapse since intercourse be accurately determined? The short answer is not often.

In living victims, the duration of sperm motility is from four to six hours. If motile sperm are found in vaginal swabs, the sexual act likely occurred less than six hours earlier. After that, the sperm die and begin to break down and fragment, and timing becomes a guessing game. First the tails are lost, leaving behind sperm heads, and then the heads and tails undergo fragmentation and destruction. The survival of sperm heads and sperm remnants in various body orifices is extremely variable, so that no accurate timeline can be established. In general, these remnants may remain in the vagina for up to six or seven days, the rectum for two to three days, and the mouth less than twenty-four hours. In cases of rape-homicide, sperm may remain in the vagina of the corpse for up to two weeks.

Elevated SAP levels can be found in the vagina for up to seventy-two hours.

Semen is a fairly resilient substance. Laundering and dry cleaning of stained clothing may or may not remove all traces of PSA and SAP, and traces of spermatozoa can sometimes be found on microscopic examination of the laundered material. If protected from extremes of temperature, harsh chemicals, and other unfavorable environmental conditions, dried semen stains may remain identifiable and usable for DNA analysis for many years.

So why is the timing of intercourse so important? Suppose a woman accuses a man she had been dating of rape. She goes to the police and states that he came to her house and forced her to have sex and that this happened just two hours earlier. She is taken for a rape exam and the man is detained for questioning. He states they last had sex two days earlier and that it was consensual. The woman confirms that encounter. If motile sperm are found, her story holds. If only heads and fragments are found, then questions are raised about her story, and his story is confirmed. Mostly.

What if he raped her but did not ejaculate or used a condom? There would be no fresh sperm, only that left from two days earlier. Rape or no rape? Unfortunately, forensic science can't resolve this. Only a judge and jury can.

VAGINAL FLUIDS

The detection of vaginal fluids is difficult but may be important in non-ejaculatory rapes and penetrations with foreign objects. Swabs can be taken from the suspect's penis or from any suspected foreign object. Testing depends on the finding of glycogen-containing epithelial cells. Epithelial cells line the vagina and glycogen is a starch that is stored within the cell.

Periodic acid-Schiff (PAS) reagent stains glycogen a bright magenta color. If epithelial cells rich in glycogen are exposed to PAS, their cytoplasm (the liquid part of the cell) will show the magenta staining. In cases of object rape, the object used is swabbed and any material obtained is spread onto a glass slide. It is then stained with PAS and viewed under a microscope. If cells with bright magenta staining are seen, the material obtained is likely vaginal fluid.

The problem with this test is that even if vaginal fluid is present, the test may be falsely negative. The reason for this is that not all vaginal epithelial cells contain glycogen. Cells from young girls before menarche contain none and those from post-menopausal women rarely do. Also, the amount of glycogen found in these cells varies with the stage of the woman's menstrual cycle. This means that a positive test is very helpful but a negative one does not necessarily mean that vaginal fluids aren't present.

SALIVA

Saliva is an important bodily fluid to the forensic examiner. It may be recovered from everything from stamps to food to bite marks. It may reveal ABO antigens, and thus blood type in secretors and may yield enough DNA for profiling.

Saliva is a digestive fluid that begins to break down carbohydrates into simpler sugars as a person chews food. Amylase is the enzyme that accomplishes this task. As with the acid phosphotase class of enzymes, amylase enzymes are found in many animals and plants.

Testing for saliva involves testing for the presence of alpha-amylase, the primary amylase found in saliva. There is no confirmatory test for saliva, only presumptive ones. The two most common use iodine and the Phadebas reagent.

Starch-Iodine Test

The starch-iodine test has been used for over one hundred years, but is rarely used today. It is simple and easy to do and depends upon two facts: iodine will turn a starch (carbohydrate) blue and alpha-amylase breaks down a starch.

Testing is done with an agar gel plate that contains a starch. Several wells are cut into the gel and then iodine is poured over the plate. The Iodine reacts with the starch in the gel and turns it blue. The suspect sample is then placed into one of the wells. If amylase is present, it gradually breaks down the starch as it diffuses through the gel, causing the blue color to fade in a circular pattern around the well. Unfortunately, this test is neither sensitive nor specific. It does not detect low concentrations of amylase, and since amylase is found in other body fluids, a positive reaction does not absolutely indicate the presence of saliva.

Phadebas Reagent

Phadebas reagent is an insoluble complex composed of a starch bound to a dye molecule. The complex is not soluble, so when it is placed in a liquid it does not dissolve and does not impart any color to the liquid. But amylase breaks down the complex and releases the dye, which is soluble and adds color to the liquid. The more amylase that is present, the more dye that is released, and the darker the liquid medium becomes. The degree of color change is measured by a spectrophotometer, which is an instrument that accurately measures color changes in liquids. The greater the color change, the higher the concentration of amylase in the sample and the more likely that it is saliva.

DNA:
YOUR PERSONAL CODE

DNA, or **deoxyribonucleic acid**, is a relative newcomer to the world of forensic science. It is also an incredibly useful tool for identification. In fact,
only DNA and fingerprints (see Chapter Twelve: Fingerprints) are absolutely
individualizing as no two people have ever been found to share the same DNA
or fingerprints. Except for identical twins, that is. They possess identical DNA
but different fingerprints. No one knows why their fingerprints are different,
but they are.

Our understanding of DNA and its uses in both medicine and forensics is a
rapidly evolving field. And like the blood chemistry discussed in the previous
chapter, it is an extremely complex subject to grasp. In this chapter, I will attempt to simplify it a bit and give you some degree of understanding how this
valuable and exciting field impacts the world of forensics.

WHAT IS DNA?

Your body is made up of approximately sixty trillion cells. Each of these cells,
with the exception of the red blood cells (RBCs) in your blood, contains a
nucleus, and it is within the nucleus that your DNA resides.

The human body has cells of many types: heart cells, brain cells, blood cells,
liver cells … you get the idea. And each of these cell types has a specific function

and works in concert with one another to produce a functional human being. But how do all these cells know what they're supposed to do? They have an instruction manual that tells them what type of cell they are and exactly what they are supposed to do. This instruction manual comes in the form of the DNA molecule.

Some of our DNA is packaged into units called **genes**. These are the basic units of heredity. The genes are in turn arranged along a long structure called a **chromosome**. Humans possess forty-six chromosomes arranged into twenty-three pairs. These pairs are numbered 1 through 22, with the final two being the sex chromosomes, called X and Y.

The DNA molecule is a polymer (long string of repeating components) of smaller molecules called **purine bases**. Though many different purine bases exist, only four are involved in the production of DNA: **guanine**, **cytosine**, **thymine**, and **adenine**. Scientists typically refer to these by their first letter: G, C, T, and A. All life is based on these four molecules.

The number of bases strung together in any given DNA strand can be in the millions or billions, and they can hook up in any conceivable order. The order in which these are linked determine the message contained within the DNA. The highly variable nature of this pattern is what makes DNA so useful for identification.

DNA is **double-stranded**, which means that it consists of paired strands (polymers) of these bases that are wound together in a double helix, a spiral-like structure. It looks like a twisted ladder (see Figure 10-1). When these bases pair up to form a double strand, each strand is a mirror image of its mate. The reason is that rules of **base pairing** dictate that C only binds with G, and A only with T. It has to do with the size and shape of these bases, but digging deeper into that is not necessary for you to understand how DNA is used in the forensic world.

Using these rules, a section of double-stranded DNA might look like this:

A-T-C-C-G-C-T-T-A

T-A-G-G-C-G-A-A-T

The term **genome** is used to refer to the total DNA within a cell. Each person has approximately three billion base pairs in his DNA—that's six billion bases in all. Since these bases can be put together in any order, the possible base sequences for any given DNA strand is literally astronomical. This is the basic reason that we are all different and the reason DNA typing (DNA fingerprinting) in the forensics lab is so accurate.

But, do we use all of our genome? The answer is yes, and no. Each DNA strand is made up of two different types of DNA: **Genes**, which make up about 5 percent of our DNA and determine our genetic characteristics and inheritance, and what is called **non-encoded DNA**, which makes up the other 95 percent. This non-encoded DNA is also affectionately called **junk DNA**.

This junk DNA supports and affects certain gene functions. And it is the DNA that is of most interest to the forensic scientist.

THE INDIVIDUALITY OF DNA

Genetic individuality is fixed at conception when a person receives half of his chromosomes, and thus his DNA, from each parent. The mother donates one chromosome from each of her twenty-three pairs to each egg she produces. Which member of each pair she donates is independent of which member of every other pair she donates. If we consider each member of the twenty-three pairs as either A or B, she would have a Chromosome 1A and 1B, Chromosome 2A and 2B, and so on. One egg could possess all A's, another all B's, another half A's and half B's, or any combination of A's and B's.

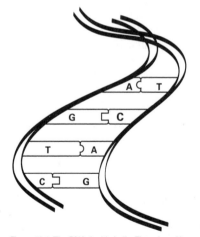

Figure 10-1: The DNA double helix. The rules of base pairing dictate that cytosine (C) must pair with guanine (G), and adenine (A) must pair with thymine (T). This pairing holds the "twisted ladder" together.

For example, one egg could be AB-BAABBA, etc., while another could be BBAABBAAA, etc. Since each chromosome has two choices (A or B) and since they are independent of one another, the possible combinations are 2 multiplied by itself 23 times. That is, $2 \times 2 = 4$; $4 \times 2 = 8$; $8 \times 2 = 16$, etc. Do this 23 times and you'll see that the mother can produce 8,388,608 different types of eggs.

Of course, the father can produce the same number of different types of sperm. Add to this that any of these eight million sperm types can combine with any of the mother's eight million egg types to produce a fertilized egg and the possibilities become huge. In fact, there are more than eight trillion possible combinations. No wonder you don't look like your sister.

It's this diversity that allows the forensic scientist to identify a perpetrator or exonerate a suspect with such a high degree of accuracy. This discriminatory power was first exposed to the public in the famous Colin Pitchfork case.

FORENSIC CASE FILES: THE COLIN PITCHFORK CASE

In 1983, fifteen-year-old Lynda Mann was brutally raped and murdered near the rural English town of Narborough. In 1986, Dawn Ashworth, also fifteen years old, met a similar fate, sending a cold panic through the community. When the police investigation hit a wall, local officials decided to try the new technique of DNA matching, which had just been developed by Dr. Alec Jeffreys at the University of Leicester. The police believed that the killer lived and worked in the area, so they asked all males in the area to submit a blood sample for testing. After screening several thousand samples, no match was made. Then, a man came forward and told police that a co-worker had persuaded him to give a blood sample in his place. The man's name was Colin Pitchfork. In 1987, the police obtained a sample from Pitchfork, a match was made, and he confessed. In 1988 he was sentenced to life in prison. This was the first time that mass DNA screening had been used to solve a criminal case.

DNA AND THE FORENSIC SCIENTIST

For many years forensic scientists searched for a method to absolutely identify an individual from materials left at a crime scene. Fingerprints were the first discovery that provided such positive proof. But fingerprints aren't found at every crime scene. Some criminals wear gloves or wipe prints from any objects they might have touched.

However, DNA-containing materials are frequently left at crime scenes without the perpetrator's knowledge. Since DNA is found in essentially every cell in the body, virtually any biological material from the criminal will reveal the perpetrator's identity. Blood, semen, saliva, hair, skin, sweat, and tears can each contain DNA evidence.

Let's look at how DNA became such a powerful forensic tool.

DNA MILESTONES

Swiss biologist Friedrich Miescher (1844–1895) first discovered DNA in 1868, but it was many years before it was truly understood what DNA was and what it did. In 1943, while working with bacteria, Oswald Avery (1877–1955), Colin MacLeod (1909–1972), and Maclyn McCarty (1911–2005) discovered that DNA carried genetic information, and in 1953, James Watson (1928–), Francis Crick (1916–2004), and Maurice Wilkins (1916–2004) elucidated the double-helical structure of the DNA molecule.

As scientists continued to analyze this molecule, it became apparent that all humans, and indeed all primates, share a large amount of the genome. This means that much of your DNA is exactly like everyone else's and also identical to that of the chimpanzees in the local zoo. If this is the case, how can DNA be used to distinguish one person from another? The key is that we share a "large amount" of the genome, but not all.

In 1984, Alec Jeffreys (1950–) and his associates at the University of Leicester discovered that each person's DNA was actually unique. By using special restriction enzymes (more on these later) that cut DNA into shorter pieces, they found that certain areas of this long DNA molecule exhibited **polymorphism** (many different forms). It turns out that these variable areas are unique in each of us, and it is the analysis of these areas that allows discrimination of one individual from another. Shortly after discovering this polymorphism, Jeffreys developed a process for isolating and analyzing these areas of human DNA. He termed this analysis **DNA fingerprinting**. It is also called DNA typing.

DNA evidence first entered a U.S. courtroom in 1985 and the first conviction based on DNA evidence in the world was in 1987 (see "Forensic Case Files: The Colin Pitchfork Case").

DNA POLYMORPHISM

DNA polymorphism is found in non-encoded junk DNA. These areas are highly variable in length and base sequence, and this is what is important to forensic DNA typing. The reason is that it has been found that certain base sequences within the non-encoded DNA segments are constantly repeated. These repeating sequences are called **satellites** or, depending on their size, **minisatellites** or **microsatellites**. These satellite sequences repeat throughout a specific location (called a locus) within the strand. Since these segments are of variable length and repeat along the length of the DNA strand a variable number of times, they are called **variable number tandem repeats (VNTRs)**.

Before we look at how these repetitive satellite sequences are used, I want to introduce a different type satellite sequence known as **short tandem repeats (STRs)**, which have further increased the discriminatory power of DNA.

STRs are tandem repeats similar to VNTRs except that they are much shorter and repeat frequently throughout the DNA chain. Also, there are many more known STRs than there are VNTRs, which gives the forensic scientist more repeats to analyze.

The length of the repeated sequence in a VNTR may be hundreds of base pairs long, but the repeating sequence in an STR is only three to seven bases long. And STRs repeat over segments of the DNA strand that is four hundred or less bases long. This means that by using STRs, even degraded or damaged DNA samples can be used for testing (discussed later in this chapter).

THE DNA FINGERPRINTING PROCESS

DNA fingerprinting or typing is complex and not easy to grasp. There are numerous techniques available and even more on the horizon as research into this field is ongoing. We'll consider the basics of some of the more common techniques—one old, two current, and one future.

The oldest DNA analysis method still in use is called **restriction fragment length polymorphism (RFLP)**. The major problem with RFLP is that it requires a rather large DNA sample that is of good quality. For this reason, many labs now use the combination of **polymerase chain reaction (PCR)** and short tandem repeats as their method for DNA analysis. As we will see, this process is automated in more sophisticated labs through a process known as **multiplexing**. Here several STRs are extracted and amplified at the same time. This allows the lab to define a number of different DNA markers in a very short period of time.

The future of DNA testing may lie in **single nucleotide polymorphism (SNP)**, where the level of differentiation falls to a single base. This technique can be easily automated, which makes it a very efficient method.

Let's look at these methods in more detail.

RESTRICTION FRAGMENT LENGTH POLYMORPHISM

This is an older, more expensive, more time-consuming, and less accurate method for DNA analysis, but it is still in use. The basic steps in RFLP are:

- DNA extraction
- DNA fragmentation and amplification
- fragment separation
- fragment transfer
- fragment tagging and visualization
- pattern matching

DNA EXTRACTION: Before the lab can analyze the DNA, it must be separated from the material that contains it. Since the DNA resides within the nuclei of the cells, it must be extracted from the cells without damaging the DNA itself. There are many methods for accomplishing this, and none are particularly better than any other. The type of tissue to be analyzed and the particular lab performing the procedure determine which method is used.

These procedures usually employ protein-destroying enzymes called **proteases**. These enzymes break down the proteins of the cell wall and other cellular structures, but do not harm the DNA, which is not a protein. The sample is mixed with a solution of salt, detergent, and a protease enzyme. The enzyme digests (breaks down) the proteins of the cells and releases the DNA into the solution. An organic solvent such as **chloroform** or **phenol** is added. The DNA is soluble in the water solution, while the protein fragments are soluble in the organic solvent. The two solvents separate—as does vinegar and oil salad dressing—with the water solvent, which contains the DNA, layering out over the denser organic one. Alcohol is then added to the DNA-water solution. This precipitates out the DNA, which is filtered. It is now ready to use.

DNA FRAGMENTATION AND AMPLIFICATION: The long DNA strands are then fragmented into smaller portions using a **restriction enzyme**, which cuts the strand at predictable locations. The location chosen is one not involved in the VNTR repeating pattern, since preservation of this pattern is necessary for determining the number of repeats. The original DNA molecule, which might be a million bases in length, is cut into fragments that might be one hundred to ten thousand bases long.

FRAGMENT SEPARATION: The fragments are separated using gel electrophoresis (see the appendix), which separates them according to size. The shorter the fragment, the faster and farther it will migrate through the gel. The reason is that the longer fragments meet more resistance as they move through the gel than the shorter ones do. In this way, the fragments are separated into groups, which will appear as bands according to length.

FRAGMENT TRANSFER: THE SOUTHERN BLOT: Now that the DNA fragments have been separated into bands so that they can be compared with other DNA samples, they have to be transferred to a medium where they can be handled. A gel simply won't work. Ever tried to pick up Jell-O? It's not an easy thing to do since gelatin isn't very sturdy. So how can we store, preserve, and compare two samples of gel? Enter Edward Southern and his technique, which bears his name: the Southern blot.

In this process, which is similar to mopping up a spill with a paper towel, a sturdy nylon membrane is placed on top of the gel. The DNA bands on the gel transfer to the nylon, retaining their positions relative to one another so that the all-important pattern of the bands is unaltered.

FRAGMENT TAGGING AND VISUALIZATION: Now that the DNA has been moved to a sturdier environment, the bands must be made visible. This is accomplished using radioisotope probes, which are simply DNA fragments tagged with a radioactive isotope such as phosphorus 32 (P-32). After the probes are attached, the nylon membrane is placed between two sheets of X-ray film and an **autoradiograph (autorad)** is made.

An autorad makes use of a standard sheet of X-ray film, but unlike the X-ray you get at the doctor's office, no external X-rays are needed. The radioactive isotopes in the tagged probe constantly release radiation that will expose the film just as X-rays will. The exposed film now reveals the band pattern of the DNA sample. This produces the familiar DNA fingerprint pattern (see Figure 10-2). It's like a personal bar code.

The autorad gives you a picture of the DNA fragment pattern at a particular locus. This alone will not give you conclusive match, since some people share similar patterns at a single locus. It may, however, exclude a suspect. When comparing a known and an unknown DNA sample, if any band in the RFLP au-

DNA fingerprint

Figure 10-2: The DNA fingerprint. Electrophoresis separates DNA sample fragments according to size, which results in columns of bands that can be compared with other samples.

torad doesn't match, the two samples in question did not come from the same person. To make a match, multiple loci must be examined. We'll look more deeply into why multiple loci are needed later.

PATTERN MATCHING

When the forensic lab must match one or more samples, the electrophoretic gel is divided into several parallel columns called lanes. A DNA sample is placed at the beginning of each lane. When the electrophoresis process begins, the fragments in each lane move and separate independent of each other. This causes each sample to separate into a series of bands determined by the size of the various fragments in each sample. A match is made when the bands in the known and unknown columns match. This comparison can be done visually or with the aid of a computer.

The samples placed at the head of each column vary. Some may be control materials, such as DNA from bacteria, viruses, or lab-synthesized DNA. These are DNA samples with fragments of known size and can be used to estimate the size of fragments in any unknown samples. More importantly, one column contains the crime scene specimen and other columns contain samples from any suspects.

For example, let's say that a perpetrator shed blood at the scene of a homicide and the crime lab found and collected it. This constitutes an "unknown" sample since its origin is not known. If the suspect list includes two people, the lab takes samples from each. These are "known" samples since their origin is known. DNA fingerprinting is then used to compare the suspects' DNA with the "unknown" crime scene DNA (see Figure 10-3).

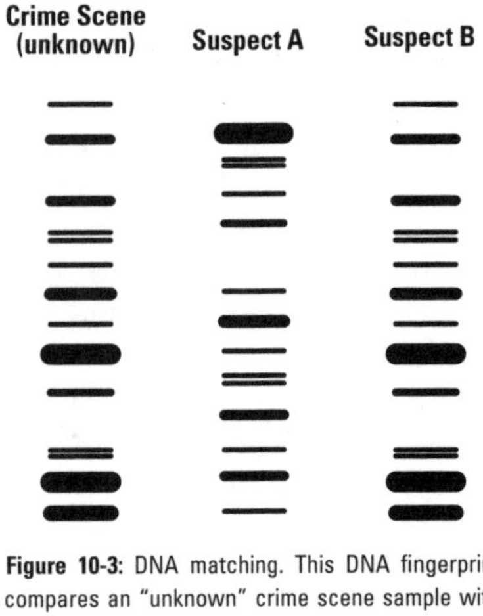

By comparing this one locus, suspect A can be excluded. This is not his DNA. A single mismatch at any

Figure 10-3: DNA matching. This DNA fingerprint compares an "unknown" crime scene sample with "known" samples taken from suspect A and suspect B. It should be apparent that the crime scene DNA did not come from suspect A, but could have come from suspect B.

locus is exclusionary. But what of suspect B? The pattern matches his DNA profile for that locus; therefore, the sample obtained at the crime scene could be his. Testing more loci will prove or disprove this.

But RFLP is on the way out as a DNA test and has yielded to the combination of polymerase chain reaction and short tandem repeat.

THE POLYMERASE CHAIN REACTION

The polymerase chain reaction (PCR) arrived on the forensic scene in 1992. This technique allows for repeatedly copying the DNA in a sample so that a larger quantity of identical DNA can be made. This process is called **amplification**. It requires as little as a billionth of a gram of DNA material.

PCR takes advantage of the method by which double-stranded DNA replicates itself in nature. Let's say that the crime scene DNA sample is a single hair follicle. Let's represent the DNA extracted from the cells of the follicle as the following:

A-T-C-C-G-C-T-T-A

T-A-G-G-C-G-A-A-T

Obviously, the actual strand would be much longer than this, but we'll use this shorter segment since, for our purposes, it is more easily visualized. PCR involves several steps: denaturing, annealing, extending, and repeating.

Denaturing is the separation of the double-stranded DNA into its two component strands. Before each strand can be copied, it must be separated from its mate. This is accomplished by heating the sample to 94°C to 96°C. The result looks like this:

A-T-C-C-G-C-T-T-A + heat =A-T-C-C-G-C-T-T-A

T-A-G-G-C-G-A-A-T

T-A-G-G-C-G-A-A-T

Annealing is the process of "priming" the copying process. Basically it's a jump-start. Short primer DNA sequences are added to the DNA sample and it is heated to 55°C to 72°C. This initiates, or primes, the duplication reaction. After attachment of the primer segments, the strands might look like this:

A-T-C-C-G-C-T-T-A   (original strand)

T-A-G-G   (primer strand)

```
A-T-C-C                  (primer strand)
T-A-G-G-C-G-A-A-T        (original strand)
```

Extending is the completion of the duplication process. Each strand is induced to manufacture its complementary strand by use of a **DNA polymerase enzyme**. This is the same type of enzyme that occurs naturally in the body. As in the body, each DNA strand serves as the template for synthesizing its complementary strand, resulting in two identical double-stranded DNA molecules.

```
A-T-C-C-G-C-T-T-A        (original strand)
T-A-G-G-C-G-A-A-T        (complementary strand)


A-T-C-C-G-C-T-T-A        (complementary strand)
T-A-G-G-C-G-A-A-T        (original strand)
```

You can see that the original single molecule of double-stranded DNA is now two identical copies.

Repeating the above three steps over and over rapidly multiplies the number of strands available for testing: 2 become 4, then 8, then 16, 32, 64, ... etc.

Very quickly the original DNA sample grows into a more usable amount. This allows for DNA testing of even extremely small samples. In many modern labs this process is automated and relatively quick.

SHORT TANDEM REPEAT

This technique was introduced in 1994. Short tandem repeats (STRs) are repeating microsatellites of DNA that are most often only four base pairs long, though they can range from three to seven. Their short sequence, multiple polymorphic types, and frequent repetition make them highly discriminatory and useful when the DNA sample of partially degraded or fragmented.

The combination of PCR and STR has become the standard in most labs. The advantages are many. It requires much smaller samples and is faster and more reliable than RFLP. It can more easily be automated so that many samples can be done in a very short period of time. Using PCR and STR analysis allows samples to be analyzed in a couple of days as opposed to a month or more using RFLP.

The process of PCR-STR shares many of the steps we saw with RFLP. After the DNA has been extracted and fragmented, it is amplified by PCR in a **thermal cycler**, an instrument that varies the temperature throughout the repeating cycles. The fragments are then separated by gel or capillary electrophoresis, the latter making use of tiny capillary tubes. The electrophoretic device is attached to a computer, which analyzes the results and prints out the DNA profile.

Though the old bar code-looking profile can be generated by this method, the more automated STR analytic systems produce a printout that looks a bit different. Here the computer displays the STR peaks on a graph. The process of comparison is similar in that if all the peaks of the graph obtained from the analysis of two different DNA samples are identical, then the two samples share a common source (see Figure 10-4).

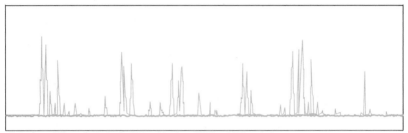

Figure 10-4: STR graph obtained with combination of PCR and STR analysis.

This process is almost fully automated now. Machines such as Applied Bio-systems' 3730 DNA Analyzer has a sample capacity of up to 384, making the analysis of many samples at once a reality.

SINGLE NUCLEOTIDE POLYMORPHISM

Single nucleotide polymorphism (SNP) is a new technique that will likely see increased use in the future. The major problem at present is that it is expensive.

We saw that RFLP fragments were fairly long, a drawback that lessens their value in degraded or damaged samples (discussed later). This problem was circumvented by the discovery of STRs, which are very short fragments. But, what if the DNA examiner could use single nucleotide bases as the standard for matching? This would increase the discriminatory power of DNA even further. This is what SNP does.

Let's say that two sequenced DNA strands looked like this:

CGATTACAGGATTA   and   CGATTACAAGATTA

If we searched for an "ATTA" STR repeat, these two strands would be indistinguishable since both have two ATTA repeats. But, with single nucleotide analysis the strands differ by a single base: The ninth base in the first sequence is guanine (G), while it is adenine (A) in the second one.

SNP can be used with restriction enzymes in the RFLP technique, or with PCR, where it can be easily automated. Theoretically, this will allow for discriminating two DNA samples based on a single nucleotide difference.

DNA'S DISCRIMINATORY POWER: A NUMBERS GAME

So, how do STRs and VNTRs work? We'll use STRs in our example since they are shorter, more discriminatory, and have replaced VNTRs in most DNA labs.

By now, you know that we each have unique DNA and we receive our DNA from each of our parents. Remember that our chromosomes are paired, one coming from each parent. This means that our DNA, which makes up our chromosomes, is also paired. And since each of these DNA strands possesses STRs, we receive STRs from both parents. Earlier we saw that there were over eight trillion possible chromosomal combinations for the child of any two parents. The same goes for STR patterns.

This means that each of us will have a variable number of STRs in any given locus of our DNA. Since the number of any given STR at any given locus can be determined, and since the number of STRs at that locus varies from person to person, we can use these facts to determine if any two DNA samples share a common source. That is, did they come from the came person?

In addition, if we know how often a given number of STR repeats is found at a locus in the general population, we can use this information to calculate the odds that the two DNA samples came from the same person. This is similar to what we saw with ABO blood typing (see Chapter Nine) where blood type AB eliminated 97 percent of the population. A single locus of STR analysis can do the same.

But, how conclusive is a match from a single locus? Not very, but if the test is repeated from several locations, the odds add up quickly. Most labs use thirteen distinct loci in their analysis.

Let's say we are dealing with a four-base-long STR such as CCTA. Let's also say that by searching a certain locus on *your* DNA we find that you received six repeats of this particular STR from one parent (one DNA strand of the pair) and eleven repeats from the other (the other DNA strand of the pair). If we checked the same locus on *my* DNA, we might find that I received five repeats of this STR from one parent and twenty-one from another. Our DNA would be very different.

But would our DNA be different from everyone else's on Earth? We couldn't tell by looking at just this one locus. There may be other people who also received six and eleven, or five and twenty-one repeats. But what if we looked at a dozen loci? What are the odds that two people would have received the exact number of repeats from each parent at each of these loci? That would happen in only one of several hundred trillion conceptions. This means that no two people have the same pattern of STR repeats and thus no two people possess identical DNA.

Let's look at another example. Say we analyze the STRs of a crime scene sample at five different loci and find the repeats at these loci as follows:

Locus 1	14 and 3
Locus 2	7 and 11
Locus 3	2 and 16
Locus 4	15 and 8
Locus 5	1 and 13

Now let's say we know that the occurrence of each of these STR repeat patterns at these loci in the general population is 1 percent, 3 percent, 2 percent, 1 percent, and 2 percent, respectively. This means that one in one hundred people share this same repeat pattern at locus 1, three in one hundred share this same repeat pattern at locus 2, and so on. If a suspect's DNA and DNA obtained at the crime scene show the exact same repeat patterns at all five loci, what are the odds that the DNA found at the scene came from someone other than the suspect? Since the inheritance of the STR patterns at each locus is independent of any other locus, the percentages (fractions) must be multiplied by each other. Like this:

$$1/100 \times 3/100 \times 2/100 \times 1/100 \times 2/100 = 12/10,000,000,000 \text{ or } 12 \text{ out of } 10 \text{ billion}$$

This means that there are only twelve chances out of ten billion, or roughly one in a billion, that the DNA found at the crime scene came from someone other than the suspect. And this was using only five loci. As we will see later, the FBI database uses thirteen loci. Now, imagine if the suspect's DNA matched the crime scene sample at thirteen loci. We would be looking at odds in the one per trillions.

Or put another way, if the STR count at all thirteen loci in a crime scene sample match the count at the same thirteen loci of the suspect sample, what are the odds that the crime scene sample came from someone other than the suspect? Astronomical would be the word.

So, DNA is a numbers game. The more loci used, the greater the odds that two matched samples share the same source.

DEGRADED DNA

Earlier, I mentioned degraded DNA. This is simply DNA that has been damaged and broken by heat, chemicals, decay, or some other process. The more degraded the sample, the more it is fragmented. Since DNA fingerprinting depends on counting the number of repeated sequences in a given locus of the DNA strand, if the DNA is already broken up, such a count becomes impossible. You can't simply put the strand back together and then count. And indeed, severely degraded DNA, which has been broken into small fragments, is of little value. But what if it is only partially degraded and the surviving fragments are fairly long?

STR analysis can still be used in many such situations. Since STRs are much shorter than VNTRs and require less lengthy DNA segments for their location and counting, the likelihood that the pattern will be disrupted is much less when STRs are used. It is for this reason that STR analysis is becoming the norm for DNA fingerprinting, and why SNP analysis might soon become the standard.

Still, if the sample is severely degraded and the lab only has a pile of very short fragments or single bases to work with, no typing can be done. Not even STR. It would be like trying to read a book in which all the sentences had been reduced to fragments and single words. *For Whom the Bell Tolls* might be indistinguishable from *The Cat in the Hat*. However, if the book were only torn into chapters, we would have little trouble distinguishing between the two. A partially degraded DNA sample would be the latter situation, while a severely degraded sample would be the former.

But with good quality DNA samples, DNA typing is highly accurate. And when analyzed properly, its discriminatory power is absolute. It will not give false results. It will give either a match or no match, but it will not point the finger of suspicion in the wrong direction.

LOCATING DNA

The first step in using DNA as a forensic tool is to locate the DNA. Without a usable sample, the crime lab will have nothing to work with, so a diligent search for DNA at the crime scene or on the victim or the suspect is critical.

DNA can be found in virtually every tissue and fluid in the human body, many of which are shed at crime scenes. Blood is the most common biological material encountered, but semen, saliva, tears, urine, bone, teeth, hair, and skin are often found at the scene, each of which can yield enough usable DNA for testing using modern techniques. Let's look at these common sources in more detail.

TISSUES: The cells of skin and other tissues contain DNA within their nuclei.

BLOOD: The red blood cells of the blood have no nuclei, so they have no DNA, but the white blood cells do. When the lab extracts DNA from blood, it is the white blood cell DNA that is isolated for testing.

SEMEN: Semen has DNA within the spermatozoa. But if the person is azoospermic (produces no sperm) or has had a vasectomy—no sperm, no DNA. The epithelial cells that line the urethra do contain DNA. The urethra is the channel that connects the bladder to the outside; as the ejaculate moves along the urethra, it collects some of the urethral cells. The DNA in these cells can often be used to develop a DNA fingerprint.

SALIVA: Saliva itself contains no cells, but it collects the DNA-containing epithelial cells of the salivary ducts as it passes from the salivary glands to the mouth.

TEARS: Like saliva, tears contain no cells, but the epithelial cells that line the tear ducts do. These cells are carried out with the tears and can be a source of DNA.

HAIR: Hair itself contains no nuclear DNA, but the follicle cells do. Hair that has been cut or has fallen out naturally does not typically have follicular material attached and is not likely to possess nuclear DNA. But hair that has been yanked out often carries follicular material with it, and this can serve as a source for nuclear DNA. Still, the hair shaft itself contains a useful, special type of DNA called mitochondrial DNA, which we'll look at shortly.

BONE: Bones have cells called osteocytes that contain DNA. DNA can be extracted from bones, sometimes even from those that are thousands of years old.

TEETH: Teeth are very hardy and are the last part of the body to dissolve away. The enamel is hard and contains no cells, but the pulp does. These pulp cells can survive for a very long time under some fairly adverse conditions. Drilling into the teeth of even very old skeletal remains can sometimes yield usable DNA.

Since DNA resides within biological materials, it is subject to the same putrefaction process that eventually destroys all human tissues. Since bacterial growth and putrefaction progresses more rapidly in warm moist environments, the best DNA samples are those that have been adequately dried and stored in a protective container. If drying is not feasible, wet samples are frozen until analyzed. If not properly collected and protected, DNA can degrade and be unusable.

How much DNA is needed? The simple answer is the more the better. However, with the use of the PCR technique, even very small samples can yield enough DNA for typing and matching. Usable DNA can come from a single hair with a follicle from an old hairbrush; a single tear or drop of blood; saliva in a bite mark or on a toothbrush, postage stamp or envelope, food, soda cans, telephones, pens and pencils, the face-side of the perpetrator's mask; or even a tooth from a one thousand-year-old mummy. A January 2004 article in the *Journal of Forensic Science* suggested that human DNA could be extracted from maggots found on a decaying corpse up to four months after death.

The case of the famous Green River Killer shows how very small and very old DNA samples can be useful.

FORENSIC CASE FILES: THE GREEN RIVER KILLER

One of the most notorious and frightening serial killers in history was known as the Green River Killer. The moniker arose because the killer dumped his victims along the Green River near Seattle, Washington. Between 1982 and 1991, nearly fifty murders were attributed to the Green River Killer. The suspect list developed by the task force assigned to the cases was nearly as long.

In April 1987, police executed a search warrant on the premises of one of the suspects, Gary Ridgway. After obtaining evidence items from his house, they requested that he undergo a polygraph, but Ridgway refused. They then asked for a saliva sample and Ridgway complied by biting on a small square of surgical gauze. Unfortunately, the semen samples taken from many of the victims were too small for current testing procedures, so the samples, as well as Ridgway's saliva, were stored. In the mid-1990s, the combination of STR and PCR analysis appeared.

Then in 2001, the lab tested Ridgway's saliva sample obtained in 1987 along with semen samples taken from Opal Mills, Marcia Chapman, Cynthia Hinds, and Carol Christensen, all killed in 1982 or 1983. Using the new techniques of PCR and STR, the samples were amplified and compared. A match was made and Gary Ridgway was arrested and charged with four of the Green River killings. However, this case took a dramatic and controversial turn on November 5, 2003, when Ridgway plead guilty to forty-eight murders in exchange for a sentence of life without the possibility of parole, thus sparing himself a possible death sentence.

This case shows that if DNA samples are properly collected and stored, they can remain useful for decades.

TRICKY CRIMINALS AND TRICKY DISEASES

Even though this absolute individuality is well established, some clever criminals still attempt to deny this fact in the hopes of winning an acquittal or overturning a conviction. Anthony Harold Turner of Milwaukee is such an example.

FORENSIC CASE FILES: THE FAKE RAPE

In 1999, Anthony Harold Turner was convicted of rape after DNA obtained from three victims matched his DNA with a probability of three trillion to one. Turner was somewhat of a self-educated DNA expert, and denied that the DNA was his. He stated that it must have come from someone with the exact same DNA. Since Turner did not have a twin brother, he was convicted. But, as he was awaiting sentencing a woman came forward saying that she had been raped. Imagine the prosecutors' surprise when the DNA obtained from this victim also matched Turner, who was safely tucked away in jail. How could this be?

It turned out that some members of Turner's family had paid the woman fifty dollars to claim that she had been raped. Where did the semen used to stage the fake rape come from? Turner managed to smuggle it from jail in a small ketchup packet.

But let's confuse the situation a bit further. There are some people walking around with another person's DNA in their blood. This was pointed out in a case worked by Abirami Chidambaram of the Alaska State Scientific Crime Detection Laboratory in Anchorage. Semen obtained from a rape victim matched that of a man who was in jail on another charge at the time of the alleged rape. Further investigation revealed that years earlier the man had received a **bone marrow transplant** from his brother. This meant that he and his brother, who

---

was not an identical twin, now shared the same DNA in their blood. This also meant that the finger of suspicion for the rape was now directed at the brother. How is it possible for these two nonidentical twin brothers to share the same DNA in their blood cells?

Bone marrow transplants are typically done in patients' suffering from certain types of leukemia or some other blood disease. The patient is given chemotherapeutic agents that kill off all his native bone marrow cells and then bone marrow from a compatible donor is infused into the patient's vein. The bone marrow material migrates to the patient's bone marrow, sets up housekeeping, and begins cranking out blood cells. This means that the circulating blood cells now have the DNA of the donor's marrow and not that of the patient. DNA testing of the blood will thus match both the bone marrow donor and recipient, a situation that is seen naturally only in identical twins.

How can the forensic DNA examiner get around this? Test other cells from the patient. Buccal cells, or cells from any other tissue in his body, will reflect his native DNA and will not match the DNA profile of his own blood. A bone marrow transplant does not change the DNA in all the recipient's cells, only those of his bone marrow and blood.

To confuse matters even further, more recently bone marrow transplants are also done in patients in whom their native bone marrow is not completely destroyed by chemotherapy before the infusion. This means that their bone marrow will be a combination of their own and that of the donor and their blood DNA will reflect this combination of native DNA and donor DNA.

Another confusing situation arises from a rare genetic condition called **chimerism**. In Greek mythology, the Chimera was composed of parts from various animals. Descriptions of this creature vary but an example would be one with a lion's head, goat's body, and a snake's tail. In humans, a chimera results from the abnormal combination of two or more fertilized (and at times nonfertilized) eggs. Let's look a bit of basic genetics.

Fraternal twins come from two separate eggs and sperm cells. They are as different as they would be if they had been born years apart. They are twins only because they shared the same womb at the same time. **Identical** twins come from a single egg and sperm. After the egg is fertilized, it begins to divide to produce more identical cells. After the first division, if the two daughter cells pull apart and then each goes on to develop a separate fetus, the two fetuses will have the exact same DNA and will thus be identical twins.

A chimera is formed when two fertilized eggs (each egg different and each fertilized by a different sperm cell as in fraternal twins) join together and go on to produce a single fetus. Here, since the fetus is the result of two eggs and two sperm cells, the child will have two different types of DNA. It's as if two fraternal twins were blended together into one person, which is essentially what happens. As you might guess, the chimeric individual would have two distinct DNA patterns. This could greatly confuse DNA testing.

TESTING PATERNITY

ABO blood typing can be used to exclude paternity, but cannot absolutely state that the man in question is the father of the child. To establish paternity, DNA is used.

The first step in this process is to profile (fingerprint) the DNA of the mother and the child. These are then compared to the profile of the suspected father. We receive all of our DNA from our parents. We get no DNA from any other source, so the child's DNA pattern should be a combination of those of the mother's and the father's. This doesn't mean the child will have every fingerprint band that each parent possesses, but it does mean that the child cannot have a band that neither parent has. Where would it come from?

In paternity testing, if the child possesses a DNA fragment that is not present in either the mother or the suspected father, then the man is not the child's parent. This fragment must have come from someone else (the real father) and paternity for the suspect father is excluded (see Figure 10-5).

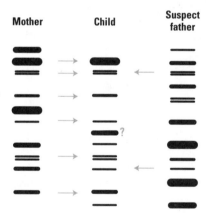

Mother Child Suspect father

Figure 10-5: DNA paternity testing. Every band in the child's DNA fingerprint must match a band from one or the other parent. If the child possesses bands that did not come from either the mother or the suspect father, the suspect father cannot be the child's parent and paternity is excluded. In this example, the child possesses a band that is not found in either the mother or the suspect father, so the suspect did not father the child.

FORENSIC CASE FILES: THE IAN SIMMS CASE

In this unusual case, paternity testing was used to obtain a criminal conviction. On February 9, 1988, Helen McCourt, a twenty-two-year-old insurance clerk in the small village of Billinge in northwest England, disappeared. She had stopped at the George and Dragon, a local pub owned by Ian Simms, to whom she may have had a romantic link. Witnesses reported hearing screams from the pub and when police confronted Simms he had several scratches on his face.

The police found a great deal of evidence: hair matching McCourt's and one of her bloody earrings in Simms's car; bloodstains on the stairway and the bedroom floor of Simms's home; and, in various areas of the county, McCourt's bloodstained coat and clothing, which also held hairs from Simms's dog and fibers from his carpet, and a length of electrical cord, which bore strands of McCourt's hair. But, McCourt's body was never found.

The problem the police faced was proving that the blood in Simms's apartment was McCourt's. With no body from which to obtain a blood sample, they turned to the girl's parents. Samples taken from her mother and father were matched against the blood found at Simms's home. At trial, Dr. Alec Jeffreys, the father of DNA fingerprinting, testified that the odds against the blood from Simms' apartment being that of anyone other than that of the daughter of the two parents was 14,500 to 1. Simms was convicted in 1989 and received a life sentence.

MITOCHONDRIAL DNA

So far, we have discussed the uses of nuclear DNA—the DNA that resides within the nuclei of our cells—but the body has other, non-nuclear forms of DNA that are extremely useful to the forensic scientist. Two of these are **mitochondrial DNA (mtDNA)** and **Y-chromosomal DNA**.

The discovery of mitochondrial DNA added an extremely useful tool to the forensic toolbox. It is useful for identification of perpetrators and human remains as well as for determination of ancestry. The first admittance of mtDNA evidence into a U.S. court occurred in *Tennessee v. Wade* in 1996.

Non-nuclear DNA is found within the **mitochondria**, small organelles that reside within the cytoplasm of the cell and serve as the cell's energy production center. A small amount of DNA is found within the mitochondria, but each cell has many mitochondria.

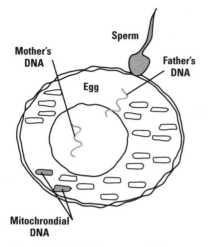

Mother's DNA

Sperm

Father's DNA

Egg

Mitochrondial DNA

Figure 10-6: The fertilization process. At fertilization, the egg supplies half of the DNA, the cell, and all the cellular structures to the fertilized zygote, while the sperm supplies only half the DNA.

Mitochondrial DNA has several characteristics that make it unique. It is passed from generation to generation by the maternal linage, mutates rarely, is found in places where nuclear DNA doesn't exist, and is exceptionally hardy.

Your mtDNA is inherited unchanged from your mother and only from your mother. And she received hers from her mother, and her mother from her mother, and so on. Why is this? At fertilization, the egg supplies the cell and half the DNA while the sperm supplies only half the DNA (see Figure 10-6). The sperm cell itself breaks down and disappears after passing its genetic material into the nucleus of the egg cell. This means that the actual cell and all the cell components (including the mitochondria) of the developing zygote come from the mother. As the cell divides and multiplies, these mitochondria are copied and passed on, generation after generation. This means that all the cells of the body contain identical mtDNA.

Since mtDNA only undergoes a significant mutation approximately once every 6,500 years, it is unchanged over many generations. This means that your mtDNA is virtually identical to your mother's, your great-great-grandmother's, and your maternal ancestors' from one thousand years ago. Thus, anyone's maternal lineage can be accurately traced over many generations and this fact can be used to prove if two people share the same maternal linage. This became important in the famous Boston Strangler case.

FORENSIC CASE FILES: THE BOSTON STRANGLER

Albert DeSalvo was convicted of the series of rapes and murders attributed to a killer known as the Boston Strangler. He confessed to many of the murders, but frequently got some of the details wrong, raising suspicion that perhaps he did not commit all the crimes he took credit for. Recently, forensic science attempted to solve this mystery.

The Strangler's last victim was Mary Sullivan. In October 2000, thirty-six years after her death, the exhumation of her body took place in Hyannis, Massachusetts. Investigators found a semen stain on her body. Tests for the presence of spermatozoa and for PSA were not possible due to degradation of the sample. However, the material did reveal the presence of mtDNA.

With DeSalvo dead and buried, blood was obtained from his brother Richard. Since the brothers should have identical mitochondrial DNA, matching the semen stain's mtDNA to Richard's would prove that Albert was indeed the killer. The result? No match. This means that even though Albert DeSalvo confessed to killing Mary Sullivan, he did not. Did he also confess to other murders that he did not commit? Was he truly the Boston Strangler? We may never know for sure, but at least in Mary Sullivan's case, he was innocent.

This case also underscores two other advantages of mtDNA. First, it is very hardy and can often be extracted from older tissues and the bones and teeth of very old skeletons. Secondly, it is found in some tissues where nuclear DNA is not.

I mentioned earlier that hair is predominantly composed of dead cellular debris, with the only living part of hair being the follicle. The cells of the follicles contain nuclear DNA, which can be used for DNA profiling. The dead cells of the hair have no nuclei, and thus no DNA. This means that hair that has been yanked out or shed with a follicular bulb attached can provide nuclear DNA, while hair that has been cut or has no bulb attached will not. But, all is not lost.

In the growth of hair, the cells of the bulb multiply, undergo change, and become incorporated into the growing hair. Part of this transformation is the loss of the nucleus from each cell. Thus, hair has no nuclear DNA. But the dead cellular debris that is incorporated into the hair shaft might contain mtDNA. If so, it can be extracted and used to identify the person who shed the hair.

Y-CHROMOSOMAL DNA

The Y-chromosome is what makes males males. It is found only in males; a father passes his Y-chromosome on to his male offspring. So, Y-chromosomal DNA is passed down the paternal linage. By testing for STR repeats on the Y-chromosome (Y-STR), it is possible to show that two or more men share a common paternal ancestry. As with mtDNA, this can be useful in genealogy and in identifying corpses and suspects. It has been shown that this technique can connect two males through their paternal genealogy across as many as thirty generations.

THE CODIS SYSTEM

CODIS stands for Combined DNA Index System. It is a database of DNA finger-prints taken from felons and from biological fluids obtained at crime scenes such as assaults, homicides, and rapes. It began as a pilot project in 1990, and then in 1994 the DNA Identification Act authorized the FBI to set up the National DNA Index System (NDIS), which became operational in 1998. This allows any CODIS-participating lab to compare DNA samples nationally.

For example, the DNA fingerprint of a crime scene or suspect sample can be plugged into the CODIS database and a computer compares it to all the profiles in the system. If a match is made to a particular individual, fresh sus-pect samples are taken and repeat testing in the crime lab is done to confirm or refute the presumptive match. Alternatively, the DNA sample could match DNA obtained from another crime scene; in this case a match would serve to link the crimes. This way evidence from two or more scenes can be consid-ered together. This alone may lead to the identity of the perpetrator.

In 1997, in an attempt to universalize the DNA testing system, the FBI se-lected thirteen STR loci as the core of their database. Laboratories that use the CODIS system examine these thirteen core loci as part of their DNA analysis, making comparing samples in the CODIS database uniform.

CODIS has already enjoyed many successes. As of September 2003, the sys-tem had registered nearly nine thousand hits. One such case was that of Nor-man Jimmerman.

FORENSIC CASE FILES: THE NORMAN JIMMERMAN CASE

In March 1989, Debbie Smith was forced from her home in Williamsburg, Virginia, and into a nearby wooded area where she was raped. Her attacker warned her that he knew where she lived and that she should not tell anyone or he would return and kill her. Debbie went to the police. Blood from the prime suspect was tested against seminal DNA obtained from the victim's rape examination. No match. In 1994, Smith's neighborhood suffered a series of sexual assaults. Another suspect attracted the attention of police, and again DNA analysis was undertaken. Again, no match.

Meanwhile, the state of Virginia began the process of developing a databank of DNA profiles taken from convicted felons. As new profiles were obtained, the Virginia Department of Forensic Services periodically matched these against unsolved crimes. One of these matches identified Norman Jimmerman as Smith's attacker. He was already serving time for robbery and abduction. His current sentence is 161 years.

A COUPLE OF ODD DNA CASES

FORENSIC CASE FILES: SNOWBALL THE CAT

In 1994, Shirley Duguay of Prince Edward Island disappeared. A few days later her corpse was discovered in a shallow grave along with a leather jacket, which was soaked with her blood and dotted with white cat hairs. Her estranged husband, Douglas Beamish, owned a white cat named Snowball. DNA in blood taken from Snowball matched that of the cat hairs found at the burial site, proving that those hairs came from Snowball and no other white cat. Beamish was convicted, marking this case the first time that animal DNA was used to gain a conviction.

FORENSIC CASE FILES: THE SCHMIDT HIV CASE

In 1994, Dr. Richard Schmidt injected his girlfriend with blood taken from one of his AIDS-infected patients. Six months later, she was diagnosed with HIV and went to the police. Sifting through Schmidt's records, investigators discovered that he had drawn blood from one of his AIDS patients on the same night that he had injected the victim. This was critical since the virus can only survive a few hours outside the human body.

The problem facing the crime lab was that HIV mutates often, so making a match between the virus taken from the unsuspecting source patient with that found in the victim could be problematic. Either could have mutated enough so that no conclusive match could be made. To get around this, samples were taken from thirty-two other HIV-positive individuals in the area. Testing revealed that the samples taken from the patient source and the victim matched almost exactly, while the others did not. Schmidt was convicted of second-degree attempted murder and sentenced to fifty years. This case marked the first time viral DNA analysis was used to convict a felon.

TOXICOLOGY:
DRUGS, POISONS, AND TOXINS

oxicology is the science of drugs, poisons, and toxins. The **toxicologist** is the scientist who deals with these substances.

The toxicologist and the toxicology laboratory are critical components of every crime lab. In fact, forensics investigations could not be adequately undertaken without this important science. Drugs and poisons are often involved in accidental, suicidal, and homicidal deaths. They may even be a contributory factor in natural deaths.

The field of forensic toxicology is involved in many diverse areas of drug and toxin detection. The well-equipped toxicology lab employs a number of sophisticated technologies for analyzing an unknown substance, evaluating drug involvement in abnormal behavior and responsibility for accidents, assessing the role of drugs or poisons in the cause and manner of death, or workplace testing for illicit drugs.

WHAT IS A POISON?

The terms *poison*, *toxin*, and *drug* are simply different ways of saying the same thing. Though you might think that a poison kills, a toxin harms, and a drug cures, these terms can be used almost interchangeably. The reason is that what can cure can also harm, and what can harm can kill.

Anything and everything can be a poison. The basic definition of a poison is any substance that, if taken in sufficient quantities, causes a harmful or deadly reaction. The key here is the phrase "sufficient quantities."

The toxicity of any substance depends on how much enters the body and over what time period it does so. For example, you probably know that arsenic is a poison, but did you know that you likely have arsenic in your body right now? If you're a smoker, you have more than a little bit. Same with mercury and cyanide. These substances are in the environment—you can't avoid them. But they are in such small quantities that they cause no real harm. However, take enough of any of them and they become deadly.

The same can be said for the medications your doctor gives you to treat medical problems. Consider the heart drug digitalis, which comes from the foxglove plant and has been used for over a hundred years to treat heart failure and many types of abnormal heart rhythms. It is also a deadly poison. Too much can lead to nausea, vomiting, and death from dangerous changes in the rhythm of the heart. It's ironic that it can treat some abnormal heart rhythms while at the same time can cause other more deadly rhythms. It's all in the dosage. The right dose is medication; the wrong dose is poison.

SEARCHING FOR POISONS

Toxicology is a marriage of chemistry and physiology, since it deals with chemical substances (chemistry) and how these substances alter or harm living organisms (physiology), particularly humans.

A forensic toxicologist deals with the legal aspects of toxicology. His job is to find and analyze toxic substances in biological materials taken from both the living and the dead, and to determine the physiological, psychological, and behavioral effects on the individual in question. For example, he might be asked to assess the state of inebriation of an automobile accident victim or to determine if someone died from a poison or if the presence of a drug contributed to the victim's death. This is often more difficult than it sounds.

When the toxicologist investigates a possible poisoning death, he must answer three basic questions:

- Was the death due to a poison?
- What was the poison used?
- Was the intake of the poison accidental, suicidal, or homicidal?

The medical examiner, not the forensic toxicologist, is charged with assigning the manner of death, but the ME relies on the findings and opinions of the toxicologist in making this determination.

Not finding a drug may be just as important. If the toxicologist finds no drugs in someone exhibiting erratic or bizarre behavior may lead to a psychiatric evaluation and diagnosis. Or perhaps the driver of a vehicle involved in an accident had a low blood level of the medication he was supposed to take for a seizure, leading to the possibility that the seizure caused the accident.

HISTORICAL PERSPECTIVE

Toxicology is a relatively new science that stands on the shoulders of its predecessors: anatomy, physiology, chemistry, and medicine. Our knowledge in these sciences had to reach a certain level of sophistication before toxicology could become a reality. It slowly evolved over more than two hundred years of testing, starting with tests for arsenic.

Arsenic had been a common poison for centuries, but there was no way to prove that arsenic was the culprit in a suspicious death. Scientist had to isolate and then identify **arsenic trioxide**—the most common toxic form of arsenic—in the human body before arsenic poisoning became a provable cause of death. The steps that led to a reliable test for arsenic are indicative of how many toxicological procedures developed.

1775: Swedish chemist Carl Wilhelm Scheele (1742–1786) showed that chlorine water would convert arsenic into arsenic acid. He then added metallic zinc and heated the mixture to release arsine gas. When this gas contacted a cold vessel, arsenic would collect on the vessel's surface.

1787: Johann Metzger (1739–1805) showed that if arsenic were heated with charcoal, a shiny, black "arsenic mirror" would form on the charcoal's surface.

1806: Valentine Rose discovered that arsenic could be uncovered in the human body. If the stomach contents of victims of arsenic poisoning are treated with potassium carbonate, calcium oxide, and nitric acid, arsenic trioxide results. This could then be tested and confirmed by Metzger's test.

1813: French chemist Mathieu Joseph Bonaventure Orfila (1787–1853) developed a method for isolating arsenic from dog tissues. He also published the first toxicological text, *Traité des poisons (Treatise on Poison)*, which helped establish toxicology as a true science.

1821: Sevillas used similar techniques to find arsenic in the stomach and urine of individuals who had been poisoned. This is marked as the beginning of the field of forensic toxicology.

1836: Dr. Alfred Swaine Taylor (1806–1880) developed the first test for arsenic in human tissue. He taught chemistry at Grey's Medical School in England and is credited with establishing the field of forensic toxicology as a medical specialty.

1836: James Marsh (1794–1846) developed an easier and more sensitive version of Metzger's original test, in which the "arsenic mirror" was collected on a plate of glass or porcelain. The **Marsh test** became the standard, and its principles were the basis of the more modern method known as the **Reinsch test**, which we will look at later in this chapter.

As you can see, each step in developing a useful testing procedure for arsenic stands on what discoveries came before. That's the way science works. Step by step, investigators use what others have discovered to discover even more.

THE MODERN TOXICOLOGIST

During his analysis, the modern forensic toxicologist sometimes searches for the poison itself, while other times he searches for the poison's breakdown products. This brings up the concept of **biotransformation**, which is the conversion or transformation of a chemical into another chemical by the body. We also call this **metabolism** and the new product produced a **metabolite**. This process is simply the body destroying or breaking down chemicals and excreting them from the body. This is why you must take most medications each day. The medication is designed to treat some medical problem, and indeed it may do that. But, to the body, the drug is also a foreign toxin and as such must be metabolized and excreted. So, you have to take another dose day after day to keep the blood level of the medication in the therapeutic level.

The metabolism of a drug or toxin typically deactivates the chemical and prepares it for elimination from the body, usually by way of the kidneys. For example, many chemicals are not soluble in water, which means they aren't soluble in urine, either. The body gets around this by metabolizing (biotransforming) the chemical in such a way that it becomes a new chemical (metabolite) that is water soluble. The metabolite can then be filtered through the kidney, into the urine, and out of the body.

Most metabolites are inactive in that they possess no biological activity and are inert as far as the body is concerned. Other metabolites are active and may have biological properties that are weaker or stronger than the original compound. They may even behave quite differently from the parent compound. For example, cocaine is metabolized into three metabolites: nor-cocaine, which possesses active properties, and benzoylecgonine and methylecgonine, which are inert.

Another example is heroin, which is made from morphine. When heroin is injected into the bloodstream it is immediately converted back into morphine—the chemical that gives the user the "high."

Since both cocaine and heroin are metabolized to new compounds very quickly, testing for either would be useless. Instead, the toxicologist tests for the presence of cocaine or heroin by searching for their metabolites. Finding them proves that the parent drug was present.

One of the reasons poisoning has been such a popular means for homicide for so many years is that most poisons cause no visible changes in the body, either in the living person or at autopsy. In the days before toxicology labs existed, the poisoner "got away with it" more often than not. After all, if there were no obvious reason for the death, it must have been natural. Since the true cause of death could not be determined, no one could be held responsible.

Of course, some toxins do leave behind visible signs, many of which have been known for years. Corrosive poisons such as acids and lye cause severe damage to the mouth, esophagus, and stomach if they are ingested. Poisonous mushrooms and chlorinated hydrocarbons such a carbon tetrachloride, which for years was used in many carpet cleaners, may cause fatty degeneration of the liver. Cyanide and carbon monoxide cause a cherry-red appearance to the blood and tissues and lead to pinkish lividity. Metallic poisons such as arsenic, mercury, and lead cause characteristic changes in the gastrointestinal tract and the liver.

But this isn't the norm. Most poisons work their mischief within the cells of the body and leave behind no visible footprints. This means the ME does not often see visible evidence of toxins at autopsy or on the microscopic slides he prepares from the body's tissues. Instead he collects fluids and tissues from the body and these are analyzed for the presence or absence of toxins by the toxicologist.

SAMPLE COLLECTION

Since toxins rarely leave behind visible clues, the ME and the toxicologist must perform specialized tests to reveal their presence. These examinations require various body fluids and tissues, and which ones are used depends on the particular drug in question and the situation under which it is tested. The goal of testing is to establish whether a particular drug is the cause of death, or a contributing factor in the death, or that it played no role at all.

The best places to obtain samples for testing are the locations where the chemicals entered the body, where they concentrate within the body, and along the routes of elimination. This means that blood, stomach contents, and the tissues around injection sites may possess high concentrations of the drug. Analysis of liver, brain, and other tissues may reveal where the drug or its metabolites have accumulated. Finally, urine testing may indicate where the drug and its metabolites are concentrated for final elimination.

During an autopsy, blood, urine, stomach contents, bile, vitreous eye fluid, and tissue samples from the liver, kidneys, muscles, and brain are obtained. If an inhaled toxin is suspected, lung tissue is also taken, and if a chronic heavy metal (arsenic, lead, etc.) poisoning is a consideration, hair samples are taken (the reason is discussed later in this chapter).

It is important that the samples be collected before embalming, since this procedure can interfere with subsequent testing or, as in the case of cyanide, completely destroy the toxin. Also, since embalming fluids may contain methanol and other alcohols, accurate alcohol testing is difficult if not impossible after this procedure.

Let's look at the most common fluids and tissues obtained by the ME or toxicologist.

BLOOD: Blood is by far the toxicologist's most useful substance since, with modern toxicological techniques, most drugs and their major metabolites can be found in the blood.

Blood is easily sampled from the living with a simple venipuncture (using a needle to draw blood from a vein, usually in the arm). During an autopsy, blood is typically obtained from several areas. The aorta (the main artery that carries blood out of the heart and to the body), both sides of the heart, and the femoral artery (in the groin area) are common locations. The samples are then placed into glass tubes and sent to the laboratory for testing. If the blood is to be analyzed for volatile chemicals, a sample is placed in a Teflon-lined screw-cap tube. Rubber stoppers should be avoided since they can react with the gases or may also allow them to escape.

The toxicologist not only determines if the toxin is present, but also attempts to assess its level in the body. This is important since low levels may be of no consequence, higher doses may have toxic effects and may have contributed to the person's actions or played a role in his death, and even higher levels may have been the actual cause of death. Blood is most often the best substance for this assessment.

Concentrations of medicines and drugs within the blood correlate well with levels of intoxication as well as with levels that are potentially lethal. **Bioavailability** is the amount of the drug that is available for biological activity. Since drugs work on the cellular level, bioavailability means the concentration of the drug that reaches the cells of the body. For most chemicals, the blood level correlates with the cellular level.

For example, the level of alcohol in the blood correlates extremely well with a person's degree of intoxication, and the lethal level of alcohol in the blood is well known. This knowledge means that the ME can use a blood alcohol level to accurately estimate a person's degree of intoxication in an automobile accident or whether the fraternity boy died from his binge drinking or from some other cause.

Or let's say that an individual takes a handful of sedative (sleeping) pills in a suicide attempt. In order for the pills to "work" they must be digested, absorbed into the bloodstream, and carried to the cells of the brain, where the concentration of the drug in the brain cells determines the degree of "poisoning." And since the amount of the drug in the blood is an accurate reflection of the amount within the brain cells, testing the blood is like testing the cells.

But, if absorption of the pills from the stomach doesn't occur, the person will have no effect from the drug. The amount of the drug present in the stomach is irrelevant since it is not available to the brain cells. So, a victim found with undigested pills in his stomach and a very low blood level of the drug did not die form a drug overdose and must have died from something else.

URINE: Easily sampled with a cup and a trip to the restroom, urine testing is a staple of workplace drug testing. It is also useful at autopsy, where it is removed by way of a needle inserted into the bladder. Because the kidneys are one of the body's major drug and toxin elimination routes, toxins are often found in greater concentrations in the urine than in the blood. However, one problem is that the correlation between urine concentration and drug effects in the body is often poor at best. All the urine level can tell the ME is that the drug had been in the blood at some earlier time. It can't tell him if the drug was exerting any effect on the individual at the time of its collection, or in the case of a corpse, the time of death.

Also, estimating blood concentrations from urine concentrations is impossible. The concentration of any drug in the urine depends on how much urine is produced. If the person has ingested a great deal of water, the urine and any chemicals it contains will be more diluted (watered down) than if the person is "dry." In addition, alcohol and drugs known as diuretics increase urine volume and decrease the urine concentration of any drugs or metabolites present. Many athletes use diuretics in an attempt to mask or dilute performance-enhancing drugs.

STOMACH CONTENTS: The stomach contents are removed from survivors of drug ingestions by way of a gastric tube, which is typically passed through the nose and into the stomach. The contents are then lavaged (washed) from the stomach and tested for the presence of drugs or poisons.

At autopsy, the stomach contents are similarly tested. Obtaining the stomach contents in any case where poison or drug ingestion is suspected is critical. However, as mentioned earlier, the concentration of any drug in the stomach does not correlate with its blood level and thus its effects on the person. It does, however, show that the drug was ingested and in what quantity.

LIVER: The liver is the center of most drug and toxin metabolism. Testing the liver tissue and the bile it produces can often reveal the drug or its metabolites. Many drugs, particularly opiates, tend to concentrate in the liver and the bile, so they can often be found in these tissues when the blood shows no traces. Where the liver might reflect levels of a drug during the hours before death, the bile may indicate what drugs were in the system over the past three to four days. Neither is very accurate, however.

VITREOUS HUMOR: The vitreous humor is the liquid within the eyeball. It is fairly resistance to putrefaction (decay) and in severely decomposed corpses it may be the only remaining fluid. Testing may uncover the presence of certain drugs.

The vitreous humor is an aqueous (water-like) fluid, which means that chemicals that are water soluble will dissolve in it. It also maintains equilibrium with the blood, so that any water-soluble chemical in the blood will also be found in the vitreous. The important thing is that the level in the vitreous lags behind that of the blood by about one to two hours. This means that testing the vitreous will reflect the concentration of the toxin in the blood one to two hours earlier.

HAIR: Hair absorbs certain heavy metal (arsenic, lead, and others) toxins and some other drugs. It has the unique ability to give an intoxication timeline for many of these substances. This will be discussed in greater detail later in this chapter.

INSECTS: In cases where the body is severely decomposed and insects have been feeding on the corpse, the maggots can be tested for drugs. And since some insects tend to concentrate certain drugs in their tissues, they may supply information that the drug was at least present in the victim.

TOXICOLOGY AND THE CAUSE AND MANNER OF DEATH

In the remote past, it was very difficult to determine why someone died, and virtually impossible to ascertain whether a poison was involved. Though modern toxicological techniques have changed things greatly, determining that poisoning was the cause of death remains one of the most difficult tasks facing the forensic toxicologist.

The ultimate responsibility for determining the cause and manner of death lies with the ME or the coroner. To do this he will rely on the circumstances of the death, the crime scene reconstruction, the autopsy findings, and the laboratory results, including the toxicology findings.

In cases where a potentially deadly poison is involved, the toxicologist must uncover the toxin, determine its concentration within the victim, and then give his opinion as to whether this level of this drug was likely lethal. To accomplish this he must consider a number of factors.

The lethal level for many drugs is extremely variable from person to person. Age, sex, body size and weight, the presence of other drugs or medications, the state of overall health, and the presence of other diseases impact a given person's tolerance to some drugs.

For example, a frequent and heavy drinker can tolerate much higher blood alcohol levels than could someone who never drank. A heavy drinker might appear completely sober at a level that would render the normal person unconscious.

Similarly, hardcore heroin addicts routinely inject doses of heroin and attain drug blood levels that would kill the average person in a matter of minutes.

In addition, some drugs are more dangerous to individuals with certain medical problems. The use of amphetamines poses a much greater risk for someone with heart disease or high blood pressure than it would for someone in good health. In this circumstance, a blood level of amphetamines that would not harm the average person could prove lethal for a person with these diseases.

So, it's not straightforward. When the ME attempts to determine the cause of death in the presence of drugs or toxins, he must consider all these factors. In the absence of other possible causes of death, and with the presence of significant levels of a potentially harmful drug, he might conclude the drug was the proximate cause of death or at least a contributing factor.

Remember that the manners of death are natural, accidental, suicidal, homicidal, and the extra classification of undetermined. Drugs and poisons can be the direct cause or at least a contributing factor in any of these.

NATURAL: A person can die of natural causes even if drugs are involved in the mechanism of death. What if a man with significant coronary artery disease (CAD) took an amphetamine or snorted a few lines of cocaine? Coronary artery disease is a very common disease in which the coronary arteries that supply blood to the heart are plugged with cholesterol plaque.

Amphetamines and cocaine are drugs that increase the heart rate and the blood pressure, both of which increase the need for blood supply to the harder working heart muscle. In addition, these drugs can cause the coronary arteries to spasm (squeeze shut), which greatly decreases the blood supply to the heart muscle. Basically, the supply of blood is reduced at a time when the need is increased, so that the person loses both sides of the supply and demand equation. The victim could suffer a heart attack (actual death of a portion of the heart muscle due to lack of adequate blood supply) or a cardiac arrhythmia (a dangerous change in heart rhythm). Either of these could kill the victim. The cause of death would be a heart attack or a cardiac arrhythmia, events that he would be prone to due to his CAD. But, the amphetamine or cocaine would be a contributory factor. This circumstance is common.

When the ME and the toxicologist confront this situation, they must assess the extent of the victim's heart disease, the amount of the drug in the body, and whether a heart attack actually occurred. If the amount of drug is low and the victim had severely diseased coronary arteries, they might conclude that the death was natural and that the drug was only a minor contributing factor. On the other hand, if his CAD was mild and the level of drug in his body was high, they might favor an accidental drug death.

But, what if the victim intentionally took a large amount of cocaine, or what if the amphetamines were given to him without his knowledge? The manner of death would then be a suicide or a homicide, respectively. The important point is that the autopsy and lab results would be the same in each circumstance. The ME would need to rely on witness statements and the results of the police investigation to sort this out. And even with this information, the picture might simply be too muddy for the ME to determine the manner of death, and it might be classified as undetermined.

ACCIDENTAL: Most accidental poisonings occur at home and often involve children. Curious by nature, children will eat or drink almost anything: prescription drugs, pesticides, household cleaners, paint thinners, weed killers, snail bait, you name it. In adults, accidental poisoning most often occurs because some product is mislabeled, usually because it has been placed in a container other than its original one. This may be in the form of medications dumped into another bottle, some toxic liquid placed in an empty liquor bottle, or the white powders of cyanide or arsenic stored in a container where they could be confused with sugar or salt.

In other situations, the death might be the result of a dosage miscalculation. Addicts often miscalculate the amount of heroin or amphetamine they are taking and die from this error. The fact that street drugs have poor quality control only adds to this problem. How much heroin is actually in the bag the addict just bought? It may be less or many times more than the bag he purchased yesterday. If the latter is the case and he injects the same dose as he did yesterday, he could easily die from an overdose.

Similarly, some people believe that if one dose of a drug is good, then two must be better. This is a dangerous assumption. Digitalis is a common cardiac medication. Sometimes a patient will decide on his own to double his dose. All is well for a couple of weeks, but as the medicine accumulates within his body, he becomes ill and can die.

Another factor in accidental drug deaths is the mixing of drugs. Alcohol taken with a sedative is notorious for causing death. Addicts often mix cocaine with amphetamines, or heroin with tranquilizers, or just about any combination imaginable, often with tragic results.

SUICIDAL: Drugs are a commonly involved in suicides. Sedatives or sleeping pills, narcotics, alcohol, and carbon monoxide (see Chapter Eight: Asphyxia, "Toxic Gases") are commonly used. Often the victim takes multiple drugs, basically whatever is in the medicine cabinet. This presents a difficult problem for the toxicologist. He must analyze the stomach contents, blood, urine, and tissues, and hopefully determine the level of each drug and assess the contribution of each to the victim's death. He may find that one particularly toxic drug was present in large amounts and that it was the cause of death. Or he might find that a certain combination of drugs was the cause.

The ME uses these findings in conjunction with information from the autopsy and from investigating officers to assess the manner of death. The finding of multiple drugs in the victim's system doesn't necessarily mean that he took them on purpose. It could have been an accidental overdose driven by the need for relief of physical or psychological pain, or someone else could have surreptitiously slipped the drugs into his food or drink, which would be a homicide.

HOMICIDAL: Though homicidal poisoning was common from antiquity to the twentieth century, it is uncommon today.

As with accidental and suicidal poisonings, homicidal poisonings occur most often at home. This means that the killer must possess knowledge of the victim's habits and have access to his food, drink, and medications. This knowledge is critical in the homicidal administration of a toxin. It is also important in solving the crime. When the toxicologist determines that the victim was poisoned, the police focus on anyone who had access to the victim.

TOXICOLOGICAL TESTING PROCEDURES

The biggest problem facing the toxicologist is that there are literally thousands of drugs and chemicals that are harmful, addictive, or lethal if ingested, injected, or inhaled. Some even absorb directly through the skin. Toxicological testing is time-consuming and expensive, and few, if any, labs can afford to perform such testing on every case. For this reason, the testing must be as focused as possible.

An understanding of the circumstances surrounding the death is important since clues at the scene often point toward a particular drug. For example, a young girl found on her bed at home with an empty pill bottle at her side would lead to one avenue of testing while a long-term addict found in an alley with fresh needle marks would follow another path. The more clues as to the likely toxin that the circumstances of the death can supply, the narrower the field of possibilities the toxicologist must consider.

THE TWO-TIERED SYSTEM

When testing for drugs or poisons, the toxicologist typically follows a two-tiered approach. Initial tests, called **presumptive** tests, are for screening purposes and are typically easier and cheaper to perform. When negative, they indicate that the drug or class of drugs in question is not present and further testing is unnecessary. When positive, they indicate that a particular substance possibly is present. By using these screening tests the number of possibilities can be greatly reduced and the toxicologist can move on to the second phase, which utilizes more focused **confirmatory** testing. These tests are more expensive and time-consuming, but are designed to establish the identity of the exact drug present. This two-tiered approach saves considerable time and money.

This same approach is used whether the toxicologist is asked to analyze blood, urine, and other materials obtained from a person (living or deceased) or to test a batch of seized material believed to be illicit drugs.

Let's say a corpse is found in an alleyway known for methamphetamine sales and use. If blood samples obtained at autopsy show a positive presumptive test for amphetamines, further confirmatory testing to identify the exact amphetamine present is indicated. If the test is negative, no further testing for amphetamines is done and the toxicologist will search for other classes of drugs.

To be doubly certain, the toxicologist prefers to find the drug or poison in at least two separate locations. Finding the toxin in the blood and the liver tissue is more reassuring than finding it in either one alone.

Or let's say that the toxicologist is asked to test a seized substance and doing so shows a positive presumptive test for cocaine. Further confirmatory testing would then be indicated. If the screening test is negative, the substance may be analyzed for other drugs, but cocaine has been ruled out.

In most labs, testing for controlled and illegal drugs consumes 75 percent of the lab's time and resources. The areas most often tested in this type of examination are blood and urine. After one of the presumptive tests shows that a particular drug or class of drugs is likely present, confirmatory testing with the combination of **gas chromatography** and **mass spectrometry (GC-MS)** or **infrared spectroscopy** are used to accurately identify which substance is present. See the appendix for details on these procedures.

Presumptive Tests

Presumptive testing comes in many varieties. Common toxicological screening tests are color tests, immunoassays, thin layer chromatography, and ultraviolet spectroscopy.

Color Tests

Tests in which a reagent (any active chemical solution) is added to blood, urine, or tissue extractions, and if the particular chemical tested for is present, a color change reaction will occur. The color change results from a chemical reaction between the drug and the reagent, which produces a new compound that imparts a specific color to the mixture. These tests are cheap, easy, and quick, and can determine if a specific chemical or class of chemicals is present in the material tested. If it does not indicate that the toxin is present, further testing is not necessary.

There are a wide variety of color tests that reveal the presence of many types of drugs. Some of the most common are:

TRINDER'S TEST: This reagent, containing ferric nitrate and mercuric chloride, turns violet in the presence of salicylates (aspirin and similar compounds).

MARQUIS TEST: This reagent contains formaldehyde and sulfuric acid and turns purple in the presence of morphine, heroin, and most opiates, and brownish orange if mixed with amphetamines or methamphetamines.

VAN URK TEST: This is a test for LSD and other hallucinogenic drugs. The reagent is a mixture of dimethylaminobenzaldehyde, hydrochloric acid (HCl), and ethanol. It turns purple to indicate a positive reaction.

DILLIE-KOPPANYI TEST: In this test, the sample is treated with cobalt acetate in methanol and then with isopropylamine in methanol. It turns violet-blue if barbiturates are present.

DUQUENOIS-LEVINE TEST: This three-step test determines if marijuana or other cannabinoids are present. The sample is treated with a mixture of vanillin and acetaldehyde in ethanol, then with HCl, and finally with chloroform. A deep purple color is a positive result.

SCOTT TEST: This is also a three-step test that uses a mixture of cobalt thiocyanate and glycerine, followed by HCl, and then chloroform. Cocaine turns blue after the thiocyanate is added, changes to pink with the HCl, and then blue once again when chloroform is added.

Other Screening Tests

IMMUNOASSAY: Immunoassays, which measure the concentration of a drug in a liquid (see the appendix), are easy, very sensitive, and useful for rapidly screening urine samples for certain drugs. However, the manufactured antibodies can also react with compounds that are very similar to the sought-after drug, a lack of specificity that makes this a presumptive test rather than a confirmatory one.

THIN LAYER CHROMATOGRAPHY (TLC): TLC (see the appendix) not only tentatively identifies many chemicals, but is also useful for separating the components of a sample. Once TLC has tentatively identified a substance, its identity is confirmed with mass spectrometry.

GAS CHROMATOGRAPHY (GC): As with TLC, GC's (see the appendix) primary use is in making a presumptive identification and separating various compounds from one another. A positive result is confirmed by using mass spectrometry.

ULTRAVIOLET (UV) SPECTROSCOPY: This test takes advantage of the fact that different chemicals absorb UV light in varying amounts (see the appendix). Since it can't identify the exact compound, it is only useful for screening.

A Typical Screening Protocol

Each lab has its own protocol for drug screening. What tests are used and in what order they are performed depend on the available staff and equipment, budgetary restrictions, and the bias of the toxicologist in charge. But most labs have certain standard screens they employ when first confronted with an unknown sample. These basic screens might include:

ALCOHOL SCREEN: GC is used to isolate and identify the various alcohols and related compounds such as acetone.

ACID SCREEN: Immunoassay of urine samples is used to detect acidic compounds such as barbiturates and aspirin.

ALKALI SCREEN: GC screens for substances that dissolve in alkaline solutions. These substances include many tranquilizers, synthetic narcotics, and antidepressants.

NARCOTIC SCREEN: Urine immunoassay reveals opiates, cocaine, and methadone.

By using these general screening procedures, the toxicologist can quickly exclude many commonly encountered drugs and narrow his area of search for those that are present. Based on these results, further screening and confirmatory tests are used to ultimately identify any unknown substance.

Confirmatory Tests

A good confirmatory test must possess **sensitivity** and **specificity** in that it must recognize the chemical in question (sensitivity) and be able to identify it to the exclusion of all others (specificity). This means that once a chemical has undergone a screening test and a presumptive identity has been established, a confirmatory test will accurately determine the true identity of the unknown substance.

The most important confirmatory test used by the toxicologist is **mass spectrometry (MS)** (see the appendix). In MS, the sample is bombarded with electrons, which fragment the chemical into ionic fractions. This fragmentation pattern is called a mass spectrum. It is different for each element and compound. This means that it gives a chemical fingerprint of the chemical being tested and can identify virtually any compound. When the mass spectrum of an unknown substance is compared to known reference standards, the identity of the unknown sample comes to light. The National Institute of Standards and Technology (NIST) maintains a database of the mass spectra of known chemicals.

In the forensic toxicology laboratory, MS is usually employed in combination with gas chromatography (GC). This combination is called gas chromatography/mass spectrometry (GC/MS). In GC/MS, gas chromatography is used to separate the test sample into components and MS is employed to identify each component. The GC/MS is as close to being fool proof as any technique available.

Though used less often than MS, **infrared spectroscopy (IR)** can also determine the chemical fingerprint of the tested substance (see the appendix). Instead of electrons, the substance is exposed to infrared light. When any light strikes an object or substance, it is transmitted (passed through), absorbed, or reflected. When exposed to infrared light, each compound transmits and absorbs the light in its own unique pattern. These unique patterns determine which compounds are present, and thus identify the chemical substance tested. This test is also used in conjunction with GC. This combination is termed GC/IR.

TESTING FOR METALS

Heavy metals and other metallic elements, such as iron, mercury, lead, copper, arsenic, antimony, and selenium, are potentially lethal and have caused accidental, suicidal, and homicidal deaths for many years. The most useful tests for detecting metals within the body's tissues are colorimetric assays, atomic absorption spectrophotometry, neutron activation analysis, and hair analysis.

COLORIMETRIC ASSAYS: These tests depend on the fact that each metallic element has a specific color when treated with certain reagents. These types of tests are centuries old and easy to do. The reagent is added to the test sample and then examined by a photometer, an instrument that accurately measures light and color. The major drawback of these tests is that they require a fairly large sample for testing.

REINSCH TEST: In this popular heavy metal screening test, the sample to be tested is dissolved in hydrochloric acid and a copper strip is placed into the solution. If a dark or silvery coat appears on the copper, one of the heavy metals is likely present.

ATOMIC ABSORPTION SPECTROPHOTOMETRY (AAS): This is perhaps the most popular method for metal detection (see the appendix). The physics involved are complex, but each metal reacts to a specific wavelength of light. A special detector examines the light before and after the sample is placed into the light path and determines its identity.

NEUTRON ACTIVATION ANALYSIS (NAA): NAA requires expensive and bulky equipment but is highly accurate (see the appendix). The test sample is exposed to low-energy neutrons where it undergoes radioactive changes and releases X-rays and gamma rays. From these rays, the presence and concentration of the metals are determined.

INDUCTIVELY COUPLED PLASMA-MASS SPECTROMETRY (ICP-MS): This is perhaps the best test for very small samples of metals, but it is expensive and not widely available at this time. This test involves using an argon torch to heat the specimen to over 6,000°C, which forms an ionized gas of the substance. This gas is then passed through a mass detector that identifies the chemical by its mass and charge.

HAIR ANALYSIS: This can be used to determine the presence of toxic heavy metals, and some other toxins, and may also give a timeline for the exposure (discussed later in this chapter).

INTERPRETING THE RESULTS

After testing has revealed the presence and concentration of a chemical substance, the hard part begins. The toxicologist must now assess what the results mean. He evaluates each of the drugs present with an eye toward the route the drug was administered and whether the concentrations played a role in the subject's behavior or death.

Route of Entry

The route of entry of the toxin is very important since it might provide a clue as to whether the victim self-administered the drug or someone else administered the drug. For example, if a drug was injected and the victim possessed no means to do so or if the injection site was in an area that made self-administration unlikely, homicide might be a stronger consideration.

Another important fact is that the concentration of the toxin is usually greatest at the administration site. Ingested toxins are more likely to be found in the stomach, intestines, or liver, while inhaled gases will be concentrated in the lungs. If injected, the drug can often be isolated from the tissues around the injection site. Drugs taken intravenously bypass the stomach and liver, directly enter the bloodstream, and are quickly distributed throughout the body. In this circumstance, the toxicologist may find high concentrations of the drug in the blood and in multiple tissues of the body, but little or none in the stomach and liver as would be seen with ingestion. This will help him determine the route of intake.

Drug Blood Level

Earlier we discussed the concept of bioavailability and how the level of a drug in the blood closely correlates with the drug's actions and toxicity. This means that finding a large amount of a toxin in the victim's stomach does not necessarily mean that the drug was the cause of death. The important fact is that drugs in the stomach will not kill. They must first be absorbed into the blood and distributed to the body.

For example, if the toxicologist found a large amount of a tranquilizers in a victim's stomach, particularly if most of the pills were intact and had not been digested, and also found a low blood concentration of the drug, he would likely conclude that the pills were taken shortly before death and played little or no role in the victim's demise.

There are exceptions. In cases of caustic acid and alkali (lye or caustic soda) ingestion, the blood levels are not important since these chemicals cause direct contact damage and do not need to be absorbed into the body to do harm (discussed later in this chapter).

Still, in most situations, blood levels are important because they correlate more strongly with the effects of the chemical in question. When the toxicologist determines a blood level of a certain chemical, he might assign it to one of four broad categories:

NORMAL: This would be the level expected in the general population under normal circumstances. An example would be low levels of cyanide. Even though this is a deadly poison, it is found in the environment, and therefore most people have low normal levels of cyanide in their blood. Smokers have even higher levels, but this would still be considered normal.

THERAPEUTIC: This is the level that your doctor strives for. If he gives you an antibiotic or a medication for high blood pressure, he wants to accomplish a blood level of the drug that will bring about a therapeutic effect. Patients with certain cardiac problems may be placed on digitalis. The doctor will periodically draw a blood test to check the therapeutic level of the drug. The reason he does this is that too little will offer less benefit to the patient and too much can cause severe problems, since digitalis is potentially a deadly poison.

TOXIC: A toxic level is one that may cause harm or death. When a prescribed drug passes the therapeutic level and reaches the toxic level it has moved from being a medication to being a poison. Using the example of digitalis, a toxic level might lead to nausea, vomiting, and a yellowish tinge to the person's vision. Or it may cause a deadly change in the rhythm of the heart. These would be toxic effects.

LETHAL: This is the level at which the drug in question would consistently cause death. In toxicology we use the term **LD$_{50}$** to measure a chemical's lethal potential. The LD_{50} of a drug is the blood concentration at which 50 percent of people would die.

From this you might assume that the toxicologist simply has to determine the blood level of any toxin and then he can determine if the level was toxic or lethal. Though that may seem logical, it is far from the truth.

Each person reacts to chemicals and toxins differently. Much of this variance can be related to age, sex, body size and weight, genetics, and nutritional and health status. An individual who is young, robust, and healthy should tolerate more of a given drug than would someone who was old, thin, and sickly. And in general that is true. As mentioned earlier, a person's habits also affect how he will react. The toxicologist must consider these facts when assessing whether a given level of a drug is toxic or lethal, or whether it contributed to the subject's behavior or death.

Acute vs. Chronic Poisoning

At times the toxicologist is asked to determine whether a poisoning is **acute** or **chronic**. A good example is arsenic, which can kill if given in a single large dose or if given in repeated smaller doses over weeks or months. In either case, the blood level could be high. But the determination of whether the poisoning was acute or chronic may be extremely important. If acute, the suspect list may be long. If chronic, the suspect list would include only those who had long-term contact with the victim, such as a family member, a caretaker, or a family cook.

So, how does the toxicologist make this determination?

In acute arsenic poisoning, the ME would expect to find high levels of arsenic in the stomach and the blood, as well as evidence of corrosion and bleeding in the stomach and intestines, as these are commonly seen in acute arsenic ingestion. If he found little or no arsenic in the stomach and no evidence of acute injury in the gastrointestinal (GI) tract, but high arsenic levels in the blood and tissues, he might suspect that the poisoning was chronic in nature. Here, an analysis of the victim's hair can be invaluable.

Hair analysis for arsenic (and several other toxins) can reveal exposure to arsenic and also give a timeline of the exposure. The reason this is possible is that arsenic is deposited in the cells of the hair follicles in proportion to the blood level of the arsenic at the time the cell was produced.

In hair growth, the cells of the hair's follicle undergo change, lose their nuclei, and are incorporated into the growing hair shaft. New follicular cells are produced to replace them and this cycle continues throughout life. Follicular cells produced while the blood levels of arsenic are high contain the poison, and as they are incorporated into the hair shaft the arsenic is, too. On the other hand, any follicular cells that appeared while the arsenic levels were low contain little or no arsenic.

In general, hair grows about a half inch per month. This means that the toxicologist can cut the hair into short segments, measure the arsenic level in each, and reveal a timeline for arsenic exposure in the victim.

Let's suppose that a wife, who prepares all the family meals, slowly poisoned her husband with arsenic. She began by adding small amounts of the poison to his food in February and continued until his death in July. In May he was hospitalized with gastrointestinal complaints such as nausea, vomiting, and weight loss (all symptoms of arsenic poisoning). No diagnosis was made, but since he was doing better after ten days in the hospital, he was sent home. Such a circumstance is not unusual since these types of gastrointestinal symptoms are common and arsenic poisoning is rare. Physicians rarely think of it and test for it. After returning home, the unfortunate husband once again fell ill and finally died.

As part of the autopsy procedure, the toxicologist might test the victim's hair for toxins, and if he did, he would find the arsenic. He could then section and test the hair to determine the arsenic level essentially month by month. If the victim's hair was three inches long, the half inch closest to the scalp would represent July, the next half inch June, the next May, and so on until the last half inch would reflect his exposure to arsenic in February, the month his poisoning began. Arsenic levels are expressed in parts per million (ppm). An analysis might reveal a pattern like that seen in Figure 11-1.

The toxicologist would look at this timeline of exposure and likely determine that the exposure occurred in the victim's home. The police would then have a few questions for the wife and would likely obtain a search warrant to look for arsenic within the home.

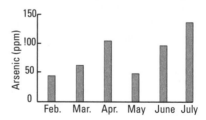

Figure 11-1: Timeline of chronic arsenic exposure. The arsenic exposure began in February and continued until May, when he was hospitalized. During this time the arsenic levels fell and he got better, but after he returned home and was again exposed to arsenic, the levels again rose until the time of his death in July.

COMMON DRUGS, POISONS, AND TOXINS

In the remote past, most poisoners favored botanical products such as hemlock, oleander, deadly nightshade, foxglove, hellebore, monkshood, opium, and many others. These were easily available and untraceable. More recently, various chemicals have been added to this long list of plant-based poisons, which has made the work of the toxicologist that much more difficult.

I said earlier that when the forensic toxicologist is faced with determining whether an individual's death or abnormal behavior is related to toxin exposure, he will use all evidence, including the results of toxicology testing, the autopsy examination, and statements from investigating officers and witnesses. To effectively use this information, he must be familiar with many aspects of drugs and poisons: He must know the chemical makeup and physiological actions of drugs and their breakdown products; understand how drugs are metabolized in the body and what the potential toxic properties of these metabolites are; know how these chemicals affect a normal person, as well as those with various illnesses and addictions; and be aware of the symptoms and signs produced by these chemicals. In addition, a working knowledge of street and recreational drugs is essential, since these are often involved in injury and death.

Obviously, a discussion of every known chemical, drug, and poison is far beyond the scope of this book. We will, however, look at many of those that crop up in real-life cases as well as in works of fiction.

We will examine the things that the ME and the toxicologist consider in assessing the effects of any of them in death, injury, or legal matters. For example, some drugs cause severe depression or addiction and may lead the user to take his own life. Others may distort perceptions to the point that the user accidentally causes self-harm through some foolish act. Trying to fly from a building would fit this description. Other drugs may cause anger, aggression, or an actual psychotic episode, and the user may commit assaults or homicides while under the chemical's influence. Some drugs are so addictive that the user will commit all types of illegal acts (robbery, assault, or murder) to obtain money to purchase them. Other substances are just downright deadly.

In each of these circumstances, it falls to the ME and the toxicologist to determine what role, if any, the drug played in the user's death or behavior. Before looking into some of the more common drugs and toxins, let's define a few terms.

Addiction or drug dependence comes in two basic varieties: psychological and physical. **Psychological dependence** occurs with many classes of drugs and can be defined as a desire for the drug's effect rather than a true physiological need. The user can stop without real harm. He might feel anxious, depressed, fatigued, or excitable, depending upon the nature of the drug that he was abusing, but with time these symptoms will fade and he will do fine. **Physical dependence**, on the other hand, implies that the chemistry of the body has been altered in such a way that abstinence from the drug could lead to severe illness or death. Physical addiction is more common with narcotics and depressants and less so with stimulants (uppers), with the notable exceptions of cocaine and nicotine.

In Greek, the word *narkotikos* means a "state of lethargy or sleepiness." As the group of drugs that derive their class name from this term, **narcotics** cause sleepiness, lethargy, and sluggishness in the user. Most are derived from the opium poppy. Others are either synthesized from materials found in the poppy (semisynthetic) or are made from scratch (synthetic). Unfortunately, the word narcotic has come to mean any powerful, illegal, abused drug. Such things as heroin and morphine, which are narcotics, are lumped with amphetamines and cocaine, which are not. In this text, the term narcotic will not refer to these latter drugs, but only to those that are truly narcotics.

It is beyond the scope of this book to cover every alcohol and drug, but we'll look briefly at how some of the more common ones affect the body and how they can be detected by the toxicologist.

ALCOHOL

Alcohol is derived from the fermentation of sugars and comes in a variety of types, with **ethanol** (ethyl, or drinking alcohol), **methanol** (methyl, or wood or denatured alcohol), and **isopropanol** (isopropyl, or rubbing alcohol) being the ones most commonly encountered. All alcohols are central nervous system (CNS) depressants. Central nervous system basically means the brain. These alcohols cause sleepiness, poor coordination, slowed movements and reactions, and distorted perceptions. In short, all the symptoms and signs you recognize in someone who is drunk. In larger amounts, they can lead to coma, cessation of breathing, and death from asphyxia.

Ethanol

Ethanol is by far the most commonly abused drug. Not only are its toxic effects potentially lethal, but the loss of coordination and poor judgment that is associated with its use can lead to violent and negligent acts. There is potential for physical addiction with alcohol and withdrawal can be an arduous and dangerous process. Without proper medical treatment, death rates from alcohol withdrawal syndromes, such as delirium tremens (DTs), can be 20 percent or more.

Alcohol in the body follows a fairly simple pathway. Once ingested, it is absorbed into the bloodstream and disseminated throughout the body, where 95 percent of it is metabolized (broken down) by the liver into water and carbon dioxide. The remaining 5 percent is excreted unchanged through the kidneys and lungs, a fact that is critical to sobriety testing.

Alcohol Metabolism

The body eliminates most toxins in what is called a **dose-dependent** fashion; that is, the higher the dose taken, the more rapidly the toxin is metabolized. A small amount activates only some of the enzymes that break down the toxin, whereas a larger amount activates more enzymes in order to handle the increased load of toxin.

Alcohol is metabolized in a **linear** fashion in that any amount of alcohol intake activates all the enzyme systems that destroy it. This means that from the first drink, the system operates at almost maximum efficiency and there is little or no ability to increase it. The average rate of ethanol destruction in the body is roughly equivalent to one drink per hour.

Why is this important? With rapid intake of alcohol, as is seen in binge drinking that is so common among college students, the body has no method for increasing the removal of the alcohol. The system is already running at top speed and excessive intake overruns the body's ability to deal with it. The result is that the concentration of alcohol in the blood will rise rapidly and this can lead to coma and death.

Sobriety Testing

The **blood alcohol content** (**BAC**) correlates very well with degree of intoxication. The BAC level is expressed in grams percent, which means the number of grams of alcohol in each 100 milliliters of blood. As the level rises, the toxic effects of the alcohol become more pronounced. A level of 0.08 is the legal limit for intoxication in most jurisdictions. An individual may be impaired at a much lower level, but at 0.08 he will be arrested. The correlation of the BAC with the signs and symptoms of intoxication are well established. These levels are for the average individual. Those who rarely drink tend to tolerate alcohol poorly, while those who drink chronically and excessively tend to handle elevated levels with fewer signs of intoxication.

- BAC of 0.03: Most people become giddy, but their motor skills are little affected. This is equivalent to a single beer or one highball in most individuals.
- BAC of 0.03 to 0.08: Coordination, reaction time, and judgment decline.
- BAC above 0.12: Nausea and vomiting can occur.
- BAC of 0.25: Slipping into a coma is likely.
- BAC of 0.30: Usually leads to a deep coma.
- BAC of 0.40 or more: Death is likely.

If a police officer detains a person suspected of driving under the influence (DUI), he goes through several steps to determine if the individual is indeed intoxicated. The first is a field sobriety test, where he will ask the person to stand on one foot, stand steady with his eyes closed, repeatedly touch one finger to his nose, walk a straight line in the heel-to-toe manner, or some combination of these. Alcohol primarily affects the coordination and balance centers of the brain and makes each of these tasks clumsy or impossible. A field sobriety test cannot be faked. Physiology conspires against the person and he stumbles, wavers, or pokes himself in the eye.

The officer may also ask the person to take a breathalyzer test (see the appendix). Remember that alcohol passes unchanged through the lungs. It goes directly from the bloodstream into the air sacs of the lungs and out with each breath. The important point is that the passage of alcohol from the bloodstream into the lungs directly parallels the BAC; the higher the level in the blood, the higher the concentration in the exhaled breath. This means that a breath test is very accurate and as with field sobriety tests, it can't be faked.

If a person fails either of these tests, blood for BAC might be obtained to determine the exact level. The arresting officer likely takes the person to a local hospital emergency room where the blood is drawn. This is particularly true if the person has been involved in an accident or has caused property damage, bodily harm, or the death of another. Most hospitals and crime labs can accurately and rapidly determine BAC. The preferred testing method is gas chromatography (see the appendix).

In suspected alcohol-related deaths, the ME can measure the BAC in cadaver blood and determine if the intoxication level was high enough to have caused or contributed to the death. However, there are problems with this determination. The BAC in some corpses actually increases due to the action of bacteria, some of which produce alcohol.

To get around this, a determination of the alcohol level in the vitreous fluid of the eye is done. Since the alcohol content of the vitreous reflects the BAC with a one- to two-hour lag, this can tell the ME what the blood level was one to two hours before death. He can use this to estimate what the level likely was at the time of the accident. For example, if he found the vitreous alcohol content was 0.21 (over twice the legal limit), it would mean the victim had been very intoxicated two hours before his demise and thus still over the limit at the time of the accident.

Embalming a body may make determination of the alcohol level at the time of death very difficult, if not impossible. During the embalming process, embalming fluid replaces most of the blood and leaves behind little for testing in most cases. It also contains alcohol, but the alcohol present is methanol, not ethanol. In this situation, the vitreous fluid can be tested for ethanol and, if present, would supply evidence that the victim had ethanol in his blood.

Methanol

All alcohols are potentially toxic, but methanol is particularly so. Methanol is the denatured alcohol used in Bunsen burners in high school science or chemistry classes. Unlike ethanol, the liver converts methanol to **formic acid** and **formaldehyde**, the same stuff the coroner uses to preserve the tissues he removes from corpses.

Methanol ingestion causes nausea, vomiting, pancreatic and other organ damage, confusion, loss of coordination, and brain damage that can lead to blindness, seizures, coma, and ultimately death from asphyxia.

Isopropanol

Isopropanol is also an intoxicant and a CNS depressant whose effects usually appear within ten to thirty minutes after ingestion, depending upon the amount consumed and whether food or other beverages are taken as well. Fifteen to 20 percent of ingested isopropanol is converted to **acetone**, which produces acidosis (excess acid in the body). This greatly complicates things. The victim appears drowsy and off balance, and possesses a staggering gait, slurred speech, and poor coordination. Nausea, vomiting (sometimes bloody), abdominal pain, sweating, stupor, coma, and death from respiratory depression may follow. Hemorrhage into the bronchial tubes (breathing tubes or airways) and chest cavity may occur.

Isopropanol also absorbs through the lungs and the skin. Not infrequently, infants experience isopropanol toxicity from alcohol-and-water sponge baths used to treat childhood fevers.

OTHER CNS DEPRESSANTS

Opiates, barbiturates, and other tranquilizers are CNS depressants. They make a person sleepy and lethargic and are called downers.

Opiates

Opiates are in the alkaloid family of chemicals and are derived from the sap of the poppy. The opiates are divided into natural, semisynthetic, and **synthetic**, depending upon their source and method of manufacture. They are narcotic sedatives (sleep producing) and analgesics (pain relieving) that produce euphoria, lethargy, and, in larger doses, coma and death from respiratory depression and asphyxia (see Chapter Eight). This is more common when an opiate is mixed with alcohol, which is also a brain depressant. Most opiates are taken either by mouth or injection, and all have great potential for abuse and physical addiction.

Natural opiates come directly from the poppy with **morphine,** a powerful narcotic much like heroin, and **codeine** being the basic ones. Codeine is found in many cough suppressants, has a low potential for abuse, and, unless used with alcohol, rarely causes death. Combining morphine with acetic anhydride or acetyl chloride produces heroin (diacetylmorphine), which is by far the most commonly abused opiate.

To test for opiates, the toxicologist will use the Marquis test as a screening procedure. If this reveals the presence of an opiate, he then attempts to determine which one. Testing for morphine and codeine are fairly straightforward, but heroin is a bit tricky. In fact, the toxicologist won't directly test for heroin. If he did, he would find none.

After injection, **heroin** is almost immediately broken down into monoacetylmorphine and then to morphine. In the living user, testing typically only reveals morphine since this two-step conversion process occurs fairly quickly.

This means that the testing cannot determine if the person used heroin or morphine, since in either case only morphine would be found.

In heroin-related deaths, the results depend on timing. If the victim died shortly after a heroin injection, the conversion process might be interrupted and the toxicologist might find both monoacetylmorphine and morphine.

Even if the heroin in the blood has been completely converted into morphine, an examination of the vitreous fluid of the eye may reveal monoacetylmorphine, which will remain in the vitreous for a much longer period of time. This proves that the victim did indeed use heroin.

The autopsy findings in individuals who die from a heroin overdose are fairly consistent. The ME usually, but not always, finds evidence of pulmonary edema, which is water in the lungs. The lungs often show evidence of talc crystals and cotton fibers, as these are used to cut and filter the heroin, respectively. When the drug is given intravenously, these crystals and fibers are carried through the right side of the heart and are filtered from the blood and trapped by the lungs.

Semisynthetic opiates are created by molecular alterations of morphine and codeine. Many medical analgesics are of this type. Hydrocodone, oxymorphone, and oxycodone (OxyContin) are examples.

Synthetic opiates are constructed in a laboratory and are not derived from either morphine or codeine. Methadone is the best known of this class because of its use in treating heroin addiction. Other synthetic opiates include meperidine (Demerol) and fentanyl drugs.

Barbiturates

Barbiturates are derived from **barbituric acid**. Known as hypnotics (sleeping pills), they include pentobarbital, amobarbital, secobarbital, butabarbital, and phenobarbital. Only phenobarbital, an excellent anticonvulsive (prevents seizures) medication, is widely used today. When mixed with alcohol, barbiturates can readily lead to coma and death from asphyxia.

The Dillie-Koppanyi test is used to screen for the presence of barbiturates in biological tissues.

CNS STIMULANTS

Stimulants or "uppers" are a commonly abused class of drugs that rev up the nervous system and pump up the blood pressure and heart rate. The ones most commonly used are amphetamines and cocaine. These drugs increase alertness, lessen fatigue, and suppress appetite. However, with continued use, they cause irritability, anxiousness, aggressive behavior, paranoia, fatigue, depression, and death.

Chronic users tend to develop **tachyphylaxis**. This means that the body "gets used to" them and their effects are lessened. The user must take ever-increasing amounts to get the same "kick" because the body produces more of the enzymes that metabolize these drugs so that they are destroyed and eliminated at a faster rate.

Amphetamines

Amphetamines belong to the phenethylamine class of chemicals and are what we term **sympathomimetics**, in that they mimic, or act like, the sympathetic side of the autonomic nervous system. This is the fight or flight response. Amphetamines rev up the body for emergency action. To do this, they increase blood pressure, heart rate, and respiration, and produce euphoria and a sense of high energy.

Ultraviolet spectroscopy can determine if a substance is in the phenethylamine class, but cannot distinguish one member from another. This class includes amphetamine, methamphetamine, ephedrine, pseudoephedrine, and phenylpropanolamine. Only amphetamine and methamphetamine are controlled substances, the others appearing in various legitimate medications. This means that finding a member of the phenethylamine class in a person's blood does not mean it is illegal. But the presence of amphetamines or methamphetamines can be useful information for the prosecution. If UV spectroscopy indicates that a member of this class is present in the sample, confirmatory testing follows.

Cocaine

Cocaine is a CNS stimulant that increases alertness, elevates blood pressure and heart rate, and raises body temperature. In higher amounts, it can lead to seizures, strokes, heart attacks, and death.

Typically, cocaine is snorted, or inhaled through the nose. When introduced this way, it rapidly absorbs through the membranes that line the nose and enters the bloodstream. Its effects are felt in just a few minutes. As with amphetamines, cocaine has the problem of tachyphylaxis so the "high" tends to diminish with repeated use. So, abusers have found even faster ways of reaching the "high" they seek.

Cocaine can be mixed with baking soda and water, and heated until all the liquid is evaporated; the solid material remaining is crack cocaine. This form has a much lower boiling point (becomes a gas at a lower temperature), which allows it to be smoked. When inhaled, this gaseous form is very rapidly absorbed through the lungs and into the bloodstream, where it is converted to methylecgonine and benzoylecgonine. Urine testing targets the latter of these two compounds and traces can be found up to three days after last use. Both immunoassay and the Scott test are used as screening tests for cocaine.

HALLUCINOGENIC DRUGS

Hallucinogens alter perceptions and mood, lead to delusional thinking, and cause hallucinations.

Delusions are beliefs that have little or no basis in reality. The person might believe that he is being watched or monitored or that his neighbor, boss, or spouse is trying to harm him.

Hallucinations are sensory experiences that are not real. That is, they are not an abnormal sensing of some sensory input; rather, the entire sensory experience is created within the person's mind. These creations may involve any or all of the senses. They may be visual, auditory, olfactory, taste, or tactile. Sometimes these sensations are so real that the person can't separate the hallucination from reality, or worse, the hallucination becomes the reality.

Hallucinations are part of severe schizophrenia and other mental disorders and can occur in victims of strokes or senile dementia. They are often seen with use and withdrawal from alcohol and other drugs. Hallucinogenic drugs are specifically designed to produce hallucinations.

The most frequently encountered hallucinogens come from the plant world (marijuana, peyote, and mushrooms) or the chemistry laboratory (LSD, STP, and PCP). Their identification depends upon both physical and chemical analyses.

Cannabinoids

By far the most commonly used hallucinogen, and one of the mildest, is **marijuana**. It goes by many street names including Mary Jane, weed, and pot. It is a cannabinoid, which means it is derived from the *Cannabis sativa* plant. The active ingredient **tetrahydrocannabinol** (**THC**) is found in marijuana at a concentration of 2 to 6 percent. **Hashish** is the oily extract of the plant and contains approximately 12 percent THC.

Though marijuana can be added to food and eaten, the most common method of introduction is through smoking. It is rapidly absorbed through the lungs, reaches peak blood levels in fifteen to twenty minutes, and usually lasts about two hours. It produces euphoria, sedation, loss of memory, reduced coordination, and also stimulates appetite.

The body breaks down THC into a series of compounds, the most important being 9-carboxy-tetrahydrocannabinol (9-carboxy-THC), which is the major urinary metabolite. Urine drug testing looks for this compound, which can be found up to ten months after last use. One problem is that even passive exposure can lead to a positive urine test. For example, if a person is in the area where someone is smoking marijuana, his urine may reveal low levels of 9-carboxy-THC.

Often the toxicologist is presented with a plant or plant material and asked to determine if it is marijuana. Identifying marijuana depends upon recognizing physical characteristics of the plant itself and establishing the presence of the active resin in the submitted materials. The plant is palm-like and the leaves have serrated edges. Under a microscope the leaves have claw-shaped hairs on the upper surface and finer hairs on the under surface. The buds are cylindrical, tightly packed, and are entwined with a red thread-like structure. An educated observer usually has little trouble identifying the plant. Chemical analysis of the plant or plant fragments reveals the presence of THC.

In suspected users, presumptive chemical testing is typically by way of the Duquenois-Levine test, which shows a purple color change in the presence of cannabinoids. A positive reaction occurs with all cannabinoids, not just THC, so it can't absolutely identify THC. But since most state laws prohibit the possession of any cannabis resin and not just THC, this test is typically all that is needed. Other presumptive tests include thin layer chromatography (TLC) and gas chromatography (GC). The advantage of GC is that it gives an indication of the amount of THC present. Confirmatory testing for THC is done by mass spectroscopy (MS).

Cacti and Mushrooms

Peyote is a small Mexican cactus that has enjoyed a ceremonial use by many native tribes for centuries. The active chemical in the plant is **mescaline**, which is a hallucinogen in the alkaloid family. Either TLC or GC can confirm the presence of the alkaloids. Further testing to identify mescaline is not necessary since the possession of plant material itself is illegal.

Mushrooms present a different problem. With marijuana and peyote the mere possession of the plant is illegal, while the possession of mushrooms is not. This means that the toxicology lab must identify the psychoactive components (psilocin and psilocybin) of the mushroom before they can be deemed illegal.

Presumptive testing with either Van Urk's reagent or fast blue B screens for the presence of psilocin and psilocybin, which turn the former reagent purple and the latter red. Often, TLC will be used to separate out the components, which are then sprayed with Van Urk's solution. Alternatively, the bands produced by TLC can be viewed under ultraviolet light, which causes the psilocin and psilocybin bands to glow. Confirmatory tests include GC/MS and infrared spectroscopy.

LSD AND OTHER HALLUCINOGENIC CHEMICALS

There are a wide variety of chemically produced hallucinogens, with the most common ones being **lysergic acid diethylamide (LSD)** and **phencyclidine (PCP or angel dust)**.

LSD is very potent and as little as 25 micrograms can produce an "acid trip" that lasts for twelve hours. Though LSD is not directly fatal, the hallucinations it produces are typically vivid and there have been many instances of users harming themselves because of these altered perceptions. The primary screening test for LSD is the Van Urk color test.

PCP is an extremely powerful drug with unpredictable effects. It comes as a powder or in a capsule or pill. It can be swallowed or smoked. PCP can cause depression, irritability, feelings of isolation, and is notorious for producing psychosis, paranoia, and violent behavior. An acute schizophrenic episode may suddenly occur many days after use. In a large enough dose, it can cause seizures and death.

Immunoassay of urine is used for PCP screening and may remain positive for a week after last use. GC/MS provide confirmation.

Other chemical hallucinogens include dimethoxymethylamphetamine (STP), dimethyltryptamine (DMT), and methylenedioxymethamphetamine (MDMA), also known as ecstasy.

DATE RAPE DRUGS

The date rape drugs are a collection of chemicals of various types that share the ability to make the user relaxed, disoriented, and compliant. Some are pharmaceutically manufactured, while others are cooked up by someone with marginal experience and a chemistry book. The major members of this group are Rohypnol (flunitrazepam), ecstasy, GHB (gamma-hydroxybutyrate), and ketamine hydrochloride.

Rohypnol, GHB, and ketamine are commonly used in date or acquaintance rapes, which is where the moniker comes from. They cause sedation, a degree of compliance, poor judgment, and amnesia for events that occur while under their influence. These properties make them effective in date rape situations.

A small amount of GHB or Rohypnol can be slipped into the victim's drink or a bottle of innocuous-appearing water. She may appear and act normally, or might seem happy, excited, pleasantly sedated, or mildly intoxicated. Neither the victim nor her friends recognize how impaired she actually is. She might leave with her would-be assailant because her judgment is impaired and euphoria enhanced. Only later will she realize that something happened, but her memory of events will be spotty or absent. This is exactly what happened with Andrew Luster's victims.

FORENSIC CASE FILES: ANDREW LUSTER

"That's exactly what I like in my room. A passed-out beautiful girl." Andrew Luster, the great-grandson of cosmetics legend Max Factor, spoke those words into his home video camera right before having sex with his "passed-out" victim. He apparently had used GHB to sedate the woman. And it wasn't the first time. After an extensive police investigation turned up tapes of several apparently unconscious women having sex with Luster, he was arrested and charged with multiple counts of illegal drug possession, poisoning, and rape. Testimony by some of his victims revealed the power of GHB. None of them remembered having sex with Luster, nor were they were aware he was videotaping the act. His sensational trial took a bizarre turn when he fled to Mexico. His trial went forward without him and he was convicted and sentenced to 124 years in prison. Luster was finally captured by bounty hunter Duane "Dog" Chapman and returned to the United States to serve his sentence.

The reactions to these drugs are unpredictable and vary from person to person.

Rohypnol (Street Names: Roofies, Roaches, Rope, Mexican Valium) is a benzodiazepine sedative in the same family as Valium and was developed to treat insomnia. Currently, it is neither manufactured nor approved for use in the United States, but is available in Mexico and many other countries. It is manufactured as white tablets of either one or two milligrams that can be crushed and dissolved in any liquid. It takes action twenty to thirty minutes after ingestion, peaks in about two hours, and its effects may persist for eight to twelve hours.

Rohypnol typically causes sedation, confusion, euphoria, loss of identity, dizziness, blurred vision, slowed psychomotor performance, and amnesia. The victim has poor judgment, a feeling of sedated euphoria, and vague or no memory of what has happened.

Ecstasy (Street Names: E, X, XTC, MDMA, Love, Adam) was first manufactured in 1912 and originally patented in 1914 as an appetite suppressant but was never marketed. It disappeared until the 1960s when it was rediscovered and became a drug of abuse. Currently, it is made in underground labs and distributed in pill or capsule form. It has amphetamine (speed-like) as well as hallucinogenic effects. The user has enhanced sensations and feelings of empathy, increased energy, and occasionally profound spiritual experiences or irrational fear reactions. It may cause increased blood pressure, teeth grinding (bruxia), sweating, nausea, anxiety, or panic attacks.

GHB comes as a white powder that easily dissolves in water, alcohol, and other liquids. Currently, it is often found as "Liquid E," a colorless, odorless liquid that is sold in small vials and bottles.

The effects of GHB appear five to twenty minutes after ingestion and typically last for two to three hours. It causes loss of inhibitions, euphoria, drowsiness, and, when combined with other drugs, increases the effects of these drugs. Users might also experience amnesia, enhanced sensuality, hallucinations, and amnesia.

Ketamine is a rapidly acting intravenous or intramuscular anesthetic agent that causes sedation and amnesia. It comes as a liquid, which is often heated and evaporated to a white powder residue. The powder can be added to a liquid such as a bottle of water, compacted into pills, or, most commonly, snorted. Whether swallowed or snorted, it takes effect almost immediately and is fairly short in its duration of action, typically forty-five minutes to two hours.

Many of its effects are similar to ecstasy, but it also possesses dissociative effects, which means the person "dissociates" from reality in some fashion. Often the user experiences hallucinations, loss of time sense, and loss of self-identity. One common form is a depersonalization syndrome, where the person is part of the activities while at the same time is off to the side or hovering overhead watching the activity, including his own actions. As mentioned earlier, this reaction is also common with PCP. Users call these effects "going into a K Hole."

Since ketamine is a sedative and general anesthetic, its potential for serious and lethal effects is real. If too much is taken, the victim may lose consciousness, stop breathing, and suffer brain damage or die.

SNIFFING

An odd, but not rare, form of substance abuse is the sniffing of volatile chemicals. This practice is also known as **huffing**. It began with glue and gasoline but has spread to include napthalene (mothballs), toluene (solvents, fingernail polish, some paints), trichloroethylene (paint thinners, correction fluid), aerosol propellants, some adhesives, and nitrates (amyl and butyl nitrate and nitrous oxide).

When the fumes of these volatile chemicals are inhaled, giddiness, euphoria, dizziness, slurred speech, headache, nausea, and vomiting may occur. Continued exposure can lead to permanent damage to the brain, liver, heart, and kidneys, loss of consciousness, coma, and death.

MISCELLANEOUS TOXINS

Cyanide is one of the most lethal chemicals known and can enter the body by inhalation, ingestion, or directly through the skin. The most common forms are the white powders sodium cyanide (NaCN) and potassium cyanide (KCN) and the gaseous hydrogen cyanide (HCN). Most poisonings are accidental, but suicidal and homicidal cyanide poisonings do occur. HCN is used in gas chamber executions. Cyanide is a metabolic poison, which means it damages the internal workings of the cells (see Chapter Eight: Asphyxia, "Hydrogen Cyanide").

Strychnine is a neuromuscular toxin that causes powerful convulsive contractions of all the body's muscles. The body adopts a posture known as opisthotonos, which means the back is arched so that only the back of the head and the heels of the feet touch the floor. Death results from asphyxia, since breathing is impossible during such violent muscular contractions. At death, rigor mortis often occurs very quickly because the muscles are depleted of ATP during these contractions (see Chapter Five: Time of Death, "Rigor Mortis"). Strychnine is rarely used for homicide since its extremely bitter taste makes it difficult to disguise in food. It is occasionally used for suicide, but since it has the deserved reputation for being very painful, this is also rare.

Mushrooms were discussed earlier (see "Hallucinogenic Drugs"). But those of the psilocybin variety are not nearly as sinister as are the mushrooms of the Amanita family, such as the death cap and death angel mushrooms. These poisonous mushrooms have been implicated in accidental, suicidal, and homicidal deaths.

The death cap is so toxic that a single mushroom can kill. The two main toxins are **amanitin**, which causes a drop in blood sugar (hypoglycemia), and **phalloidin**, which damages the kidneys, liver, and heart. The real treachery of these mushrooms lies in that fact that the symptoms—nausea, vomiting, diarrhea, and abdominal pain—are slow to onset, typically beginning six to fifteen hours after ingestion, but can be delayed as much as forty-eight hours. In general, the later the onset of symptoms, the worse the chances for survival. This is because the toxins go to work on the liver and other organs almost immediately, but since symptoms are delayed for many hours, the victim doesn't know to seek medical help until it is very late. At autopsy, the ME finds severe damage to the liver and the toxicologist might find a low level of sugar in the blood, as well as the amantin and phalloidin toxins.

Ethylene glycol is the major ingredient in many antifreeze solutions. In the body, ethylene glycol breaks down into several compounds, the most important being **oxalic acid**. When oxalic acid is absorbed into the bloodstream, it reacts with calcium in the blood to form calcium oxalate. This reaction consumes the blood's calcium, and low levels can cause a cardiac arrest and death. The calcium oxalate is filtered through the kidneys where it can clog up the microscopic tubules and severely damage the kidneys. At autopsy, the ME finds the crystals in the tubules of the kidney. Oxalic acid is also found in raw (not properly cooked) rhubarb, which can lead to accidental poisonings. It is rarely if ever used for suicide or homicide. Ingestion of this plant can irritate the gastrointestinal tract and cause mouth, throat, and esophageal pain and possibly bleeding. In those who die from this plant, the autopsy reveals a burned and irritated mouth, esophagus, and stomach, low blood calcium levels, and calcium oxalate sludge in the kidneys.

Heavy metals are dangerous metallic elements such as arsenic, mercury, lead, bismuth, antimony, and thallium. Arsenic was the major homicidal poison for hundreds of years but is not frequently used now. One reason is that it works slowly. Even a large dose will take hours to kill someone. And since the death is very painful, the victim will often seek medical help before death and survive. It is occasionally used as a chronic poison.

The most common arsenical compound used in homicidal poisonings is arsenic trioxide, which is a white powder. A dose of 200 to 300 milligrams is usually lethal. Symptoms begin about thirty minutes after ingestion and include nausea, vomiting, abdominal pain, bloody diarrhea, a metallic taste in the mouth, and a slight garlicky odor to the breath. Arsenic severely damages the lining of the stomach and intestines and the ME will easily see this at autopsy in those who die. He will also find fatty deposits in the liver, kidneys, and heart.

Lead poisoning is uncommon and usually occurs in an industrial setting. Occasionally children will peel away and eat wall paint that contains lead. Even though lead has not been a component of interior paints for decades, many older buildings still have layers of old lead-based paint. Lead poisoning can cause anemia, nausea, vomiting, abdominal pain, weakness, numbness, and seizures. To test for these metallic toxins, the toxicologist will employ the Reinsch test or one of the colorimetric tests for screening and atomic absorption spectrophotometry or neutron activation analysis for confirmation (see the appendix).

Insulin is a naturally occurring hormone that is essential for life. It is also synthetically manufactured and is a life-saving treatment for many diabetics. On occasion, diabetics die from an accidental overdose of insulin, but it has also been used for suicide and homicide. In fact, for many years it was considered to be an almost perfect murder weapon. The injection of a large dose dramatically drops the level of sugar in the blood, and since the brain needs a continuous supply of nutrition, death occurs very quickly. And since insulin is normally found in all of us, how could its presence raise suspicion? Now, insulin levels can be determined by radioimmunoassay and if the level at autopsy is found to be very high, the ME searches for a rare insulin-secreting tumor in the pancreas. If he finds no tumor, it is logical to suspect that insulin has been administered by someone else and the ME launches a search for hidden injection sites on the corpse.

Succinyl choline is an injectable drug that paralyzes every muscle of the body and prevents all movement, even breathing. Death is from asphyxia. It has also been considered a nearly perfect murder weapon.

After injection, it is very quickly metabolized by the body and leaves behind little evidence of its presence. However, since the 1980s the gas chromatography and mass spectrometry (GC/MS) combination has allowed for detection of the drug's metabolites. If the ME suspects that this drug has been used, he takes blood samples as well as excises the tissues around any suspected injection sites and sends these materials to the toxicologist. Toxicological testing using GC/MS is directed toward finding metabolites of the drug, which, when found, proves that the drug was at one time present in the victim. This sophisticated testing was a direct result of the Carl Coppolino case.

FORENSIC CASE FILES: THE CARL COPPOLINO CASE

Carl Coppolino and his wife, Carmela, were both physicians who moved from New Jersey to Longboat Key, Florida. On the night of August 28, 1965, Carl called his friend Dr. Juliette Karow and told her he had found his wife dead of an apparent heart attack. Dr. Karow came to the Coppolino home, agreed with Carl's assessment, and ultimately signed Carmela's death certificate, stating that her death was due to a coronary thrombosis. The Sarasota County Medical Examiner also agreed, so no autopsy was performed.

Slightly more than a month later, Carl married wealthy socialite Mary Gibson. This angered his neighbor Marjorie Farber, who had followed Carl to Florida to resurrect their affair. Marjorie visited Dr. Karow and told her that Carl had helped her kill her own husband, William, back in New Jersey. She said that Carl, who was an anesthesiologist, had given her a syringe filled with a liquid and instructed her how to inject her husband with it. She managed to inject only a small amount of the drug into her husband. She panicked and called Carl, who came over and finished off William by strangling him. Carl returned home and then Marjorie called the Coppolino's home, saying that her husband had died of an apparent heart attack. Ironically, it was Carmela who had gone to Marjorie's home and, as

---

a physician, had pronounced William Farber dead and signed his death certificate, stating that his death was due to coronary thrombosis.

After Marjorie's revelations, an investigation into both deaths followed, and New York Chief Medical Examiner Dr. Milton Helpern performed an autopsy on each of the victims. Carl was acquitted of the death of William Farber in New Jersey, but Halpern was well aware that Carl was an anesthesiologist and guessed that he might have access to many anesthetic drugs, including the muscle paralytic drug succinyl choline, which at that time was essentially impossible to find in a corpse. Dr. Halpern brought toxicologist Dr. Charles J. Umberger into the case. After months of research, Umberger finally managed to isolate some of the metabolites of succinyl choline, one of which was succinic acid. He then found large quantities of this acid in the brain tissues of Carmela Coppolino. Carl was convicted of second-degree murder in Florida.

Corrosive chemicals are typically strong alkalis (lye) or acids (hydrochloric acid, sulfuric acid). When ingested, these chemicals severely corrode or "burn" the tissues of the mouth, esophagus, and stomach, which may lead to severe bleeding, shock, and death. These corrosives are rarely weapons for homicide. Most ingestions are accidental and involve children. At autopsy, the ME has no trouble determining the cause and mechanism of death. The damage to the mouth, esophagus, and stomach is extensive and readily visible. Usually an open container near the victim indicates the particular caustic substance used, but if not, samples are taken from the mouth and stomach for analysis by the toxicologist.

PART III

THE CRIME SCENE
AND THE
CRIME LAB

FINGERPRINTS:
A HANDY IDENTIFICATION TOOL

Fingerprints are extremely powerful tools in criminal investigations. They are often the only way police can identify criminals and solve crimes, some of which are decades old. Though a well-accepted standard now, the recognition of the individuality of fingerprints by police, scientists, and the courts did not happen overnight.

If you look closely at your finger pads (the fleshy surface you use for touching and gripping), you will see very fine lines that curve and circle and arch. These lines are composed of narrow valleys called **grooves** and hills known as **friction ridges**. When you see an inked fingerprint, you are looking at the pattern of the friction ridges.

These ridges have a practical purpose. They give your fingers traction and allow you to pick up a glass, a pin, a piece of paper, or a speck of lint. Over the centuries, we learned that these ridges also serve as a unique "signature" for each of us. And as the population of communities grew, this became increasingly important.

When the world was poorly populated and people existed in small nomadic communities of thirty to fifty individuals, everyone knew everyone else. But, as populations grew, settled into ever-expanding cities, and developed systems of government, identifying others became much more difficult.

This fueled a search for a reliable method for identifying people. Most people could not read, write, or sign their name, and this made proving identity for legal matters very difficult.

The two most important characteristics of any method of identification are that it be absolutely individual and that it remains unchanged throughout the person's life. It is also important that it be easily obtained and, for criminal investigations, be frequently left behind at a crime scene. Fingerprints fit these requirements perfectly. But it took several centuries and the astute observations of many scientists and criminal investigators before this tool became an accepted standard.

THE HISTORY OF FINGERPRINTS

The evolution of fingerprints as a method of absolute identity was a long, slow process journey of nearly three thousand years. Let's look at some of the milestones in this development.

PREHISTORY: Early pot makers "signed" their works with an impressed finger or thumbprint, which identified the work as their own.

1000 B.C.: Chinese used fingerprints to "sign" legal documents and even criminal confessions. It is unclear whether this was a ceremonial practice or a true method of personal identity.

CA. 1000 A.D.: Quintilian, a Roman attorney, exonerated a blind man accused of murdering his own mother by showing that a bloody palm print found at the scene had been placed by someone else in an attempt to frame the unfortunate man.

1685: Marcello Malpighi (1628–1694), professor of anatomy at the University of Bologna, was the first to recognize fingerprint patterns when he wrote of the "varying ridges and patterns" he saw on human fingertips. He was the first to use the terms *loops* and *whorls* in describing these patterns.

1823: Johannes Purkinje (1787–1869) of the University of Breslau devised the first system for classifying fingerprints. He listed nine basic patterns and laid down rules for their individual classification. These rules and patterns are the basis for today's classification systems.

1858: In order to prevent fraud in contracts and pension distributions, Sir William Herschel (1833–1917), an English civil servant stationed in Bengal, India, required that the natives sign contracts with a hand imprint. He is perhaps the first European to recognize the individuality of such prints. He also kept a record of his own prints and showed that they did not change over a fifty-year period, a discovery that was of paramount importance to the development of fingerprints as a forensic tool.

1880: Henry Faulds (1843–1930), a physician and surgeon at Tsukiji Hospital in Tokyo, Japan, wrote that fingerprinting could be used for personal identification and suggested that it might be useful for identifying criminals. He also recognized that latent (invisible) prints could be exposed by dusting them with powder and used this method to exonerate a man accused of thievery. The man's prints were checked against one the thief had left on a window, but they didn't match. Days later the real thief was found, his prints matched, and he confessed.

1883: Mark Twain (1835–1910) understood the discriminatory power of fingerprints and used the technique in his book *Life on the Mississippi*, and again later in *The Tragedy of Pudd'nhead Wilson* (1893–1894).

1892: Sir Francis Galton (1822–1911) published his classic textbook, *Finger Prints*, the first book on the subject. He described three patterns within the prints that he called loops, arches, and whorls. More importantly, he gave convincing evidence that no two prints were identical.

1892: Argentina became the first country to use fingerprints to solve a crime. In June 1892, Francisca Rojas murdered her two sons and cut her own throat. The investigation centered on a man named Pedro Ramón Velázquez, but Juan Vucetich (1858–1925), a police official in Argentina, became convinced that fingerprints could be used to identify criminals and devised a classification system that is still in use in most of South America. Vucetich matched a bloody fingerprint found at the scene to Rojas' right thumb and she confessed.

1897: Herman Welcker (1822–1899) compared his own prints taken in 1897 with ones he had taken forty-one years earlier in 1856 and found they were unchanged, thus supporting the findings of Sir William Herschel.

1899: Sir Edward Richard Henry (1850–1931) devised a classification system based on five types of prints. His system is the basis for those used in Britain and America today. Henry was appointed head of Scotland Yard in 1901 and adopted a fingerprint identification system in place of anthropometry.

1902: Burglar Harry Jackson became the first person in England to be convicted by fingerprint evidence when he left his thumbprint at the scene of his crime.

1903: The New York State Prison system instituted the first systematic use of fingerprints for criminal identification in the United States.

1910: Thomas Jennings became the first U.S. citizen convicted of a crime by use of fingerprints. Tried for murder in Chicago, Jennings was convicted and the verdict was upheld on appeal, making his case a landmark in the use of fingerprint evidence in court.

Near the end of the nineteenth century, fingerprints weren't the only identification method being studied. In fact, the field of anthropometry vied with fingerprints to become the standard method for identification. Until an odd and landmark confrontation between the two methods settled the issue, that is.

ANTHROPOMETRY AND BERTILLONAGE

Anthropometry (*anthrop* means "human"; *metry* means "to measure") is defined as the study of human body measurements for use in anthropological classification and comparison. Simply put, it is the making of body measurements in order to compare individuals with each other.

Using anthropometry, French police officer Alphonse Bertillon (1853–1914) developed the first truly organized system for identifying individuals in 1882. Believing that the human skeleton did not change in size from about age twenty until death and that each person's measurements were unique, he created a system of body measurements that became known as **bertillonage**. According to Bertillon, the odds of two people having the same bertillonage measurements were 286 million to one.

This belief led Bertillon to state that all people could be distinguished from one another by key measurements, such as height, seated height from head to seat, length and width of the head, right ear length, left little finger length, and width of the cheeks, among others. His greatest triumph came in February 1883, when he measured a thief named Dupont and compared his profile against his files of known criminals. He found that Dupont's measurements matched a man named Martin. Dupont ultimately confessed that he was indeed Martin.

For many years, this system was accepted by many jurisdictions, but by the dawn of the twentieth century cracks began to appear. The measurements were inexact and subject to variation, depending upon who made them. And because the measurements in two people who were of the same size, weight, and body type varied by fractions of a centimeter, flaws quickly appeared and the system was soon discontinued. Its death knell tolled with the famous Will West case.

FORENSIC CASE FILES: THE WILL WEST CASE

Though landmark in its importance, this case was an odd comical coincidence. On May 1, 1903, Will West came to Leavenworth Penitentiary in Kansas. The records clerk apparently thought that the man looked familiar, but the new inmate denied ever having been in the prison before. As part of his intake examination, anthropometry was performed and officials were surprised to find that Will's measurements exactly matched those of William West, another inmate at Leavenworth. The two men even looked eerily similar as if they were twins.

They were brought together into the same room, but each stated that they were not brothers. Fingerprints were then used to distinguish between the two Wills after which Leavenworth immediately dumped anthropometry and switched to a fingerprint-based system for identifying prisoners. New York's Sing Sing prison followed a month later.

But was the similarity between Will and William West just a bizarre coincidence? Not really. A report in *the Journal of Police Science and Administration* in 1980 revealed that the two actually were identical twins. They possessed many fingerprint similarities, nearly identical ear configurations (unusual in any circumstance except with identical twins), and each of the men wrote letters to the same brother, same five sisters, and same Uncle George. So, even though the brothers denied it, it seemed that they were related after all.

Bertillon reluctantly agreed to add fingerprints to his bertillonage profile. However, he only added those of the right hand, which proved to be a huge mistake.

FORENSIC CASE FILES: THE MONA LISA THEFT

On August 21, 1911, the *Mona Lisa* was stolen from the Louvre Museum in Paris. The thief left a clear thumbprint on the glass that protected Leonardo Da Vinci's masterpiece. To assist investigators, Alphonse Bertillon added his profiles to the investigation. Unfortunately, he had no classification system to streamline the search through his thousands of data cards, which resulted in he and his assistants spending several months digging through his files. They found no matches. Two years later, the police apprehended Vincenzo Perugia and his prints matched the one found at the crime scene.

It turned out that Perigia's prints were among those in Bertillon's possession all the time. Why no match? The print found at the scene was from Perugia's left thumb, while Bertillon's files only contained that of the right. This unmasked yet another flaw in Bertillon's anthropometric system and finally put it to rest once and for all.

RIDGE PATTERNS

Fingerprints are more accurately termed *friction ridge prints*, since it is the ridge patterns that are the basis of printing and comparison. Their use for identification depends upon three principles:

INDIVIDUALITY: Fingerprints are individual and are not shared by any two people, including identical twins. Twins share the same DNA (see Chapter Ten: DNA) but not fingerprints.

STABILITY: A person's fingerprints remain unchanged throughout life, a fact confirmed by the work of William Herschel and Herman Welcker. Fingerprints develop in utero (in the womb) and remain unchanged from birth to death. Unless the damage is deep within the tissues, if someone burns or shaves off the pads of his fingers, the prints will disappear for a while, but as the skin repairs itself and the wounds heal the print reappears.

Severe damage that involves the deeper layers of the skin may leave a permanent scar and keep the prints from reemerging. Nonetheless, completely obliterating a print is difficult, and any scars left behind by the attempt to do so will create new individual characteristics an examiner can use for making a match.

COMMON PATTERNS: Fingerprints have general patterns that allow for a systematic method of classification, reducing the number of records that must be searched when looking for a match.

Once it was proven that fingerprints were individual and remained unchanged for life, a system for effectively using this knowledge became imperative. With an ever-increasing population, matching print after print by hand would have severely limited its usefulness. Some system for narrowing the search had to be devised.

FINGERPRINT CLASSIFICATION SYSTEMS

The purpose of any classification system is to add order to chaos by finding common traits among items. The same is true for fingerprint files. They are useful only if they can be stored in great numbers and can be quickly searched. The FBI has more than 200 million fingerprint files. Organizing the prints into groups makes the search for a match to an unknown print much easier.

BASIC PRINT PATTERNS

Whorls, loops, and arches are still the basis for fingerprint identification and matching because, although everyone has them, how many and where they are located is unique. Not only do the patterns vary from person to person, but they vary from finger to finger in any given individual. We each have ten unique prints, one on each of our digits. Let's look at each of these basic patterns.

Arches

Arches are ridgelines that rise in the center to create a wave-like pattern. They are subgrouped into **plain** (see Figure 12-1) and **tented** (see Figure 12-2) varieties. Tented arches possess a sharper central rise than do plain arches. Only 5 percent of all pattern types are arches.

Plain arch

Figure 12-1: Plain arches have a low central rise.

Tented arch

Figure 12-2: The tented arch rises more sharply than does a standard arch.

Single loop

Figure 12-3: A single loop occurs when one or more ridges double back on themselves.

Double loop

Figure 12-4: A double loop is two loops nested against one another.

Target whorl

Figure 12-5: Target whorls look like a bull's-eye.

Spiral whorl

Figure 12-6: Spiral whorls look like clock springs.

Loops

Loops have one or more ridges that double back on themselves to produce a loop pattern. Loops make up 60 percent of all patterns seen and come in many varieties, some **single** (see Figure 12-3) and some **double** (see Figure 12-4). Single loops are further divided into two types depending upon the direction the ridges flow in relation to the two bones of the forearm—the radius and the ulna: **Radial loops** flow downward and toward the radius or the thumb side; **ulnar loops** flow toward the ulna or little finger side.

Whorls

Whorls look like little whirlpools of ridgelines and comprise 35 percent of all patterns seen. They are subgrouped into: **plain whorls**, which are either concentric circles like a **target** (see Figure 12-5) or **spirals** (see Figure 12-6) like a wound spring; **central pocket loop whorls** that resemble a loop with a whorl at its end; **double loop whorls** comprised of two loops that collide to produce an S-shaped pattern; and **accidental loop whorls**, which are similar to central pocket loop whorls but with subtle differences.

THE HENRY CLASSIFICATION SYSTEM

Sir Edward Richard Henry, an inspector general of the British police in

India's Bengal province, worked on a fingerprint classification system for many years and completed it in 1899. The Henry System, with a few modifications, is still used in the United States and Great Britain.

It is somewhat complicated and I won't go into great detail, but a brief look is worthwhile. At its heart lies the presence or absence of whorl patterns on the various fingers as revealed by the ten-finger print set. Scores are assigned based on which fingers have whorls, with some fingers getting higher scores than others.

First, Henry paired the fingers in a numerator/denominator scheme as follows:

R. Index	R. Ring	L. Thumb	L. Middle	L. Little
R. Thumb	R. Middle	R. Little	L. Index	L. Ring

If a whorl pattern is seen on either of the first pair (right index and right thumb), it is assigned a value of 16 points, on the second pair (right ring and right middle) 8 points, the third 4 points, the fourth 2 points, and the fifth 0 points. Any finger having an arch or a loop pattern is given a value of 0. Finally, 1 is added to both the numerator and denominator.

Let's say that a whorl appeared on both the right index finger and the right thumb. According to the scheme, each of these would receive 16 points and would be indicated by placing a 16 in both the numerator and denominator at the first position of the sequence. If neither had a whorl, both numerator and denominator would have a 0. Further, if a whorl appeared on the right thumb but not the right index, then the numerator would be assigned a 0 and the denominator a 16. In these situations, the first position in Henry's chart would, respectively, look like this:

$$\frac{16}{16} \quad \frac{0}{0} \quad \text{and} \quad \frac{0}{16}$$

So, a set that showed whorls on only the right index and little fingers and the left middle and ring fingers would have a score of:

$$\frac{16 + 0 + 0 + 2 + 0 + 1}{0 + 0 + 4 + 0 + 0 + 1} = \frac{19}{5}$$

Using Henry's scoring system, files are separated into 1,024 groups. Only those prints with the same overall score as the print in question need to be examined. This greatly focuses the search. The actual match is made by hand. That means that the system does not make the match; it simply reduces the number of files agents must wade through.

One major drawback to Henry's system was that it required a complete ten-finger set of prints. Otherwise the overall score could not be calculated. But criminals rarely leave behind a full set of prints at a crime scene. This proved to be a major obstacle for law enforcement until computers and the Automated Fingerprint Identification System (AFIS) hit the scene.

THE AUTOMATED FINGERPRINT IDENTIFICATION SYSTEM

AFIS was established in 1977 through collaboration between the FBI and the National Bureau of Standards (now the National Institute of Standards and Technologies). With the growing numbers of print sets in the FBI's database, some method for storing, retrieving, and matching became a necessity. Imagine hundreds of agents sitting at hundreds of desks looking through thousands of print cards, searching for a match to the partial print left behind by a serial killer. The wheels of justice would indeed move slowly.

The AFIS computer scans and digitally encodes fingerprints, storing this information in massive databases. It can then search thousands of these files each second and attempt to match them to an unknown ten-print set or even a single print.

Once the computer makes a match, an agent trained in fingerprint evaluation hand-checks the prints to see if they indeed match. Even in the computer age, the trained human eye makes the final match.

An example of the power of such rapid searches is illustrated by the famous Night Stalker case in California.

FORENSIC CASE FILE: THE NIGHT STALKER

Between June 1984 and August 1985, a series of brutal rapes and murders occurred throughout Southern California and the Bay Area, putting the entire state on edge. The killer became known as the Night Stalker because he entered his victims' homes at night through unlocked doors, often after he had cut the phone line. He shot any adult males present, then raped the female victims, often in the bed next to where the woman's spouse lay dead or dying. Sometimes he then killed his female victim, and other times he did not. Survivors described him as a thin, foul-smelling Hispanic male with bad teeth.

His final victim was a Mission Viejo, California, woman whom he had raped in the bed next to her boyfriend who had been shot in the head. Both survived the attack. The woman saw her attacker leave in an orange Toyota station wagon and called 911.

Earlier, a teenager working on his motorcycle in his garage saw the station wagon enter and then leave the neighborhood. He wrote down the license plate number, and the next morning called police and gave it to them. The stolen car was found abandoned two days later, but a partial latent fingerprint was lifted from the vehicle.

The print was sent to Sacramento where it was entered into the newly installed AFIS system and within hours a match was made. It was estimated that to perform a by-hand match of the print against the 1.7 million print cards in the Los Angeles area alone would have taken an agent sixty-seven years.

The print revealed that the Night Stalker was Richard Ramirez, a twenty-five-year-old drifter from El Paso, Texas. Once his likeness went out over the media, residents of East Los Angeles recognized him and overpowered him as he attempted to steal another car. The police arrived in time to save him from an angry mob. On November 7, 1989, he received a death sentence.

As you can see, fingerprints have made great strides and sit beside DNA as the only two absolutely individualizing type of evidence. But to use them, they must be found.

LOCATING AND COLLECTING FINGERPRINTS

Fingerprints are sometimes readily visible, while at other times they require a diligent search. A print left in grease, paint, or blood on a wall will be much easier to find than one left on a trash bag by a hand not contaminated with any visible substance. Yet, each can be critical to solving the crime.

Fingerprints are of three basic types:

Patent prints are visible to the naked eye. They occur when the perpetrator of the crime gets a substance such as blood, ink, paint, dirt, or grease on his fingers and leaves behind a visible print.

Plastic prints have a three-dimensional quality and occur when the perpetrator impresses a print into a soft substance such as wax, putty, caulk, soap, moist paint, and even cold butter.

Latent prints, by definition, are invisible and can't be seen without special lighting or processing.

How do latent prints come about? The friction ridges on the inner surfaces of fingers, palms, and the soles of feet have tiny pores that are the outlet openings of sweat glands. Although these glands secrete sweat that is poor in oils, sweat glands in other areas of the body secrete a more oil-rich sweat. When fingers touch these areas or hair, they pick up oils, salts and grime. Other substances are collected from environmental surfaces you touch. A person deposits this residue whenever his finger pads contact another surface.

So, latent prints come from "dirty" fingers. Freshly washed hands will leave fainter latent prints than will fingers that are contaminated with sweat and grime. It is the job of the crime scene technicians and police to locate, expose, and collect these hidden prints.

The best surfaces to search for latent prints are the murder weapon, any tools or objects left behind by the criminal, opened drawers or out-of-place furniture, and entry and exit points. In short, any place the perpetrator may have touched.

Both patent and plastic prints are visible and can be easily photographed, and the photo can be used for matching. Often an angled light is used to increase contrast, but little else is needed to make these prints recordable. Latent prints require special handling and the criminalist has a toolbox full of methods for exposing and collecting them.

SIMPLE INSPECTION

To reveal latent prints, the simple approach is often best. An angled light from a flashlight with or without the aid of a magnifying glass may bring it into focus. Also, because the oils of a latent print will fluoresce (glow) when exposed to some laser and ultraviolet lights, these light sources may snap it into view. Once revealed in this manner, it can be photographed.

Print Powders

Fingerprint powders adhere to the moisture and oils of the latent print residue and expose the pattern of the friction ridges. The powders come in a variety

---

of colors and types. The color chosen should impart the greatest degree of contrast with the background surface. Black (made from carbon black or charcoal) and gray (made from aluminum or titanium powder) are used most often, but white or another light color is used when the background is dark.

Magnetically sensitive powders may also be used; they, too, come in varying colors. These powders are used with a special magnetic "brush," which is actually not a brush at all. It has no bristles and makes no actual contact with the print, which means it is less likely to damage or smear it. Passing the device over the print deposits the powder, and as with standard powder, the print snaps into view. Magnetic powders are better suited for slick surfaces such as shiny magazine covers, coated cardboard, and plastic bags or containers, where standard powders are less useful.

Other specialized powders are fluorescent. After these are applied, the print will fluoresce under a laser light.

Once the powdering process is complete, the print is photographed and then "lifted." Lifting is done by gently laying the sticky surface of a strip of transparent tape over the print. The print pattern sticks to the tape, which is then peeled away and placed on a card for later examination and matching.

Latent prints on more porous surfaces must be treated with chemicals, which reveal print patterns by reacting with some component of the print residue. The reaction creates another compound that is more clearly visible. Common chemicals used for exposing prints include cyanoacrylate, iodine, ninhydrin, and silver nitrate.

Cyanoacrylate Vapor

Cyanoacrylate is a component of Super Glue. In fact, Super Glue is 98 percent cyanoacrylate and it has become an extremely useful forensic tool. For use in exposing fingerprints, the glue must be heated and vaporized, but since it has such a low boiling temperature, little heat is required. The released vapors bind to the amino acids in print residues, revealing the latent print in white.

The item to be treated is often placed in a **fuming chamber** and exposed to the vapor. A fuming chamber is simply an airtight box that will prevent the gaseous glue from escaping. A few drops of the glue are put into a pan, which is placed over a heating element, and after a few minutes vapors fill the chamber and begin to react with the print.

The fumed print is quite hard and stable, as you might expect from Super Glue. It actually fixes the print to the surface it is on so that it can later be presented in court exactly as found. For example, if a print on a crowbar used in an assault is fumed with cyanoacrylate and stained, the crowbar itself can be collected and taken into court. The jury will not only see the print, but the location of the print on the weapon.

Once a print has been exposed with cyanoacrylate, it can be photographed as is or under an angled light. It can also be powdered just as other prints are and at times it can be treated with a fluorescent dye, which after binding to the print, glows under a laser or UV light. This, too, can be photographed.

Rather than setting up a fuming box at the crime scene, police now frequently use a handheld wand. This gadget heats a small cartridge of Super Glue mixed with a fluorescent dye. The wand releases fumes that are directed at the latent print. In this way, the cyanoacrylate "fixing" and the fluorescent dying of the print occur at the same time.

Iodine Fuming

When heated in a fuming chamber, solid crystal iodine releases iodine vapors, which combine with the oils in the latent print to produce a brownish print. The print fades quickly, so it must be photographed right away. Or the print can be fixed by spraying it with a solution of starch in water. This solution will preserve the print for several weeks or months.

Ninhydrin

Ninhydrin (triketohydrindene hydrate) has been a staple of law enforcement for many years and is fairly easy to use. The object that holds the latent print is dipped in or sprayed with a ninhydrin solution. The reaction of the ninhydrin with the oils of the print produces a purple-blue print. One drawback is that this reaction is extremely slow, so the print may take several hours to appear. Heating the object to 80° to 100°F hastens the reaction.

Silver Nitrate

Silver nitrate is a component of photographic film. When a latent print is exposed to silver nitrate, the chloride of the salt (sodium chloride) molecules in the print residue reacts with the silver to form silver chloride. This colorless compound "develops" when exposed to ultraviolet light, revealing a black or reddish brown print.

BLOODY PRINTS

Latent or faint prints left by a blood-soaked finger can present special problems. They are often too faint to photograph and the usual powders may not expose them well enough. Sometimes, but not always, a laser light may cause the print to luminesce so it can be adequately photographed. When this isn't possible or doesn't work, luminol or Amido black might help.

Luminol

Luminol was discussed in detail in Chapter Nine. Though it is better suited for larger pattern impressions such as shoeprints, it can occasionally help with fingerprint exposure. It reacts with the blood's hemoglobin, causing it to fluoresce when viewed in dark conditions. The glow doesn't last long, so once the print is exposed it must be photographed.

Luminol reacts with extremely small traces of blood—down to parts per billion. It can find blood where none seems to exist. Scenes that are many years old or have been cleaned or painted over still hold traces of blood, and luminol will reveal them. Because luminol is so sensitive in locating blood residue, it not only locates very dilute traces of blood but also helps reconstruct a crime scene by uncovering a bloody trail.

Amido Black

Amido black is also called Naphthalene blue-black. It reacts with blood proteins and turns the bloody print a blue-black color. The print is then photographed for later comparisons.

DIGITALLY ENHANCING PRINTS

More often than not a print or partial print is unclear and its minute detail is fuzzy or difficult to see well. Digital technology can help remedy this. The print is scanned into a computer and then subjected to one of many programs that can enhance and clean up a photo. Changing the light, contrast, clarity, and background patterns can make a previously obscure print jump into view. This makes the hand-matching process faster and more accurate.

GLOVE PRINTS

Some criminals wear gloves to prevent leaving behind prints. Thin latex surgical-type gloves are sometimes so thin that the friction ridges still protrude and their pattern might be left on a smooth surface if the glove is contaminated with blood, grease, paint, or some similar substance. In addition, there have been cases where the perpetrator tossed aside these gloves after use and his fingerprints were obtained from inside the gloves' fingertips.

But even using leather or cloth gloves is no guarantee of anonymity. Though the person's fingerprints are not left, the pattern of the glove fingertips or palm might be. If the glove has defects, such as snags in cloth gloves or creases and scars on the surface of leather ones, these can leave a distinctive patterned print at the scene. If the gloves are located and the examiner is able to match the print to defects in the gloves, this can be strong evidence that the gloves in question were used during the commission of the crime. This would be similar evidence to shoeprints or tire tracks (see Chapter Fourteen).

BLOODSTAINS:
PATTERNS TELL THE STORY

Violent crimes, suicides, and accidents often involve the shedding of blood, and the resulting bloodstains can be the key to determining exactly what happened and in what sequence. In cases of criminal activity, these stains are often key to the crime's solution. The analysis of bloodstain patterns is partly science, but mostly art. Science tells us how blood behaves, but understanding the messages hidden within its patterns requires knowledge, experience, and common sense.

From a forensic point of view, blood provides the ME and the crime lab with a wealth of information. The analysis of blood can be divided along biological and physical lines. The analyses in Chapter Nine dealt with blood as a biological fluid, and in this chapter we'll deal with its physical properties—those it shares with other liquids. The bloodstain pattern at the crime scene can be used to determine the cause and manner of death and to reconstruct the crime scene.

BLOODSTAIN PATTERNS

It is unknown exactly when bloodstain patterns were first used in criminal investigation, but it was mentioned in an English court proceeding as early as 1514. In 1895, the first published work on bloodstain pattern recognition appeared. Authored by Polish scientist Dr. Eduard Piotrowski, it cataloged the results of his extensive studies of bloodstains. In 1939, Sorbonne forensic scientist Victor Balthazard (1872–1950) published his considerable work on blood patterns. The famous case of *State of Ohio v. Samuel Sheppard* was seminal in the use of bloodstains in U.S. courtrooms.

FORENSIC CASE FILES: THE SAM SHEPPARD CASE

This famous case of Dr. Samuel Sheppard inspired the popular television series and movie *The Fugitive*. The real case began on the night of July 4, 1954, when Dr. Sheppard's wife, Marilyn, was brutally murdered in her home. Dr. Sheppard said an intruder attacked and bludgeoned his wife to death, while he attempted to protect her but was knocked unconscious. When he awoke, he examined his wife for signs of life, including checking her pulse in her neck, and then called for help.

The home appeared to have been ransacked as if the attacks were part of a home invasion robbery. But police found inconsistencies in the crime scene bloodstain pattern.

Sheppard had no blood on his hands, body, or clothing. Such stains would be expected had he been the one to bludgeon his wife; their absence would seem to exonerate Sheppard. But this complete lack of blood on Sheppard and his clothing raised many questions. Because of the brutal nature of the attack, the killer would have been covered with blood and some of that blood should have been transferred to Sheppard during their struggle. In addition, Sheppard had no blood on his hands, which would be likely if he had checked for a pulse in his wife's blood-covered neck.

Sheppard said that his watch, wallet, ring, and keys were missing. He believed that the killer must have taken them and, indeed, the police found a green bag with the missing items not far from the house. Again, the bag and wallet had no blood on them as would be expected if the killer handled them with his bloody hands. And wouldn't Sheppard's pants, wrists, and hand have blood transfers as the killer removed Sheppard's wallet, keys, watch, and rings? No such stains were found, which meant that whoever took those items and placed them into the bag did so with clean hands.

However, several fine blood spatters were found on the face of Sheppard's watch. These spatters were produced by flying blood droplets and would indicate that the watch had been near the victim at the time she was struck. Had they came from contact with the victim's neck as Sheppard felt for a pulse, the stains would have been in the form of transfer smears and not spatter droplets.

Police determined that most likely Sheppard bludgeoned his wife to death, cleaned the blood from his hands and body, trashed the house to make it look as though a burglary had occurred, and placed his watch and the other items in the green bag and tossed the bag where police would find it. The spatters on his watch went unnoticed. Based on the blood, or lack of blood, as well as other evidence, Sheppard was convicted of murder. The case didn't end there, and over the decades the family of Dr. Sheppard have returned to court to clear the doctor's name in what is viewed by many to be a wrongful conviction. Dr. Sheppard was posthumously declared innocent, but his story remains controversial to this day.

Blood is frequently found at crime scenes that involve violent bodily injury. An analysis of the bloodstain patterns might allow the ME to determine:

- the origin of the bloodstains
- the type of weapon used
- the direction from which an object struck the victim
- the relative positions of the victim and the assailant or assailants
- the locations and movements of the victim and assailant during the attack
- the number of blows or gunshots delivered to the victim
- the truthfulness of any suspects and witnesses

CHARACTERISTICS OF BLOOD

Blood is a complex substance, consisting of both liquid (plasma) and solid (cellular) components. As a liquid, it shares many physical properties with other liquids in that it moves and flows as gravity dictates and tends to pool in low-lying areas. It spreads to cover a surface or to conform to the shape of any container. It possesses viscosity, a measure of its thickness, and surface tension properties. Surface tension is an elastic-like property that results from the attraction of a liquid's molecules for each other. It is the force that holds a liquid together and that pulls a falling drop into a spherical shape.

However, unlike water and most other liquids, blood possesses biological properties. It is more viscous (thicker) than water, and of course it clots. Within its liquid plasma are cellular elements such as red blood cells, white blood cells, platelets, and various proteins, many of which are involved in the clotting process. When blood clots, it separates into a solid dark-red clot and clear yellow liquid called serum.

Plasma and serum are often used interchangeably, but they are quite different even though they appear similar to the naked eye. **Plasma** is the liquid portion of whole, unclotted blood. It contains the proteins that are involved in the clotting process as well as other protein materials. It can be separated from whole blood in a centrifuge, a device that rapidly spins a test tube of blood, causing the cells to settle in the bottom, leaving the plasma on top. **Serum** is the liquid remaining after the blood has clotted and retracted into a clump. It is devoid of the clotting proteins since they have been consumed in the clotting process.

Blood will remain a liquid as long as it's inside the body's vascular system and is moving. At death, the heart stops and the blood stagnates and clots. Also, when blood leaves the body, it will clot in just a few minutes.

SHEDDING BLOOD

Blood is shed from the body in several ways. It can drip, ooze, flow, gush, or spurt, and each of these leaves a distinctive bloodstain pattern. If unchecked, any continuous blood loss can lead to death from **exsanguination** (bleeding to death).

As blood flows from the body, it begins to pool and clot. Normal clotting time for blood is from three to fifteen minutes. This is extremely individual and may be affected by certain diseases, such as hemophilia and some types of leukemia, as well as various medications, like heparin and Coumadin. When blood begins to clot, it first forms a dark, shiny, jelly-like mass. With time, the clot begins to contract and separate from the yellowish serum. Investigators can use this as a rough guide to estimate the time lag since the blood left the victim's body. If still liquid, the bleeding occurred only a few minutes before. If it is a shiny and gelatinous pool, the bleeding likely occurred more than thirty minutes earlier, and if separated into clot and serum, it is probable that several hours have passed.

Corpses do not bleed. At death, the heart stops, the blood ceases to circulate, and bleeding stops. Within minutes, the blood begins to clot within the vessels and tissues of the body. This means that any bloodstains that resulted from spurting or gushing of blood must have occurred before death. Impact spatters and splashes may occur after death, but only through the actions of the assailant, such as if he continues striking the victim or steps in a pool of blood.

The mechanisms by which blood leaves the body can be divided into two categories: passive and projected. Passive mechanisms depend upon the action of gravity alone and include oozes and drips. Projected blood results when some force other than gravity is applied. Arterial spurts, castoff blood, and impact spatter are examples. Each of these types of blood loss creates a unique stain pattern. These are called **bloodstain patterns** or **blood spatters**.

PASSIVE BLOODSTAIN PATTERNS

Passive stains are the result of the effects of gravity. That is, the blood is not ejected or forced from the body by some other force, but rather moves passively under the influence of the force of gravity. Blood that oozes or drips from the body will "move downhill" and will tend to collect in the lowest areas near the injured or deceased person. This could be a floor drain or a low corner of the room. Stairs, ramps, or any steeply angled floor may carry the blood a considerable distance before it clots. Gushing or fast-flowing blood will gather in larger amounts and is capable of traveling further from the body than oozing blood. A slow ooze will clot before moving too far from the body.

Blood may drip from an injured person's wounds, a blood-covered weapon, the assailant's hands, a tabletop, or any elevated object that is coated with blood. If a person is shot or stabbed in the shoulder, blood might run down his arm and drip from his fingers. The assailant who is carrying a bloody knife or bludgeon likely drips blood in his wake. Blood on a bed or tabletop might ooze over the edge and fall to the floor.

Typically, a drop is formed when a small amount of blood breaks away from a larger blood source. Because of the surface tension of the drop, it will be spherical and remain so until it strikes some surface or until it is itself struck by another object. Drops do not break apart into smaller drops simply by falling through the air. If the drop strikes a table edge or is struck by a swinging arm or weapon, it will break apart. But if unmolested, it will fall as a sphere until it reaches the floor or some other surface.

When a falling blood drop strikes a flat surface it splashes in all directions, creating a circle of spatter around the point of impact. The diameter and shape of this spatter pattern depends on the size and speed of the drop, the angle of impact, and the nature of the surface it strikes.

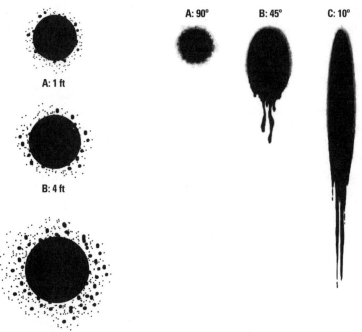

A: 1 ft

B: 4 ft

C: 7 ft

Figure 13-1: Vertical blood drop. The diameter of the bloodstain produced by a drop of blood falling vertically onto a smooth surface increases with the distance traveled: 1 foot (A), 4 feet (B), or 7 feet (C).

Figure 13-2: Angled blood drop. The shape of the stain pattern depends on the angle of impact. The circular pattern seen in a 90-degree approach angle (A) progressively elongates as the angle becomes more acute, as is seen in impact angles of 45 degrees (B) and 10 degrees (C).

A blood drop picks up speed as it falls until it reaches terminal velocity, its maximum free fall speed. The terminal velocity is approximately twenty-five feet per second and is only reached after a fall of twenty to twenty-five feet.

The spatter pattern of a drop of blood increases in size as the drop falls from an inch up to about seven feet, where it produces a circle of nearly an inch in diameter. Above that height, no significant increase in spatter diameter is seen. The size range for a single drop varies from approximately 13 mm to 22 mm, depending upon the distance traveled and the size of the drop (see Figure 13-1).

If a drop approaches at a right angle (90 degrees) to the surface, the spatter pattern will be a symmetric circle around the point of impact. If it strikes from a more acute angle, the spatter is an elongated elliptical pattern with the narrow or pointed end aiming in the direction of the drop's travel (see Figure 13-2).

Using trigonometric functions, it is possible to calculate the **angle of impact** by measuring the dimensions of the stain (see Figure 13-3), a determination that is critical to the accurate reconstruction of the sequence of events at a violent crime scene. The formula uses the width (W) and length (L) of the stain and is:

$$\text{Angle of impact} = \text{arc sin } W/L$$

An area of confusion results from what are called **secondary** or **satellite** spatters. If a large drop of blood falls onto a hard surface, small secondary droplets may surround the original circular stain. Since these have directionality, they are elongated. The confusion arises from the fact that the elongated "tails" of these satellite droplets tend to point toward the direction from which they came and not the direction they were traveling.

The nature of the surface impacted will significantly alter the size and character of the spatter (see Figure 13-4). Hard, smooth surfaces, such as glass, glazed tile, or polished marble, create much smaller spatters than rough, irregular surfaces such as unfinished wood or concrete.

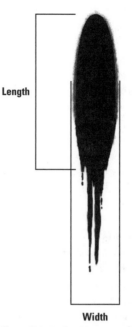

Length

Width

Figure 13-3: Angle of impact calculation. A blood drop's angle of impact can be calculated by measuring its width and length.

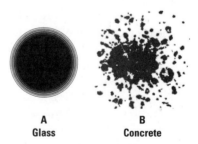

A
Glass

B
Concrete

Figure 13-4: Target surface and spatter shape. The character of the struck surface alters the spatter pattern of a blood drop. A smooth surface (A) creates a small, round spatter while a rough surface (B) causes a very irregular spatter.

Earlier I said that the dead don't bleed. That's true under almost all circumstances, but there are situations where a body might continue to shed blood after death ... for a few minutes anyway. This is called the perimortem period—the time around the time of death.

Take the example of someone killed by a throat slash. He falls dead fairly quickly and the heart stops in short order. But in this situation, the major arteries and veins of the neck, which hold a good deal of blood, have been sliced open. The force of gravity might cause the blood within the vessels to flow through these openings and exit the body. A victim who is lying on his side or face-down might continue to leak blood from these vessels until they are empty or until the blood clots. This can take several minutes so that a pool of blood might collect near the neck of the victim even after death has occurred.

PROJECTED BLOOD SPATTERS

Projected blood spatters occur when an influence other than gravity acts on a blood source. This influence might be a naturally occurring internal force, such as the heartbeat or breathing of the victim, or it may be an external force such as a gunshot or blunt-force trauma. The disseminated bloodstains tend to vary in size and shape and can be produced by several different mechanisms, including stabbings, beatings, gunshots, arterial bleeding, expired blood (blood from airways blown out of the nose or mouth), castoff blood, and splashing. A single stain is not a spatter, since a pattern of stains is required for spatter analysis.

A single gunshot may produce a spatter pattern, but a single blow with a blunt object (a baseball bat, board, or similar item) typically does not. A bullet that enters and exits the body damages tissue, causes immediate bleeding, and carries blood and tissue with it through the exit wound. This produces a characteristic spatter pattern on any object "downwind" from the exit point.

But with a victim who is repeatedly struck in the head, the first blow strikes only skin and hair, and thus does not cause a spattering of blood. It does, however, cause damage and bleeding so that the bloody scalp becomes a **blood source**. A blood source is any collection of blood, in this case on and within the scalp. Subsequent blows to the same area cause spattering of this collection of blood. So, the initial blow produces the blood source and subsequent blows produce the spattering.

Figure 13-5: Point of convergence. Lines drawn through the long axis of each bloodstain intersect at the point of convergence, which indicates the location of the blood source.

Spatter patterns aid the ME in determining the blood source, the source's location at the crime scene, and the mechanism that produced the spatters. This is critical since it can show the positions of the assailant and the victim at the time the attack occurred. This is accomplished by locating the **point of convergence** and the **point of origin** of the spatter. Finding the point of convergence (the location of the blood source) requires the use of simple plane geometry, while the locating the point of origin (the three-dimensional location of the blood source) employs three-dimensional solid geometry. It's actually quite simple, so let's look at how each of these points is located.

Just as we saw with blood drops, the individual droplets that make up the spatter strike nearby surfaces with varying angles of impact and directionality. The impact angle is the angle of approach relative to the surface struck, while the directionality is the direction from which it approached.

The directionality of each stain is used to locate the point of convergence (see Figure 13-5). It is a two-dimensional location that is determined by the convergence of imaginary lines drawn through the long axis of two or more spatters.

At the crime scene, strings are stretched along the long axis of each stain. The strings intersect at the point of convergence. If the angle of impact of each stain is added to this measurement, the point of origin is revealed (see Figure 13-6). This is done by using a protractor to angle each of the imaginary lines or strings to correspond with each stain's angle of impact. Today, laser lights are sometimes used instead of strings and computer programs are available to help with the calculations.

In the crime scene analyst's report, he usually gives a range of possible points of origin of the blood source. For example, after analyzing spatter patterns on the floor, wall, and sofa at the scene of a violent attack, he may state that the point of origin was four to six feet from the wall, two to four feet from the sofa, and four to six feet above the floor. This would indicate that

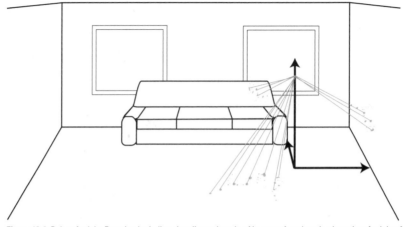

Figure 13-6: Point of origin. By using both directionality and angle of impact of each stain, the point of origin of the stains is revealed.

the victim of the blood-shedding trauma was standing near the wall and the sofa. If he found that the proximity to the wall and sofa were as above, but the distance to the floor was only one to two feet, then most likely the victim was lying on the floor when struck.

A **void pattern** also helps with crime scene reconstruction. A void pattern is an absence of blood spatters in an area where the examiner would expect to see them. This might indicate where the attacker was standing. For example, if someone is severely beaten and blood spatters are found on the walls, floor, and furniture in every direction except to one side of the victim, it is likely that the attacker was standing at that position during the attack and intercepted the spattered blood. Here, the blood droplets would be on the attacker and not on the floor or other objects.

Similarly, if a spatter pattern is found on a suspect's body or clothing, it means he was present at the scene at the time of the attack. Spattering of blood can only occur during the impacts that produce them, so if the suspect had spatters on his clothes, arms, or face, he must have been in close proximity to the victim at the time of the attack. Someone who came along after the attack and accidentally got blood on his clothing would not show a spatter pattern, but rather blotches or smears. These stains are called transfer patterns.

This information can help investigators confirm or refute a suspect's statement, regarding whether he was at the scene during the attack. For example, let's say a husband states that he came home and found his wife on the floor, beaten and bleeding, and tried to perform CPR. He explains that this was how he got blood on his hands and clothes. And indeed he could have smears and blotches of blood on his clothes and body from just such contact with his wife. But what if he also had spatter stains on his arms or pant legs? These could not be present unless he was near the victim at the time the blows were delivered. He would have a bit of explaining to do.

So, the analysis of blood spatter patterns can reveal the blood source and the source's location at the crime scene. It can also provide clues as to the mechanism that produced the spatters.

SPATTER CLASSIFICATION

Classifying spatter patterns helps determine what produced them. Was the blood shed as a result of a gunshot, a blow to the head, or a severed artery? There are two methods for classifying projected blood spatters: one using the mechanism by which the spatter was produced and the other by using the velocity with which the blood was shed. Using these, the ME or blood spatter expert can determine how the spatter was produced, and this in turn helps reconstruct the events of the crime and test the veracity of suspect and witness statements.

MECHANISM: IMPACT, PROJECTION, AND COMBINATION SPATTERS

One classification system uses the mechanism that produced the stains, dividing them into three major types: **impact**, **projection**, or **combination** spatters.

Impact spatters typically occur with beatings, stabbings, gunshots, or any other circumstance where the victim is "impacted" by a foreign object. Projection spatters result from arterial bleeding, castoff blood, and expired blood. Arterial bleeding occurs whenever an artery is torn, severed, or punctured and blood is pumped through the defect by the beating heart.

Castoff stains occur whenever a blood-soaked object, such as a bat or pipe, is swung. The swinging action "casts off" droplets of blood, which may be found on the floor, walls, ceiling, or any nearby object.

Expired blood results when the victim's lungs or airways contain blood and the victim is breathing. Each expiration sprays blood from the victim's mouth and nose.

Often the spatters found at a crime scene are a combination of these. For example, a victim who is stabbed in the chest or neck may leave a combination of impact spatters from the force of the attack, castoff spatters from the arc of the knife, arterial projection spatters if a major artery is damaged, and expired blood from the injured and bleeding lungs or trachea.

SPATTER VELOCITY: LOW, MEDIUM, AND HIGH

The other spatter classification method categorizes spatters by the force with which the impacting object strikes and the resulting velocity of the blood as it leaves the blood source. This system divides spatters into low-, medium-, and high-velocity spatters.

Low-velocity spatters come from an object moving less than five feet per second. This results in larger spatters, which are typically 4 mm or greater in diameter. These types of spatters are produced by several mechanisms. Drops that fall under the influence of only gravity, such as blood dripping from a wound or a blood-soaked weapon, are common examples.

If the dripping source is standing still, the drops fall vertically and create circular stains. But, if the source is moving, such as a fleeing injured victim or an escaping assailant who is carrying a blood-covered weapon, the drops strike the floor at an angle, producing elongated stains with projections extending in the direction of movement. Such information is vital to the criminalist who is attempting to analyze the crime scene.

Let's suppose that an assailant with blood on his hands stands near the body of his victim. He drips blood onto the floor, leaving a round bloodstain pattern for each drop. If he begins to move around in the house, the drops that fall no longer strike the floor from a vertical or 90-degree angle, since as he moves the drops leave his hands with a forward motion. The resulting stains are oval with the elongated tail pointing in the direction of travel. They would appear similar to the angled impacts shown in Figure 13-2. The criminalists can use this to determine the assailant's movements within the crime scene and perhaps to determine his escape route. Following his trail may lead to a discarded murder weapon or other evidence.

Arterial bleeding is also considered low velocity. If an artery is damaged during an assault, suicide attempt, or accident, the blood loss may be in the form of gushes or spurts, depending on the size of the artery, the extent of the damage, and whether clothing or some other object covers the injury. A freely spurting artery results in a spatter pattern that is linear and cascading in nature (see Figure 13-7). Its distance from the wound, length, and volume declines steadily as the blood loss increases and the victim's blood volume and blood pressure declines.

Another low-velocity blood source is castoff blood. This is blood that is cast off or flung from a bloody object due to centrifugal force. Castoff patterns result when a weapon is used to deliver a series of arcing blows, and thus are typically found on walls and ceilings. The resulting spatter pattern is a fairly uniform trail of droplets that reflect the arc of travel of the object (see Figure 13-8). Determining the point of convergence and the angle of impact of these castoff stains will reveal the assailant's position at the time he swung the weapon. In some cases, it is possible to estimate the perpetrator's height and even his handedness, or at least which hand struck the blows.

In addition, the number of castoff patterns found will indicate the minimum number of blows to the victim. Because every swing of the weapon may not produce castoff stains, there may have been more blows delivered, but there can't be fewer.

Figure 13-7: Arterial blood spatters. Arterial bleeding occurs in rhythmic spurts. If the blood strikes a vertical surface, it produces long, linear, or arcing stains that "bleed" downward under the influence of gravity.

Figure 13-8: Castoff blood spatters. Blood cast off from a moving weapon typically forms a linear bloodstain pattern.

Medium-velocity spatters come from objects moving between five and one hundred feet per second. These spatters are typically smaller than stains from low-velocity droplets and vary from 1 to 4 mm in size. Medium-velocity spatters come from impacts with blunt or sharp objects and from expirated blood.

Spatters from impacts with a blunt object are distributed in all directions in a radial pattern. As with low-velocity spatters, an analysis of directionality and impact angle of the stains can help locate the point of origin. And as mentioned before, a void pattern in the omnidirectional spray can indicate the position of the attacker.

If the wounds are to the face, throat, or lungs, blood mixes with the exhaled air, creating a fine spray and producing a mist spatter pattern. This misty pattern may be found on and around the victim as well as on the attacker. These spatters would indicate that the victim lived for a while after delivery of the fatal blows.

High-velocity spatters result when an object strikes at a speed above one hundred feet per second. The resulting spatters tend to be very small, usually less than 1 mm in diameter. They tend to appear as mist-like stains. Gunshots and high-speed machinery injuries usually produce this pattern.

A bullet, which moves at very high velocity, will of course produce a high-velocity spatter pattern. These patterns may be seen near either entrance or exit wounds, but they arise from different mechanisms. When associated with the entrance wound, it is called **blowback** or **back spatter**. In this situation, the direction of travel of the droplets is opposite to the path of the bullet. These types of spatters might be found on the shooter or the weapon, even inside the barrel of the gun in very close-range shots. If the misting is found near the exit wound, it is termed **forward spatter**, since the droplets follow the direction of the bullet. These are likely found on the wall, furniture, or any other object that is near the exit wound.

TRANSFER PATTERNS

Another form of bloodstain pattern is a **transfer pattern**, which occurs when an object soaked with blood contacts an unstained object. Bloody fingerprints and footprints are commonly seen. If the perpetrator brushes against or kneels in a bloodstain or wipes the weapon or his hands on his shirt, he transfers the victim's blood to his clothing. Matching the blood from such a transfer stain to the victim's blood shows that the suspect and the victim were in contact with one another during or after the blood-shedding event.

As with finger and shoeprints, blood-soaked fabric can leave behind a recognizable pattern. Let's say a perpetrator kneels on the floor next to his victim and unknowingly transfers blood to the knee of his pants. After his escape, he leans against his car door and transfers the stain, along with the weave pattern of his pants. This stain, coupled with DNA matching of the blood to the victim, could link the suspect to the crime scene and the victim.

BLOOD SPATTERS AND CRIME SCENE RECONSTRUCTION

The ME uses passive, spatter, transfer, and void patterns to reconstruct the crime scene and to determine the sequence of events that led to the victim's injury or death, which in turn might reveal whether a suspect or witness is being truthful about the circumstances of the crime.

Documenting bloodstain and spatter patterns is essential and must be done in a timely and logical fashion. Police, fire, and rescue personnel, as well as family, friends, and other unnecessary foot traffic, can alter or contaminate the blood evidence. For this reason, control of the scene must be immediate and consistent (see Chapter Two: Evidence, "The Crime Scene"). Indoor scenes, unless they are high-traffic public places, can usually be preserved long enough to obtain the needed information, while outdoor crime scenes, which are subject to environmental influences, and public places require more urgency.

Bloodstains are carefully photographed in an orderly sequence. The photographer initially captures an overall view of the scene and then gradually moves in on individual stains. The latter are photographed closely enough to reveal all needed detail and a ruler or other measuring device is included for scale.

In homicide cases, initial attention is given to the body and any associated bloodstains or spatters. After removal of the body, other spatters are addressed.

Bloodstain analysis might also indicate that the body was moved or that someone attempted to clean up the scene. Long smears might reveal the path of a dragged body and faint smears and streaks on a freshly cleaned floor could indicate an attempt to clean up the scene.

Some bloodstains may be latent (invisible to the naked eye). Luminol (see Chapter Nine: Serology) is frequently used to expose these hidden stains. Even in well-scrubbed scenes, luminol can often reveal bloody tracks and drag marks, which may indicate the perpetrator's movements or escape route or whether the body was moved. It can also expose mop and wipe marks left behind by the attempted clean up.

After adequate photographs have been obtained, crime scene analysts begin to examine the stains for directionality and impact angle. The criminalists run a web of lines or employ laser lights to determine the points of convergence and origin. Once they complete their analysis, they create a report that includes the locations of the victim and the assailant at each stage of the attack, the number and type of injuries inflicted, and the exact sequence of events. Let's look at a couple of examples of this art.

THE ART OF CRIME SCENE RECONSTRUCTION

First we'll return to the example of the husband who came home and found that his wife had been bludgeoned to death. He says that he checked to make sure she was dead, walked to the kitchen and called the police, and then waited on the porch for their arrival. A reasonable and believable sequence of events. But, what if the victim is stretched out on the living room floor and the amount of blood around the body seems meager in view of the violence of the attack? What if no spatter patterns are found on the floor, wall, or furniture near the body? Such evidence suggests that the victim had not been attacked where she lay. What if an examination of the kitchen revealed that the floors had been freshly cleaned? What if one leg of the husband's pants showed a very fine spatter and several tiny drops of the victim's blood were found on the carpet between the kitchen and the location of the body?

This evidence would refute the husband's story in many ways and would elevate him to the top of the suspect list. The spatter analysis would suggest an entirely different scenario beginning with the fact that the victim was likely killed in the kitchen and moved to the living room, probably in an effort to deflect the investigator's attention away from the true crime scene. The kitchen was then cleaned, but the drops on the carpet that fell while moving the body went unnoticed by the husband. Luminol might reveal drag stains where the body was moved, mop strokes where the kitchen floor was cleaned, and wipe marks from where he cleaned the cabinets or kitchen table. Even worse news for the husband is the spatter pattern on his pant leg, which would indicate that he had at least been present at the time of the attack.

Let's look at a second example.

John comes home from work two hours early one day and finds that the back door to his house has been pried open. As he enters, he hears someone moving around upstairs, so he goes to his den where he keeps a handgun locked in a drawer. Taking the weapon, he climbs the stairs and enters his bedroom where he surprises a burglar, standing near a chest of drawers and rummaging through his wife's jewelry case. The burglar charges him and John manages to get off a single shot, which hits the intruder in the upper arm. But the thief strikes John in the side of the head twice with a metal pipe. The gun falls to the floor and John retreats into the hallway, his attacker in pursuit. John heads toward the bathroom in the hopes of locking himself inside, but doesn't make it. He is clubbed to the floor, rolls to his back, and attempts to defect the blows. He is struck in the head several times before he loses consciousness. The attacker strikes John three more times, killing him. He then returns to the bedroom, takes the jewelry box, rushes down stairs, and out the back door.

Using fingerprints and the AFIS system (see Chapter Twelve: Fingerprints, "The Automated Fingerprint Identification System"), the police quickly identify the perpetrator and arrest him at his home. He admits to the robbery but says that the killing was in self-defense. Will the blood spatter patterns at the scene expose his lie?

IN THE BEDROOM: The bullet that entered the thief's arm would produce high-velocity spatter over the carpet, the chest of drawers, and perhaps the bed or any other nearby furniture. There would also be medium-velocity spatter on the floor and doorway from the blows to John's head. DNA analysis could easily determine whose blood was where and firearms examination (see Chapter Sixteen: Firearms Examination) would reveal that the gun was the weapon that fired the bullet through the thief's arm. Also, using gunshot residue techniques and perhaps fingerprints, it would be shown that indeed John had pulled the trigger. So far, the perpetrator's story holds up.

IN THE HALLWAY: Blood drops from both men would be found on the hardwood floor of the hall and the shape of these drops would indicate that both were moving toward the bathroom at the end of the hall. Also, bloody shoeprints might help in this regard. Near the bathroom, blood spatter analysis would show that several blows were delivered to the now unarmed John and defensive wounds on his hands and arms would indicate that he defended himself.

Spatters from the killing blows would cover the floor, wall, and the door leading into the bathroom. The point of origin of these spatters would indicate that John had been on the floor when the killing blows were delivered.

Based on the bloodstain evidence, the criminalist would be able to reconstruct the scene and determine the exact sequence of events. The fact that John was unarmed, on the floor, and in a defensive posture would refute the killer's claim that he had killed John in self-defense. The perpetrator would not only face burglary charges but also perhaps murder charges. He could easily have fled with John injured and down, but he chose to continue his attack until he had killed him.

IMPRESSIONS:
SHOES, TIRES, TOOLS, AND FABRICS

The criminalist is often confronted with various types of pattern evidence for identification and comparison. We saw in earlier chapters how finger, palm, and foot print patterns, DNA patterns, blood spatter patterns, and even the braid pattern of rope ligatures are useful in criminal investigations. But these are not the only such pattern evidence found at crime scenes and presented to the crime lab.

Shoes, tires, and tools often leave behind patterns and impressions. In most cases, these yield only class evidence, but by examining wear and tear and damage marks, the criminalist might be able to individualize the evidence.

For example, the tread pattern of a shoe might identify the size as well as the manufacturer of the product. This narrows the search for the perpetrator by focusing investigative efforts on the sellers and buyers of the particular shoe. But even if the perpetrator is found, wearing shoes of the same size and brand does not mean that his shoes left the impressions at the crime scene. It simply means that they could have. It does not exclude him or anyone else who wears similar shoes from the suspect list. But, if it can be shown that the wear pattern or areas of specific damage to a suspect shoe exactly match that of the impression found at the crime scene, this would individualize the evidence and point the figure more directly at the owner of the shoes.

IMPRESSIONS

SHOE IMPRESSION EVIDENCE

Shoe manufacturers produce shoes in many styles, shapes, and sizes. Some have plain, leather soles with few distinguishing features while others, particularly athletic shoes, have intricate, easily recognizable tread patterns.

In the course of the day, a person's shoe tread contacts a wide array of surfaces. Hardwood or tile floors, carpets, soft soil, rain-soaked sidewalks, mud, grass, and snow are all commonly encountered. The soles tend to pick up dirt, oil, grease, moisture, and debris and then deposit these substances on other surfaces, leaving behind shoeprints.

Crime scene shoeprints, like fingerprints, can be patent (visible), latent (invisible), or plastic (three-dimensional).

These deposited prints and impressions can help crime scene investigators in many ways. They can associate a suspect with the crime scene, help with scene reconstruction, link several scenes together, and indicate the minimum number of participants in the crime.

SCENE AND SUSPECT ASSOCIATION

The most important function of shoe impressions is to associate a particular person with the crime scene. Often this is enough to cast a cloud of suspicion over the individual. For example, if a shoeprint is found at the scene of a murder, robbery, or rape and the print belongs to someone who has no legitimate reason to be there, the simple finding of the print is strong evidence against the person. Why else would his shoeprint be at the scene?

But, even if the person has a plausible reason for his shoeprints to be found in the area of the crime, the prints still may be useful in confirming or rebutting his alibi or story. If the person's bloody shoeprints were found at a homicide scene, it would suggest that he participated in or was at least present during or after the commission of the crime. He might say he was never at the scene, but his shoeprints in the victim's blood would say otherwise.

The manufacturer, size, and style of the shoe can be determined from the shoeprint. The FBI keeps a database of thousands of footwear sole patterns that a print can easily be checked against. This determination can be used to include or exclude a suspect as the possible perpetrator. If the suspect owns, or it can be proven that he has owned, an identical size and style of shoe, he cannot be eliminated as a suspect. The finding of the sole pattern of the uncommon and expensive Bruno Magli shoes at the murder scene of Nicole Brown Simpson and Ronald Goldman and the photos of O.J. Simpson wearing the exact same model and size were crucial in the civil judgment against him.

Alternatively, if it can be shown that the suspect neither possessed nor ever had possessed such a shoe, he might be excluded from consideration.

CRIME SCENE RECONSTRUCTION

Shoe impressions also help with crime scene reconstruction. A suspect whose shoeprints are found at the scene might say he stumbled into the scene, but had nothing to do with the crime. Here, the finding of his prints in areas he says he never entered could be crucial to refuting his story. For example, a neighbor says he walked next door to borrow a cup of sugar and saw the woman who lived there lying on the kitchen floor bludgeoned to death. He says the door was unlocked so he checked her for a pulse, called 911, and waited for the police. He went nowhere else in the house. If the police then discover his shoeprint in the woman's bedroom near her empty jewelry box, his story immediately becomes suspect.

Prints may also indicate the points of entry and exit. Investigators know these areas are common places to search for shoeprints, and that they often aid in reconstructing the sequence of events surrounding the crime. Plastic shoeprints in the soft soil of a flower garden beneath a pried-open window and matching dirt and grime prints on the floor inside the home indicate the point of entry. Or partial prints matching his shoes found on pieces of glass from a broken window at the point of entry can be damaging evidence. Prints left on tile or wooden floors, stairs, countertops, windowsills, ladders, and chair seats reveal the perpetrator's movements within the crime scene area. If prints are found in several rooms of a house that has been burglarized, the search concentrates in those areas.

Prints found near an open rear door might indicate the exit route and a search for more evidence along that path would be instigated. Following shoeprints through the crime scene helps investigators focus their search for evidence. Following the exit trail may lead to where the perpetrator tossed a weapon or articles of clothing, such as a mask or gloves. The best evidence tends to be left in the perpetrator's wake.

SCENE LINKAGE

A shoeprint can link several crimes. If an identical print is found at several different crime scenes, it indicates that the same perpetrator is involved in each. This linkage can be crucial. Besides the shoeprints, each scene might have other evidence that taken alone is of little help, but when considered together could be significant. For example, let's say that prints left by a certain brand of men's athletic shoes, size ten, are found at several murder scenes. At one scene, a blonde hair is also found, at another, gray carpet fibers from a Toyota, at another, red wool clothing fibers, and at yet another blood spatter patterns that suggested the killer was left-handed and approximately six feet tall. Viewed piecemeal, this evidence would tell the investigators little, but with the shoeprints linking the crimes, a clearer picture emerges. The focus is now on a six-foot, left-handed male who drives a Toyota with gray carpets and wears a red wool shirt or jacket. This still does not provide conclusive identification, but it does construct a better profile of the perpetrator and helps investigators focus their search and narrow their suspect list.

MINIMUM NUMBER OF PARTICIPANTS

Multiple shoeprints indicate that more than one person was involved. If investigators find three distinct types of prints, they can state that at a minimum three persons were involved. There could have been more, with some of the perpetrators failing to leave behind shoe impressions, but there can't be less.

CLASS AND INDIVIDUAL SHOEPRINT EVIDENCE

Shoe impressions are most often class evidence in that they identify the manufacturer and size of the shoe. But occasionally they are distinctive enough to be individualizing (see Chapter Two: Evidence, "Class vs. Individual Characteristics").

Each person wears out the soles of his shoes a little differently than everyone else. The wear pattern tends to be more prominent in some areas than in others, since some people walk more on the outside of their feet, others favor the heel, and still others shuffle along on the balls of their feet. How a person's foot strikes the ground determines how the shoe sole will wear.

The surfaces people frequently walk over vary as well. The wear pattern of an office worker would be greatly different from that of a construction worker or a coal miner. A shoe that walks over smooth surfaces, such as carpets and

Figure 14-1: Minimal shoe tread wear pattern. This tread shows minimal wear and damage to the sole.

Figure 14-2: Extensive shoe tread wear pattern. This sole shows more extensive wear.

wooden floors, suffers much less damage than would one that frequently travels over gravel or rough concrete.

Pick a well-worn pair of your own shoes and examine the soles and you will see that the original tread pattern is worn in some areas more than in others. Now, examine the soles of someone else's shoes and you will see that the wear pattern is different. One pair might show minimal wear (see Figure 14-1) while another might reveal more extensive wear (see Figure 14-2).

This means that each of you would leave a different shoeprint. A print made by one of the shoes could be matched to the shoe that made it and exclude the other one. The wear pattern makes the print individual evidence and not simply class specific. Such an individualized pattern often allows the criminalist to positively identify a suspect shoe as the exact shoe that left the impression at the crime scene. Of course, the shoe must be located and tested fairly soon after it left the crime scene impression or further wear and tear can make individual matching impossible.

Other damage and foreign materials can also serve to individualize the print. Cuts, nicks, scratches, and gouges in the sole or a stone trapped in the tread can make the shoeprint distinctive. A print revealing a gouge or a small, embedded rock found at the crime scene positively identifies that a suspect's shoe possesses the exact same gouge or rock pattern as the one that left the print. As with wear patterns, if weeks or months have gone by before the shoes are located and examined, any gouges or cuts might have lost some of their characteristics and an embedded rock may have come loose. Under these circumstances, the individualizing characteristics are lost or altered and a positive match cannot be made.

GAIT PATTERNS

Shoeprints might also give insight into the person's gait, or how he walks. Is his stride long or short? Is his stance wide or narrow? Is he pigeon-toed or slew-footed? Though this is generally unreliable evidence, the stride length and step width may give an indication of height or whether the person has a limp or expose any unusual characteristics of the perpetrator's gait. Widely spaced, short stride-length impressions are not likely to have been left by a tall, thin suspect.

GATHERING SHOE IMPRESSION EVIDENCE

Protecting the crime scene involves protecting all the evidence, including shoe impressions. Investigators must be mindful of where perpetrators might have walked and use every means to avoid these areas until the prints can be recovered. Also, exclusionary shoeprints are obtained from all law enforcement personnel who visit the crime scene. This prevents later confusion when prints are examined at the crime lab and allows the examiner to exclude prints that belong to investigators. Often, investigators slip surgical booties over their shoes to avoid such confusion.

I said earlier that shoeprints can be patent, latent, or plastic. The crime scene handling of these prints employs different techniques.

Two-Dimensional Impressions

Two-dimensional shoeprints can be either patent or latent. Most usable prints are left on firm, smooth surfaces such as wood, tile, or linoleum flooring, glass, plastic, or paper, but occasionally they are also found on carpeting, concrete, and other less even surfaces.

Patent prints are usually made by mud, grease, paint, blood, or some other transferable material. When a person steps into blood or paint, the liquid coats

---

the sole of the shoe so that when he walks on another surface, the liquid is transferred to the new surface in a pattern that reflects the shoe's sole pattern.

Patent prints are by definition visible and can often simply be photographed. Prints in mud or blood are typically easily seen and captured on film. Others may require an angled light or a high-intensity light source to produce a clear photograph. Regardless, care is taken to obtain the photographs at a 90-degree angle relative to the print. This lessens distortion of the image so that more accurate comparisons can be made. A ruler is always included in the field so that accurate size determination can be carried out.

Latent prints are not readily visible to the naked eye and are deposited by shoes that are relatively clean. Shoe soles constantly pick up and deposit debris, most often in the form of oils, dust, and fine dirt. When the shoe then contacts a clean surface, a faint print is left. Even clean and dry shoes can leave prints on glass, hard-surfaced floors, tables, or countertops that have been polished or waxed, or on surfaces that have a faint film of grease or grime.

Searching for latent shoeprints is as meticulous as a search for latent fingerprints. Near the victim and around points of entry and exit are typically the most fruitful areas to search.

Latent shoeprints are handled in a manner similar to fingerprints (see Chapter Twelve: Fingerprints, "Locating and Collecting Fingerprints"). They may be dusted with fingerprint powder and either photographed or lifted with special adhesive tape. For latent dust or fine dirt prints, an **electrostatic lifting device** may be used. This device uses high-voltage electricity to create an electrostatic charge that transfers the print to a lifting film specifically designed for this purpose.

Latent blood prints can often be exposed by the use of luminol (see Chapter Nine: Serology).

Let's say the perpetrator in a robbery-homicide kills the victim in the living room of her home and then walks upstairs and takes jewelry from her bedroom. As he walks on the bloody carpet near his victim, his shoe soles pick up blood. Then when he walks across the room and up the stairs, his bloody shoeprints are transferred to the flooring. These tend to fade from view as more and more of the blood is wiped from his shoe soles with each step. Later during the crime scene evaluation, his trail will be visible and easily followed for several steps, but will eventually disappear. However, if luminol is sprayed over the carpet and the stairway, the previously invisible shoeprints come to

---

life, glowing in the darkened room. The perpetrator's every movement within the house can be seen.

Three-Dimensional Impressions

Plastic shoeprints are those made in soft, malleable materials such as mud or snow. Before the impression is manipulated or casted, it is photographed. Angled light helps bring out depth and detail. Impressions in snow and sand create special problems since they are white and contrast is poor. This can be resolved by coating them lightly with a dark spray paint.

Once the impression has been photographed, a cast can usually be made. Though Plaster of Paris was used in the past, **dental stone**, a hard, durable plaster, is most often used today. Dental stone comes as a powder, which is dissolved in water. First, a metal or wooden frame is placed around the impression. The dental stone mixture is then carefully poured into the shoe impression and allowed to set. This can take from twenty minutes to a couple of hours, depending on ambient temperature and humidity. Near the end of this setting process, the criminalist making the cast scratches his initials into the base so that he can easily and accurately identify it later in court. The casting is then placed in a dry place for approximately twenty-four hours so that it will further harden. This results in a three-dimensional model of the shoe sole, which can be used to match against the shoes of any suspects.

In soft mud and sand, the weight of the plaster or dental stone can deform or change the impression. In this situation, before the casting process is undertaken, it is useful to spray the impression with shellac or an acrylic lacquer, which will harden and support the impression.

Impressions left in snow have other problems: They are easily deformed and snow is prone to melting. Dental stone and plaster are of little use in this circumstance. However, all is not lost. Snow Print Wax, a product that stabilizes snow impressions, can be applied before a cast is made.

A special form of three-dimensional shoe impression occurs when someone steps on a carpet, leaving behind faint indentions in the pile. The indention will fade with time. This is called depression hysteresis. (*Hysteresis* is a Greek word that means "to lag or be delayed." The impression remains or lags behind the footstep.) Sometimes an angled light reveals these impressed footprints. Alternatively, **interference holography** can be used. This technique makes use of a split laser beam to create a holographic image of the print. Though great detail is not revealed, the size and overall structure of the shoe can be determined.

Impression Matching

Once the crime scene (unknown) shoeprint has been photographed, lifted, or casted, it can be compared to a print obtained from a suspect (known) shoe. The sole of the suspect shoe is coated with ink and its sole pattern is transferred to a sheet of paper or acetate. A visual inspection determines if the shoes possess the same tread pattern and general wear patterns. A magnifying glass, or in some cases a low-power microscope, may be used to reveal small cuts and scars, which are the key to matching any individual characteristics.

Once the criminalist has completed his examination, his report may say one of three things: The impressions match, they do not match, or the results are inconclusive, meaning that neither a match nor the exclusion of the unknown print is possible.

TIRE IMPRESSION EVIDENCE

Before the invention of the automobile, criminals, and everyone else for that matter, moved about on foot or by horseback. This restricted mobility meant that most crimes were committed close to the perpetrator's home. After all, how far could he walk or ride a horse in an hour or two? But, with the advent of the automobile, criminals became extremely mobile and could commit crimes in widely spread areas, traveling from state to state, even country to country. This created major problems for law enforcement as they had to greatly broaden their search for evidence. But it also led to new avenues of forensic investigation since a vehicle's tires can leave behind tire tracks or tire impressions.

Today, cars typically travel over paved roads, and though they can't leave impressions in firm asphalt or concrete, they might still leave tracks. If the car rolls through mud, paint, or blood, these substances can be picked up by the tire and transferred to the pavement. Tires also pick up grease and grime from the roadway, and if the tire then passes over a piece of paper or a cardboard box along the roadside, clearly visible tracks can be left behind.

Even in the absence of mud or other foreign substances, tires can deposit impressions on paved roads in the form of latent tracks. These come from the extender oils used in tire manufacturing to make the tires more pliable. The amount of any of these oils present in a given tire varies from manufacturer to manufacturer and with the age of the tire. However, these oils can be deposited on the roadway as the tire passes over its surface. They fluoresce under ultraviolet light, exposing the tread pattern, which is then photographed.

Since tar also fluoresces under ultraviolet light, this technique is not useful on tar-covered roads.

Occasionally, tires leave behind plastic, three-dimensional impressions when they pass over softer surfaces, such as dirt roads, soft shoulders, mud, snow, and many off-road surfaces such as lawns or fields. Each of these can retain an impression of the vehicle's tires.

TIRE TRACK CHARACTERISTICS

Tires are produced in a wide variety of styles and sizes. Each manufacturer makes several different lines, each with its own tread design, and each of these in varying sizes. These tire tread patterns are analogous to tread patterns on shoes.

As with shoeprints, tire tracks tend to be class evidence, but wear patterns can individualize the impression. A particular tread design might point to a particular manufacturer and tire size, but cannot usually indicate the exact tire that made the impression. Matching a crime scene tire impression to a known design stored in a database narrows the search for suspects so that investigators can focus their attention on vehicles with similar tires.

Tires possess several design features that help with classification and identification (see Figure 14-3). The tread is wrapped around the tire's circumference in alternating **ribs** (high points or ridges) and **grooves** (depressions). There are also transverse grooves called **slots** that run at more or less 90 degrees to the circumferential treads. This cross-hatching effect breaks up the ribs into more or less square islands called **lugs**. On the surface of the lugs are small grooves called **sipes**. These features are fairly standard and appear on most tires.

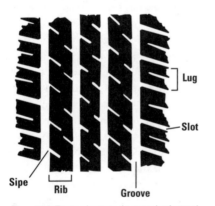

Figure 14-3: Tire tread pattern. An example of a tread pattern, showing the most common design features.

Two other important elements, tread wear bars and noise treatments, are also useful in identification. **Tread wear bars** (also called wear indicators) are bars of rubber that are placed in the grooves at scattered points around the tire. They are raised above the floors of the grooves about one-sixteenth of an inch, which is much lower in height than the tread ribs and lugs. Their purpose is to show the degree of tread wear, and when fully exposed they indicate that the tire should be replaced. Obviously, a tire would have to be significantly worn before these bars would appear in a two-dimensional impression, but they might be clearly visible in a three-dimensional one.

The other tread design feature is called **noise treatment**. If you look at a car tire carefully, you will see that the tread design is not simply a monotonous repetition of ribs, lugs, and grooves. There are minor variations in the sizes of each of these design elements. Typically, the lugs tend to be of three different sizes, though on better tires there may be as many as nine. The purpose of this variation in lug size is to improve traction and reduce noise. At high speeds, tires tend to vibrate. If the tread design is completely uniform, this vibration will increase due to the development of harmonic waves. This creates more tire noise. A slight variation in design pattern prevents this harmonic buildup and decreases tire noise.

The importance of these design elements to the forensic investigator lies in the fact that each of these varies from manufacturer to manufacturer and can aid in determining the maker and the type of tire in question. Several databases of tread designs, including an extensive one maintained by the FBI, are available to facilitate this process.

Besides helping to determine the exact type and style of the tire, track evidence can also reveal information about the car itself. Track width, or **stance**, can be measured from the center on one tire to the center of the tire opposite it. If the tracks found show that the vehicle was turning, it is at times possible to determine the **wheelbase** (distance between the center of the front wheel hubs and the center of the rear wheel hubs) and the **turning radius**. These characteristics vary among vehicle models and may help narrow the field of search. For example, a Cadillac has a wider stance, longer wheelbase, and wider turning radius than a Volkswagen Beetle.

TIRE IMPRESSION MATCHING

As with shoeprints, tire track evidence tends to be class specific rather than individualizing. However, tires are constantly subjected to wear and to road hazards, which produce defects that make the tire unique and distinguishable from others of the same model and size.

Wear patterns vary greatly from tire to tire and car to car. If all tires were perfectly aligned and balanced, wear would be more uniform, but this is rarely the case. Instead, tires wear more on one side than the other or more down the middle. The wear pattern may not be circumferentially uniform so that flat spots or islands of excess wear occur. Cuts, tears, gouges, and accumulated debris such as rocks and nails add a unique quality to the tread impression.

At times, impressions from two, three, or all four tires can be recovered at the scene. It is important to collect each and to determine their relative locations on the vehicle. A new car, with new tires, will have the same brand at all four positions, but older cars may have one or more replacement tires. Maybe the replacement tires are all of one type, or maybe they vary, which can be extremely important individualizing evidence. For example, if impressions obtained from a crime scene reveal that the vehicle possessed a different brand of tire at each position and a suspect vehicle is identified that has the same four brands in exactly the same positions, that is very strong evidence that particular vehicle left the impression. Couple this with matching wear patterns and defects on each of the tires and the match becomes extremely conclusive.

OBTAINING TIRE IMPRESSIONS

Tire tracks may be two-dimensional or three-dimensional. Two-dimensional tracks are found on firmer surfaces and extraneous materials such as paper or cardboard. Three-dimensional impressions occur in soft soil, mud, snow, and other malleable surfaces.

Two-Dimensional Impressions

Two-dimensional impressions are typically photographed. It is important that the photo be taken at a 90-degree angle to prevent distortion and that a ruler is placed near the track for later size determination.

Tread patterns are obtained by "inking" the suspect tire and rolling it down a long piece of white paper to compare crime scene (unknown) impressions with those of the suspect (known) vehicle. It is important to capture the entire tread since the noise reduction patterns and all individualizing defects are the keys to making an individual match. Obtaining only a foot or so of the pattern might miss this critical information.

Three-Dimensional Impressions

Before any other manipulation is carried out, three-dimensional impressions are photographed, usually employing angled light to add detail and depth. After this, investigators can proceed with casting the impression. The technique is similar to that for plastic shoe impressions and typically employs dental stone, though Plaster of Paris is still used at times. A good cast produces a model of the tire tread that can be directly compared to the tread from any suspect vehicle. These castings are better for comparisons than photographs since they possess more detail and accurately reflect depth and design element contour and expose any unevenness in the tire tread pattern.

TOOL MARK EVIDENCE

Tool marks are any impressions or marks left by tools, including screwdrivers, crowbars, chisels, shears, cutters, and presses. The principle behind tool mark analysis is that no two tools are identical. First of all, there are variations in the manufacturing process. Even mass-produced products have minor flaws that distinguish them from one another. Secondly, with use, the tip, sides, and cutting edges of the tool develop nicks, scrapes, striations, and other minor defects. These minor, even microscopic, defects allow for individual characteristics to be identified when the tool is used.

Tool marks fall into three classifications: indented, sliding, and cutting.

Indented marks occur when a tool is pressed into a soft material such as putty, caulking, or thick paint. A screwdriver tip wedged into a caulked window seal to pry open the window often leaves behind an indented mark in the soft caulking. Class characteristics such as width and thickness might be revealed from this type of mark and can be used to determine the size of the screwdriver used. But matching the indented mark to a particular screwdriver is difficult if not impossible.

Sliding marks occur when a tool moves across a stationary surface. Chisels, screwdrivers, and crowbars typically produce sliding marks when wedged into a doorjamb or window seal, leaving behind a pattern of lines or striations in the wood and paint. These striations vary from tool to tool and reveal both manufacturing and use defects. At times, these might be sufficiently distinct to yield a conclusive match with a suspect tool.

Cutting marks are left by tools, such as wire or bolt cutters, that slice through materials. They leave behind lines and striations along the cut edge of the severed object. Since many of these cutting tools are ground by hand, the striation pattern is unique to the particular tool used and might allow the examiner to state that the pattern is so sufficiently unique that it could only have been produced by the particular tool in question. The best cut surfaces for comparison are those made in soft metals such as copper and lead, which tend to retain the microscopic detail of the tool's blade.

Other types of tool marks include indentions produced by hammers and marks left by drill bits. Safecrackers often use these tools and sometimes the marks they leave behind can identify the instrument used in the robbery.

TOOL MARK LOCATION AND COMPARISON

At the crime scene, the best place to look for prying tool marks is at points of entry, such as windows, doors, cabinets, and safes. Cutting marks are typically found on chains and lock hasps.

All marks are carefully examined and photographed and, if possible, re-moved to the lab for further processing. A door, window, lock, or chain may be taken in its entirety to the lab. Casts are made of any indented marks that cannot be moved. Several casting materials are available, but the most versatile seems to be rubberized silicon, since it can maintain the minute detail of the impression and not damage the indented object.

One important caveat is that under no circumstances should the suspect tool be placed into contact with the impression. That is, no effort should be made to "fit" the suspect tool into the indented tool mark. This could alter the impression and make it inadmissible in court, if not completely useless.

In the crime lab, the comparison microscope (see the appendix), which places two images side by side and allows for viewing the smallest details, is the most useful tool for making tool mark comparisons. Under the scope, mi-croscopic lines, grooves, and striations in the mark can be readily seen. When a suspect tool is found, the examiner attempts to match it to the cut object ob-tained from the crime scene. For this comparison he must make a known cut using the suspect implement. This is best done in some soft material such as lead. Lead has the advantage of not only retaining the striations and defects of the blade, but also its softness does not damage or alter the blade. This is criti-cal since the blade is the evidence, and any alteration of it might make it inadmissible in court. The crime scene (unknown) cut surface is then compared to the lab-produced (known) cut surface under the comparison microscope (see Figure 14-4).

Sometimes making a comparison cut through soft lead is not adequate for making an accurate comparison. In this circumstance, the examiner might re-create the crime scene cut as closely as possible by attempting to cut the same material in the same manner. For example, if a bolt cutter was used to cut a lock hasp and the lab possesses both the cut lock and a suspect bolt cutter, the examiner uses the cutter to cut a similar lock

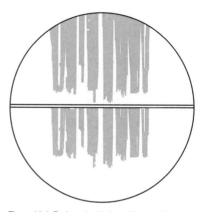

Figure 14-4: Tool mark striations. Marks obtained at the crime scene (unknown) and those made in the lab by the suspect tool (known) as seen through the comparison microscope.

hasp. He attempts to use the same angle and pressure as was used by the perpetrator and then examines the crime scene and the lab-produced cuts with the comparison microscope.

It's not quite that simple because bolt cutters and similar devices produce a special problem for the examiner. The severed bolt or lock hasp is typically smaller than the device's cutting edge. That is, the blade is much wider than the object that it cuts. But if an accurate comparison is to be made, the lab-produced cuts must be made by the same portion of the cutting blade. The examiner could make several cuts using different areas of the blade, but this would be time-consuming and could damage the blade, making further comparisons impossible.

Fortunately for the examiner, there are chemical tests that reveal traces of the cut object or material on the cutting edge of the tool. For example, many locks possess zinc coatings. Testing the blade for zinc may reveal exactly where on the blade the cut was made. This allows the examiner to make a similar cut at the same place and thus make a more accurate comparison.

The examiner might also be called on to make a comparison of pressed imprints. Many illegal drug labs compress their product into tablets. The presses used for this often leave behind distinguishing marks on the surface of the pill, and microscopic examination of the press and the suspect pills may lead to a match.

FABRIC IMPRESSIONS

As with fingers, shoes, and tires, fabrics, leathers, and other materials can also leave behind impressions. The most common fabric impressions come from gloves (see Chapter Twelve: Fingerprints, "Glove Prints"). Like fingertips, gloves pick up grease, dirt, and grime and can deposit either patent or latent prints on surfaces. Sometimes the deposited patterns can be used for comparison with a suspect glove.

Leather gloves tend to crease, wrinkle, and crack with use, and the pattern of these defects may allow for individualization of a print to a specific glove. Gloves made from cotton and other fabrics may leave behind an imprint of their weave pattern. Pulls, snags, tears, and other imperfections may make the print individual enough for conclusive matching to a suspect glove.

Glove prints are handled in a manner similar to fingerprints. Patent prints are photographed and latent prints are dusted with fingerprint powder and then photographed and lifted. And as with fingerprints, prints left in dust can be lifted using an electrostatic device. A piece of plastic film is placed over the print and an electrostatic charge is added. This causes the dust to attach to the film, which can then be photographed.

Other fabrics may also leave impressions. Blood, oil, grease, or dirt on clothing can be transferred to a wall or other object by contact. A killer who kneels next to his bleeding victim might later transfer a bloody fabric pattern on a floor, wall, or door. Fabric impressions from the clothing of hit-and-run victims have been found in the dirt and grease on car fenders and bumpers. A perpetrator might sit on an uncovered chair, countertop, or car fender and transfer a unique pocket-stitching pattern to the surface. Leaning on a tabletop might leave behind the weave pattern of a knitted sleeve or tweed jacket. The possibilities are almost endless.

TRACE EVIDENCE:
SWEATING THE SMALL STUFF

ocard's Exchange Principle, introduced and discussed in Chapter Two, states that whenever any two objects contact each other, a transfer of materials occurs. In the early 1900s, Professor Edmond Locard showed that he could use traces of dust to determine whether a particular individual had been in a certain place. He reasoned that we all constantly pick up and leave behind tiny pieces of our environment, and indeed we do.

Locard's Exchange Principle is the underlying reason each crime scene is secured and access to it controlled. Everyone who enters the scene adds and takes away trace materials; this contamination might render any evidence found useless at trial. Obviously, if the first officers on the scene do not yet know a crime has occurred, or if they must disarm and apprehend a suspect or assist a victim, some contamination will occur. The same is true for medical and rescue personnel who must help the injured. These situations make the criminalist's job much more difficult.

Nowhere is Locard's Exchange Principle more clearly demonstrated than in the location, collection, and analysis of trace evidence.

Modern criminals are clever, or at least they think they are. They know to wear masks and use the dark of night to avoid being identified by any witnesses. They've learned the importance of wearing gloves or wiping away

---

fingerprints. They know not to leave behind blood and semen, which contain their individual DNA pattern. This has been termed "The CSI Effect." Criminals see all the *CSI*-like TV shows, both fictional such as *CSI: Crime Scene Investigation*, and factual, such as the numerous shows on TruTV, Discovery Channel, and A&E. And they learn a great deal about criminal investigations and forensic techniques from these shows.

Yet, despite all this information, criminals continue to be tracked down, arrested, and convicted. Very often this is the direct result of tiny bits of evidence. Evidence the perpetrator doesn't see and doesn't realize he is leaving behind or carrying away on his shoes and clothing.

Transferability is an important characteristic of most trace evidence. It clings to clothing, hides in shoe seams, nestles into hair, and settles into nooks and crannies. And it is typically very durable, in that it survives for months or years.

As we saw in Chapter Two, the major value of trace evidence is that it creates an association or link between suspects, places, and objects. In many situations, trace evidence is the only evidence that connects the suspect to the crime scene. This evidence must be carefully documented, photographed, collected, and protected from contamination before it is presented to the crime lab for detailed analysis.

Trace evidence is predominantly class rather than individualizing evidence (see Chapter Two: Evidence, "Class vs. Individual Characteristics"). This means it can exclude a suspect but can rarely absolutely implicate him. For example, if a blonde hair is found at a crime scene and the suspect has black hair, he is eliminated as the source of the hair and the police must develop another suspect. But, if the suspect's hair matches that found at the crime scene, he remains a suspect. The hair may be his or it may be from someone else with similar hair.

ANALYZING TRACE EVIDENCE

The analysis of trace evidence requires a thorough investigation of its physical, optical, and chemical properties. Since most trace evidence is very small, it can't often be adequately examined with the naked eye. Nor are its optical or chemical properties easily determined. Fortunately, the modern crime lab possesses a wide array of magnification systems, including the compound microscope, the comparison microscope, the stereomicroscope, and the scanning electron microscope (SEM), as well as a number of analytical devices and techniques such as the energy dispersive X-ray spectrometer (EDS), microspectrophotometry, X-ray diffraction, neutron activation analysis, and infrared spectrophotometry. Each of these will be mentioned in this chapter and discussed in detail in the appendix.

Initially, most types of trace evidence are inspected with the naked eye under good lighting conditions. Indirect or angled light can often bring out details by creating depth and shadows in everything from soil and plants to paint and glass. Ultraviolet and laser lights may expose certain fibers and hair. But the minute detail of the substance requires that the evidence be viewed through some type of magnification system.

These microscopic techniques are useful for determining the physical properties of hair, fibers, glass, and paint, and these alone may exclude certain evidence as having shared a common source with a bit of crime scene evidence. But if the two pieces of evidence (the unknown crime scene sample and the known or control sample) are similar physically, then an analysis of the evidence's optical and chemical properties must be undertaken.

TYPES OF TRACE EVIDENCE

The bulk of trace evidence investigation involves hair, fibers, glass, paint, soil, and plant materials. Each of these can be brought to or carried away from the crime scene by the perpetrator without his knowledge. And since these materials often possess distinguishing characteristics, they may help link the guilty party to the scene of the crime. Let's look at each of these.

HAIR

Hair, both human and animal, is frequently found at crime scenes. The ME attempts to determine if the hair is from the victim, the perpetrator, the family dog, or some unknown source. As with virtually all forms of trace evidence, hair is considered class evidence, since at the present time we can't individualize hair to an exact source, unless a portion of the follicle is attached from which DNA can be extracted (see Chapter Ten: DNA).

Hair is small, easily shed, clings to clothing and other materials, and goes unnoticed by the perpetrator. It is hardy and survives for a long period of time, even many years after a body has undergone putrefaction. Many toxins, particularly heavy metals such as arsenic, can be found in hair (see Chapter Eleven: Toxicology).

Hair analysis predominately deals with its structure and chemical characteristics. Its value as evidence depends on how confidently the examiner can use these characteristics to match hairs from known (the suspect) and unknown (the crime scene) sources. It is essential to note that hair varies not only from person to person but also from one area of an individual's body to another. A person's head, pubic, and axillary (armpit) hair are often very different.

The forensic use of hair analysis is not new. In fact, it was one of the earliest forensic techniques—the first paper on its use was published in France in 1857. Microscopic examination of hair was widely used by the turn of the century, and in 1931 Professor John Glaister (1856–1932) published his landmark book on the subject, *Study of Hairs and Wools Belonging to the Mammalian Group of Animals, Including a Special Study of Human Hair, Considered From the Medico-Legal Aspects*. It is now a common forensic technique that has been used to solve many cases, including the famous Atlanta child murders case (see Chapter Two: Evidence).

To help you understand how the criminalist uses hair as evidence, let's look into the nature of hair itself.

Structure of Hair

Hair is an appendage of the skin, as are fingernails, and it grows from a pocket of specialized cells called a **follicle**. The shaft of the hair possesses three parts (see Figure 15-1): The central core is the **medulla**, the surrounding portion is the **cortex**, and the thin outer coating is the **cuticle**. The examiner looks at each of these areas when he attempts to match two hairs.

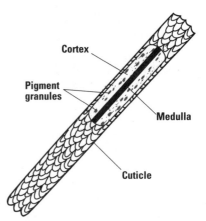

Figure 15-1: Hair shaft structure. The hair shaft consists of a central medulla, a pigment-containing cortex, and a scaly cuticle.

MEDULLA: Though the medulla actually contains a collection of cells, it appears as if it is an empty or mud-filled central canal. The width of the medulla relative to the overall width of the hair is called the **medullary index**. In most animals, this index is greater than 0.5, which means that the medulla is more than half the thickness of the hair. In humans the medulla is typically narrow with an index of approximately 0.3, which means that the width of the medulla is only about one-third the width of the hair shaft. This fact is useful in distinguishing between human and animal hair.

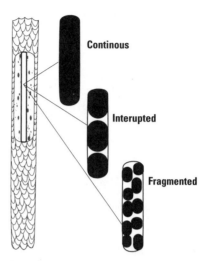

The material within the medulla may appear to be solid and continuous, interrupted, or fragmented (see Figure 15-2). The pattern varies greatly; this fact is extremely useful when comparing two hairs. If the medulla of two hairs (crime scene and suspect's) are of the same width, share the same color, and possess the same pattern, then they could have shared

Figure 15-2: Hair medullary patterns. Some hairs have no medulla, but those that do are continuous (A), interrupted (B), or fragmented (C).

a common origin, namely the suspect. If not, the suspect did not shed that particular hair at the scene.

Not all hairs have a medulla. Human head hairs possess either no medulla or one that is fragmented. The notable exception is that, in those with a Mongoloid racial background, the medulla is typically continuous.

In animals, the medulla material might appear fragmented or disjointed, or may contain cells arranged in various patterns. For example, the medulla of cat hair resembles a string of pearls. These characteristics help the criminalist determine the species of origin. He can refer to databases of hair types from various animals to help make the match.

CORTEX: In human hair, the cortex is the largest portion of the shaft and is the component that contains the hair pigment, which gives hair its color. The pigment particles show highly variable color, shape, and distribution patterns that help determine race and are important to matching and identification. The cortex may also contain tiny air pockets called **cortical fusi** and other structures such as **ovoid bodies**. Under microscopic examination, these various patterns are used to seek a match.

If two hairs share the same color and distribution pattern of pigment, fusi, and ovoid bodies, then the examiner can say that they likely shared a common origin.

CUTICLE: The cuticle, the layer of cells that cover the surface of the shaft, looks like the scales on a fish or like roofing tiles. These scales overlap and always point up the shaft and away from the bulb. They are of three basic types and tend to vary by species. **Coronal** (crown-like) scales give the hair a mosaic surface appearance and are rarely seen in humans, but are common among rodents. **Spinous** (petal-like) scales tend to be somewhat triangular in shape and are not found in humans but are typical of cats. **Imbricate** (flattened) scales are found in humans and many other animals. The examiner can use the scale pattern to determine if the hair is human and to match one hair to another.

Hair Analysis

For the criminalist to make a comparison, he must have the unknown (crime scene) hair as well as known hair samples from the victim and any suspects. The known hair samples should be taken from various areas of the victim's and the suspect's body. Typically, fifty hairs are removed from various parts of the head, several pubic hairs are pulled, and in sexual assault cases, the pubic region is combed for foreign hairs and other trace materials.

The examiner then uses a comparison microscope (see the appendix) to view the two hairs side by side. He first compares their color and width. If these do not match, they did not come from the same source and further analysis is not necessary. If these characteristics do match, he then examines the medulla (if present) and determines if the two hairs share the same distribution pattern. Similarly, he compares the color and distribution pattern of pigment in the cortex. Lastly, he determines if the two share a common cuticle pattern.

By using infrared microspectrophotometry (see the appendix), the examiner might be able to determine if the hair has been dyed, bleached, or treated, and, if he has a complete strand, how long ago the last treatment was. Since hair grows approximately a half-inch a month, a one-inch segment of undyed or unbleached hair near the root would suggest that the last treatment was two months earlier. This may be another point of comparison.

Similarity among all these characteristics is essential for a match. But, as I mentioned earlier, even a match is not absolute proof that a particular individual shed the hair in question. Yet, it is still important evidence. A study performed by the Royal Canadian Mounted Police showed that if a crime scene head hair matches a suspect's head hair in all the above respects, the odds that the crime scene hair came from someone other than the suspect is 4,500 to 1. With pubic hairs, the probability falls to about 800 to 1.

Race, Sex, and Age

It would be helpful if the criminalist could accurately determine the race, sex, and age of the person who shed a particular crime scene hair, as this would significantly narrow the suspect pool. In some cases this is possible, but these determinations are neither easy nor absolute.

The general nature of the hair (color, thickness, curliness) can sometimes separate the source along broad racial lines. Caucasoids tend to have straight or wavy hair with a round or oval cross-sectional shape and a finer, more evenly distributed cortical pigment pattern. Those of Negroid ancestry have curly hair that is flat to oval when viewed in cross section and the cortical pigment is denser and unevenly distributed. Unfortunately, these characteristics are not completely reliable.

Neither age nor sex can be determined with any degree of accuracy. Certain dyes may be more likely used by women than men, but this is not consistent. Infants tend to have short, fine hair, but this too is not predictable.

Site of Origin

One of the first questions the examiner must answer is where on the body the unknown hair likely came from. Is it a head hair, a pubic hair, or one from some other location? Since he wants to match the crime scene hair with hair taken from the same location of any suspect, this determination is essential. Though not always true, in general, hair taken from different body areas tend to have different cross-sectional geometry. Head, eyebrow, and eyelash hairs are more likely round while axillary hairs are oval. Beard hairs tend to be triangular.

Manner of Removal

Was the hair in question yanked out or cut? Such a determination may indicate what happened between the perpetrator and the victim and may help with reconstruction of the crime scene. Microscopic examination of the hair root may reveal tissue adhering to the root. Since yanking hair from the scalp often rips out follicular tissues as well, this finding suggests that the hair was forcibly removed rather than fell out naturally. A cut edge indicates that some sharp instrument was employed to cut the hair. In such situations, it is often possible to determine what instrument did the cutting.

Individual Chemical Characteristics

Many of the chemicals within the human body can also be found in hair. By using techniques such as neutron activation analysis (NAA), which can detect over a dozen different chemicals, the chemical content of hair can be determined.

FORENSIC CASE FILES: JOHN VOLLMAN

In 1958, the body of sixteen-year-old Gaetane Bouchard of Edmundston, Canada, turned up in a gravel pit near her home. She had been stabbed several times in the chest. Near the pit, police found tire tracks and two chips of green paint that appeared as if they had been chipped from an automobile by flying gravel as the car drove away. Witnesses said they had seen Gaetane earlier in a light green car with a man. Friends told police that Gaetane had been seeing John Vollman, a twenty-year-old musician from across the border in Madawaska, Maine.

Indeed, Vollman owned a light-green 1952 Pontiac. An examination of the car showed that the paint was chipped and one of the chips found at the scene seemed to match one of the defects. This was confirmed by microscopic analysis. At autopsy, a single hair was found clutched in the victim's hand. This hair along with hair from Vollman were subjected to what was at that time the new technique of neutron activation analysis and they were found to be very similar in chemical content. Based on these findings, Vollman changed his plea from not guilty to guilty of manslaughter. This was the first murder case in which "atomic evidence," as it was called in 1958, led to a conviction.

Since it is rare for two people to have the exact same chemicals in their hair, comparing the types and amounts of these substances might allow the forensic examiner to determine if two hairs likely came from the same person.

Hair and DNA

I said earlier that hair was predominantly class evidence, but there are circumstances where it can supply DNA, which is highly individualizing (see Chapter Ten: DNA, "Mitochondrial DNA"). Hair production and growth occur when follicular cells die, lose their nuclei (and DNA), and are incorporated into the hair shaft. This means that the hair shaft is composed of cellular debris and possesses no nuclear DNA. The follicle (bulb) is composed of living cells, which do possess DNA. If during their struggle hair is pulled from either the victim or the assailant, the follicular tissue often remains attached and can serve as a source of DNA, which can be used for DNA fingerprinting and matching.

Occasionally, mitochondrial DNA (mtDNA) can be extracted from the hair shaft. Since the hair is built from cellular remnants, and since the cell cytoplasm houses mtDNA, it is possible to obtain a usable sample of mtDNA from the shaft of the hair. Here, even cut or follicle-less shed hair can be useful in identifying the source of the hair.

For example, if the mtDNA of a hair found at a crime scene matches that from hair taken from the suspect's siblings or other maternal-line relative (mother, grandmother, etc.), it proves that the person shedding the hair at the scene shared a maternal lineage with the suspect's relatives. This means that either he was there or one of his relatives was. Since Granny didn't likely commit the crime, he must have. This evidence is not as strong as a nuclear DNA match, but it is very powerful.

FIBERS

Fibers are everywhere. Clothing, carpet, car mats, bedding, towels, and a thousand other things people use every day are made from various fabrics, which of course are composed of fibers. Because fibers are so common and come in such a wide variety of types, they are important types of trace evidence. Like hair, they are easily shed, transferred, and transported, and are almost never noticed by the criminal. They can be found on the victim's or suspect's body, hair, or clothing, as well as at the scene of the crime. After they are collected, the crime lab attempts to identify the manufacturer or the source of a particular fiber, or to match one fiber to another.

Time is critical in collecting fiber evidence. Studies have shown that fibers clinging to the clothing of a victim or a suspect are lost quickly. By four hours,

80 percent have fallen away and by twenty-four hours, 95 percent are lost. For this reason, a search for trace evidence on the clothing of the victim and of any suspects is done as soon as possible. Fibers are lifted from clothing, furniture, or other surfaces with tape or by vacuuming.

Fibers Classifications

Fibers are classified into three basic types: natural, manufactured, or synthetic.

NATURAL FIBERS come from various animals, plants, and minerals. These are often easily identified and compared by microscopic inspection alone. It might seem odd that animal hair would be considered a fiber, but when it is woven or used to manufacture clothing and other household items, it is considered to be a fiber rather than a shed animal hair. Examples are wool, mohair, cashmere, and silk. Plant fibers include cotton, hemp, flax, and jute. By far, the most commonly used natural fiber is cotton. When examined under a microscope it has an easily recognizable "twisted ribbon" pattern. Undyed white cotton is so common that it is of little evidentiary value. Natural fibers, such as asbestos, can also be derived from minerals.

MANUFACTURED FIBERS are also called REGENERATED FIBERS. To make them, raw cotton or wood pulp is dissolved and cellulose is extracted. The cellulose is then "regenerated" into fibers. Rayon, acetate, and triacetate are common examples.

SYNTHETIC FIBERS come from POLYMERS, which are substances made up of a series of single molecules (**monomers**) strung together to make long molecules that can be thousands of monomers in length. The molecule looks like a long chain, each link representing a monomer. The properties of the polymer depend on the chemical structure of the repeating monomer.

Polymer fibers are made by melting a polymeric material and then extruding it through the very fine holes of a spinnerette. The material passes through the spinnerette as a thin fiber that quickly hardens and can then be woven into fabrics. Nylon and polyester are synthetic fibers.

Fiber Identification and Comparison

The fiber analyst is often asked to determine the likely source of a fiber. Is it a carpet fiber, and if so, who manufactured it? Or he may be presented with several fibers and asked to assess whether they came from a common source. Does the fiber on the victim's clothing match fibers taken from the floor mats of the suspect's car? In order to make these determinations, he evaluates the fiber's physical, optical, and chemical properties.

In the lab, he first examines the unknown fiber under a stereomicroscope in order to assess its diameter, shape, color, shine, curls, and crimps, and to look for any attached debris. When matching two fibers, he uses a comparison microscope so that he can compare the two fibers side by side.

Microspectrophotometry is used to determine the fibers true color without the problem of observer variance (see the appendix). In fiber analysis, visible light microspectrophotometry is favored over its infrared light counterpart. This device analyzes the exact wavelength of the light and can determine if the colors of two fibers are indeed identical or merely appear so.

When the film is exposed to **polarized light**, the reflective index of the fiber can be estimated; this, in turn, can help determine its makeup. The **reflective index** is a measure of how the fiber reflects light of various types. Different materials reflect visible, ultraviolet, and infrared light in varied and characteristic ways. Comparing the reflective index of two fibers can help determine if they are similar.

The examiner then views the cross section of the fiber to determine if it is single-stranded or multi-stranded—or if it is tri-lobed, that is, if it appears as if three strands were melted together into one.

If the fiber or piece of fabric has been damaged, a scanning electron microscope can be used to examine fine structural and surface details. These might reveal exactly how the damage occurred. Was it torn, cut, or rent by a bullet?

Another useful characteristic of many fibers is known as its **refractive index (RI)**. When light passes from one medium to another, it is refracted (bent). A stick dipped into a swimming pool or a bowl of water appears to be bent even though it is actually straight. The cause of this phenomenon is that light moves at different speeds in different mediums—faster through air and slower through water. This causes the light to bend so that the stick appears that it, too, is bent. The degree of this bending is called the refractive index. Fibers possess different RIs, and this difference can be used for identity and comparison.

A similar property is called **birefringence**, or double refraction. When light is passed through some synthetic fibers, it is refracted twice and emerges as two different waves of polarized light, each with its own refractive characteristics. A comparison of the birefringence of two fibers is useful for identification and comparison.

If the compared fibers vary in any of the above characteristics, they do not match and could not have come from the same material. If they are similar in all these physical and optical properties, the examiner might then move forward with testing the fiber's chemical makeup.

Two commonly used procedures for the chemical analysis of fibers are the combination of a scanning electron microscope (SEM) with an energy dispersive X-ray spectrometer (SEM/EDS) and the combination of gas chromatography with mass spectrometry (GC/MS) (see the appendix). Each of these reveals the chemical composition of the fiber and of any pigments or treatments that may have been added to it during the manufacturing process or as a later alteration. In fact, GC/MS can separate and identify each chemical found in the fiber or any applied treatments. For example, the presence of tin and bromide might indicate treatment with a fire retardant, while titanium oxide reveals the presence of a delustering product (lessens the fiber's luster or shine).

These chemical determinations can often indicate the manufacturer of the fiber or may serve to more strongly match one fiber to another. After the criminalist analyzes the physical and chemical properties of any known and unknown fibers, he might be able to say that the two very likely came from the same source. Or, if the fibers differ in any of their characteristics, he would conclude that they did not share a common source.

GLASS

As with other types of trace evidence, glass analysis rarely gives individualizing evidence; it gives class evidence, which makes it more useful to exclude than to include a given suspect. The best the examiner can hope for is to be able to state that two pieces of glass are similar and could have come from a common source. The operative word here is "could." Maybe they did, maybe they didn't.

For example, after comparing two pieces of glass, if the examiner finds that they are dissimilar in physical, optical, or chemical properties, he can confidently say that they did not come from the same source. Alternatively, if they share the same class characteristics (color, shape, surface characteristics, and optical and chemical properties), he can say that they could have shared a common source, but can't state that as fact. Thus, the evidence can be exclusionary, but not necessarily proof positive. The notable exception is the matching of lines of fracture.

Glass products are all over—windows, cups, plates, car headlamps, everywhere you look. Glass comes in many sizes, shapes, types, and colors, and varies greatly in its chemical composition. It breaks easily and typically scatters fragments when it does. These tiny slivers and chips can attach to weapons, shoes, and clothing, and settle on the perpetrator's skin and in his hair. The perpetrator who shatters a window, breaks a vase, or drops a glass object risks transferring these fragments to his clothing.

Characteristics of Glass

Glass is produced by heating a mixture of sand (silica or silicon dioxide), limestone (calcium carbonate), and soda (sodium carbonate). During the process certain other chemicals are added to alter the characteristics of the glass. Various impurities also creep into the final product. The analysis of the chemical makeup of these additives and impurities is useful in matching or excluding an unknown sample.

Glass has a hard, smooth surface, and is an ideal substrate for fingerprints and shoeprints. For example, if an intruder smashes a window to enter a home, he might accidentally touch a piece of glass while crawling through the opening, or perhaps step on a large piece of a broken glass that has fallen to the floor. In either case, he could unknowingly transfer clear and usable fingerprints or shoeprints.

Broken glass can also injure the perpetrator, causing bleeding. If the point of entry or exit is a broken window or a sliding door panel, the perpetrator can easily suffer a scrape or cut and be completely unaware of the injury, and that he is leaving behind blood or tissue—and thus DNA.

Glass Analysis

Glass analysis includes two basic evaluations: identification and comparison. The glass examiner will use the physical and chemical properties of the glass to make these determinations.

IDENTIFICATION: Identifying an unknown sample of glass is often crucial to solving a crime. The examiner is often given a piece of glass and asked to identify its source: a broken drinking glass, windowpane, or car headlamp. If he is able to make that determination, he then attempts to identify the likely manufacturer.

Since different glass manufacturers use different manufacturing components, processes, and techniques, analyzing the physical, optical, and chemical properties of glass often indicates who made it and when. For example, a shard of

---

glass from a car windshield or headlamp might reveal the make, model, and year of a car used in a crime or involved in an accident or hit-and-run.

COMPARISON: The examiner is also frequently asked to compare two separate pieces of glass and determine if they share a common origin. Did the chip of glass found on the suspect's clothing come from the shattered window at the crime scene?

Physical Properties

The first step in glass analysis is to look at the color, thickness, shape, pattern, and opacity of the sample submitted. Often these characteristics alone provide a clue to the source or show that two pieces could or could not have come from the same piece of glass. A shard from a window, a shattered crystal bourbon glass, an eyeglass lens, and an automobile windshield would each appear very different.

Unfortunately, this isn't always enough. Let's say the examiner is comparing pieces of a broken drinking glass found at the crime scene (known) with a piece found in a suspect's pant cuff (unknown). The two samples might have the same color, shape, and thickness, but that doesn't necessarily mean they were once part of the same glass. The examiner's next step is to determine if the two pieces of glass possess the same density. **Density** is a measure of weight to size. A one-inch square of dense glass weighs more than an identical-sized piece from less dense glass.

Comparing densities requires a cylindrical container filled with liquids of different densities. The liquids most often used are **bromoform** and **bromo-benzene**. They are mixed together, the piece of glass is added, and then one or the other of the liquids is added until the glass is suspended, neither rising nor sinking. At this point, the glass and the liquid mixture possess the same density. Since the densities of the liquids are known, the density of the mixture, and thus of the glass, can be easily calculated.

If the known piece of glass has been suspended in this way, the unknown piece can be added. If it too remains suspended, the densities of the two are identical. If the unknown fragment either sinks or floats, the two pieces of glass do not share the same density and thus could not have come from the same source.

But, even if the two samples share the same physical characteristics and density, they still could have come from different sources. To help solve this, the examiner would then turn to the sample's optical properties.

Optical Properties

Various glass products transmit, reflect, and refract light in different ways. **Transmitted light** passes through the glass, **reflected light** bounces off it, and **refracted light** passes through but its path is refracted (bent), as in a prism. Different types of glass differ in one or more of these optical properties. If the two samples of glass share each of these optical properties, then they could have come from the same source. If not, then they did not.

The RI is tested by submerging the piece of glass in a liquid, such as **silicon oil**, that changes its RI according to its temperature. The oil is then slowly heated. At the point where the piece of glass seems to disappear, the RIs of the glass and the oil are equal. Since the RI of the silicon oil at any given temperature is known, measuring the temperature yields the RI of the glass.

One problem with matching two pieces of colored glass is that each person sees or perceives color differently. To get around these individual variations, the process of optical examination is automated and employs special optical and computer equipment that can evaluate the true color, transparency, and reflectivity of a glass object. These methods remove observer variation from the process.

If the two samples match in all the above characteristics, the examiner would next look at the chemical nature of the glass in question.

Chemical Properties

During the manufacturing process, various substances are added to glass to change its color, transparency, texture, and strength, as well as its reflective and refractive properties. Cookware and glassware need to be relatively heat- and shock-resistant. This is achieved with the addition of boron. Less sturdy glass is found in windows, which often have a high sodium and calcium content due to the addition of inexpensive soda lime. Colored glass often contains lead and other pigments. Lead is added to make crystal sparkle, while magnesium oxide adds strength to plate glass and aluminum oxide does so to bottle glass.

The forensic chemist tests for these additives and any impurities in the glass with an eye toward matching the chemical makeup of any known and unknown samples.

It bears reiteration that if at any step in the testing process the two samples differ in any of their physical, optical, or chemical properties, the examiner can state with confidence that they did not come from the same source and further testing is unnecessary. If they are identical in every respect, then that is strong evidence that they shared a common source, but it is not absolutely conclusive.

Glass Fractures

Though none of the above properties can absolutely prove that two pieces of glass were once one, the fracture pattern might. If the known and the unknown samples are physically and chemically identical and also fit together in a jigsaw fashion, this is extremely strong evidence that they were at one time joined into a single unit. For example, let's say that a piece of car headlamp is found attached to the clothing of a hit-and-run victim. If a suspect car with a broken headlamp is found and the glass bit exactly fits into the gap, the examiner would feel confident that the piece came from that exact headlamp. The operating principle here is that no two things fracture exactly the same way.

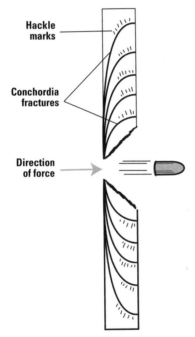

To determine if two pieces of glass were once part of the same object, the examiner often employs a microscope. If the fracture line of a piece of glass found at the scene is compared to a similar piece found in the possession of a suspect, and if the two edges are a perfect fit, the two pieces were once one.

The lab might also be asked to determine how and why a glass object, such as window, fractured. The pattern of the breaks and cracks seen in a window give the examiner a clue as to the speed and direction of the impact; this helps him determine what object likely caused the break. Was the object moving at a low velocity, such as a rock or fist, or at a higher rate, such as a bullet or explosive shrapnel?

Figure 15-3: Conchoidal fracture lines. Conchoidal fracture lines tend to curve out and away from the point of impact. Hackle marks also reveal the direction from which the force was applied.

Hackle marks

Conchordia fractures

Direction of force

Cracks in windows and other flat plates of glass tend to be radial and concentric. **Radial cracks** spread outward from the point of impact in a spoke-like configuration. **Concentric cracks** are a series of progressively larger circles around the point of impact. Overall, the cracked window might look like a spider web.

Certain characteristics of a break allow the examiner to determine the direction from which the impact came. This can be critically important in crime scene reconstruction. Did the bullet penetrate the window from outside in, or was it fired from within the house? Did a perpetrator break the window and enter, or did someone within the house break the window in an attempt to stage the scene and make a domestic homicide look like a breaking-and-entering murder?

Stress-fracture lines known as **conchoidal lines**, which radiate away from the impact site (see Figure 15-3), can help make this determination. Viewed through the thickness of the glass, these lines tend to curve out and away from the point of impact. Looking more closely at these conchoidal fractures, smaller lines that radiate in a perpendicular direction from edges that face away from the impact site may be seen. These are called **hackle marks**.

If a projectile such as a bullet strikes a window and penetrates it, but does not completely shatter it, it may leave a hole with or without surrounding fracture lines. On the side of approach, the bullet creates a rather clean hole, while on the opposite side, a small cone-shaped plug of glass is forced out. Simple visual inspection of the impact site reveals the projectile's direction of travel.

If multiple bullets or other projectiles fracture the glass, it is often possible to determine the order in which they struck. Typically, the radial fractures caused by the second object do not cross those of the first. That is, they end when they encounter glass that is already fractured (see Figure 15-4).

These findings can be extremely important in corroborating or refuting suspect and witness statements and in reconstructing the events surrounding the crime. They can also be useful in assigning culpability.

Let's say two gang members decide to do a drive-by shooting of a rival gang member while he is sit-

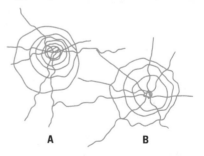

Figure 15-4: Intersecting fracture lines. Impact radial fracture lines end abruptly at those produced by a previous impact. In this case, fracture B followed fracture A.

ting in his car. The driver fires through the victim's car window and begins to drive away. His accomplice then takes the gun and fires again. Both bullets pass through the window and strike the victim, one in the shoulder and the other in the head, killing him. Since both bullets came from the same gun and both men have gunshot residue on their hands (see Chapter Sixteen: Firearms Examination, "Gunshot Residues"), which of the shooters was the actual killer? Was it the first bullet (the driver) or the second (the passenger)? The dilemma is resolved when analysis of the fracture lines in the victim's car window reveal that the second bullet was the killing shot.

PAINT

Like glass, paint is everywhere. Walls, cars, and many types of objects are covered with paint. It is common for paint chips and smears to be transferred from one painted surface to another or to a victim or perpetrator during the commission of a crime.

For most crime labs, automobile paint constitutes the most common samples submitted for evaluation. As with other trace evidence, the examiner might be asked to determine the origin and manufacturer of the paint or to compare two samples to determine if they likely share a common origin. Often an analysis of the paint's physical and chemical properties will determine the paint manufacturer and ultimately the make, model, and perhaps the year of the automobile involved in the accident. This is critical in hit-and-run investigations.

Occasionally, paint or paint chips from a house or other property are brought to the examiner. A perpetrator might walk across a freshly painted floor or brush against a freshly painted wall. He might then transfer this to his car, home, or belongings. Or he might get paint on the tools he used to break into a home or office.

An analysis of these transfers can be critical to placing a suspect at the crime scene.

To determine if two paint samples came from the same source, the examiner must answer three questions:

- Do the samples share identical physical and chemical properties?
- If multilayered, do the layers appear in the same sequence and thickness?
- If a chip, does its fracture edge match that of the area of paint loss?

Paint Analysis

Paint is a complex liquid whose four basic parts are binders, pigments, extenders, and modifiers. **Binders** are typically natural or synthetic resins to which the pigments are added. **Pigments** add color and may be organic (most blues and greens) or inorganic (most reds, yellows, and whites) in nature. Common chemical pigments include titanium oxide, which is white, and iron oxide, which is a component of many red pigments. Pigments tend to be expensive and manufacturers will use as little as possible to achieve the desired hue and concentration of color. **Extenders** add solid bulk, which increases the covering capacity of the paint. **Modifiers** change the gloss, flexibility, hardness, and durability of the paint. An example is lead oxide, which toughens paint and makes it resistant to weather. The type and proportion of each of these varies greatly from paint to paint and are the basis for analyzing paint in the crime lab.

The painting of an automobile is a multistep process that results in laying down several layers of paint products. Though the composition of each layer varies from manufacturer to manufacturer, the types of coatings used are similar. Common layers are:

ELECTROPLATED PRIMER: An epoxy resin electroplated to the car's metal to provide corrosion and rust protection.

PRIMERS: Placed over the electroplated primer to smooth out imperfections and provide a base for the color coat.

BASECOAT: Also called the color coat; the layer that gives the car its color.

CLEAR COAT: Several coats of clear acrylic or polyurethane, which add shine, depth, and protection for the color coat.

An analysis of each of these coats, together or individually, can lead to the manufacturer, make, model, and production year of the vehicle. Each can also serve as a point of comparison between two paint samples.

Occasionally, the analyst is asked to determine the manufacturer of a particular paint sample. Often color alone can make this distinction, particularly with automotive paints, since some colors are unique to a particular automaker. To aid the examiner, there are several comprehensive databases of home and automobile paint. But since paints with similar colors are often quite different chemically, the examiner employs chemical analyses to make or exclude a match.

The lab might also be asked to determine if a known sample and an unknown sample came from the same source. Once again the physical and chemical properties of the paint come into play.

The initial analysis looks into the paint's physical properties such as color and luster. As we saw with fibers, microspectrophotometry can be applied to paint to determine its true color without the problems of observer bias. In this case, the use of infrared microspectrophotometry is favored over the one employing visible light (see the appendix).

Next, layers or coats are examined for the thickness and sequence of colors if several have been used. The sequence of colors on a car that has been repeatedly repainted can be highly suggestive evidence if the crime scene sample and the suspect car display identical order and thickness in each layer.

Let's say a paint chip is recovered from the clothing of a hit-and-run victim and this chip shows that the car had been repainted several times. Maybe the original color was red, but the vehicle was repainted in order black, a different shade of red, and finally yellow. If a suspect vehicle is located and a sample is taken for comparison and this sample shows the exact same colors in the exact same sequence and thickness of layers, the odds are unlikely that another vehicle could have been serially repainted in this fashion. And what if the chemical analysis of each layer of the crime scene sample matches those of the suspect vehicle? Time to book him.

The chemical examination of paint includes an analysis of any binders, pigments, extenders, and modifiers. To do this, the examiner will use the combination GC/MS (see the appendix) with a slight twist. Since the paint chip is a solid, the process used is called **pyrolysis gas chromatography (Py/GC)**. Pyrolysis is the conversion of a solid into a gas by using high heat. In Py/GC, the chip is vaporized and the resulting gas passes through the GC column and is separated into its various chemical components. It then undergoes mass spectrometry, which reveals the "chemical fingerprint" of the components of the paint and allows for an accurate comparison of the submitted paint samples.

In addition, the use of scanning electron microscopy (SEM) and energy dispersive X-ray spectrometry (EDS), a combination termed SEM/EDS (see the appendix), offers a much higher resolution for separating the layers of the paint as well as the ability to perform an elemental analysis of each layer. Alternatively, infrared spectrophotometry (often used in conjunction with GC) has the ability to analyze the chemical nature of the paint as does **X-ray diffraction (XRD)** and **analytic electron microscopy (AEM)**. These latter two techniques can accurately identify the various polymeric forms of paint additives. For example, some paints contain titanium oxide, which comes in three polymorphic forms. These diffraction techniques can distinguish these forms, and this might serve as the basis for comparing two otherwise very similar paints from one another. Each of these techniques is discussed in the appendix.

Finding that a known and an unknown sample are chemically identical can strongly suggest, though not absolutely prove, that the two samples came from the same source.

But, by far, the most individualizing evidence in paint analysis is physical match of the edges of a paint chip. Just as we saw with glass analysis, if the edges of a known and unknown paint chip can be shown to perfectly fit in exact jigsaw fashion, this is fairly conclusive evidence that the two are from the same source. Stereomicroscopic, comparative microscopic, and scanning electron microscopic examinations of the chips can aid in this matching process (see the appendix).

SOILS AND PLANTS

Soil and plant materials are also trace evidence, since they are typically left behind or carried away from crime scenes in small quantities. Either can provide evidence that links a suspect to the scene of the crime. The lab is often asked to analyze soil taken from crime scenes, or from a suspect's shoes, clothing, or car tires or from tools such as shovels.

Soil is not simply dirt. It is a complex mixture of minerals, plant and animal matter, and tiny particles of man-made products including glass, paint, asphalt, concrete, and other materials. It varies greatly from region to region and from locale to locale in a given area. For example, the soil in the Kansas heartland is much different from the red clay of Alabama. And the soil in a California beach-front community will differ greatly from soil in a downtown Los Angeles park.

If a known sample of soil is compared with unknown sample obtained from a suspect's car or shoes and the two match physically and chemically, the examiner can say that the two samples likely came from the same place. This can place the suspect at the scene of the crime or can at least cast doubt on his story of where he picked up the innocuous-appearing dirt on his shoes.

Soil analysis begins with a visual and microscopic inspection and progresses to determination of color, consistency, pH (a measure of soil acidity), and mineral content. Any foreign substances, such as plant material or animal hair are also searched for. Let's say a suspect says he has never been near a beach community where a crime has occurred, yet patches of sandy soil from the area are found on his car tires and floor mats. This could cast doubt on his story. Similarly, if a corpse has been found at a nearby stable, the finding of horse hair and flecks of horse manure in a dirt sample taken from a suspect's boots might indicate that the soil came from a horse farm and not from the suspect's backyard as he said.

If the known and unknown samples are similar physically, chemical analyses are then done to determine if two samples are chemically similar. GC/MS can be used to identify many constitutes of the sample and X-ray diffraction is useful for examining and comparing any minerals present in the soil.

Another technique known as **differential thermal analysis (DTA)** is also useful. The principle behind this analysis is that soils absorb and release heat at differing rates. In this test, a sample is placed into a specially designed furnace and heated. The point at which it breaks down, melts, or boils is determined. This point can be compared with other soils and their thermal properties can be said to match or not.

Plant materials have great forensic significance. They may be included in a soil sample or may be found on corpses, clothing, flooring, car mats, tools, and any number of places. Leaves, stems, pine needles, bark, flower petals, seeds, and pollen might be submitted for analysis.

Since various plants are native to different areas, the identification of any plant products can help determine the place of origin of the soil sample. For example, if pine needles are found on the floor near a homicide victim, and there are no pine trees near the residence, it is likely that the killer brought them with him on his clothing or shoes. A determination of the particular species of pine tree might narrow the area of search for the suspect.

Pollen, which comes from flowering plants, can be extremely useful to the forensics examiner. Pollen grains are tiny and rarely noticed, yet they are highly distinctive for their plant of origin. They may be found on clothing, in a victim's or suspect's hair, and even in envelopes that contain threatening letters or ransom notes. Microscopic identification of pollen found on a suspect might reveal that he had been in an area where the particular plant was in bloom, and this might serve to link him to a nearby crime scene. There are several pollen reference databases that help with species identification.

Finally, DNA might play a role (see Chapter Ten: DNA). Let's say a corpse is found along a roadside and, on examination, bits of pine needles and a fine dust of pine pollen are found in the victim's hair. Let's further say that

---

the nearest pine trees are a mile away, where a vagrant is found sleeping beneath one of them. Pine needles on his clothing, his sleeping bag, and the nearby ground are similar to those found on the victim. Yet, the vagrant denies that he has ever seen the victim. DNA from the needles and pine pollen obtained from the victim could be compared with the DNA from the needles and pollen found on the vagrant. A match would indicate that the materials found on the victim didn't come from just any pine tree, but from the specific tree under which the vagrant was found.

DUST

Dust is different from soil. It is any finely powdered substance, including coal dust, flour, cement or stone dust, tiny paper fibers, and many other products. If these are located at a crime scene or on a murder victim, the investigators have a great deal of useful information. The type of dust material might suggest that the killer had a specific occupation or a particular hobby. If similar dust can be located at a suspect's residence, car, or place of work, it provides a connection between him and the crime. Perhaps not enough to win a conviction, or even to file charges, but it may help direct further investigation and focus the police more closely on the suspect.

Let's say traces of cement and brick dust are found on the carpet near a slain elderly woman. Further, her son, who stands to inherit a good chunk of money from her estate, works at a construction site not far from the crime scene and works with a mason who is laying brick and mixing cement. If investigators can analyze and compare the dust from the crime scene with products obtained at the work site and show that they are physically and chemically identical, the son will need a good lawyer.

CHAPTER 16

FIREARMS EXAMINATION:
MORE THAN GUNS AND AMMUNITION

This area of forensic investigation is popularly called ballistics. That term is incorrect but it's difficult to shake such common practices. **Ballistics** is actually the science of projectile motion, which means how a bullet, artillery shell, rocket, or other hurled object travels. How firearms work and how guns and ammunition are identified and compared is the job of the **forensic firearms examiner**.

In Chapter Seven, we looked at what bullets do to the human body and how the coroner evaluates such injuries. In this chapter we will look at guns and ammunition and how their identification and comparison can solve the many crimes in which guns play a role.

Deaths from gunshots may be accidental, suicidal, or homicidal. In the latter situation, evidence provided by the gun or the ammunition often proves to be the perpetrator's undoing. As part of his duties, the forensic firearms examiner might be asked to:

- analyze bullets and shell casings to determine what type of weapon fired them
- help with crime scene reconstruction by estimating the distance between the gun muzzle and the victim or by working out the trajectory of the bullets
- match a bullet or shell casing to a particular weapon

- compare bullets or shell casings obtained at different crime scenes with the hope of linking the two crimes to one another

To perform his duties, the firearms examiner must be familiar with all types of firearms and ammunition and must understand the inner workings and ballistic characteristics of each.

WEAPON AND AMMUNITION COMPONENTS

Guns are typically classified as **handguns**, **rifles**, or **shotguns**. A handgun can be held and fired in one hand, while rifles and shotguns are typically held against the shoulder and fired from that position. Handguns are further classified as **revolvers, semiautomatic pistols**, or **machine pistols**. While shotgun barrels are smooth-bored, rifles and handguns have **grooves** cut into the inside of the barrel. The areas between the grooves are called **lands**. This means that the lands are the high points and the grooves are the valleys between the lands. These grooves spiral down the barrel and impart spin to the bullet, which greatly increases the weapon's accuracy.

Rifle and handgun cartridges have several components. The **bullet** (the actual projectile) fits into a **shell casing** that is filled with smokeless powder. It is the explosion of this powder that propels the bullet from the gun. The shell casing remains in the cylinder of a revolver until manually removed, while in most automatic weapons, it is ejected.

The shell casing usually retains marks, such as the impression left by the firing pin as well as breechblock marks. The good news for the examiner is that these marks tend to be highly individual to the particular gun that fired the cartridge.

In automatic and semiautomatic weapons, the casings typically show extractor and ejector marks. These result from the mechanism that ejects the spent cartridge and seats a new one in the firing chamber. These also vary among weapons and may serve to match a shell casing to a particular gun.

True gunpowder is rarely seen today, except in self-loaded ammunition, since it has been replaced by **smokeless powder**. Yet, the term *gunpowder* remains in common usage for both types of explosive powder. Depending on their chemical composition, these smokeless powders are termed single-, double-, or triple-based. Single-based powders contain **nitrocellulose** as the only explosive component. Double-based powders contain nitrocellulose and **nitroglycerin**, while triple-based ones also contain **nitroguanidine**.

Powders also contain **stabilizers** such as **diphenylamine** and **ethyl centralite**. Other additives include **plasticizers** (to reduce the absorption of moisture by the powders) and **flash suppressants**. The chemical makeup of the powder and the type and amount of each of these additives varies among manufacturers.

The base or bottom of most cartridges possesses a centrally located cup of primer. These are called **centerfire** cartridges. When the shooter pulls the trigger, the gun's firing pin strikes the primer cup and ignites the primer. The primer in turn ignites the powder, which explodes and produces large amounts of gases, predominantly carbon monoxide, carbon dioxide, and nitrogen oxide. These gases force the bullet from the shell casing and through the barrel.

Some shells do not have a primer cup, but instead have the primer around the rim of the shell. The guns that use these types of cartridges, typically .22 caliber weapons, are termed **rimfire** weapons because the firing pin strikes the rim of the shell, not the central area.

BULLET AND SHELL CASING EXAMINATION

Interestingly, the first use of "ballistic" evidence to solve a crime did not involve a bullet, but rather the paper wadding used in arming a muzzle-loaded weapon. The value of bullet striations came later. The major events and discoveries that led to modern forensic firearms examination include:

1784: In Lancashire, England, Edward Culshaw was lethally wounded by a shot from a muzzle-loading flintlock pistol. A surgeon removed from Culshaw's wound a bit of paper wadding that had been used to pack the powder in the gun. The paper proved to be a jigsaw match for paper found in the pocket of the chief suspect, John Toms, who was convicted of the crime.

1835: In a case of breaking and entering and burglary in which a servant suffered a gunshot wound, Henry Goddard (1866–1957), one of Scotland Yard's Bow Street Runners, noticed an odd "bump" on the fired bullet that he had dug from the headboard of the servant's bed. He then examined the servant's own bullet mould (bullets were handmade then) and saw that the mould had a defect that matched the mark on the bullet. He concluded that the man had made the bullet in his own mould, and had thus shot himself to cover his theft, and that no outsider had been involved.

1863: The bullet that killed Confederate General Stonewall Jackson was found to be a 0.67 caliber ball, the size used by Confederate forces. Since the Union

---

troops used a 0.58 caliber ball, the killing bullet must have been fired by one of Jackson's own men.

1864: Union General John Sedgwick fell to a Confederate sniper, who fired from a distance of eight hundred yards. The caliber and the hexagonal shape of the bullet indicated that it had come from an English-made Whitworth rifle, imported by the Confederacy for use by snipers.

1889: Alexandre Lacassagne (1843–1924) discovered that marks found on bullets recovered from shooting victims could be matched to a particular gun barrel by simply counting the number of grooves.

1898: Dr. Paul Jeserich (1854–1927) used a microscope to compare the striations on two bullets fired by the same gun.

1913: French Professor Victor Balthazard (1872–1950) stated in his paper "Archives of Criminal Anthropology and Legal Medicine" that each fired bullet carried with it unique marks.

1920: Physicist John Fisher invents the helixometer, a probe fitted with a light and magnifying glass, which allowed a detailed examination of the inside of a gun barrel.

1920: The Sacco and Vanzetti case brought firearms examinations to the public attention.

1923: In New York City, Charles Waite, Philip Gravelle, Calvin Goddard, and John H. Fisher established the Bureau of Forensic Ballistics to offer firearm identification services throughout the United States.

1925: Gravelle and Goddard invented the comparison microscope, which revolutionized firearms examinations.

FORENSIC CASE FILES: SACCO AND VANZETTI

This case cemented firearms examination techniques as viable tools in forensic investigations. On April 15, 1920, security guards Alessandro Berardelli and Frederick Parmenter were shot dead by two men who absconded with more than $15,000 of payroll money. The only evidence found at the scene were several shell casings, which were manufactured by three firms: Remington, Winchester, and Peters. Two days later, the getaway car was found and traced to an earlier robbery, which ultimately led police to Nicola Sacco and Bartolomeo Vanzetti. Sacco had a .32 caliber handgun, the same caliber as the murder weapon, and a total of twenty-nine bullets manufactured by Remington, Winchester, or Peters. The two were arrested and charged with double murder.

Since the two men belonged to an anarchist movement that advocated violent political change, the case became America's first "Red Scare." The defense team put together an alliance of anarchist, communist, and union leaders called the Sacco-Vanzetti Defense Committee, who labeled the trial a "witch hunt."

The case hinged on proving that the killing bullets came from Sacco's gun. A match was made and Sacco and Vanzetti were convicted and sentenced to death. But, that didn't end the story. Not even close.

Because of continued protests by anarchists, in June 1927, a committee was formed to look into the case. America's leading ballistic expert Calvin Goddard of the Bureau of Forensic Ballistics in New York entered the case with two new forensic tools: the comparison microscope and the helixometer. The former allowed side-by-side comparison of two bullets while the later was a probe fitted with a light and magnifying glass, which allowed a detailed examination of the inside of a gun barrel. Again, the match was conclusive.

On August 23, 1927, the two killers died in the electric chair. Yet the controversy persisted. In 1961 and again in 1983 the case was reexamined and on each occasion Goddard's findings were confirmed.

WEAPON TYPE

A gun found at a crime scene or confiscated from a suspect can provide a great deal of evidence. It might be matched to the killing bullet or to bullets from other crime scenes. It can serve as a substrate for fingerprints and trace evidence such as blood, hair, and fibers from the perpetrator that cling to the weapon. **Blowback** of blood and tissues from the victim in close-range shootings might provide the only link between the victim and the weapon in cases where no bullet is recovered.

But what if only a bullet is found? With no gun to compare it to, how can the forensics team use this piece of evidence?

Let's say a bullet is removed by the ME at autopsy and presented to the firearms examiner so he can attempt to determine the type of weapon that fired the bullet.

The examiner first attempts to identify the caliber and type of bullet. If the bullet is intact, or mostly so, the caliber can be determined by a simple measurement. If it is severely deformed, it can be weighed, which doesn't give the exact caliber but eliminates some calibers. For example, the weight of .22 caliber and .44 caliber bullets are very different. If the bullet is heavy, then a .44 or .45 caliber weapon is more likely the gun of origin.

The type of jacketing, if any, is easily determined, which often helps identify the type of weapon used. A fully jacketed bullet is typically fired from a rifle, while a simple lead bullet most likely came from a small-caliber handgun.

Earlier, I said that different manufacturers produce barrels with different numbers and widths of lands and grooves and with different directions and degrees of twisting. The examiner uses these rifling characteristics when confronted with an unknown bullet. This places the weapon into one of several categories.

COLT TYPE: Six broad grooves, narrow lands, and a left-hand twist.

BROWNING TYPE: Six broad grooves, narrow lands, and a right-hand twist.

SMITH & WESSON TYPE: Five lands and grooves of equal width and a right-hand twist.

WEBLEY TYPE: Seven broad grooves, narrow lands, and a right-hand twist.

MARLIN TYPE: Marlin rifles use a technique known as **microgrooving**, which leaves between eight and twenty-four narrow grooves inside the barrel.

Armed with this knowledge, if the examiner is given a .32 caliber bullet recovered at autopsy and he finds ballistic striations consistent with the bullet having traveled down a barrel with five lands and a right twist, the weapon was likely a Smith & Wesson. Investigators can then focus on .32 caliber handguns manufactured by Smith & Wesson.

To help firearms examiners in these determinations, the FBI maintains a database known as the General Rifling Characteristics (GRC) file. It is a listing of land, groove, and twist characteristics of known weapons.

BULLET EXAMINATION

The lands and grooves inside a rifled barrel not only impart spin to the bullet but also cut into its side, leaving behind marks called **striations**. These marks are linear and parallel to the long axis of the bullet. They lie at the heart of ballistic comparisons. As you would expect, they are more prominent on soft lead bullets and may be extremely faint or absent on metal or Teflon-jacketed ones.

Each rifled barrel possesses minute characteristics that differentiate it from all others. For one thing, the manufacturer's rifling tool cuts through each metallic barrel a little differently. Also, the cutting or etching equipment itself becomes worn and damaged with each use. This progressive wear and tear produces rifling patterns that vary from barrel to barrel.

In addition, the grooves and lands undergo wear and damage with repeated firing of the weapon, which adds even more individual characteristics to the barrel and thus to any bullet that travels through it. This means that bullets fired from the same gun share the same striation patterns, while those fired from different guns do not.

With an intact bullet, striation comparison is usually easy, but unfortunately the examiner rarely receives an undamaged bullet. More often, he gets bullets that have struck bones or walls or other solid objects, and they are usually misshapen or fragmented. Still, if the bullet is not severely deformed, it can provide a wealth of information.

During the collection and handling of any crime scene bullet, great care must be taken not to damage or alter it. Whether removed from a body in surgery, at autopsy, or from a wall at the crime scene, the bullet is handled carefully. For example, a bullet grasped by a surgical instrument or pried from a doorjamb might be damaged and extraneous marks might be added to the striation pattern, making matching the bullet to a suspect weapon difficult or impossible.

If the bullet is more or less intact, a microscopic examination will reveal the rifling pattern imprinted on it. We've already seen that the number of grooves and the direction and degree of twist can help determine the type and manufacturer of the weapon. This is considered class evidence since it cannot pinpoint exactly which gun fired the bullet. But when viewed under magnification, smaller, individualizing striations are visible; these are what the firearms examiner looks at when he is analyzing a bullet.

These individualizing striations are useful in many situations. For example, multiple bullets found at a crime scene can be compared to see if they came from one gun. If not, more than one weapon was used. Or, bullets collected at two different crime scenes can be compared to determine if the same gun fired them. If so, this strongly connects the two crimes. Most importantly, a bullet removed from a homicide victim can be compared against a suspect weapon. A match means that the murder weapon has been identified, which might be the key to identifying the killer. Similarly, if a victim is shot by two assailants, matching the killing bullet to one of the guns indicates which shooter would face the more serious charges.

The first step in this comparison process is to obtain an intact bullet fired by the suspect weapon. The examiner, using similar ammunition, discharges the weapon into a test-firing chamber. This may be a bullet trap or a water trap, either of which captures the bullet without damaging it. The lab-fired bullet (known) can then be compared with the crime scene bullet (unknown) by using a comparison microscope, which places images of the two bullets side by side (see the appendix).

It is important to note that the two bullets do not have to match in every detail. In fact, they essentially never do. The reason is that each bullet that travels down the barrel alters the barrel slightly and leaves behind soot and grit. These changes within the barrel along with the deposited foreign materials alter the imprint left on the next bullet. This means that the two bullets will have slightly different markings. Though the two bullets do not need to be identical, a match requires that identical patterns be found on at least three consecutive striations on each bullet.

Silencers, which muffle the sound from the gun muzzle, can also leave markings on the bullet, but these are unpredictable. A bullet thus marked may not match the gun if the silencer is not also available for the test firing.

Also, the bullet could have important trace evidence attached. Paint, fibers, bits of glass, and other materials can cling to the bullet as it passes through or ricochets off walls, doors, bricks, and windows. Small bits of flesh and blood may also be found. These microscopic bits can on occasion be the key to solving a case or to reconstructing a crime scene.

For example, a husband might say that his wife ran away from home. Family and friends insist she would not do that. During their investigation, the police find a bullet embedded in a basement wall and the crime lab discovers it holds a speck of blood, which is then matched to DNA obtained from the missing woman's hair in her hairbrush. Even without a body, such evidence could lead to an indictment.

Shotguns do not have rifled barrels. They fire a wad of pellets (shot) rather than a single bullet, so striation comparisons are not part of the examination of shotgun ammunition. After a shotgun has been discharged as part of some criminal activity, the shot can often be extracted from walls or furniture, for example, or from victims, either in surgery or at autopsy. The size of the shot does not determine the gauge of the shotgun but does give information about the ammunition used. The various sizes of shot are numbered, with the lower the number the larger the pellets within the shotgun shell. For instance, a No. 8 shot is smaller than a No. 4. They vary in size from 0.05 inch for No. 12 shot to 0.33 inch for OO shot, also called double-O buckshot. The examiner can measure the diameter of any recovered shot and estimate what size shot was used.

SHELL CASING EXAMINATION

At some crime scenes, bullets are not found and the only ballistic evidence available is one or more shell casings. These casings often carry several types of marks that are of interest to the ballistics examiner. As with bullets, the comparison of multiple casings found at one scene, or casings found at different scenes, or casings from a test-fired suspect weapon, may provide important information. Useful shell case markings include:

FIRING PIN IMPRESSIONS: Whether the casing is centerfire or rimfire, the firing pin impression is usually unique enough to make a match.

BREECHBLOCK MARKINGS: The breechblock is basically the back wall of the firing chamber. When the powder in the casing detonates and pushes the bullet down the barrel, Newtonian physics dictates that the casing is forced back against the breechblock. This leaves an impression on the bottom of the casing.

EXTRACTOR AND EJECTOR MARKINGS: Automatic and semiautomatic weapons have mechanisms that remove the spent shell from the chamber and eject it from the weapon (ejector) and that extract the next bullet from the clip and set it in the firing chamber (extractor). These extracting and ejecting mechanisms leave their own unique scratches and marks on the sides of the shell casings.

Each of these unique marks on the shell casing can be viewed and compared with a comparison microscope. They might be distinctive enough to individualize the casing to a particular weapon. The power of such evidence was first brought to the public's attention after the infamous St. Valentine's Day Massacre and reinforced by many other cases such as the odd Branion murder case.

FORENSIC CASE FILES: THE ST. VALENTINE'S DAY MASSACRE

During the Roaring Twenties, Prohibition led to warfare among the many crime families in several major U.S. cities, since whoever controlled the flow of illegal alcohol would be assured a hefty income. Nowhere was this war more evident than in Chicago where Al "Scarface" Capone squared off with George "Bugs" Moran.

On the evening of February 14, 1929, seven of Moran's men waited in a Clark Street warehouse for a shipment of hijacked liquor. Moran himself was late arriving, which ultimately saved his life. As he approached, he saw five police officers enter the warehouse, so he retreated. The "police officers" were actually Capone's men. Inside the structure, they lined Moran's seven men up and massacred them with Thompson submachine guns (Tommy guns).

The real police arrived shortly after and ultimately recovered seventy shell casings from the scene and later several bullets from the victims. Because of the high-profile nature of the case and because of his expertise in firearms examinations, cardiologist Dr. Calvin Goddard, who became famous during the Sacco and Vanzetti Case, was called in. He determined that the shell casings were from Thomson submachine guns, and using the newly developed comparison microscope, he determined that none of the Thompsons owned by the Chicago Police Department were the murder weapons. This meant that the killers had impersonated police officers and Capone immediately became the primary suspect. Police raided the home of one of Capone's hit men and found two Thompsons, which Goddard identified as two of the murder weapons.

Two businessmen in Chicago were so impressed with Goddard's work that they helped fund the establishment of the Scientific Crime Detection Laboratory (SCDL), the first independent crime lab, at Northwestern University in 1929. Following this model, the FBI set up its own crime lab in 1932.

FORENSIC CASE FILES: JOHN BRANION

On December 22, 1967, Dr. John Branion left a hospital in south Chicago, passed by his home, picked up his son from nursery school, and then went to the home of a friend who was to have lunch with the Branions. The friend couldn't make lunch, so Dr. Branion went home, arriving just before noon. Upon entering his house, he found his wife, Donna, dead on the floor of a utility room. She had suffered multiple gunshot wounds. He called the police.

Firearms expert Burt Nielson examined the shell casings recovered at the scene and the bullets removed from the victim at autopsy and determined that the weapon was a .38 caliber. He also noted distinctive markings on the casings that he recognized as ejector-type markings that could only have come from a Walther PPK. Branion was a gun collector but had told detectives that he did not own a Walther. A warranted search of Branion's home turned up a Walther PPK brochure, an extra ammunition clip, and a Walther branded target, all of which bore the serial number 188274. Police also found two boxes of .38 caliber ammunition, one full and the other missing four cartridges. Mrs. Branion had been shot four times.

Police contacted the importers of Walther handguns in New York and learned that the Walther PPK bearing the serial number 188274 had been shipped to Chicago and sold to James Hooks, a friend of Dr. Branion. Branion was convicted and sentenced to a long prison term. He was released on bond while he undertook an appeal of his conviction. By 1971, with his appeal going nowhere and facing a return to prison, he fled to Uganda, where he enjoyed the protection of the dictator Idi Amin. He even served as Amin's personal physician. Unfortunately for Dr. Branion, Amin was toppled and Branion was extradited back to the United States to serve his sentence.

OTHER FIREARMS EXAMINATION TECHNIQUES

In addition to testing gun types and bullet markings, the forensic firearms examiner is charged with finding other information about the gun, including how far away it was fired from the victim, and how to identify the gun's owner.

SCATTER PATTERN ASSESSMENT

One of the important determinations in the investigation of any gunshot is the firing distance. This is the distance between the gun muzzle and the victim. An estimate of this distance can be the difference in a gunshot death being deemed an accident, suicide, or homicide. It can also serve to reconstruct the events of the crime and to support or refute suspect and witness statements.

We saw in Chapter Seven how this distance affects the anatomy of entry wounds. Remember that when a gun is fired, hot gases and burned and unburned gunpowder particles follow the bullet out of the barrel. The ME can usually estimate the firing distance by the effects of these substances on the wound. But sometimes the victim is shot through clothing. In this case, the hot gases and unburned powder that would normally cause tattooing and charring of the victim's skin are intercepted by the clothing. The ME is left with few, if any, distance markers on the victim's skin. Enter the firearms examiner.

As with gunshot entry wounds, the residue pattern on the garment depends on the firing distance: The further the distance, the wider the spread of the residue—up to a point. Once the firing distance exceeds the distance the gases and particles travel, no residue pattern is produced.

To accurately estimate the distance, the examiner uses the suspect weapon and similar ammunition and performs a series of test firings into similar fabric from several different distances. It is important to use the same weapon and similar ammunition in order to make the test an accurate representation of the actual shooting event. He then compares the residue pattern on the test shots with those on the crime scene garment and estimates the firing distance.

Let's say a victim has been shot in the chest through his shirt, and that the firearms examiner uses the weapon and similar ammunition to perform test firings at four, ten, and eighteen inches, as well as two and three feet. He then compares the residue pattern on the test garments with that of the victim's and finds that the closest match is with the eighteen-inch test shot. He then estimates the firing distance at approximately eighteen inches.

A similar comparison can estimate the firing distance when a shotgun is the weapon involved. This was discussed in detail in Chapter Seven.

GUNSHOT RESIDUES

When a gun is fired, the primer and the powder within the cartridge explode, forcing the bullet down the barrel followed by most, but not all, of the explosive gases and particulate matter produced by the explosion. However, some of these materials escape through the breech and other openings in the weapon. This is particularly true of revolvers, which tend to "leak" more gases than other types of weapons. The chemical and particulate components of these gases, called **gunshot residue (GSR)**, cling to the shooter's hand, arm, clothing, face, and hair, They may also settle on nearby walls or furniture as well as on the victim's skin and clothing in close-range gunshots.

Wind and rain often lessen or change the pattern of spread of the residue cloud so that GSR may be found in areas where the examiner would not expect to, and not in areas where he would. On light clothing, the GSR pattern may be readily visible as a smudge or smear, whereas on dark, multicolored, or bloodstained clothing, the pattern may be obscured. Infrared photography often reveals GSR stains among these patterns. The pattern may also be revealed by the **Griess test**. This test uses a sheet of photographic paper or a sheet of acetic-acid-dampened filter paper. Either is pressed over the area and then immersed in Griess reagent, which reacts with the inorganic nitrites in the GSR, revealing the pattern.

The ultimate goal of GSR analysis is to place the gun "in the suspect's hand." Unfortunately, the residue cloud isn't that cooperative. Simply being near the gun when it was discharged or handling the gun afterward can leave behind GSR on an innocent person.

GSR tends to fade rapidly and is usually dissipated after about two hours. It can also be wiped or washed away. For this reason, testing should be accomplished as soon after the gun is fired as possible.

The suspect's hands, face, and clothing should be inspected and samples obtained. The old paraffin test, where melted paraffin was used to pick up the residue from the shooter's hands, is rarely used anymore. Instead, sampling is done by swabbing the suspect's hands, arms, and clothing with a moist swab or filter paper.

Chemical analysis looks for the byproducts of primer and gunpowder combustion, which are predominantly the metals lead, barium, and antimony. To identify these, the swab or filter paper is treated with diphenylamine, which turns a blue color when positive. Unfortunately, other substances such as fertilizer, tobacco, cosmetics, and urine can yield false positive results. This means that the presence of GSR must be confirmed by more specific confirmatory tests such as neutron activation analysis and atomic absorption spectrometry (see the appendix). A positive result is the finding of elevated levels of barium and antimony.

Sometimes GSR is found not on the shooter's hands, but on his clothing or in his hair. A scanning electron microscope (SEM) can often locate these tiny GSR particles (see the appendix). SEM is often paired with energy dispersive x-ray spectroscopy (EDS), which gives a "chemical fingerprint" of the substance tested. Using SEM/EDS, the finding of lead, barium, and antimony in such small particles is highly suggestive that the particle is indeed GSR. This technique was developed in 1974 by J.S. Wessel, P.F. Jones, and R.S. Nesbitt.

RESTORING SERIAL NUMBERS

Sometimes it's obvious that a particular gun was the murder weapon. It is found at the crime scene, along the perpetrator's escape route, or where it was discarded, and the forensic firearms examiner matches the gun to the bullets removed from the victim. But that information doesn't identify the gun's owner or who fired it. In this situation it is useful to discover if anyone had registered the gun. Even if the registered owner is not the killer, he might have given the gun to someone, or it might have been stolen and the murder and the gun theft can be linked. Comparing the evidence in the two cases would move the investigators closer to identifying the perpetrator.

But criminals are clever. They often attempt to grind or file away the gun's serial number in the hopes that the weapon can't be traced. If so, the examiner has a few tricks he can employ in these situations.

The most common are **magnaflux, chemical and electrochemical etching**, and **ultrasonic cavitation**. Each relies on the changes in the structure of the gun's metal that follows the serial number stamping process. When the metal is pressure-stamped, not only is the metal indented with the numbers, but also the metal beneath the numbers is stressed and undergoes structural changes.

MAGNAFLUX: This is only useful if the weapon is composed of iron-containing metals. The gun is placed in a strong electromagnetic field or beneath a strong magnet, which magnetizes the weapon. The lines of magnetic force in a magnetized object usually run parallel to each other, but the disordered metal beneath the stamped numbers disrupt this order. The gun is then sprayed with a special oil in which iron-like particles are suspended. The particles tend to collect in the areas of disordered metal, thus revealing the hidden number. The major advantage of this process is it is nondestructive and doesn't alter the weapon.

CHEMICAL AND ELECTROCHEMICAL ETCHING: These are destructive processes, which limits their use. They involve the painting of an etching solution over the area in question. The chemical eats the disordered metal faster than the surrounding metal, and thus brings the numbers into view. Adding an electric current (electrochemical etching) hastens the process. Either of these must be done carefully, since over-etching will destroy the evidence forever.

ULTRASONIC CAVITATION: This technique is similar to chemical etching and is also a destructive process. The gun is placed in a special ultrasonic bath and exposed to very high-frequency vibrations. This causes cavitation, a process in which tiny bubbles form along the surface of the metal. With continued exposure, the cavitation begins to eat away the metal. The process is fastest in the areas of disorder and, as with chemical etching, the serial number might be revealed.

NATIONAL BALLISTIC DATABASE SYSTEMS

What if the ballistics examiner is given only a single bullet or shell casing and no suspect weapon to match it against? As mentioned earlier, he can often determine the type and manufacturer of the weapon that fired the bullet, but that's about as far as he could go. Now, thanks to computer technology, he might also be able to compare the ballistic markings with databases of markings taken from weapons used in other crimes. Several databases of this type exist at present.

DRUGFIRE: The FBI developed this ballistic identification system in the 1990s, though it has recently been replaced by IBIS.

INTEGRATED BALLISTICS IDENTIFICATION SYSTEM (IBIS): IBIS is maintained by the Federal Bureau of Alcohol, Tobacco, Firearms, and Explosives (BATFE or ATF, as it is commonly called). This computer-based system stores digital photos of fired bullets and shell casings.

NATIONAL INTEGRATED BALLISTIC INFORMATION NETWORK (NIBIN): NIBIN is a joint venture between the FBI and the ATF that uses the IBIS system to compare ballistic markings.

These databases remain incomplete, but if images of the bullet or shell casing from the same weapon that fired a crime scene bullet or casing is in the IBIS system, a match will serve to connect two scenes. IBIS computers can rapidly compare hundreds of records and separate out possible matches. Then an experienced firearms examiner can make the final match.

ARSON INVESTIGATION:
FIRES AND EXPLOSIONS

Arson investigations are extremely difficult to conduct, and where explosions are involved, they become even trickier. The fundamental problem is that the crime scene and the evidence typically are severely damaged if not completely destroyed. Such is the nature of fire and explosives.

The investigator uses both physical and chemical evidence to determine if the fire was accidentally or intentionally set. Fires started by natural causes are rare, except as the result of lightning strikes.

THE NATURE OF FIRE

Fire is almost a living, breathing entity. It consumes fuel materials and oxygen and produces heat and light. From a chemistry perspective this is called **oxidation**, which is when a substance combines with oxygen, or some other **oxidant**, to produce another substance. Oxidative reactions are characterized by a transfer of electrons from one molecule to another, a reaction that results in the release of energy. Such reactions are also termed **exothermic**, or energy-producing, reactions. In the case of fire, this energy is released as light and heat.

It may surprise you that the process of rust formation is also an oxidative process. In this case, iron (Fe) combines with oxygen (O_2) to produce iron oxide (Fe_2O_3), or rust. This is an extremely slow process and may take months or years, and since it is so slow, no detectable heat or light is produced.

Fire is the same basic reaction, except that it occurs more rapidly. Fire results when a fuel source combines with oxygen in an oxidative reaction that produces light, heat, and various byproducts of combustion such as carbon monoxide (CO) and carbon dioxide (CO_2). When a fuel source such as methane gas (CH_4), which is a flammable hydrocarbon (any compound composed of hydrogen and carbon atoms), burns, it combines with oxygen to produce water (H_2O) and CO_2. The equation for this reaction is:

$$CH_4 + 2\ O_2 = CO_2 + 2\ H_2O + \text{heat and light}$$

One molecule of methane combines with two molecules of oxygen to produce one molecule of carbon dioxide and two molecules of water. Heat and light are byproducts of the reaction. An explosion is simply a violent and sudden version of this same process.

So, rusting, burning, and exploding are similar oxidative processes with the difference being the rate of the reaction.

But, simply bringing oxygen and a flammable fuel such as paper or gasoline together will not produce fire. Something else is needed. That something is heat. This triad—fuel, oxygen, and heat—must be present for a fire to begin. Remove any one of these and no fire will occur.

As you might expect, the removal or suppression of any of these will extinguish or slow a fire that is already in progress, while the addition of one or more will accelerate it. For example, spraying water on a fire extinguishes it because it lowers the temperature, blocks oxygen from reaching the fuel, and in some circumstances dilutes the fuel. This reduction in the three necessary components dampens or extinguishes the fire. On the other hand, adding gasoline or oxygen increases the fire's intensity.

If the initiation of a fire requires heat, exactly how much is needed? It depends on the fuel.

The temperature at which fire starts is called the **ignition temperature,** and it varies widely from substance to substance. The ignition temperature for gasoline is quite different from that of wood. However, in the presence of oxygen, either will ignite when the proper amount of heat is applied. Once combustion occurs, the fire continues because the fire itself produces enough heat to continue the burning process. This is true of all exothermic, or heat-producing, reactions.

The fuel consumed in a fire can be solid, liquid, or gas. In structure fires of homes or other buildings, all three types of fuels are usually present, either as part of the structure or as an igniter or accelerant in the case of arson. Solids include wood, drapes, carpets, furniture, and roofing materials. Liquids could be gasoline, paint thinners, alcohol, or any other flammable substance. Gases could be natural gas or the vapors from any flammable liquid.

But, in order for any of these three general types of fuels to ignite, they must first be in a gaseous state. Put another way, flammable gases will ignite, but before solids or liquids can burn, they must be converted to a gas.

Fire requires that a gaseous fuel mix with the gaseous oxygen in air. It will then ignite when sufficient heat is present. With gases such as natural gas, this is self-evident, but what about liquid and solid fuels? With a liquid fuel, the applied heat must be sufficient to vaporize (turn into gas) the fuel. This temperature is called the **flash point**, the lowest temperature that will vaporize a liquid fuel. It varies from liquid to liquid. Gasoline possesses its characteristic odor because it is an extremely **volatile** liquid. You detect the odor when the vapors from the gasoline reach your nostrils. When gasoline catches fire, it is the vapors that are burning, not the liquid gasoline. The heat from the fire continually vaporizes the gasoline, thus supplying gaseous fuel to continue the burning.

The same is true for solids, which burn only when enough heat is applied to convert the solid to gas. This process is called **pyrolysis**. In the case of wood or paper, the heat turns the surface of these solids to a gas, which then can mix with oxygen and ignite. When you see wood burning, what you are actually seeing is the burning of a very thin layer of "wood gas" over the surface of the wood. If the temperature is too low for pyrolysis to take place, the solid may still burn. We call this smoldering. It is a slow flameless burn. But, add heat or oxygen and the smoldering burn might generate enough heat for the pyrolytic reaction to occur and the fuel will burst into flames. Blowing, fanning, or using a bellows to direct air at a fire causes a smoldering log to burst into flames, thus the term "fanning the flames."

The bottom line is that neither solids nor liquids will burn openly. Only gases can intermingle with oxygen and ignite.

Spontaneous combustion is basically a self-starting fire. This rarely occurs because the conditions required are uncommon. A collection of rags soaked with certain oils and placed in a poorly ventilated container can combust spontaneously. The mechanism appears to be an accumulation of heat from the slow oxidation of the oils. If the heat rises to the ignition temperature of the oil, fire is likely to occur. Occasionally, home and industrial fires begin in this manner. More often, however, arsonists attempt to use this fairly rare occurrence as a defense.

Explosives are fuels that are capable of undergoing very rapid oxidation. These reactions are so rapid that the oxygen in the air is not enough to cause the oxidative process. Explosives get around this by containing their own oxygen in the form of oxidizing agents. For example, black powder is composed of sulfur, carbon, and potassium nitrate. Since potassium nitrate contains oxygen, it serves as the oxidizing agent.

ARSON

When there are suspicious circumstances surrounding a fire, arson investigators are brought in to determine the source and cause of the fire. **Arson** is a fire purposely set, most often to look like an accident.

ARSON MOTIVES

Why do people intentionally set fires? The reasons are many and varied, but arson invariably has a payoff. Common ones include:

FINANCIAL GAIN: Insurance fraud is at the heart of many arson cases. Perhaps quick money is needed and the insurance on the home or warehouse is greater than the property's market value. Or a torched home might contain money or insured valuables such as jewelry or art work. A search for remnants of these items must be undertaken since they might have been removed before the fire was started. This way the perpetrator not only has the insurance money, but also the intact insured items.

COVERING ANOTHER CRIME: Arson is often used to cover another crime, such as theft. Maybe an employee has embezzled from the company and attempts to cover his crime by destroying all the financial records in a fire. Or perhaps an employee has stolen goods from a company warehouse and hopes that a fire will hide this fact. After all, if the inventory is destroyed, how can anyone determine if any stock is missing? For this reason, a fire scene is always searched for signs of breaking-and-entering and theft.

REVENGE OR TERROR: A grudge or deep-seated hatred for another might lead the arsonist to set fire to a home or business. Or an individual or a group might burn a structure in order to create fear or make a political statement.

PSYCHOPATHOLOGY: Some individuals have a pathological love for fire and start them simply because it is exciting. In these cases, the fire feeds some deep psychological need. These people often become serial arsonists.

SUICIDE AND MURDER: Fire is rarely used for suicide or murder because it is simply too painful for the former and too unpredictable for the latter. However, it is often used in an attempt to disguise or cover a murder. The killer's hope is that the fire will make the true cause of death impossible to determine. Unfortunately for the killer, a structure fire rarely is hot enough, nor does it burn long enough to completely destroy a body. When cremated, bodies are typically exposed to temperatures in the range of 1,500°F or higher for two hours or more. This reduces the body to ashes and bone fragments. A structure fire does not often do this. In fact, even bodies that are significantly charred are often remarkably well preserved internally, allowing the ME to search for signs of trauma, poisons, and other causes of death.

ARSON INVESTIGATION

After the firefighters have pulled people safely away from the structure, extinguished the fire, and prevented it from spreading, fire investigators then step in and attempt to determine if the fire was accident or intentional.

The investigation of a suspected arson revolves around the answer to two questions:

- Where was the fire's point of origin?
- What was the cause of the fire?

Point of Origin

Locating the **point of origin** is the cornerstone of fire and arson investigation. Materials found in the area where the fire began help the investigator determine if the fire was accidental or intentional, and whether any **igniters** (the heat source that ignited the fire) or **accelerants** (substances that facilitate the start and spread of the fire) were used. For example, the finding of a point of origin near an overloaded wall outlet would favor an accidental fire, while finding one in a corner of a warehouse, far removed from any electrical source and near a charred gasoline can, would suggest arson. Similarly, the partially burned remains of rags, paper, or other combustible materials near the point of origin would suggest arson, as would the finding of igniter residue, such as remnants of matches or a road flare. Much to the dismay of many arsonists, these types of materials often survive even very destructive fires.

When a fire investigator approaches a charred structure, he must do so with extreme caution and only after he has received clearance from a structural engineer. If not, collapsing floors, falling beams, broken glass, sharp nails, smoldering materials, noxious gases, and asbestos (in older buildings) can pose a hazard to the investigator. However, it is imperative that the investigation and the collection of evidence begin as soon as possible after the fire has been extinguished and the structure has been deemed safe to enter. Time is the enemy because many of the volatile substances that cause or accelerate a fire rapidly dissipate.

While the structural inspection is underway, the fire investigator interviews witnesses, and from this often obtains important clues. Someone may have seen the fire in its earliest stages and this may help with locating the point of origin. The color of the flames and smoke may be helpful, since many accelerants and combustible materials produce characteristic flame and smoke colors. For example, gasoline produces a yellow flame and white smoke. Wood yields a red and yellow flame and gray or brown smoke. Rubber and some petroleum products give off red-orange flames and black smoke. The investigator can use this information to help locate the point of origin and determine if an accelerant was used.

Locating the fire's point of origin requires an understanding of how fire moves through a structure. Fires typically spread laterally and vertically so that once the point of origin has been located, the investigator can often follow the path of the fire as it spreads through the structure. This is often possible even in heavily damaged structures. Conversely, backtracking along the fire's route of spread may lead to the origin point. The investigator searches for a V pattern in the burned material. Since fire tends to rise and spread, it often produces a V-shaped area on a wall or other vertical surface. The point of origin is typically at the foot of the V.

It's not always that simple, though. In significantly burned structures, the walls are often severely damaged or collapsed. But typically the greatest degree of damage is near the point of origin, so the investigator searches for that area. He also knows that it is in this area that any igniters or accelerants are most likely to be found. Unfortunately, many things obscure and confuse the issue and the investigator must consider them all.

Wind, drafts from open windows, the airflow pattern of the particular structure, stairs, elevators, and many other things can alter the way the fire spreads and where it burns the hottest. Materials used in construction and decoration, such as plastics, paints, insulating or sound-retarding materials, synthetic carpeting, and wall coverings, can create confusing "hot spots" and patterns of spread. Stored fuels and other flammable liquids interfere not only with the location of the true point of origin but may also make the search for accelerants difficult, since they themselves are accelerants. Also, the arsonist may have started multiple fires within the building or may have sloshed a path of gasoline or other accelerant throughout or around the structure. In this case the fire may have multiple points of origin. A fire with multiple points of origin is virtually always arson.

The intensity of the fire at any particular location can be estimated by assessing its effect on structural materials. Steel beams might buckle if the fire is extremely intense. Glass tends to melt around 1,500°F. Cracking and flaking of walls and floors (spalling) indicate an area of high heat. Wooden beams, floors, and walls can char, leaving an alligator-skin-like pattern. If so, the smaller "scales" tend to be near the hottest point of the fire. If the building is equipped with a system of smoke detectors, the timing with which they went off helps determine the path the fire took through the structure.

Liquid and gaseous fuels present special problems for the investigator. Liquids spread and conform to the shape of their container. If gasoline is poured on a floor, it will spread across the room, run down the stairs, and seep into the baseboards. When ignition occurs, the fire follows the liquid and spreads rapidly. Here the point of origin is widespread. Gaseous fuels, such as natural gas, diffuse in all directions until they fill a room or the entire structure. When an ignition source is added, they may explode. In this situation, finding an exact point of origin may be impossible.

Cause of the Fire

Once the point of origin is defined, a search for potential causes follows. This requires an examination of the circumstances and factors that brought the fire and the fuel into contact in this place at this time. Particular attention is given to human factors, because if a human is involved, the fire is not natural and must be either accidental or intentional.

The next step is a thorough search of the area near the point of origin for igniters and accelerants. Potential ignition sources, such as electrical wiring, oil lamps, candles, cigarettes, fireplaces, sophisticated electrical timers, or poorly ventilated oil-soaked rags (a source for potential spontaneous combustion), are sought. An analysis of these potential ignition sources aids the fire investigator in categorizing the fire as natural, accidental, or intentional. A natural fire results from such natural occurrences as a lightning strike, while accidental sources could be frayed wiring, an overloaded circuit or extension cord, a smoldering cigarette, or a pile of oily rags. The presence of an electrical or combustible timing device of course suggests arson.

Igniting and timing devices may be simple or complex, with the most common being a match. Often the arsonist lights the fire and tosses the match aside, believing that the resulting fire will completely destroy it. However, match heads contain **diatoms**, single-celled organisms that are found in diatomaceous earth such as is used in match production. These tiny creatures possess silica-containing shells, which are very tough and survive fires. Interestingly, match manufacturers use different materials that contain different diatom species, which can be distinguished from one another by their shell structure. Identifying these shell remnants can indicate that a match was used and also possibly identify the brand.

Another low-tech device is a candle placed on a pile of paper. When the candle burns down, it ignites the paper and the fire takes off. A cigarette laid across an open book of matches beneath curtains is equally as simple. Or the ignition source might be a complex electrical timing device. Sometimes the igniter and an accelerant are combined, as in a Molotov cocktail. This is typically a glass container filled with a flammable liquid. A cloth "fuse" is stuffed into a hole in the jar's lid or the bottle's neck. Then the cloth is lit, and the device is tossed into the building. Crude, but effective. A thorough search may reveal candle residue, a cigarette butt, the remains of the electrical device, or the neck of the bottle with cloth remnants inside.

Accelerants

An accelerant is any substance that promotes or accelerates the intensity and the progress of the fire. Arsonists almost always use accelerants. Simply dropping a match onto a pile of paper or tossing a cigarette on a sofa is too unpredictable. The arsonist wants to be sure that the fire will take hold and burn.

Accelerants may be solids, liquids, or gases. Solid accelerants include paper, black powder, and kindling wood. Liquids include gasoline, kerosene, alcohols, and paint thinners. Typical gaseous accelerants are natural gas and propane.

Liquid accelerants, particularly gasoline and kerosene, are by far the most commonly used fire accelerators. Even if the structure is severely damaged, traces of these accelerants remain. They soak into carpets and brickwork, seep into baseboards and crevices, and settle into areas beneath the fire. Remnants survive most fires, and investigators make a diligent search for them in any suspicious fire. Since obtaining samples from where accelerants were likely used gives him the best chance of finding and identifying them, the investigator uses several techniques to narrow his search.

Accelerants intensify fire, so the easiest first step is to look for the visible signs that indicate the fire burned faster and hotter than would be expected in a given area. These signs include:

ALLIGATORING: The surface of wood exposed to a severe heat is covered with rolling blisters that resemble alligator scales.

CRAZING: Intense fires crack glass in an irregular pattern.

SPALLING: Chipped, flaked, and discolored bricks or concrete indicate an intense fire.

CHAR DEPTH: A normal fire burns wood to a depth of approximately one inch for each forty-five minutes. A deeper, faster burn indicates a hotter fire.

The arson investigator might employ specially trained dogs that sniff out traces of accelerants, or perhaps a detector such as a vapor trace analyzer (VTA). This "artificial nose"—actually a specialized gas chromatograph—is extremely sensitive and tests for flammable hydrocarbon residues in the air around sites of accelerant residue. The VTA has a nozzle, a heating element, and a temperature gauge. A sample of the air and any accelerant vapors it might contain is drawn in through the nozzle and passed over a heating element. If the sample burns, it raises the temperature within the device, causing a needle in the temperature gauge to rise. A bump in the temperature is presumptive evidence that a flammable residue is present. Further samples are taken and returned to the lab for more thorough analysis.

Once accelerant-rich areas are located, samples for testing are obtained. The sooner this is done the better since most accelerants are volatile petroleum-based hydrocarbons, such as gasoline and kerosene, and their vapors will dissipate with time. To prevent loss of this crucial evidence, any materials gathered must be placed in nonporous, sealed containers. Sealed cans, such as clean paint cans, and glass jars are best. Plastic bags are not advisable, since the plastic can react with the hydrocarbons and the volatile gases might escape through the damaged material.

ARSON INVESTIGATION

If possible, the examiner not only takes sections of the charred carpet but also samples of the same carpet from any unburned areas. This gives him an uncontaminated substrate against which to compare the suspect sample. This is important since many carpets, linoleum flooring, and tile adhesives contain volatile hydrocarbons, which can test positive for accelerant residues. A comparison of the burned and unburned segments can separate a foreign hydrocarbon from those naturally occurring in the burned material.

All the materials—charred wood, pieces of carpet, furniture remnants, even empty bottles that are suspected of having held a flammable liquid—are collected and taken to the crime lab. The first step in the analysis is to extract any accelerant chemicals from the debris. The most common methods used for this are:

STEAM DISTILLATION: The charred material is heated and the steam is collected and condensed. The resulting liquid contains any volatile hydrocarbons.

SOLVENT EXTRACTION: The sample is placed in a container with a solvent such as chloroform, carbon tetrachloride, methylene chloride, or carbon disulfide. Hydrocarbons will be leeched from the material as they dissolve in the solvent and are then separated and analyzed.

HEADSPACE VAPOR EXTRACTION: The material is placed in a closed container. The natural volatility of the hydrocarbons creates a vapor-rich gas above the material in the container's "headspace." Heating the sample slightly accelerates this process. The vapor is then removed from the container with a syringe and tested.

VAPOR CONCENTRATION: The sample is heated in a closed container, which also contains charcoal. Volatile hydrocarbons leave the sample and absorb into the charcoal. The charcoal is then removed and the hydrocarbons are extracted by using a solvent.

Once any volatile hydrocarbons have been extracted, they are analyzed to determine their nature and type. By far, the most useful tool for this procedure is the gas chromatograph (GC) (see the appendix). Since gasoline, kerosene, and other commonly used petroleum-based accelerants are actually mixtures of various hydrocarbons, the GC device separates them into their components. These are then compared to known standards and the identity of the substance is revealed.

Usually GC is all that is needed for identification, but if further delineation of the sample is necessary, the GC may be combined with mass spectroscopy

(GC/MS) or with infrared spectroscopy (GC/IR). Either of these give a molecular "fingerprint" of the substance.

Each batch of gasoline produced varies slightly in its chemical makeup and additive content. Though it is not possible to determine the exact manufacturer of a given sample, a comparative analysis between the unknown sample and those taken from nearby or suspect service stations may trace it to a particular station. Though this is not completely reliable, the examiner might be able to say that it is at least possible that the sample came from a particular source. An investigation into who purchased gasoline at that location during a particular time period might lead investigators to a suspect.

HOMICIDAL FIRES

Sometimes a body turns up among the fire debris and the coroner and homicide investigators are called in. The purpose of their investigations is to identify the corpse and to determine the cause of death and whether the manner was accidental or homicidal.

The coroner uses whatever is available to identify the victim (see Chapter Four: Identifying the Body). Depending on the condition of the body, physical characteristics such as stature, age, sex, tattoos, birthmarks, and surgical scars and appliances can help. Surgical appliances are man-made devices placed inside the body and range from artificial hips to pacemakers to metal rods inside bones.

Fingerprints, dental matching, and DNA might also be useful. However, fingerprints might not be obtainable and the corpse could be so severely damaged that no usable DNA survived the fire. But even in severely burned bodies, many of the internal organs do survive, and DNA can often be obtained from these organs or from the bone marrow or dental pulp. This is particularly true for the hardier mitochondrial DNA (see Chapter Ten: DNA, "Mitochondrial DNA").

One question the ME must answer is whether the victim was alive at the time the fire started. If so, an accident is possible. If not, homicide becomes a more likely manner of death, since dead folks don't usually start fires. Determining the cause and manner of death depends on careful evaluation of the fire scene and the autopsy. The ME looks at things such as the position of the body, the carbon monoxide level of the blood and tissue, the presence or absence of soot in the lungs and airways, and the nature of the burns.

BODY POSITION: The position of the body can be telling. For example, if the corpse is found on a bed, the cause of death is smoke inhalation, and the fire's origin is found to be a cigarette in contact with bedding, the death would likely be accidental. But what if the victim is a nonsmoker? Why would he be smoking (unless he was a clandestine smoker)? Or could the cigarette be the arsonist's chosen igniter, thus making the death homicidal? Interestingly, the ME can often measure the nicotine level in the victim's urine, where a high level would indicate that he was indeed a smoker.

On the other hand, what if the victim's burned corpse is found bound and gagged in the basement with a gunshot wound to the head? Here, the manner of death is clearly homicide. Homicide would also be likely if stab wounds, strangulation marks, or significant trauma, such as bone fractures, were present.

A common misconception is that if a body is found curled into a fetal position it means the victim was alive at the time the fire started and suffered great pain before death. This is simply untrue. A burning corpse will often assume a "pugilistic position" or a boxer's posture. The legs and arms are flexed and the fists are tucked beneath the chin. This posture is due to contraction of the body's muscles as the fire "cooks" and dehydrates them.

CO LEVEL: Most deaths in fires are due to asphyxia from smoke and carbon monoxide (CO) inhalation (see Chapter Eight: Asphyxia, "Toxic Gases"). CO is a byproduct of the combustion of organic materials such as wood. The ME tests the victim's blood and tissues for its level. A normal level is less than 10 percent, though in smokers, it may be slightly higher. In victims of CO asphyxiation, the level ranges from 45 to 90 percent. The finding of a high level suggests that the victim died from smoke and CO inhalation, while a low level favors the victim being dead at the time the fire started.

CO poisoning not only causes death directly, but can also prevent the victim from escaping the fire. As the blood CO level rises, the person's ability to think and move appropriately declines. At a CO level of 30 percent, dizziness and confusion appears; at 50 percent weakness, loss of coordination, and disorientation occur; and at higher levels loss of consciousness and death follow. This means that the victim might have been alive and had time to escape, but the toxicity of the CO prevented him from doing so.

Another autopsy finding in victims of CO poisoning is a high level of **carboxyhemoglobin**, which occurs as CO combines with the blood's hemoglobin. Carboxyhemoglobin imparts a bright, cherry-red color to the blood, muscles, and organs of the victim. When the ME sees this, he will suspect that CO inhalation played a role in the death and will then proceed to prove this by assessing the CO level in the blood and tissues.

AIRWAY SOOT: In addition to a high blood CO level, the finding of soot in the mouth, throat, lungs, and airways would suggest that the victim was alive and breathing as the fire burned. Conversely, if the CO level is low and no soot is present in the airways, another cause of death must be considered.

NATURE OF THE BURNS: When a living person suffers a burn, the body immediately begins the repair process by diverting extra blood flow to the area, causing the surrounding tissues to become **hyperemic**. This is a big word meaning that the tissues are filled with blood, which also brings in many white blood cells (WBCs) to begin the repair process. If the ME performs microscopic examinations of the burned tissues and sees increased blood and WBCs in the surrounding areas, the victim was alive at the time the tissues burned. If the victim was already dead, no reaction could occur since the heart was not beating and no blood could flow into the area.

Also, an examination of any blisters on the skin might help. The fluid that collects inside blisters that occur during life tend to be rich in protein, while those that occur after death are not. The ME can often test the protein level and determine if the blistering occurred pre- or post-mortem.

So, burns with surrounding hyperemia and many WBCs and blisters filled with protein-rich fluids indicate that the victim was alive at the time of the fire. If the opposite is the case, then the victim was likely dead, due to homicide or smoke inhalation or some other cause, before the fire reached him.

Let's look more closely at the situation of the burned body that is found bound, gagged, and shot. The ME performs an autopsy and blood CO levels to determine the cause of death. The question is: What killed the victim? The gunshot or the fire? The finding of high blood CO levels and soot within the lungs and bronchial tubes would lead the ME to conclude that the victim lived through the gunshot and died as a result of CO inhalation. Or, if a low blood CO level is found, the gunshot is the likely cause of death. This may be critical to prosecutors if there were two perpetrators in the crime. One pulled the trigger and the other started the fire; one is the murderer and the other an accomplice. The charges filed against each depends on the ME's findings.

EXPLOSIONS

An explosion is an extremely rapid oxidative reaction. The key to any explosive device is confining the explosive material. If ignited in an unconfined space, the material simply burns, while if tightly packed into a container, ignition results in an explosive reaction.

Detonation releases a large amount of expanding gas, which compresses the surrounding air in a concussive wave. This wave travels at high speed and does severe and sudden damage to anything in its path. This creates numerous problems for the investigator, since the explosive device and any surrounding structures are heavily damaged, if not completely destroyed. Unless a secondary fire occurs, determining the point of origin is usually easy, but finding fragments of the device or any igniters or timers may be more difficult.

Explosives are deemed high or low by the speed of the pressure wave they produce. **Low explosives** typically move at rates of 1,000 meters per second or less, while **high explosives** may reach up to 8,500 meters per second.

The most commonly used low explosives are black powder and smokeless gunpowder. Gunpowder, which consists of nitrocellulose (nitrated cotton—cotton treated with nitric acid) with or without nitroglycerine, may be purchased, while black powder can be easily made with charcoal, sulfur, and potassium nitrate. Another easily made explosive is a combination of sugar and potassium chlorate. Bombers don't need to be chemists, and unfortunately a great deal of bomb-making information is easily available on the Internet.

High explosives are further subdivided into **initiating** or **noninitiating**, depending upon their sensitivity to heat, friction, or mechanical shock.

INITIATING EXPLOSIVES: These are very sensitive to heat, friction, and shock, which means that they have a great potential for unexpected detonation. For this reason, they are rarely used in home-manufactured bombs. More often, they are found in primers and blasting caps, where they are used to initiate other less sensitive noninitiating explosive materials. Mercury fulminate and lead azide are commonly used in this fashion.

NONINITIATING EXPLOSIVES: These are more stable and less likely to be accidentally detonated. They require a fuse or some type of initiating device to set them off. They are the most commonly used materials in commercial and military applications. Examples are dynamite, trinitrotoluene (TNT), pentaerythritrol tetranitrate (PETN), and cyclotrimethylenetrinitramine (RDX). Though dynamite is still available, it and other nitroglycerine-based explosives have largely been replaced by ammonium nitrate-based explosives.

Ammonium nitrate-fuel oil (ANFO) is an easily made explosive material. Ammonium nitrate, found in fertilizers, is an oxygen-rich oxidant. Bombs produced from this substance were involved in the Oklahoma City and 1993 World Trade Center bombings.

Searching the scene of a bombing requires the same attention to detail as with an arson scene. The finding of fragments from the explosive device, the igniter, and any timer may be crucial to determining the type of explosive used, and ultimately the person responsible. Besides locating these fragments, the search is directed toward the collection of debris to test for unexploded residue, which is almost always present.

Microscopic examination of the debris may reveal black powder and gunpowder, which are easily recognizable by the color and shape of their particles. After this inspection, the debris is rinsed with a solvent such as acetone, in which most explosives are soluble. The resulting solution is then analyzed, using thin layer or gas chromatography as well as mass spectroscopy and infrared spectroscopy (see the appendix), and the particular explosive used is identified. Once this is known, investigators can focus their efforts on the sellers and buyers of this particular product. This information can also serve to link two or more separate bombings.

Serial bombers are similar to serial arsonists in that they typically have deep-seated anger toward someone or an institution such as a company or the government. At times, the bombings are meant to deliver a political message or cause terror. But, as with most serial offenders, serial bombers develop habits. They repeatedly use materials and set up situations where they feel comfortable. This means that they tend to use the same types of explosives and timing or triggering devices over and over. An analysis of the explosive material and of any devices associated with the bomb can often link several bombings and ultimately lead to the perpetrator.

QUESTIONED DOCUMENTS:
HANDWRITING AND FORGERY EXAMINATION

Documents lie at the heart of many criminal enterprises. An embezzler alters the company books to obscure his theft. A kidnapper sends a list of written demands. And an altered check, lottery ticket, or will can divert a large amount of money into the wrong hands. The analysis of these documents by the forensic document examiner can be key to solving these crimes.

As we have seen with most other forensic techniques, document examination dates back many more years than one might imagine. In 1609, François Demelle published the first scientific treatise on the subject in France. And in Germany, the 1810 chemical testing of the ink dye used in a document known as Konigin Hanschritt is believed to be the first use of document analysis in the legal arena.

The documents that come to the attention of the modern document examiner may be handwritten, typed, or photocopied, complete or fragmentary, or simply a signature. They can be letters, checks, wills, lottery or claim tickets, receipts, ledgers, ransom or hold-up notes, harassing letters, driver's licenses, contracts, or deeds. They can be counterfeited currency or stamps. They might even include writings and symbols scrawled on walls, doors, or any other object.

The term **questioned document** is applied to any document whose source or authenticity is in question. When criminal investigators come across such documents, the forensic document examiner will be asked to:

- determine if a document is authentic and was produced by the person and at the time it was purported to be
- determine if the document has been altered
- expose damaged or obliterated writing
- compare handwriting, personal signatures, and typewritten or photocopied documents
- determine the age and source of papers and inks

To tackle these tasks, the examiner uses all of his skills and experience as well as several microscopic, photographic, and chemical techniques. This is an exacting art that can't be completely covered in this book, but hopefully by the time you finish reading this chapter you will have a feel for the many unique duties and talents of the forensic document examiner.

HANDWRITING

No two people write alike. There may be similarities, but on close inspection, the writing varies. Each person's writing style is personal, unique, and results from unconscious, automatic actions. Also, people never write the same way twice. Don't believe me? Quickly write your own signature a dozen times and take a close look at them. Each is a little different, isn't it?

Now repeat this experiment while holding the paper up against a wall or while standing over a table. Try using different types of writing instruments. What do you see? There will be even greater differences between these and the original signatures. The reason is that our handwriting is not only different each time but is also affected by our position and by whether we use a pen, pencil, or crayon.

These and many other variables create problems for the document examiner, and he must take all of them into consideration.

Let me make one other thing clear up front. When a forensic document expert examines handwriting, he is concerned only with the physical characteristics of the writing. He does not attempt to determine the writer's personality type. This is the job of a graphologist, and graphology is not an accepted forensic science.

LEARNING TO WRITE

Each of us has a personal and individual writing style that develops over years. We all learned to write early in life and in basically the same way. In fact, in the United States, only two basic writing systems are used: the

Palmer system, introduced in 1880, and the Zaner-Blosser system, which first appeared in 1895.

People are first taught to print and later to write in script, invariably beginning with the alphabet. They learn to copy each letter in both upper and lower case, and then progress to words and how to print and write them. Early in this educational process many people possess very similar styles because the system teaches everyone to form letters in the same way. This lends certain shared **class characteristics** to writing. But with time and repetition, a style and flow to a person's writing appears, so that each person develops his own style—a personal signature, so to speak. These personal characteristics become **individual characteristics** to the eye of the document examiner and are the basis for handwriting identification and comparison.

The point is that writing is a slowly progressive learning experience. Lettering goes from big block letters to flowing script only after years of practice. It is not until the late teens that a person's penmanship becomes unique, ingrained, and individual. After that, handwriting style changes little. But it does change and certain conditions may alter it dramatically.

As a person ages, his style undergoes a slow, steady metamorphosis. Not dramatic, but enough to recognize. This is important when comparing older documents, since new samples of the author's handwriting might differ from what he wrote twenty years earlier. If he has suffered some illness, such as a stroke or Parkinson's disease, these changes may be significant. Fatigue, stress, impaired vision, hand or arm injuries, an awkward writing position, and intoxication with drugs or alcohol can also alter the person's handwriting. The examiner must be cognizant of all these variables.

HANDWRITING COMPARISON

When comparing two documents or signatures to determine their authenticity, the examiner must have at his disposal examples (called **exemplars** or **standards**) of the person's writing that he knows are authentic. That is, if he wants to determine if a certain person wrote a certain questioned letter, he needs samples of that person's writing as a basis for comparison. And since a person's writing is a little different each time he puts pen to paper, the more examples the examiner has the better; he must get a good grasp of the individual characteristics and the range of variation that appears in the writing if he is to make an adequate comparison.

To begin his comparison, he looks for points of similarity and points of difference between the known standards and the questioned document. He will assess such things as:

OVERALL FORM: This includes the size, shape, slant (right, left, or vertical), proportion (relative height), and the beginning and ending strokes of the letters. Does the writing slant one way or the other, or employ angles, loops, or curves to make various letters? How do the individual letters begin and end?

LINE FEATURES: These deal with writing speed and fluidity, the amount of pen pressure applied, the spacing of the letters and words, and how the letters are connected. Does the writing flow or is it broken and hesitant? Is it written firmly or lightly? Are the letters and words crowded or spread out? Are the words written in a single smooth line or was the pen lifted in the middle of certain words?

MARGINS AND FORMAT: This is the overall layout of the writing. Are the page margins wide or narrow? Are the written lines parallel with each other and the top of the page, or do some show a rising or falling slant?

CONTENT: Grammar, punctuation, and word choice are part of the comparison. Are there consistent mistakes in spelling and punctuation? Do certain phrases and grammatical constructions repeat? Does the writing reveal the author's ethnicity or educational level?

If the examiner has a sufficient number of standards, he can usually determine if the questioned document and the standard share the same authorship. Problems arise if he has only a few examples. These may not be sufficient for him to get a "feel" for the person's writing style. Another problem is that the standards may have been written using a different instrument and under different circumstances. For example, comparing a questioned letter to a known writing on a wall might be impossible. If no usable known standards are available, the examiner may request the person to write something on similar paper and with a similar instrument.

This brings up the concept of requested and nonrequested standards. **Nonrequested standards** are documents or signatures of known authorship. **Requested standards** are writings or signatures a person produces at the request of the examiner.

For example, the examiner might be asked to determine if a check is forged. Besides the signature on the questioned check, he needs a copy of the real account holder's signature. Such nonrequested standards can usually be obtained from the bank. Or the examiner may simply ask the suspected forger to write his signature (actually the signature on the check, which he claims is his) several times. These requested standards are written on the same type of paper and with a similar writing instrument as those used on the check in question.

Nonrequested writings have several advantages, most importantly that they reveal the writer's true writing habits. They also often contain words and phrases that the writer frequently uses, which can be strong evidence against him. For example, old letters or notes may contain phrases that are identical to those used in a ransom note. The major disadvantage of these nonrequested standards is that they must themselves be authenticated. If they can't be, they are of little value to the examiner.

Another problem with nonrequested standards is that everyone's handwriting can change as a result of aging, certain medical conditions, and a host of other reasons that I mentioned earlier. For this reason, the examiner attempts to obtain documents written by the suspected author that were written around the same time as the questioned document. For example, if he is asked to authenticate a twenty-year-old handwritten will, he would want documents written by the purported author twenty years ago. These would reflect his style at the time the will was prepared much better than more recently written documents.

The major advantage of requested writings is that their authenticity is unquestioned—the examiner can actually watch the person write. Another advantage is that the examiner can dictate exactly what he wants written, such as words or phrases from the questioned document. This allows him to compare the writing word for word. If the content of the document contains information that he wants to withhold from the suspect or that is sensitive to the ongoing investigation, he can ask that he write sentences that are quite different but that include many of the words and phrases used in the questioned document.

A major disadvantage of requested writings, though, is that this situation makes some people nervous or causes them to concentrate too much on the writing process, which can lead to changes in their "normal" signature and introduce minor changes that make an accurate comparison more difficult.

Also, the person might attempt to purposefully disguise his writing style. For example, let's suppose the questioned document is a ransom or extortion note or a threatening letter. Obviously, if the suspect is the author of the note, he does not want his handwriting to match that of the document and would attempt to disguise his handwriting. Sometimes such efforts are successful and a match can be difficult or impossible.

One way around this is to have the suspect write a great deal of material. Not just a page, but several pages. It might be easy for him to alter his style for short passages, but the more he writes the more his natural style will come through. Another trick is to dictate the same material to the writer several times. If he is attempting to disguise his handwriting style, he will likely use different devices with each attempt. Basically, he forgets what he did in the last draft so he must make up changes "on the fly." A good examiner can then find the hidden style elements and the devices used to disguise them within the requested writing and make a comparison.

But what if a suspected forger refuses to give a sample of his writing? Can't he plead that it violates his Fifth Amendment right not to incriminate or testify against himself? The short answer is no. The Supreme Court decided in *Gilbert v. California* that handwriting was part of identifying physical characteristics and was not under the protection of the Fifth Amendment. Further, in the case of the *United States v. Mara*, the court also decided that this did not violate the Fourth Amendment protection against unreasonable search and seizure. This means that the court can order the suspect to produce handwriting standards even if he refuses.

Once he has either requested or nonrequested standards in hand, the examiner places the known and questioned documents side by side and visually inspect the writing. He first looks for gross likenesses or differences. If he finds significant differences, the comparison can end and he can state that the two documents were not written by the same person.

The most evident gross feature of script is the slant. Taller letters such as *T*s and *L*s most readily display the slant of a person's writing. These letters may lean right, left, or remain fairly vertical. Other common distinguishing features are the size and shading of the letters, the spacing between letters and words, and the relative height of letters.

If these gross characteristics are similar, he proceeds to evaluate more subtle characteristics, such as the beginning and ending strokes of certain letters. These include such things as broad, looped terminal strokes and ending flourishes. For example, the tail of letters, such as *y* or *j*, may be straight, angled, hooked, or looped.

He then addresses such things as pen pressure, writing speed, and pen lifts. Pen lifts are simply the lifting of the pen from the paper during writing. Some people write words without breaking contact with the paper, while others lift the pen and write in a noncontinuous fashion. These motions are ingrained and repetitive and are difficult to disguise.

No single feature makes an accurate comparison, but a combination of features might allow the examiner to determine that the writings came from the same person. This is obviously a very subjective judgment. Based on his findings, the examiner might say that the documents absolutely match, match with a high probability, probably match, or do not match, or his evaluation is inconclusive and he can't say one way or the other.

If the writing in question is script or a signature, a trained examiner can usually determine if a particular individual created it. If the questioned document is printed, this task is much more difficult since many of the distinguishing features of writing are not present in printed text.

Fortunately for law enforcement, most criminals are not very smart. This is often evident in written documents where misspellings are common. When the suspected writer of a forged document or a ransom note is asked to produce a requested sample for comparison, the examiner asks him to use the same words that were misspelled in the note. More often than not, the suspect, if he is the author of the note, misspells the words in the same fashion. He doesn't know how to spell the word so he doesn't know he did anything wrong.

In the infamous Charles Manson murders in 1969, the words "Healter Skelter" were written in blood on a refrigerator door at the LaBianca crime scene. It was apparently a misspelling of the title of the Beatles song "Helter Skelter" from their famous White Album. The incorrect spelling was used in the trial of Manson and his followers, who were convicted of the murders.

As we saw with fingerprints, ballistic patterns, and DNA databases, several handwriting databases also exist. The FBI maintains the National Fraudulent Check Center, the Bank Robbery Note File, the Anonymous Letter File, and the Forensic Information System for Handwriting (FISH), which contains scanned and digitized documents. A questioned document can be compared with these reference files, and if a match is made, a forensic document examiner can make a visual confirmation.

FORGERY

Forgery is legal terminology, not a forensic determination. It is defined as the writing or alteration of a document with the "intent to defraud." The document examiner can determine if a document was written by someone other than the stated author or if the document has been altered in any way, but the "intent to defraud" is decided by a judge and jury.

Criminal investigations often involve forged documents, such as handwritten wills and contracts or signatures on checks, wills, and contracts. Even ransom notes and threatening letters are forged in the hopes of casting suspicion on someone else. Since forged writing is not natural, even the most careful and gifted forger leaves behind evidence of his efforts.

The two most common methods of forgery are **freehand simulation** and **tracing**. Freehand methods are simply an attempt to copy the signature, while tracing involves placing the document over the original signature and tracing its lines. Either technique leaves clues that result from the forger writing in a manner that feels unnatural to him.

Common clues to forged writing include:

PRIOR DRAWING: The forger often uses a pencil to lightly trace a signature and then go back and write over the traced signature with ink.

FORGER'S TREMOR: This is a very fine shakiness to the writing from the forger's attempts to make an exact copy.

UNEVEN SPEED AND PRESSURE: Careful writing and tracing are not smooth and flowing as is natural writing. The forger uses varying speeds and pen pressures as he carefully creates each letter.

HESITATIONS: These are very common and result from the writer's starting and stopping frequently in his efforts to be exact.

UNUSUAL PEN LIFTS: Since copying and tracing are tedious, the forger frequently lifts the pen from the page to check his work.

PATCHING AND RETOUCHING: Mistakes are common in this tedious writing. The forger must continually add, remove, and repair marks.

BLUNT BEGINNINGS AND ENDS: Beginning and ending strokes of almost anyone's natural writing are very difficult to duplicate, so forged words are often relatively blunt on both ends.

To the naked eye, many of these defects may pass unnoticed, but under magnification with either a simple magnifying glass or a microscope, they are easily seen. In the case of prior drawing, a microscopic examination of the writing often shows both the pencil and the ink lines. The examiner may also use infrared light in this situation, since some inks become transparent under infrared light but graphite from the pencil will not. This means that the pencil lines can be seen beneath the ink.

DISGUISED WRITING

A special form of forgery is **disguised writing**. In this situation, the forger attempts to change or disguise his own writing. Many ransom notes and threatening letters are written this way so that the author can deny ownership at a later date. Alternatively, a suspect might attempt to disguise his writing when confronted with an incriminating letter that he wrote in his natural handwriting. He may change the size, slant, and form of some letters. But, despite his best efforts, much of his own writing style slips through. Certain letter formations, slants, or flourishes sneak into the script without the forger noticing. It is very difficult to hide these ingrained writing motions and an expert examiner can often find them.

ALTERED DOCUMENTS

Forgers often attempt to remove, add, or change portions of a written document for a wide variety of reasons, including financial gain or creation of an alibi. It might be as simple as changing a date or as complex as attempting to erase and rewrite a portion of the document or a signature. Perhaps a change in the date or dollar amount on a contract or check will bring a financial windfall. Maybe the gain of money or property will follow the addition of one name and the removal of another from a will. Or a signature on a sign-in sheet may provide an alibi. These changes are called erasures, obliterations, and alterations.

Erasures are common and easily accomplished with a rubber eraser, a knifepoint or other sharp instrument, sandpaper, or even a fingernail—anything that will scrape or rub away the unwanted marks. Fortunately, most of these are readily visible with the naked eye, often with the use of oblique (angled) light, which reveals the imperfections left on the paper or the indented remnants of erased writing. If not, the examiner can use a magnifying glass or microscope with oblique lighting to expose the erasures.

If a rubber eraser was used, tiny fragments of the eraser and the ink nestle into the fibers of the paper. With ultraviolet or infrared light, these may fluoresce (glow) and become visible. Also, dusting the page with **lycopodium powder**, which clings to and exposes the tiny rubber particles that invariably remain, can help.

Exposing erasures is important because even if the original words or marks can't be visualized, the examiner at least knows that the document was altered. This alone may be proof of a crime and make many legal documents null and void.

Obliteration is a bit more aggressive than simple erasing, which is not needed if the person simply obliterates or severely damages the paper that the words or signature is written on. Fire is most often the chosen method. Once the paper is burned, the writing is lost forever, right? Not exactly. If the paper is charred but intact, reflecting light at various angles off the paper's surface may expose the contrast between the ink and the charred paper background. The page can then be photographed.

Of course, handling charred pages is very difficult as they are extremely fragile and easily crumble. One way around this is to spray them with a solution of **polyvinyl acetate** in acetone. This stiffens the paper and makes handling much easier. The pages can then be floated on a solution of alcohol, chloral hydrate, and glycerin and photographed, sometimes using infrared light. Alternatively, a form of **autoradiography** can be used. In this technique the pages are sandwiched between two photographic plates and placed in a dark room for two weeks. The plates can then be developed and often the writing is revealed.

Sometimes chemicals such as oxidizing or bleaching agents are used to remove writing. These chemicals react with ink to produce a colorless compound and the writing disappears. But, under a microscope, the examiner can see remnants of the ink as well as discoloration of the paper in the area of treatment.

A more modern method of obliterating writing is by use of a laser, which vaporizes the ink. It also burns the paper fibers in the area and these can be seen under a microscope.

Alterations are used when a simple obliteration of words isn't enough. The forger needs to replace the obliterated words or numbers with others. Common examples are changing the amount of a check or the date on a contract or will. If the writing is obliterated before other writing is added, the examiner sees the above-mentioned changes in the underlying paper. He then analyzes the new writing and compares it to the old for differences in technique.

If the forgery is exceptionally well done and simple inspection doesn't reveal the changes, the examiner uses a microscope to expose the small differences in the original and the altered portions of the writing. He might also see subtle changes in ink color, line thickness, double lines, and pen pressure. If a ballpoint or roller ball pen was used, defects in the ball of either may be seen. One pen may have a very smooth, flawless ball, while the other may have an uneven or defective ball that leaves behind gaps and imperfections in the written line. The same is true for pencil leads and fountain pen nibs.

Overwriting is another form of alteration. Instead of erasing anything, the forger adds to or overwrites a portion of a document. Maybe change a 4 to an 8 or add a zero or two to a check. If the forger uses the same ink as the original writer, these types of changes can be extremely difficult to uncover. But, most often the forger does not have access to the pen or the ink used for the original writing and must make do with one of similar color. A careful examination of the inks used most often reveals the areas of alteration.

Though the two inks might seem identical under normal light, they usually appear very different when exposed to ultraviolet (UV) or infrared light. Depending upon the chemical makeup of the inks, UV light may cause them to fluoresce, fade from view, or appear unchanged. Each ink reacts differently, so one may fluoresce and the other fade from view, thus revealing that two different inks were used. Infrared light is invisible to the unaided eye, so it is usually coupled with photography to capture the image of the writing. **Infrared photography**, which is basically photographing the page under a blue-green light with infrared-sensitive film, often can distinguish the two inks very clearly. If these light techniques don't help, it may be necessary to examine the chemical contents of the inks to show that they are indeed different.

Indented Writing

Whenever something is written on a pad and the written page is removed, the remaining second page is **indented** by the path of the pen over the removed page. If the side of a pencil lead is then rubbed back and forth over the surface of the page, the "invisible" writing appears. This indented writing is also called **second page writing**. Of course, the forensic document examiners would never use this pencil method, since the pencil's markings could destroy or damage the evidence.

Sometimes a simple angled light exposes indented writing, and when it does, the page can be photographed. A more sensitive method is the use of an **electrostatic detection apparatus (ESDA)**, which was developed by Foster & Freeman USA, Inc. in 1978. It can, on occasion, uncover indented writing several pages below the original page. It's interesting that no one knows exactly how ESDA works, only that it does.

In ESDA, the page in question is covered with a Mylar sheet and placed on a porous metal plate. A vacuum is applied, which pulls the Mylar tightly against the page. The Mylar is used to protect the page, which is potential evidence, against damage. Static electricity is produced in the Mylar sheet-page combination by passing an electric wand over them. Though this process charges the entire surface of the Mylar, the charge is greatest in the indentions. Black toner similar to that used in copy machines is poured or sprayed over the Mylar. It attaches to the surface in proportion to the degree of charge, which means the indentions retain the greatest concentration of the toner. This reveals the indentions and thus the writing. It can then be photographed and preserved, and the original page (the real evidence) has not been damaged or altered in any way.

Paper and Ink

Sometimes the forensic document examiner must determine if a document has had pages added or if it was actually created at a certain time. To do this, he may resort to analysis of the document's paper or ink. If the pages of a document are of different types of paper, it might mean that pages have been added or exchanged. Or if the paper or ink was not manufactured until after the purported date of the document, something is amiss.

Most paper is made of wood or cotton and often has chemical additives that affect its opacity, color, brightness, strength, and durability. During the manufacturing process, coatings, fillers, and sizings are added. **Coatings** improve the appearance and surface properties of the paper, some making the paper better for copiers or printers, others better for writing. **Fillers** add color, strength, and surface texture. Common ones include titanium oxide and calcium carbonate. **Sizings** make the surface less porous to ink, so writing and printing will be sharp and clear. The types and amounts of each of these vary among manufacturers and paper types; chemical testing can distinguish one type and manufacturer from another.

Let's say the examiner is asked if each page of a will, contract, or other multipage document was created at the same time. That is, were pages added to it at a later date? By analyzing the chemical content of each page, he can determine if they are all the same type and from the same manufacturer, and he might even be able to distinguish among various lots of paper.

He also looks for **watermarks**, which are translucent designs in the paper that can be seen by holding the page up to a light. These usually indicate the manufacturer, the date of its production, and often for whom the paper was made. Attempts to forge a watermark are usually easily spotted. The reason is that a true watermark has fewer fibers than the rest of the page. This is what makes it visible when held up to a light. Forged marks are added images, and thus have an underlying fiber density equal to the rest of the page.

Paper analysis played a key role in revealing that diaries purported to have been written by Adolf Hitler were modern forgeries.

FORENSIC CASE FILES: THE HITLER DIARIES

On February 18, 1981, Gerd Heidemann, an employee of German publisher Gruner + Jahr, claimed to have found some lost diaries of Adolf Hitler. He said he had received the documents, which were handwritten in almost illegible German script, from a wealthy collector whose brother was an East German general. Heidemann's boss, Manfred Fischer, agreed to purchase the twenty-seven-volume diary along with a previously unknown third volume of *Mein Kampf* for 200,000 marks.

Fischer then began the authentication process by sending portions of the documents along with samples of Hitler's handwriting to Dr. Max Frei-Sulzer of the Zurich police forensic department and to Ordway Hilton, a world-renowned document examiner in Landrum, South Carolina. Unfortunately, neither Dr. Frei-Sulzer nor Hilton were aware that the handwriting samples came from the same source as the diaries themselves, so as expected, both men determined that the writings were from the same hand and, therefore, the documents were authentic.

Bantam Books, *Newsweek,* and publisher Rupert Murdoch entered into a bidding war for worldwide publication rights. Murdoch flew in Hugh Trevor-Roper, a renowned British historian, who, working under the same deception as Frei-Sulzer and Hilton, reached a similar conclusion. *Newsweek* ultimately won the bidding for the price of $3.75 million.

Fortunately, at the request of Gruner + Jahr, the West German police forensic department conducted their own examination and discovered that the paper on which the diaries were written contained Blankophor, a whitener that did not exist until 1954. In addition, the bindings contained threads of viscose and polyester, neither of which existed in the 1940s. Further, none of the inks used were widely available during World War II, and finally, a measurement of chlorine evaporation from the ink revealed that the documents were less than a year old.

Sometimes the key to determining authenticity lies in the ink used. Inks that appear the same physically may be very different chemically. This can help the examiner determine if the same ink was used for each page or word of a document, and can also reveal whether a particular ink existed at the time the document was supposedly prepared. For example, the ballpoint pen was first publicly marketed in 1945, so a document prepared with this type of instrument could not be older than that.

One nondestructive method for ink comparison is microspectrophotometry (see the appendix). This allows the examiner to accurately determine if the colors of the two inks match. If they do, it is likely they came from the same batch.

Another comparison method is thin layer chromotography (TLC) (see the appendix). For this test, very small samples of the inked paper are punched from the written lines using a thin hollow needle. The tiny piece of paper is placed in a test tube, and a solvent, which dissolves the ink, is added. A drop of the solvent solution, which now carries the ink, is placed on a paper strip along with drops of several known control inks. The strip is dried and then placed into another solvent, which migrates up the paper strip, dragging the inks along with it. The distance each of the inks migrates along the strip is determined by the size of its molecules, which separates the inks into bands. If inks from two pages of a questioned document are tested in this fashion, and if they yield different bands, the writing on the two pages was done with two distinctly different inks.

The examiner also has several ink reference databases at his disposal, such as the Ink Library, which is part of the United States Secret Service Forensic Services Division's Questioned Document Branch. In addition, the U.S. Treasury

Department maintains an extensive database of the TLC patterns of commercial inks. More recently, many manufacturers have begun adding fluorescent dye "tags" to their products so that they can be more easily identified. Since the tags change annually, the year of manufacture can be readily determined.

Even with all these sophisticated techniques available to the forensic document examiner, some forgery cases are very difficult to unravel. Just how clever experienced forgers can be is illustrated in the Mormon Forgeries case.

FORENSIC CASE FILES: THE MORMON FORGERIES

On October 15, 1985, in Salt Lake City, Utah, two pipe bombs exploded, one killing businessman and Mormon bishop Steve Christensen and the other grandmother Kathy Sheets. The package that killed Mrs. Sheets was addressed to her husband, Gary, also a bishop in the Mormon Church. The next day a third bomb exploded in the car of Mark Hofmann, a young man who dealt with historical documents. Hofmann survived and told police that he had seen a strange package sitting in his car, and when he reached for it, it exploded. Bomb investigators knew immediately that Hofmann was lying since crime scene reconstruction evidence indicated that Hofmann had been kneeling in the car seat, working with the bomb when it detonated. Hofmann became the lead suspect in the other bombings, since it was felt that he was likely preparing a third bomb for delivery when it accidentally went off.

Police soon learned that Hofmann was somewhat of a whiz at locating ancient documents. In fact, he had recently discovered not one but two copies of the *Oath of a Freeman*, a seventeenth-century work that was the first document ever printed in America. Amazingly, prior to Hofmann's discoveries, no copies were known to exist. He had also found what became known as the "White Salamander Letter," a document that undermined the very tenets of Mormonism and greatly embarrassed the church. The police discovered that Hofmann had sold many historical documents to the Mormon Church. However, they also uncovered evidence that these documents were forgeries. Did Hofmann plant the bombs in an attempt to cover his forgeries?

The case became long and complex, but ended when Hofmann was confronted with evidence that proved he had forged his "discoveries." Hofmann confessed to the bombings and the forgeries in exchange for a life sentence rather than face a possible death sentence in court. He also told investigators how he pulled off the forgeries, which were so realistic that many experts had deemed them authentic.

The original *Oath of a Freeman* had been printed by Stephen Daye, who also printed the *Bay Psalm Book*. Hofmann purchased a cheap copy of this book, cut out the letters, and rearranged them into *Oath of a Freeman*. He then used this model to create a printing plate, which he used to print the two copies of the *Oath*. He added wear patterns to the letters, to simulate the changes that would be seen with repeated use in a real printing press, by grinding down portions of some letters and rubbing the entire plate with steel wool. This gave the printed document realistic printing defects.

But for the documents to stand up to the rigorous scrutiny that he knew would follow, he needed to "age" the paper and the ink he used. The paper was the easy part. He simply used paper pilfered from the flyleaves of other seventeenth-century books in the Brigham Young University library. He even burned one of these pages to produce the carbon black he needed to make the "ancient" printing ink he needed. He did this because he feared the examination of his discoveries might include carbon-14 dating of the ink. If it came from seventeenth-century paper, the C-14 dating would reflect this. He mixed the carbon black with linseed oil, beeswax, and tannic acid, which he obtained by boiling a seventeenth-century leather book binding in distilled water. Through this process he produced "old" ink. But, ink oxidizes with age and turns from dark black to a rusty hue. To simulate this effect, Hofmann used a combination of peroxide (an oxidizing agent) and a hand iron, which added heat and sped up the process. All these precautions meant that if the ink were visually and chemically tested, it would appear as if it had been prepared in the seventeenth century.

But, the prosecutors who handled the bombing-murder case brought in forensics document examiners George J. Throckmorton and William Flynn, and they proved to be Hofmann's undoing. After examining the documents, they discovered several things wrong. Letters with "tails" such as *Y* and *J* seemed to overlap with taller letters such as *L* and *T*, when the former appeared in the line above the latter. This overlapping was a product of Hofmann's pasting together of the letters when he made the template for his press and would not be possible with the handset type used in the seventeenth century. In handset type each letter is a raised figure on a small cube and the cubes are lined up on a page-sized holder in the proper order to produce the words and sentences, line by line, down the page. This means that each letter is "within" the area of its cube and overlapping is not possible.

They also noted evidence of scorching on the paper and ink from the hand iron and what is called the "alligator effect." This is the cracking and breaking of the ink from the use of chemical oxidants to artificially "age" the ink. Natural aging doesn't produce such changes. They found many other problems with the documents, and at the end of the day, the very clever Hofmann failed to deceive the even more clever document examiners.

Typewriters and Photocopiers

Typewriters are frequently used to write threatening letters and ransom and extortion notes, since criminals believe this will make the letter untraceable. Not true. When a typewriter is involved, the two most common questions asked of the document examiner are:

- What make and model typewriter produced the document?
- Was the document prepared using this particular suspect's typewriter?

The answer to the first question relies on class characteristics, while the answer to the latter requires the identifying of individual characteristics.

To identify the make and model, the examiner must have a database of typefaces used in various models, both old and new. Most manufacturers use either pica or elite typefaces, but the size, shape, and style of the letters vary so that a particular manufacturer can be identified. This alone narrows the search for the exact machine that produced the document.

In order for the examiner to determine if a particular machine produced the questioned document, he searches for individual characteristics of the typewriter. These include misaligned or damaged letters, abnormal spacing before or after certain letters, and variations in the pressure applied to the page by some letters. For example, a certain letter can have nicks or spurs that would be imprinted on the page, or a letter could lean to one side or be slightly higher or lower than the others. These defects can be compared to a suspect typewriter and offer powerful individualizing characteristics.

This type of comparison was a critical part of the famous Leopold and Loeb case of 1924.

FORENSIC CASE FILES: LEOPOLD AND LOEB

Nathan Leopold and Richard Loeb were new kinds of killers—"thrill killers." On May 21, 1924, nineteen-year-old Leopold and eighteen-year-old Loeb murdered classmate Bobby Franks with a chisel to see what it felt like to kill someone and to see if they could get away with it. Even though Franks was dead, they sent a ransom note as part of their attempts to deflect the investigation. Unfortunately for them, Leopold left his glasses at the crime scene. The spectacles had an unusual hinge, which allowed police to trace them to a Chicago optometrist who said he had written only three similar prescriptions, one to Nathan Leopold. The investigation ultimately led to a match between the ransom note and a typewriter Leopold used in his law study group. Despite the efforts of famous defense attorney Clarence Darrow, the two boys were convicted and sentenced to life in prison.

One problem with typewriter comparison arises with the IBM Selectric typewriter. This model has an interchangeable type-head sphere. This means that the typewriter must have the same sphere that was used to prepare the document in place at the time of the examination. Obviously, if the sphere has been replaced and the original discarded, no match can be made.

In typewriters that use ribbons, the examiner might be able to use this to link the typewriter to the document. If the typewriter possesses a single-pass ribbon and if the ribbon used to type the document is still in place, the message can simply be read from the ribbon itself. But, even if the ribbon has been used in several passes, portions of the message might be retrievable. There is one caveat with typewriters that use ribbons, however: In order to compare a typed document to a particular machine, the examiner must prepare a comparison document by using the machine to type it. When he does this, he must use a similar ribbon and it must be in a similar condition. The reason for this is that a worn or lightly inked ribbon will reveal minor defects in the typeface, whereas a heavily inked, new ribbon might obscure them.

What if the original typewriter was used to add a line or a paragraph to a document? How would the examiner know that this had occurred? Since the typeface would be identical, it's possible that he couldn't uncover the alteration. But, when a page is placed into a typewriter a second time, its alignment is often slightly off. This might be very subtle, but the examiner has a way around that. He places a specially made glass plate that possesses an etched grid pattern over the page. Any imperfection in the alignment of the added lines or paragraphs may then be readily visible.

Unfortunately, typewriters have given way to computers, which connect to printers that may use daisy wheel, dot matrix, ink-jet, or laser technologies. These vary very little so that the examiner can't often distinguish one from another. If the suspect printer is available, the examiner may find subtle changes in how it jets and lasers certain letters. This is more difficult and less often possible than matching a typewriter to a document.

At times, a photocopied document can be matched to a particular copy machine. A copy machine takes an image on a page and duplicates it onto another. It does this by a complex series of events. First, a lens focuses the image of the page onto a drum, which has been charged with static electricity and coated with selenium or another light-sensitive substance. The drum retains the image as it is bathed with a toner that attaches to the surface of the drum in proportion to the strength of the electrostatic charge. This toner image is then transferred to the blank page, which is then exposed to a fixing agent.

The mechanisms within the machine that pull the paper onto and remove it from the copy surface can leave marks on the page, or the cover glass, camera lens, or drum might have scratches or defects that mark each page produced. Occasionally, these marks can be identified and matched to the machine that produced the page in question.

ART FORGERY

Art forgers are a special breed. They need to be smart, meticulous, and talented. After all, if you are going to copy a master, you'd better know how to handle a brush. Yet, the methods to uncover their forgeries are similar to those employed by document examiners. The creation of *Christ With the Adultress*, purported to have been done by Dutch painter Johannes Vermeer in the 1600s, is an example of just how clever art forgers can be.

FORENSIC CASE FILES: THE VERMEER FORGERIES

Prior to and throughout World War II, the Nazis purchased and stole art from all over Europe and Russia. Many of the works were secreted within bunkers, caves, and mines during the war. After the war ended, a cache of such paintings was uncovered in an Austrian salt mine and among them was a work titled *Christ With the Adultress*, which appeared to be a previously unknown work by Johannes Vermeer. An investigation traced the painting to Han van Meegeren, another Dutch painter. Since he had sold the piece to the Nazis, he was arrested as a collaborator.

Van Meegeren confessed that the work was a forgery, but authorities didn't believe him until, while under house arrest, he produced other astonishing forgeries. He then told investigators that his original intention was to create fakes, trick art experts, and then expose their ignorance. He apparently had created many such forgeries during the run-up to World War II. He deviated from his original plan when he found he could sell the works for a good deal of money to the Nazis.

So, how did he create fake works that fooled the experts? First, he needed canvases from the seventeenth century, the period in which Vermeer painted. He purchased lesser works of that time period and, using pumice, removed most of the original art. He then ground his own pigments, much as did Vermeer and other painters of the time. But he couldn't simply add his pigments to conventional oils like linseed oil, as these require many years to completely dry and crack, as would be the case in a painting that was truly three hundred years old. He instead used a synthetic phenol-formaldehyde resin (known as Albertol or Ambertol), which dried and hardened quickly. Using this mixture, he created his paintings and then dried them in an oven at 105°F for an hour. After a coat of varnish, he rolled the canvas over a drum to "crack" the paint. Ink was then spread over the painting and allowed to seep into the cracks to "age" them. After a second coat of varnish, the painting was ready for viewing.

Examiners then analyzed this painting and many others that van Meegeren had produced over the years to ascertain if he was truthful about his methods. Chemical analysis showed that phenol-formaldehyde resin was indeed present and that a blue pigment used in some of the paintings was not available until the nineteenth century. X-rays revealed remnants of the original underlying paintings on the canvases he had used. *Christ With the Adultress* was indeed a 1930s forgery.

CRIMINAL PSYCHOLOGY:
ASSESSING THE MIND

The study of the psychology behind criminal activity falls to the forensic psychologist and psychiatrist. Though people often use the terms psychologist and psychiatrist interchangeably, they are quite different. A doctor of psychology possesses a PhD, while a psychiatrist has a medical degree. The psychiatrist must go through four years of medical school, as would any other physician, and then complete a residency in psychiatry.

Clinical psychologists are trained to test and interview patients in order to determine their mental state, competence, and sanity, and to offer counseling. A clinical psychiatrist does all this but in addition is a medical doctor, which allows him to perform psychotherapy and employ medications in his treatment regimens.

FORENSIC PSYCHOLOGY

As we saw in our discussion of pathologists (see Chapter One: Forensic Science), the work of the clinical psychologist or psychiatrist and his forensic counterpart are quite distinct. The former attempts to analyze and treat his patient with the hope of improving his mental health, while the latter tries to dissect the criminal mind to search for motives, competency, and sanity in the criminal arena. **Forensic psychiatry** is, by definition, the legal aspects of psychiatry.

HISTORICAL MISSTEPS

Society has always searched for a method to identify the "bad guys." The rationale is simple: If criminals can be identified and put away, the public will be safe. If not, the public is at risk. This fear is fueled by such seemingly "normal" serial killers like Ted Bundy, John Wayne Gacy, and most recently Dennis Rader, the BTK Killer. These guys weren't slobbering monsters and wild animals—at least in outward appearance. This is discomforting to most people.

Because of this, there has been a long, historical search for methods to identify the "criminal type." Let's look at a couple of the more famous people who have delved into this arena.

German physician Franz Joseph Gall (1758–1828) developed the field of phrenology around 1800. He believed that criminality could be determined by reading the "bumps" on a person's head. The concept was that the criminal's brain was abnormal and since the brain resided within the skull, the abnormality would in turn alter the shape and contour of the overlying bone. He believed that feeling for these changes could detect the abnormal brain and identify the criminal personality.

Cesare Lombroso (1835–1909), a professor of psychiatry and director of a mental asylum in Pesaro, Italy, published his book *The Criminal Man* in 1876. In it he states that criminals can be identified and classified by their physical characteristics. Attributes that indicated criminality included: cleft palates, poor teeth, long arms, an asymmetric head shape, prominent jaw or cheekbones, large ears, a hawk nose, fleshy lips, extra fingers or toes, and other physical "defects." In his article "Criminal Anthropology," published in *The Forum* in 1895, he suggests that not only could these features point out the criminal element, but also that some characteristics indicated the type of crime the person would likely commit. According to Lombroso, assassins had prominent jaws and pale faces and ravishers short hands, narrow foreheads, and light hair, while pickpockets possessed long fingers (this actually makes sense) and black hair.

These theories and many others have long since fallen by the wayside, as of course they should, but the search for the "criminal mind" continues. Profiling, which will be discussed later in this chapter, is one such endeavor. In addition, there are studies underway that utilize such high-tech devices as CT scans, MRIs, and PET scans to evaluate the brain function of criminals. The goal is to develop techniques as wide ranging as a better lie detector to identifying those with brain disorders that could lead to aberrant behavior.

Modern forensic psychiatrists and psychologists take a more reasoned and scientific approach to evaluating suspects and criminals than did their predecessors.

THE ROLE OF THE FORENSIC PSYCHIATRIC PROFESSIONAL

The forensic psychiatric professional might be called upon to perform several functions, including:

- testing of a suspect for mental illness
- assessing a perpetrator's sanity
- establishing a perpetrator's mental state at the time the crime occurred
- determining competency to stand trial, offer testimony, sign contracts, and perform other actions
- evaluating suspects for signs of deception and malingering
- profiling perpetrators and victims

To perform these duties he uses various medical records, examinations and tests, psychiatric tests and interviews, police and witness reports, and crime scene evidence.

The medical (clinical) and legal (forensic) aspects of psychiatry have widely divergent goals and methods.

The clinical psychiatrist's primary goal is to develop rapport and a trusting relationship with the patient. If successful, the patient will open up and tell the psychiatrist what he needs to know in order to develop the proper treatment plan. The process is cooperative and the psychiatrist does not make moral or value judgments about the patient.

Forensic psychiatry is the opposite. It is adversarial rather than cooperative. It is judgmental in that the legal system is designed to make moral judgments concerning responsibility. The goal is not to treat the individual but rather to dissect his personality so that motives can be revealed. This means that the subject and the forensic psychiatrist are often at odds.

In the clinical arena, the patient has every reason to be truthful. After all, both he and his physician want him to get better. In the forensic setting, the person has many reasons to lie. If guilty, the person wants to hide the truth of his actions and his thoughts. He wants his motivations for the crime in question to remain buried, and to do this he might fabricate or exaggerate symptoms in order to create an insanity defense. He likely views the psychiatrist as an enemy rather than a health care professional.

The forensic psychiatrist is often involved in both criminal and civil matters. In the criminal arena, he might be brought to the case by the prosecution, the defense, or the judge to be involved in homicides, robberies, and kidnappings, or cases of assault, battery, and sexual misconduct. He might be asked to assess the role of alcohol and drugs in the defendant's conduct, or to determine a person's sanity or competency to stand trial, or to assess the subject's understanding of reality and responsibility and offer a judgment as to the suspect's state of mind at the time of the crime. He might also offer investigators information for use in witness and suspect interrogations.

In civil cases, the psychiatrist is asked to determine competency to sign wills and contracts, manage personal affairs, vote, offer testimony, or stand trial. He might also become involved in spousal and child abuse cases, or disputes involving child custody, sexual harassment, disability, or emotional suffering.

In cases of apparent suicide, the psychiatrist might perform a psychological autopsy to determine if the victim likely took his own life. Interviews with family, friends, and co-workers can often reveal the victim's behavior during the period before the tragedy and determine whether drugs and alcohol, financial problems, or social difficulties could have contributed to his death.

PSYCHIATRIC TESTING

Before the forensic psychiatrist can delve into a subject's psyche, he must first make certain that no illnesses or treatments that could interfere with his evaluation are present. Medical problems such as strokes, certain liver or kidney diseases, and head trauma, as well as many medications, can alter the subject's ability to think, understand, and reason, and this might impact the examiner's assessment of the subject. For example, a stroke may have altered the person's reasoning abilities so that he can't form complete and coherent thoughts. It may have damaged areas of the brain that control speech, hearing, emotions, and any other brain function. Since these can greatly affect the subject's performance on the various psychiatric tests, medical problems must be addressed before any psychological testing is undertaken.

Many prescription and illicit drugs alter brain function. Medications for seizure disorders, diabetes, heart disease, insomnia, weight loss, and essentially every known sedative and mood elevator can affect psychiatric testing.

To rule out these medical problems before any psychiatric testing is undertaken, the subject would undergo a complete medical history and physical examination with special attention to his neurological status. A review of his medical, work, and military records would be done. If the subject is a suspect in a crime, police and witness reports, crime scene photos, and autopsy reports (in cases where a death was involved) would be reviewed. Blood testing and perhaps specialized brain testing such as an electroencephalogram (EEG) or an MRI or CT brain scan might also be done. If these examinations are normal, the psychiatrist would then proceed with his evaluation and testing.

The goal of his testing is to search for any significant psychiatric disorders, such as schizophrenia, and to establish the subject's thought processes and his cognitive (reasoning) abilities. One important area that the forensic psychiatrist must address is the suspect's likely state of mind at the time of the crime. Was he capable of understanding what he did and that his acts were harmful or illegal? This is often difficult to determine.

In court, one side or the other almost invariably argues that these tests are fraught with problems in that they assess the suspect's past and present mental state but do not necessarily determine his state of mind at the time of the crime, so any such determination is merely conjecture. This is in many ways true, but with properly conducted tests and interviews the psychiatrist can most often formulate an accurate assessment.

Psychiatric testing falls into several categories: personality inventories, projective tests, and intellectual and cognitive assessments. Different psychiatric professionals employ different tests, but we will consider some of the more common ones.

PERSONALITY INVENTORIES: These tests, designed to determine the subject's basic personality type, are highly standardized and reliable. Common ones are the **Minnesota Multiphasic Personality Inventory (MMPI)**, the **Millon Clinical Multiaxial Inventory (MCMI)**, and the **California Psychological Inventory (CPI)**. Since these are commonly given in schools and the workplace, you've likely taken one or more of these at some time during your life.

PROJECTIVE TESTING: These tests evaluate personality and thought processes. They are less standardized and more subjective than the above-mentioned personality inventories. Common ones include the Rorschach test, projective drawing, and the thematic apperception test.

In the **Rorschach test**, or the ink blot exam, the subject is shown a series of abstract ink blots and is asked to describe what he sees. His descriptions might reveal something about his personality, his thought processes, and his connection to reality, and might also offer a clue to his inner fantasies.

Projective drawing is similar except that the subject produces the drawings, which are then analyzed. He might be asked to draw a house, a car, a tree, a member of the opposite sex, or a frightening scene or situation. His drawings might reveal his inner thought processes and fantasies. For example, if he draws images of a house that is on fire, a woman who has been stabbed, or a leafless tree with broken branches, these constructs might provide a look into his inner world.

In the **thematic apperception test (TAT)**, the person is shown pictures of common situations and asked to make up a story to go with the images. Again, his inner thoughts and fantasies might be revealed. For example, after viewing a photo of a man and a woman talking, he might then relate a tale of how the two are planning their wedding or that they are arguing over money or that they are saying negative things about him. Each of these answers would indicate a different psychiatric state.

INTELLECTUAL AND COGNITIVE TESTS: These are designed to assess the subject's intelligence, mental competency, thought processes, and ability to understand his behavior. In forensic evaluations, the suspect's ability to understand situations and his own actions are critical in determining his level of responsibility and competency to stand trial. The most common intelligence test is the **Wechsler Adult Intelligence Scale (WAIS)**, which assesses **intelligence quotient**, or **IQ**.

After these tests are completed and evaluated, the forensic psychiatrist interviews the subject, during which he probes deeper into any areas of concern uncovered by the testing process. This is where his training and experience comes into play. Because of the complexity and range of these interviews, and because different psychiatrists use different interview techniques, a complete discussion of this subject is far beyond the scope of this text. However, two interview techniques deserve mention: hypnosis and the use of drugs during the interview process.

Hypnosis induces a subject into an altered state of consciousness. This is used to help suspects and witnesses recall certain events and details. One problem is that it is fairly easy to fake hypnosis, so any information obtained by this technique needs corroboration. Also, persons who are under the influence of hypnosis are often highly "suggestible," so the mere asking of questions may alter their memory for certain events. These new "memories" will become part of their real memory, which renders the validity of any future interviews and court testimony suspect. Some courts allow testimony from previously hypnotized witnesses while others do not.

Though there is no such thing as a "truth serum," certain drugs such as sodium pentathol can lower inhibitions and defenses. Pentathol is a narcotic that makes the recipient drowsy and euphoric, and might also make him talkative. As with hypnosis, any information gleaned in this fashion is suspect and would likely be challenged in court.

Based on the testing and interview results, the psychiatrist offers an opinion as to the subject's psychiatric state, competence, and sanity.

COMPETENCE AND SANITY

The forensic psychiatrist might become involved in all three phases of the criminal justice process: pre-trial, trial, and post-trial. During the pre-trial phase, he could be asked to determine the suspect's competency to stand trial, offer testimony, understand his rights, work with his attorneys, and confess. Courts do not usually accept confessions from someone who is incompetent or mentally ill.

Competency to stand trial involves the defendant's ability to understand the charges against him, the possible consequences of the charges, the workings of the courtroom, and the roles of the judge and the attorneys. If he has no understanding of these matters, he can't be fairly tried. For example, he may harbor delusions that the judge is his grandfather or that the judge and the attorneys are involved in a conspiracy to "get him." Either delusion would be counter to reality and could affect his ability to participate in his own defense. A competency examination can also determine if the subject is competent enough to confess, testify, waive his Miranda rights (the right to remain silent and to have council present), accept or refuse an insanity defense, or be executed.

Common mental disorders that lead to a determination of lack of competence include:

- mental retardation (resulting from congenital or developmental abnormalities, or from brain injuries or infections)
- severe drug or alcohol addiction
- organic brain syndromes (structural or functional brain abnormalities) such as strokes, tumors, or infections
- severe neuroses that lead to paranoid or severe anxiety states

- psychoses and schizophrenias where there is an altered perception of reality

During the trial, the forensic psychiatrist might take the stand in order to offer an opinion regarding the suspect's mental state at the time of the crime. If the person was mentally ill—temporarily or permanently—at the time he committed the crime, he might present a defense based on insanity.

In the post-trial or sentencing phase, the psychiatrist might be asked to address the defendant's need for admission to a treatment facility as opposed to a prison, or to offer his opinion regarding the defendant's level of dangerousness, or the likelihood of him committing future criminal acts. In death penalty cases, he may even be asked to comment on a convicted person's competency to be executed.

It is important to know that **insanity** is a legal and not a medical term. A psychiatrist can't diagnose insanity. Only a judge or jury can make that determination. Psychiatrists can diagnose mental disorders and advise the court as to their findings, but the final say comes from the law, not medicine.

Legal insanity is a slippery, poorly defined term that varies among jurisdictions. However, most jurisdictions use the **M'Naughten Rule**, which dates to the early nineteenth century in England, as the yardstick for determining sanity. It is primarily a statement of the defendant's cognitive ability in that it asks whether the perpetrator suffered from any mental disorder that prevented him from understanding the nature and the consequences of his actions. In other words, an individual could be found not guilty by reason of insanity if he did not know at the time of the crime's commission that his actions were illegal or if he was incapable of altering his illicit behavior.

Congress passed the Insanity Defense Reform Act of 1984, which states that a person can be found not guilty by reason of insanity if "the defendant, as a result of a severe mental disease or defect, was unable to appreciate the nature and quality or the wrongfulness of his acts." The term *appreciate* is vastly different from the word *know*. It implies a higher degree of understanding than simple knowledge.

Both the M'Naughten Rule and the Insanity Defense definitions address the fact that a crime has two parts: One is the criminal activity, termed the *actus reus*, while the second part is the *mens rea*, or the criminal intent.

Diminished capacity is a special form of "insanity," and like true insanity its definition varies among jurisdictions. The basic tenet of diminished capacity is

---

that certain conditions present during the commission of the crime reduced the person's ability to alter his actions or to distinguish between right and wrong. In other words, the perpetrator was not capable of forming a specific criminal intent or could not act in a purposeful manner. This may relieve the person from criminal guilt or at least reduce the degree of his crime. For example, a person suffering from paranoid delusions secondary to chronic cocaine or methamphetamine abuse might not have been capable of planning a murder. This may change his degree of liability from first- to second-degree murder.

LIES AND DECEPTIONS

Criminals lie. Always have and always will. If they didn't, police investigation would be an easy job. The criminal would simply walk in and confess. But, that's not the case. Whether it's forgery, establishing a false alibi, staging a crime scene, or lying in court, the criminal will alter, distort, and manufacture the truth to his own ends. In other situations, a witness's identification of a suspect may be erroneous or an innocent person may offer a false confession. Though their intent is not to lie, the result is still false information.

Distortion, exaggeration, and deception present problems for the forensic psychiatrist. As I stated earlier, the relationship between the forensic psychiatrist and the suspect is mostly adversarial. Regardless of whether the suspect views the psychiatrist as an enemy or as a possible ally in his deceptions, he is extremely likely to lie. After all, if he can convince the psychiatrist that he's telling the truth, or that he remembers nothing of the crime, or that he's insane, he will have an ally in the courtroom.

Let's say the suspect is indeed guilty of a horrid rape and murder. He might say that he likes and respects women, when the exact opposite is the case. He lies about past interpersonal and sexual experiences and alters or completely fabricate his beliefs and inner feelings. Or he might go the other way and exaggerate his own negative actions and feelings in the hope that he will be declared incompetent or insane, and thus avoid responsibility for his actions. Often these exaggerations revolve around symptoms the suspect believes will lead to a well-known, though controversial, diagnosis such as post-traumatic stress disorder (PTSD), multiple personality disorder (MPD), or another disorder that could render him incompetent for trial.

Even though psychiatrists are trained and experienced in detecting deception, they still occasionally fall prey to a clever suspect. The case of Hillside Strangler Kenneth Bianchi is one famous example.

FORENSIC CASE FILES: KENNETH BIANCHI

During the 1970s, a series of brutal rapes and murders occurred in Los Angeles. The bodies of the victims were dumped in plain sight on hillsides throughout Los Angeles County, which earned the killers the title of the Hillside Stranglers. Through a long and complex investigation, the police finally arrested Angelo Buono in Los Angeles and his cousin Kenneth Bianchi in Bellingham, Washington.

Using knowledge he got from college psychology classes and from the movies *The Three Faces of Eve* and *Sybil*, Bianchi concocted an insanity defense that revolved around his alleged MPD. Bianchi said that his evil alter ego, Steve, made him kill the young women and that he, Kenneth, was innocent and a pawn of the evil Steve. He was so good that he fooled several psychiatric professionals.

Finally, Dr. Martin Orne, an expert in hypnosis, evaluated Bianchi and managed to bring out Steve. Though initially convincing, Bianchi made several mistakes. While he was Steve he referred to Steve as "he" rather than "I" on several occasions. If he were truly Steve at that time, he would not use the third-person pronoun "he." Also, at one point, he was introduced to an imaginary someone whom Kenneth knew but Steve didn't. He acted out a handshake with the non-existent person. "Seeing" this imaginary person, much less shaking hands with him, would mean that he was hallucinating (seeing something or someone that was not really there), and this is not part of MPD. Finally, Dr. Orne told Bianchi that it was very unusual for an MPD victim to have only one other personality and that most had several. Almost immediately, "Billy" was born, giving Bianchi three separate personalities.

After his ruse was exposed, Bianchi confessed and agreed to testify against his cousin Angelo in exchange for favorable treatment by the court.

Malingering is a special form of deception. In this case, the subject attempts to make any physical or mental defects appear worse than they are or manufactures them completely. Alternatively, he might try to make a defect less severe than it actually is. Fortunately, the MMPI and several other tests include scales that indicate such deceptions.

EYEWITNESS ACCOUNTS

It would seem that an eyewitness to a crime would be solid evidence. After all, the witness actually saw the perpetrator and the criminal act. No guesswork or supposition is involved. Case closed, right? Not exactly.

Eyewitnesses are notoriously unreliable. Numerous studies have attested to this fact. For example, in 1974 Robert Buckhout published an article in *Scientific American* titled "Eyewitness Testimony." It related the results of an experiment in which fifty-two people witnessed a purse snatching. Only seven of the witnesses were able to identify the thief. This is typical of the many other studies done in this area.

Doesn't make sense, does it? Seems counterintuitive.

Unfortunately, memory isn't that simple or that reliable. Creating, storing, and recalling memories is a complex sequence of neurological events. It's not just simply storing an image or a sound or some other sensory input. It requires a delicate and exact communication among several areas of the brain.

A person's ability to recall the details of any event fades with time, and the natural tendency is to fill in any blanks with what the person believes should have happened. And this unconscious effort is colored by one's beliefs, prejudices, motives, and expectations. Add to this the stress of witnessing a frightening or threatening event and the conditions are ripe for false or altered memories. This isn't necessarily a malicious attempt at deception, but rather just the way the human brain works.

Earwitness testimony is even more problematic. People are occasionally asked to identify a perpetrator by his voice, but unless the voice is exceptionally distinctive, this is an unreliable exercise.

FALSE CONFESSIONS

False confessions are more common than you might think. It is difficult for most people to grasp why this is so, but there are several reasons.

A false confession may serve to deflect the police from another crime. For example, the suspect may confess to stealing a car or robbing a store, but say that he knows nothing of the murder that occurred at the same time in another location. If he is guilty of the robbery, he could not possibly be the killer. Or perhaps a friend or family member might confess to a crime in order to protect the real culprit.

But what of the people who simply confess for no apparent reason? Many psychological factors come into play. Low self-esteem, fear of the police, a need for fame, or a need to please the authorities or another person may all play a role. Many people have deeply hidden feelings of guilt, real or imagined, and might feel a need to confess to something so that they will be punished for this buried guilt. The use of alcohol or drugs can cloud judgment and lead to confusion, false memories, and fabrications, which in turn can lead to a false confession.

Certain police interrogation tactics might also lead to false confessions. Isolation and fatigue can break down resolve, so that a confession is deemed easier than continuing with the interrogation. If the good cop/bad cop routine is employed by the interrogators, the suspect might confess to the good cop, thinking that he will protect him from the other and from the legal system.

SERIAL AND MULTIPLE OFFENDERS

Serial offenders have always created special problems for law enforcement. Whether they are serial rapists, bombers, or killers, the episodic nature of their crimes and the fact that they often have no apparent connection to their victims have forced law enforcement officials to develop new techniques for dealing with these types of offenders.

Most murders have readily visible motives such as financial gain, revenge, or to cover another crime. Financial gains from insurance policies, wills, contracts, and marriage or partnership assets lay the foundation for many homicides. Anger and revenge for some wrong, real or imagined, motivates some murderers. Murder to cover crimes such as embezzlement or extortion, or to hide extramarital affairs, is not rare. Occasionally, spouses and children are murdered so that the killer can be free of social responsibilities.

For these reasons, the earliest stages of any homicide investigation focus on people who know and could possibly profit from the victim's death. This is a rational approach since the overwhelming majority of homicides occur between people who know one another. But this is not the case with most serial killers and rapists. Their motives are more private and personal and may not be readily apparent. More often than not, even when the motive is discovered, it seems totally irrational. But not to the killer.

CLASSIFICATION OF THE MULTIPLE MURDERER

Multiple murderers are those who have killed more than one person. They are classified according to the location and sequence of the killings into mass, spree, and serial types.

MASS MURDERERS: Those who kill more than four people in one place at one time would fit this classification. These killers often have a clear agenda and want to send a message. This is the killer who walks into his workplace and shoots several people in a rapid-fire assault. The attack often ends with the killer taking his own life or in a "blaze of glory" with the police killing him in an exchange of gunfire. The motive is often some perceived wrong by his co-workers or employer. Examples are the University of Texas Tower shooter Charles Whitman, Columbine killers Eric Harris and Dylan Klebold, and Virginia Tech University killer Seung-Hui Cho.

FORENSIC CASE FILES: CHARLES WHITMAN

On August 1, 1966, a bright, sunny day in Austin, Texas, Charles Whitman snapped and became one of America's most notorious mass murderers. After killing his wife and mother, the ex-Marine climbed the twenty-seven-story tower on the campus of the University of Texas, armed with an array of rifles and handguns. He laid down a lethal barrage of gunfire on everyone in sight, striking people as far away as five hundred yards. He even hit a plane that carried a police sniper. Before he was himself gunned down by police officers Ramiro Martinez and Houston McCoy, Whitman managed to kill sixteen and wound thirty-one people. His motives were never truly known, but he did leave a letter that suggested he wanted to die dramatically and did not want his wife or mother to suffer the humiliation that would certainly follow his actions.

FORENSIC CASE FILES: THE COLUMBINE MASSACRE

At 11:19 A.M. on April 20, 1999, eighteen-year-old Eric Harris and seventeen-year-old Dylan Klebold, wearing trench coats, military fatigues, and ski masks, entered Columbine High School near Littleton, Colorado, armed with rifles, automatic weapons, shotguns, and homemade pipe bombs. Their explosive rampage began in the cafeteria, where fellow students were taking their lunch break, and ended in the library, where the two killers took their own lives. In between, the two killed one teacher and twelve students and wounded two-dozen others. Diaries and a videotape made by the boys the morning of the massacre revealed a deep-seated hatred of many of their classmates.

FORENSIC CASE FILES: VIRGINIA TECH UNIVERSITY MASSACRE

On April 16, 2007, Seung-Hui Cho, a student at Virginia Tech University in Blacksburg, went on a killing spree. By the time he finished, he had become the deadliest mass murderer in modern U.S. history. At approximately 7:15 A.M., Cho entered a dorm and fatally shot two people. But Cho was just getting started. He fled the scene, changed clothes, grabbed more weapons and ammunition, and went to the post office, where he mailed a package of papers and a video to NBC News. He then launched a second attack that lasted nine minutes. He fired 174 rounds, killing another thirty people and wounding many others. He then turned his weapon on himself. The materials received by NBC were found to be Cho's written and videoed manifesto in which he railed against "rich kids" whom he believed participated in "debauchery" and were "deceitful charlatans." This type of long-standing, deep-seated anger at a group of people is typical of mass murders.

SPREE KILLERS: These individuals kill several people at two or more locations with the killings linked by motive and with no "cooling-off" period between. The spree killer goes on a rampage, moving from place to place, city to city, even state to state, leaving bodies in his wake. It is as if an underlying rage pushes the perpetrator to act, and once he begins, he doesn't stop or deviate from his goal. As with mass murders, the spree often ends in suicide or a confrontation with law enforcement. Andrew Cunanan offers an example of a spree killer.

FORENSIC CASE FILES: ANDREW CUNANAN

Andrew Cunanan was often described as a "high-class male prostitute" who catered to wealthy older men. He lived and played in a world of wealth and hedonism until late 1996 when his world began to unravel. In mid-April 1997, he threw himself a going away party in San Diego, telling most people that he was moving to San Francisco. However, he apparently told others that he was going to Minnesota to "settle some business." He then bought a one-way, first-class ticket to Minneapolis. On the night of April 27, 1997, he used a hammer to beat twenty-eight-year-old Jeffrey Trail to death in the Minneapolis apartment of Cunanan's lover, David Madson. The spree had begun. Five days later, at a lake some fifty miles away, he shot Madson in the head and fled in the red Jeep that the two had taken from Trail's home.

Cunanan drove to Chicago where he took up with seventy-two-year-old real estate mogul Lee Miglin. After torturing and killing Miglin with pruning shears and a garden saw, Cunanan headed east in Miglin's Lexus. On May 9, he shot and killed William Reese in Pennsville, New Jersey, stole the dead man's red Chevrolet pickup, and headed south. Cunanan was now on the FBI's Ten Most Wanted Fugitives list.

He ended up in Miami, Florida, where on the morning of July 15, he shot Gianni Versace twice in the head in front of Versace's residence, Casa Casuarina. On July 25, police were summoned to the boathouse where Cunanan was hiding by its caretaker, Fernando Carreira. As with many spree killers, Cunanan took his own life before police could apprehend him.

SERIAL KILLERS: These offenders kill several people at different times and locations with a cooling-off period between the killings. The cooling-off period, which may be days, weeks, months, even years in duration, distinguishes serial from spree killers. The catalog of serial killers includes some very famous names: Ted Bundy, John Wayne Gacy, Henry Lee Lucas, Gary Ridgway, Jeffrey Dahmer, Randy Kraft, Dennis Rader, and many others.

THE PSYCHOPATHOLOGY OF SERIAL OFFENDERS

This is obviously a huge and controversial subject. There are many theories as to where these offenders come from and what triggers their aberrant behavior, and I'm not going to attempt to enter that fray. I will, however, give you some of the more accepted theories regarding what drives these criminals.

Society has always had difficulty understanding and dealing with serial offenders. Whether serial rapists or serial killers, these individuals seem so far removed from the rest of society that a rational method for dealing with them has been and is still out of reach. They are typically **psychopaths** or **sociopaths**, two terms that are often used interchangeably. These individuals tend to be self-centered (egocentric and narcissistic), manipulative, emotionally shallow, and devoid of empathy and remorse. They can often lie with impunity, fool even the cleverest interrogator, and occasionally pass a polygraph examination.

Serial rapists and serial killers have a great deal in common. In fact, they may be exactly the same, just at different stages in their psychopathological derangement. Many serial killers begin their adventures with rape and then progress to murder to cover the crime or to increase their enjoyment.

Current thinking is that these individuals cannot be reliably rehabilitated. This is obviously controversial, but one fact remains: There are many laws that are designed to protect the public from these criminals. These types of offenders are given long sentences, and while serial killers are rarely released from prison or a mental facility, sexual predators often do get out eventually. When they are released, they are watched constantly. Neighborhoods that sexual predators move into are notified of their presence.

These are not new concepts. As early as the 1930s, laws mandated that sexual offenders be evaluated and treated by medical professionals, and by the 1960s such programs were in place in virtually every state. It soon became clear to those charged with diagnosing and treating these sexual predators that these offenders were different. They didn't fit into the usual diagnostic categories and did not respond to the usual treatment regimens. By the 1990s, many states closed these specialized treatment centers and longer prison sentences became the norm.

What makes these types of offenders resistant to treatment?

It appears that the psychosexual pathology that drives these offenders becomes ingrained early in life, and it only grows in strength as the individual matures through puberty and into adult life. Many, but not all, come from backgrounds of physical, psychological, and sexual abuse. They often insulate themselves from this abuse by creating a protective world rich in fantasy. In some, as these fantasies develop, they take on sexual and violent characteristics ‸ can brew for years, even decades, before the offender begins to act

There is little doubt that fantasy plays a powerful role in the s‸ violent crimes. Early on, his fantasies might be amorphous a‸ he mentally plays it out over and over, year after year, it b‸ Often the fantasy is simple, but in the more imaginativ‸ an elaborate scripted play. In many, sexual and vi‸ mingle until the two are inseparable.

When the offender goes on the hunt for victims, he is in fact seeking a character in his fantasy play. He looks for a certain type of person or one with a specific look. Ted Bundy sought women with dark hair, parted in the middle. This was the character he needed for his fantasy.

This brings up an important fact about these fantasies—they tend to be very specific. Each of us has different fantasies, and one person's fantasy would not necessarily appeal to another. But when you fantasize, the details and the feel remain the same, evoking the same emotions with each fantasy. So it is with the serial offender. The difference is that these individuals tend to have sexually violent fantasies, which they may ultimately act out.

But it is these specific details of the fantasy that make it possible to develop a profile of the killer. Since the fantasy is specific and repetitive, certain elements of the criminal act will be specific and repetitive. This is manifested in the killer's signature.

SERIAL OFFENDER PROFILING

Profiling is more an art than a science. It is basically looking at the evidence and making a best guess as to the type of individual that would commit the crime in question. The profiler looks at the crime scene, autopsy data, victim, and likely pre- and post-crime behavior of the killer to make this assessment. How did the killer gain access to the victim? What did he do to the victim? Did he try to cover his tracks, and if so, how? What is it about this victim that attracted the killer? What motive or fantasy drove the killer to harm this person in this manner at this time in this location?

In serial murder cases the offender is often termed the **unknown subject**, or **unsub** for short. An analysis of the crime scene may offer clues to the type of unsub the police are to search for. Such an analysis has become known as **offender profiling**. Though profiling may not lead to the exact individual, it often helps the police narrow the focus of their investigation. Profiling might suggest the unsub's physical and psychological makeup, the area where he lives or works, what behaviors he may have exhibited before the crime and what he is likely to do after the crime, and where other evidence is likely to be located. Lastly, the crime scene may reveal aspects of the unsub's modus operandi (MO) and his signature.

Besides the usual investigative techniques, law enforcement officials have asingly turned to criminal profiling to help track serial offenders. Since these are often "stranger" killings, the usual connections between the killer and the victim are not present. But there is always a connection of some type. Something in the killer's psyche drives him to attack a particular victim at a particular place and at a particular time.

Criminal profiling evolved from studies done by the FBI's Behavioral Science Unit (BSU), now known as the Investigative Support Unit (ISU). The studies, which included a series of jailhouse interviews with convicted serial killers, were designed to gain insight into violent criminals. Certain commonalities among these types of offenders appeared, which gave investigators a better understanding of these violent offenders, and a useful investigative tool evolved. Crime scene analysis for clues to the offender's personality and motives and offender profiling have continued to gain popularity and are now considered critically important in tracking serial offenders. The premise is that the perpetrator not only leaves behind physical evidence but also behavioral and psychiatric evidence. Understanding this evidence is the key to finding the perpetrator.

This understanding added the critical "who" to the "how" and "why" that crime investigators have traditionally used. When confronted with a serial or stranger murder victim, the profiler uses the "how" and "why" to make a judgment of "who." That is, "what type of person" would commit this particular crime in this particular manner?

One of the basic tenets of profiling is that behavior reflects personality. How a person acts derives directly from his personality and psychological needs and fears. Profiling seeks clues to the perpetrator's personality from his behavior, not only at the crime scene but also before and after the criminal act. These clues provide insight into the killer's motives, his level of intelligence and sophistication, and his reasons for selecting this particular victim.

Often the killer "poses" the victim. This posturing could be to shock whoever finds the body, or it could be a recreation of his fantasy mental image. The pose could be degrading, angelic, or anything in between; it often reveals how the perpetrator feels about the victim. If he harbors a hatred for the victim, or the person the victim is representing (his mother, prostitutes, or all women), the posing will reflect this.

The first major success of criminal profiling, in a mid-twentieth-ce̶ case known as the Mad Bomber, came long before the art of prof̶ into existence.

FORENSIC CASE FILES: THE MAD BOMBER

On November 16, 1940, an unexploded bomb was found on a window ledge at the Manhattan office of Consolidated Edison, the power company known as Con Ed or Con Edison. Attached was a hand-printed note that said, "Con Edison Crooks— This is for you." In September 1941, a second unexploded bomb was found. Three months later, after the attack on Pearl Harbor, the bomber sent a letter to police in which he stated that, out of his sense of patriotism, he would send no more bombs until the war was over. Though he sent many letters over the years, he remained true to his word, and no further bombs turned up until well after World War II.

Then on April 24, 1950, another unexploded bomb was found in a phone booth at the New York Public Library. Between 1951 and 1955 over a dozen bombs were set, many of which exploded, and letters from the bomber that expressed a deep anger at Con Ed kept arriving. On December 2, 1956, a very powerful bomb exploded in Brooklyn's Paramount Theater, injuring several people. This prompted police to bring in psychiatrist Dr. James Brussel, who was known for his uncanny ability to analyze crimes and to speculate as to what type of individual could be the culprit.

After reviewing the Mad Bomber's letters and the police reports, Dr. Brussel concluded that the person responsible was a middle-aged male who was paranoid, introverted, and held a deep-seated grudge against Con Edison. He told police that the man likely had issues with and may have been fired from the company. He was well educated, probably of Slavic decent, lived with an older female relative, and was extremely neat and meticulous in his work. He would be good with tools and, when captured, would be neatly dressed, likely in a double-breasted suit, buttoned.

Indeed, in one letter the bomber had given the date of September 5, 1931, for an incident that had particularly enraged him. Checking Con Ed's records, police found that a boiler explosion had occurred at Con Ed on that date and that George Metesky had been injured. Metesky had subsequently written a letter of complaint to the company, and when this was checked against letters from the Mad Bomber, many similar phrases appeared. When police arrested Metseky at his home, they found he was fifty-four, of Polish extraction, unmarried, and living with two older sisters. He was also wearing a double-breasted suit, buttoned.

If actions speak to personality, then looking at the characteristics of the crime scene should offer clues to the perpetrator's mental state. One basic method of categorizing offenders from crime scene evidence divides them into organized, disorganized, or mixed offenders.

Organized offenders are more sophisticated in their approach and show evidence of planning. They tend to be of average or better intelligence, employed, and have social relationships, such as spouses and families. Even though they are driven by their fantasies, they maintain enough control to avoid being impulsive. They prepare and even rehearse. They tend to target specific victims or types of victims and use control measures, such as restraints, to maintain victim compliance. They bring the tools they need to gain access to and control of the victim and avoid leaving behind evidence. They generally hide or dispose of the body and most likely will have a "dump site" already selected.

Disorganized offenders are the opposite. They usually live alone or with a relative, possess lower than average intelligence, are unemployed or work at menial jobs, and often have mental illnesses. They act impulsively, as if they have little control over their fantasy-driven needs. They rarely use ruses to gain the victim's confidence, but rather attack with sudden violence and overwhelm the victim. The crime scene is often messy and chaotic. They do not plan ahead or bring tools with them, but instead use whatever is handy. The body is typically left at the scene and little attempt is made to avoid leaving behind evidence. Sexual contact with the victim may occur after death.

Mixed offenders possess characteristics of both the above types and leave behind a mixed scene. They often show evidence of planning and a sophisticated MO, but the assault itself may be frenzied or messy. This might indicate some control over deep-seated and violent fantasies.

To help streamline and standardize the process, profilers have developed categories of **descriptors**. These "describe" the type of individual that would perpetrate the crime. Some of the descriptors used in serial killer profiling are:

AGE: Most serial killers are in their twenties or thirties. Organized offenders tend to be older and more mature than disorganized ones.

SEX: Almost all are male. Sexually sadistic serial killers are driven by fantasies, which in turn are driven by testosterone, the male sex hormone. A mixture of sexual and violent impulses is at the heart of these types of killings.

RACE: Most don't cross racial lines. White offenders kill whites; black offenders kill other blacks. Though not universal, this trend speaks to the specificity of the perpetrator's fantasies. He will seek out victims of a certain age, sex, and ethnicity as dictated by his personal and specific fantasies.

RESIDENCY: Organized offenders may be married, have a family, and be well liked by their friends. Disorganized offenders, because of their mental instability and immaturity, tend to live alone or with a family member.

Proximity of the perpetrator's home to the crime scene is also important. Disorganized offenders tend to kill close to home because the immediate area is a comfort zone for them. Since they are mentally unstable, movement out of this zone is stressful. On the other hand, organized offenders are usually more mobile and have a broader range. Though their first few victims may be close to home, with experience, their comfort zone expands and so do their predatory boundaries.

SOCIAL SKILLS: Those who use a ruse to ensnare their victims, as Ted Bundy did, typically possess good social skills (organized), whereas those who use a blitz-style attack are less comfortable with conversation (disorganized).

WORK AND MILITARY HISTORY: Organized offenders more often have a stable work history and are more likely to have left any military service with an honorable discharge. Disorganized offenders are often simply too "crazy" to hold a job long term or complete military service.

EDUCATIONAL LEVEL: Organized offenders tend to have more schooling than their disorganized counterparts. Again, the discipline and pressure of school is not handled well by a disorganized person.

Using these descriptors, the profiler can create a "picture" of the type of person that likely committed the crime. This in turn can help the police hone in on a specific suspect. Profiling also plays an important role in the interrogation of suspects. Knowing the type of individual that would commit the criminal act in question can help the investigators design questions and leverage any pressure points, which might snare the suspect in a web of lies or even produce a confession.

Profiling also helps determine whether or not a crime scene is "staged." Staging means changing the appearance of the scene so that it will look as if the murder took place in a different manner and for a different reason (see Chapter Two: Evidence, "The Stage Crime Scene"). A classic example would be the husband who kills his wife in a fit of anger and then empties drawers and closets, knocks over furniture, and breaks a door lock or window to make it appear as though a burglar committed the crime. When the investigators discover that the wife was severely bludgeoned and stabbed twenty times, the light of suspicion falls on the husband. A burglar would not engage in such overkill. He would kill and run. Overkill is usually personal and anger is a common underlying drive.

Trophies and Souvenirs

Many criminals take things from the crime scene. Objects of value, such as money, jewels, electronic equipment, and things that can be sold, are commonly stolen. Offenders also remove incriminating evidence, such as the murder weapon or a used condom. Serial offenders tend to take objects that have no monetary or evidentiary value, but rather hold some personal meaning to them as **trophies** or **souvenirs**. These may be clothing, jewelry, hair, photos, and even body parts from the victim.

The terms *trophy* and *souvenir* have been used interchangeably, but differences between the two exist. The distinction lies in how the offender feels about the victim. If he views the victim as a conquest, he views the taken object as a trophy of his triumph. When he later handles it, it will remind him of his domination of the victim. If he sees the victim as a cherished member of his fantasy, the object is a souvenir, and he will use it to relive the experience and make it part of his masturbatory fantasies.

MO vs. Signature

Simply put, **modus operandi (MO)** is the method used to commit the crime. Did the perpetrator drive or walk to the scene? Did he bring weapons and tools with him or simply use what was available? Did he break a window, jimmy a door, or use a ruse to gain entry or overpower the victim? Did he take things of value from the scene? Did he restrain or harm the victim? All of these speak to his method of doing things. Each of these is necessary to conduct the crime and get away with it.

Modus operandi is not a new concept. It dates back to Major L.W. Atcherley, a police constable in England, who developed a ten-point system for dealing with a perpetrator's MO. He looked at such things as the location of the crime, the point and method of entry, any tools used to gain entry or commit the crime, types of objects taken from the crime scene, time of day, alibi, accomplices, methods of transportation to and from the scene, and any unusual features of the crime. Scotland Yard later adopted many of his techniques.

It is important to point out that MO can evolve over time. As the unsub learns better ways to commit his crimes, he might change his mode of entry, his ruse, his disguise, the time of his attacks, the weapon used, and any other aspect of his MO. Whatever will make his efforts more effective and help him avoid detection might be modified.

A **signature** is an act that has nothing to do with completing the crime or with getting away with it. These are acts that are important to the offender in some very personal way. Torturing or overkill of the victim, post-mortem mutilation or posing, and the taking of souvenirs or trophies are signatures. These are actions driven by the killer's psychological needs and fantasies.

Unlike MO, the signature never changes. The perpetrator may refine it, but the basic signature remains the same. For example, if a serial killer poses his victims in a religious manner, such as praying or in a crucifixion posture, he might later add details such as candles, crucifixes, and other ceremonial objects. The details of the signature have changed, but its basic form and theme remains the same.

The reason for the stability of the signature lies in its driving force: the unsub's fantasies. These fantasies develop early in life and become refined into an obsession over years of mental reenactment. During the crime, he forces the victim to respond in accordance with the script the unsub has rehearsed in his head thousands of times. His signature actions are solely to live out this personal fantasy, and since this fantasy never changes, the signature remains intact. In the above situation, the religious posing and paraphernalia are an important aspect of the killer's fantasy, and since this is the reason he committed the act in the first place, all his victims are treated the same way.

This signature is useful in profiling the killer. Religious posing might indicate some issue with religion, church, or a priest, and this would be incorporated into his profile. Also, the signature might serve to link a series of crimes. If several victims are found posed, bound, or killed in a similar manner, the wise investigator would search for other linking clues, since linking crime scenes is often crucial in tracking the killer.

FORENSIC CASE FILES: CARMINE CALABRO

In 1979, the body of twenty-six-year-old schoolteacher Francine Elveson was found on the roof of her apartment building. She was nude and had been object raped with a pen and an umbrella and mutilated. Her body was placed in a position that reflected the shape of the Chai (the Jewish symbol of good luck). She was known to wear a Chai pendant, but it had apparently been taken as a souvenir by the killer.

The FBI profile of the killer suggested that he was disorganized, since there seemed to be little planning and the scene suggested a fantasy-driven murder. This means he was likely a white male, twenty-five to thirty-five years old, unemployed, and knew the layout of the building and the victim's habits. In addition, he likely knew the victim or had at least seen her. He knew that the apartment house's roof would be private enough for him to complete his assault and murder and escape. The ritualistic and sadistic nature of the murder, and the fact that he did not rape the victim himself but used objects, suggested that he was sexually inadequate and had no stable relationships with women. He likely had some form of mental illness and probably had been in a psychiatric hospital at some time.

This profile caused police to focus on Carmine Calabro, a thirty-year-old, unmarried, unemployed male who often visited his father, who lived in the victim's apartment building. He was undergoing treatment at a psychiatric hospital and had been absent without permission at the time of the murder. He was convicted when his dental anatomy matched bite marks on the victim's body.

Victimology

The perpetrator isn't the only one profiled. Evaluating the victim can add to the offender profile and might offer valuable information to narrow the search for the killer. The study of victim characteristics, called **victimology**, is basically an assessment of the person's risk of becoming a victim as a result of his personal, professional, and social life. A detailed understanding of the victim's lifestyle and habits provides clues as to why this particular victim was selected at this location and time. This information can divide victims into high-, medium-, and low-risk.

High-risk victims are those who are frequently in high-risk situations. Prostitutes, particularly those who "walk the streets," obviously fall into this category. They typically work at night, interact with strangers on a regular basis, willingly get into cars with strangers, and, in short, are easy targets. Other high-risk behaviors include drug use, a promiscuous lifestyle, nighttime employment, and associating with people who possess criminal personalities.

Low-risk victims are those who stay close to work and home, don't visit areas unfamiliar to them, have a steady job and many friends, don't use drugs, and lock their doors at night.

Medium-risk victims fall between these two.

Why the offender selects a particular victim is determined by both the perpetrator's fantasy needs and the victim's vulnerability. Some victims are merely grabbed as a victim of opportunity. High-risk victims place themselves in vulnerable positions much more often than do low-risk victims, but either could simply be in the wrong place at the wrong time. Other victims are taken because they fit the starring role in the perpetrator's fantasy. The offender might spend days or weeks "cruising" for just the right victim, the one who most closely matches his fantasy. He ignores other potentially easy victims because they are not "right."

A special form of victim profiling is the **psychological autopsy**. It is performed when the manner of a victim's death is not clear. Was the victim's death an accident, suicide, or homicide? To help make this determination, the forensic psychiatrist will look into the victim's medical, school, work, and military history; interview family, friends, and associates; and evaluate autopsy, police, and witness reports. The goal is to assess whether the victim was in a stressful enough situation and the type of person to take his own life. Or was his lifestyle such that he was an easy target for a killer?

Geographic Profiling

In nature shows on television, the narrators often discuss a certain predator's domain or hunting range. Game wardens use these boundaries to narrow their search for an illusive lion or tiger. Profilers do the same with serial killers.

An analysis of the pattern of the perpetrator's assaults can yield valuable information that might ultimately lead to his apprehension. This analysis is known as **geographic profiling**. It is based on the premise that serial offenders, like lions and tigers, have a certain "comfort zone" within which they feel free to carry out their crimes. The geographic profiler would like to know where the victim was abducted, where the actual assault or murder took place, and where the body was dumped. If several assaults have occurred, the profiler has several such locations to work with. He can then locate these points on a map and define the killer's domain.

This might show that the murders are clustered in a small area, which would indicate that the killer is not very mobile and might not possess a car or have a job. Or the range could be broad, indicating that the perpetrator is highly mobile and may possess a vehicle with high mileage that he uses to troll for victims. Whether the range is narrow or broad, the perpetrator likely resides or works within or near this comfort zone.

It is important for investigators to determine which victim was killed first. This is often straightforward if the victims are found shortly after the crime. But, if the victims are street dwellers or prostitutes, whose disappearance might go unnoticed, the date of their abduction might not be known. And if the bodies are dumped in remote places, the order in which the victims were killed might not be the order in which the bodies are found. In such cases, a forensic anthropologist is brought in to assess the approximate time of death (see Chapter Five: Time of Death). Why is this important? The comfort zone for most serial killers usually begins small and grows with each killing. This means that the first victim was probably abducted close to the killer's home or workplace, and this knowledge can be crucial to identifying the killer.

LINKING CRIMINALS AND CRIME SCENES

Linking several crime scenes can link evidence, and this is turn might help narrow the suspect pool, possibly to a single individual. Suppose a crime scene in Phoenix is linked by signature to similar scenes in Los Angeles and Las Vegas. Also suppose that a witness in Phoenix saw a tall man leave the area in a blue van, a shoeprint in Los Angeles revealed the killer wore a certain size and model of athletic shoe, and hair found at the scene in Vegas suggested that the killer dyed his blonde hair black. Each piece of evidence alone is fairly meager, but together they present the police with a suspect who is tall, dyes his hair black, wears athletic shoes, and drives a blue van. That's a lot more to go on. But, how does this linkage happen?

As with the Automated Fingerprint Identification System (AFIS), which allows the matching of fingerprints from various crime scenes and suspects (see Chapter Twelve: Fingerprints), the FBI also created other databases to deal with serial offenders. The first was the **National Center for the Analysis of Violent Crime (NCAVC)**. It serves as a repository for violent crime data throughout the country. This led to the development of the **Violent Criminal Apprehension Program (VICAP)** and **PROFILER**, which maintains profiles on serial murderers.

Data from crime scenes are entered into these databases. When an investigator is confronted with a murder or a series of murders, he can create a profile of the scene in question and compare it with others from around the country in the hopes of linking the two crimes. For example, if an investigator is analyzing a murder scene in which the victim was strangled with a knotted rope, violated with an object, and had her hands hacked off, he can plug this information into a profile and compare the scene with those in the VICAP and PROFILER databases. Any crimes with similar characteristics are identified and the investigator looks into them to see if perhaps the same perpetrator committed both crimes. If other evidence shows that this is the case, he has linked the two murders and this might ultimately lead him to the killer.

Forensic psychiatry is a difficult if inexact science. In fact, it is more art than science. Whether performing mental status tests, assessing competence, determining the veracity of what a subject says, or profiling an unsub, the forensic psychiatrist must use his training, experience, and common sense to make a "best guess." In psychiatry, nothing is ever certain.

AFTERWORD

I hope your journey through this book was informative and fascinating. I hope you learned many new things and achieved a better understanding of what forensic science can and cannot do. I hope you more than once rummaged around on the Internet to explore more fully some topic that struck a chord or piqued an interest in you. Most importantly, I hope you had fun. I surely did while researching and writing.

Visit my Web site at www.dplylemd.com and you'll find articles and questions from writers about all kinds of forensic topics. And if you feel so moved, drop me a note and let me know what you thought of *Howdunit: Forensics*.

—D.P. Lyle, M.D.

FORENSIC SCIENCE TOOLS

BREATHALYZER: Indiana State Police Captain R.F. Borkenstein invented the breathalyzer in 1954, and though it has undergone many changes since then, the basic concept is the same. This device captures and analyzes expired air. With its valve turned to the TAKE position, the subject blows into a mouth-piece, which leads to a collection chamber where the breath is trapped. The valve is then turned to the ANALYZE position, exposing the captured breath to a mixture of water, silver nitrate in sulfuric acid, and potassium dichromate. Any alcohol in the expired air is immediately oxidized into acetic acid, a reaction that destroys the potassium dichromate in proportion to the amount of alcohol. This means that the more alcohol that is present in the breath, the more of the potassium dichromate that is destroyed.

The breathalyzer also contains a spectrophotometer, a device that measures light absorption. In this case, the spectrophotometer measures the absorption of light at a certain wavelength by potassium dichromate. Obviously as the po-tassium dichromate is destroyed, its concentration drops, and its absorption of the light decreases. The spectrophotometer measures this change. The degree of change is correlated to the amount of alcohol in the breath, and since the amount of alcohol in an expired breath is a direct reflection of the blood alcohol level, the breathalyzer is an accurate indirect measure of the level of alcohol in the blood.

Gas chromatography (GC) rapidly separates mixtures of compounds into individual components. The gas chromatograph (see Figure A-1) does this by measuring how fast each component moves through a column of inert gas such as nitrogen or helium. This gas is called the **carrier gas** since it carries the unknown gaseous sample along as it circulates through a glass or metal column. Basically, the liquid sample is injected into one end of the column where it is heated and vaporized. The gaseous vapor enters the column and flows with the moving carrier gas until it reaches a detector. Various compounds move at different speeds and are thus separated from one another during this transit and arrive at the detector at different times. The time it takes for a chemical to reach the detector is called its **retention time (RT)**, and this varies from chemical to chemical. The detector then sends a signal to a recorder, which prints a graph that represents the RT of each of the com-

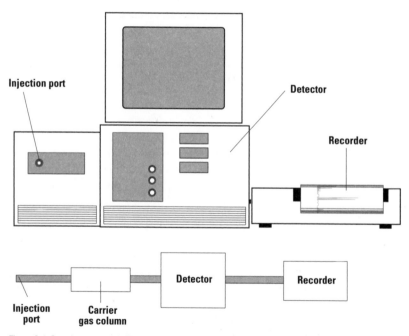

Figure A-1: Gas chromatograph. The gas chromatograph consists of an injection port, carrier gas column, detector, and graphic recorder and printer.

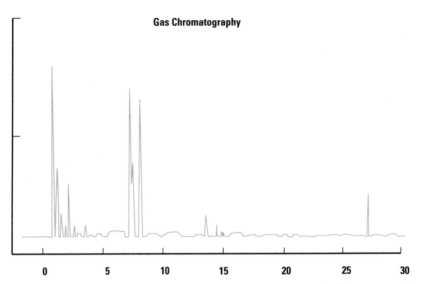

Gas Chromatography

0　　　5　　　10　　　15　　　20　　　25　　　30

Figure A-2: Chromatographic peaks. The gas chromatographic peak pattern separates different compounds from one another. Each component of an unknown mixture of compounds moves along the column at its own specific speed. The detector recognizes the arrival of each and signals the recorder, which creates a spike for each component. In this chromatograph, each peak represents a different component of the unknown substance tested.

pounds detected. The graph is called a chromatograph (see Figure A-2). Often this is all that is needed to determine the composition of the unknown sample, but if further information is needed, GC can be combined with either mass spectroscopy or infrared spectrophotometry, which are discussed below.

Pyrolysis gas chromatography (Py/GC) is used whenever the sample to be tested is a solid. The solid must be heated and converted into a gas (this process is called **pyrolysis**) and then the gas product is subjected to gas chromatography as described above.

Liquid chromatography is similar to GC except that the samples are tested in a liquid form. The sample is dissolved in a liquid solvent and this is then passed through a stationary absorbent material. Each dissolved compound flows along the absorbent material at a different rate and will reach the far end of the material at a different time. This difference serves to separate and often identify the chemical nature of the sample.

Thin layer chromatography (TLC) is also similar to GC in that it can separate and presumptively identify hundreds of compounds at once. The main difference is that it uses a thin layer of absorbent material, usually silica gel, instead of a gas column. In this test, silica gel (or whatever is used for the layer) is spread over a glass plate. The samples to be tested are dissolved in a solvent and then placed in a row on the gel near the bottom of the glass plate along with known standards (mixtures of known composition). After the samples and standards dry, the plate is turned on end and placed into a closed tank, the bottom of which contains a liquid solvent. As the solvent soaks into the gel and begins to rise up the plate by capillary action, it creeps past the samples and standards, collecting each along the way. Each chemical migrates up the plate at different rates. When the solvent reaches the top of the plate, the plate is removed and dried. Each of the chemicals will have a different length of migration, which separates them from one another.

The plate must then be sprayed or dipped in various reagents, which react with various compounds to produce a color reaction. By determining the length of migration vs. the known standards, and by looking at which reagents bring about a particular color change, the presence and type of chemicals in the sample can be determined. The results can then confirmed and refined with mass spectrometry.

GEL ELECTROPHORESIS: **Electrophoresis** is the process of separating molecules or molecular fragments, such as DNA fragments, according to some physical property, such as size or electrical charge. The basic principle is that the material to be separated is placed at one end of an agarose gel (sort of like Jell-O) and an electrical current is applied. This causes the material to move from one end of the gel toward the other. The various components of the material migrate at different speeds, according to their size, shape, or electrical charge. Smaller, uniformly shaped, and highly charged materials move faster and farther. The opposite is true for larger materials, which encounter more resistance from the gel. This results in bands of separation in which each band contains a different component of the original material. This technique is used in some methods of DNA fingerprinting.

IMMUNOASSAYS: **Immunoassays** involve an antigen-antibody reaction. The substance searched for is the antigen and the testing reagent is the antibody. An antibody will react only with an antigen that it recognizes and will ignore all others. In this test, an antibody specific for the substance in question is added to the sample. A positive reaction is an agglutination or "clumping" of the antigen-antibody complex. If a reaction occurs, the substance tested for is present. A fluorescent "tag" is often added to the antibody so that the reaction can be "read" by the glow of the fluorescent antigen-antibody complex. If such a radioactive "tag" is used, the process is termed a **radioimmunoassay**. This is useful in many serological (blood) procedures.

INDUCTIVELY COUPLED PLASMA-MASS SPECTROMETRY (ICP-MS): This test is rapidly becoming the test of choice for very small metal samples. The major drawback is that it is expensive. This test involves using an argon torch to heat the specimen to over 6,000°C, which forms an ionized gas of the substance. This gas is then passed through a mass detector that identifies the chemical by its mass and charge.

MICROSCOPES: **Compound binocular microscopes** are basically two scopes joined together so that each eye looks through one of the parallel scopes. This is the most common type of microscope used in schools, hospitals, and forensic labs. Light can be cast on the object to be viewed from above, at an angle, or from below, so that the light passes through the specimen. Magnifications can reach 1,200 times or more. Attachments can supply polarized or other types of light, which can aid in the viewing of certain objects. The scope can also be fitted with a micrometer, which serves as a rule for measuring the physical dimensions (length, width, thickness) of very small objects.

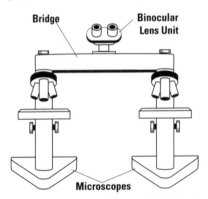

Figure A-3: Comparison microscope. This is basically two microscopes joined by a bridge and allows for the side-by-side viewing of two objects.

Comparison microscopes allow for the side-by-side comparison of two objects. Invented in 1925 by Philip Gravelle, the comparison microscope is basically two microscopes joined by a bridge (see Figure A-3). The bridge contains a series of lenses and mirrors that project images of the two objects into a single binocular lens unit. The viewer sees a circular field divided in half, with the object under the left-hand scope on the left and that under the right on the right (see Figure A-4). Microscopic details of the two specimens can then be compared. It is most often used in tool mark and ballistic comparisons.

Polarized light microscopes allow for the viewing of materials under polarized light, which will bring out details not visible under standard light. In normal light, the light wave oscillations move in all planes, while in polarized light, the wave oscillations all move in one direction or plane. When an object is viewed under polarized light, there is less scatter of the reflected light so the object appears sharper and its colors clearer.

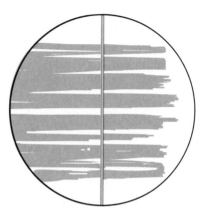

Figure A-4: Comparison microscope field of view. This scope allows for the side-by-side comparison of such things as rifling marks on bullets.

Stereomicroscopes are binocular scopes (one eyepiece and viewing tube for each eye) in which the two scopes are separated by an angle of 10 to 15 degrees. This gives the viewed object a three-dimensional appearance. Things such as layers of a paint chip, the texture of a fabric, the surface markings of glass, or the curliness of a hair are best seen in stereo.

Scanning electron microscopes (SEMs), which became commercially available in the early 1920s, can attain magnifications up to 100,000 times, though rarely are magnifications above 20 to 25 thousand needed in forensics work. Where a standard microscope uses light to view an object, an SEM uses an electron beam. This beam is swept over the object and viewed through electromagnetic lenses. This not only greatly magnifies the image but also gives it incredible clarity. It is used to examine very small objects, define tiny details, and identify things such as gunshot residue (GSR).

When combined with energy dispersive X-ray spectrometry (EDS) (see below), the combination (SEM/EDS) becomes an exceptionally powerful identification tool. The SEM locates tiny particles and the EDS reveals their elemental makeup, thus identifying the substance.

NEUTRON ACTIVATION ANALYSIS: This procedure is cumbersome and requires a nuclear reactor, which is no small expense. In this technique, neutrons are fired at the sample, colliding with its various components. This causes each component to release radiation at its own unique energy level. Measuring the emitted radiation reveals the chemical makeup of the sample. This process is useful in the analysis of paint, soil, hair, metals, and many other substances.

SPECTROSCOPY, SPECTROMETRY, AND SPECTROPHOTOMETRY: **Atomic absorption spectroscopy (AAS)** uses the absorption of light by gaseous atoms to identify various chemicals. This means that any solid or liquid materials must first be vaporized before they are submitted to AAS. It is most often used to assess the amount of various metals, such as lead, iron, arsenic, and many others, within the test sample. An example would the determination of arsenic levels in the hair of a victim of chronic arsenic poisoning.

Infrared spectroscopy (IR) depends upon the absorption of infrared light by the sample being tested. Each compound has a different infrared absorption spectrum and can be identified in that manner so that IR basically gives the "chemical fingerprint" of the tested compound. It is often used with GC, a pairing called GC/IR, and this combination is highly accurate for separating and identifying a mixture of compounds.

Energy dispersive X-ray spectrometry (EDS) analyzes the light and color characteristics of very small objects. When combined with the SEM (see above), a combination called SEM/EDS, it can define structures less than one micron (one millionth of a meter) in size and can accurately define the chemical characteristics of the material.

Mass spectroscopy (MS), like infrared spectroscopy, can give the "chemical fingerprint" of a compound. In this test, rather than the infrared light used in IR, the sample is bombarded with a beam of high-energy electrons, which fragments the compound. These fragments then pass through an electric or magnetic field where they are separated according to their mass. The fragmentation pattern of the unknown sample is then compared to known fragmentation patterns and the composition of the unknown substance is determined. As with IR, it is often used in conjunction with gas chromatography, a combination known as GC/MS. By using GC/MS, virtually any substance can be separated and identified.

Microspectrophotometry is used to measure the light and color characteristics of trace evidence while eliminating the problems of observer bias and variability. Each person sees light and color a little differently. One person's red might be another's orange. With microspectrophotometry, the exact color of an object or material, as well as its light transmission, absorption, and reflection characteristics, can be accurately and measurably determined. It works with either standard white light (visible light) or with infrared light and is extremely useful when examining paint chips, colored fibers, and dyed or treated hair.

Ultraviolet (UV) spectroscopy takes advantage of the fact that different compounds absorb or reflect UV light in different amounts and at varying wavelengths, which serves to separate tested samples into classes. This means that each compound or class of compounds absorbs UV light more strongly at a specific wavelength and less so at other wavelengths. The magnitude of the absorption at the wavelength of maximum absorption give an indication of the concentration of the chemical in the sample. This is an extremely useful test for the forensic toxicologist.

X-RAY AND ANALYTIC ELECTRON DIFFRACTION: **X-ray diffraction (XRD)** is a test in which the sample is bombarded with a monochromatic X-ray beam and the scattering of the beam is measured. This reveals how the atoms and molecules in the substance are arranged and gives a "chemical fingerprint" of the substance. This is useful with materials such as paint since it can distinguish among the various polymeric forms of chemical additives such as titanium oxide.

Analytic electron microscopy (AEM) is similar to XRD except that the diffracted beam is a stream of electrons rather than X-rays. It is used to analyze very small samples, even particles as small as a single micrometer in size.

INDEX

FORENSICS